李宗恩先生文存

The Collective Writings of Mr. Chung-Un Lee

李宗恩 著　李维华 编

纪念李宗恩先生诞辰 125 周年

《民国医学教育家李宗恩》李维华编著

《李宗恩先生编年事辑》虞云国 李维华编著

《李宗恩先生文存》李宗恩著 李维华编

目　录

前　　言

我出生在北京协和医院。当时妈妈在小儿科当总住院医，爸爸是公共卫生系的助教，爷爷是协和医学院的院长，一家三代住在外交部街 59 号内 41 号楼。妈妈后来告诉我，我出生的那一天特别热，她简直就是浸泡在汗水里。其实，那时热的还不只是北京 6 月的天气，1956-1957 年春正是 1949 年后中国知识分子的“小阳春”，包括协和医学院在内的医学教育工作者们热情高涨，爷爷还在《人民日报》上发表了他在政协会议上的发言《更好地向科学进军》[1]。谁知天有不测风云，转眼间爷爷成了中国医药界的头号右派，被发放到西南边陲的昆明，我们也搬到了妈妈后来工作的儿科研究所宿舍。之后的 4 年，我们和爷爷天各一方，年老体弱的爷爷在千里之外和奶奶相依为命，于 1962 年 3 月初客逝他乡。

此后的年月里，爷爷一直是我心中的一个迷。家里人很少提起他，即使我们问起爷爷的事情，爸爸妈妈也沉默不语。文革时红卫兵来抄家，我们才知道自己是黑五类，只有滚出去的份儿。年幼的我自然不能理解这些政治上的风云变幻，所以心里一直有个大大的问号：爷爷怎么就从协和医学院院长突然变成了大右派？后来，经过 5 年在中国学医、5 年在美国读博、4 年博士后、在美国医学院从教 20 余年，我对医学教育也算有所了解，但更不明白人人尊敬的医学院院长怎么变成了右派。为了解开这个谜，我在工作之余走访了贵阳医学院档案馆、协和医学院档案馆、贵州省档案馆、洛氏基金会档案馆、格拉斯哥大学档案馆、伦敦热带病和卫生学院档案馆、台湾中研院近代史所档案馆和在北京的国家图书馆。十几年的时间，几万英里的旅程，每次找到一篇爷爷的论文、讲演稿、报刊文章或手稿，我都激动不已。渐渐地，一位独立思考、严谨治学的医学研究者，一位不畏艰辛、敢作敢当的医学教育家的形象浮现在我的眼前。

[1] 《人民日报》1957 年 3 月 23 日。

抗战爆发之前，爷爷李宗恩在协和医学院工作了近 14 年，共发表热带病学研究论文 29 篇，其中第一作者 11 篇。他的研究涵盖了当时危害中国人民健康的几种主要寄生虫病，包括丝虫病、血吸虫病、疟疾和黑热病。为摸清这些疾病的传染源和传播途径，李宗恩深入疾病流行区，探询病人、搜集标本，捕捉蚊虫、孑孓、钉螺、病犬，又在协和医学院内科实验室用科学的方法"大胆假设，小心求证"，然后制定防病措施，再在临床实践中详细比较各种诊断和治疗的方法。李宗恩在研究中（1）不盲从盲信：他根据中国人的低蛋白饮食而罕有糙皮病的观察，挑战当时流行的糙皮病病因说，认为笼统的蛋白缺乏并不一定会引起糙皮病；（2）动脑动手：他多次设计实验仪器和方法，解决实验中的各种疑难问题；（3）培养下一代本土热带病科学家：30 年代起，他多次与诸福棠、钟惠澜、王季午、袁贻瑾、刘纬通等发表文章，这些研究在他离开协和之后仍旧继续；（4）注重实际观察：他对科学态度的解释为："避免主观，注重客观。主观太强，理智容易给感情蒙蔽，会不知不觉地走入错路。[1]"这种科学的态度，就是他一生治学、办事的态度。

抗日战争的爆发改变了李宗恩的生命轨迹。虽然当时协和医学院并不受战争的影响,[2] 但李宗恩视民族利益高于一切，毅然决然地放弃了自己的热带病研究和协和医学院的优越条件，接受国民政府教育部的任命，出任国立贵阳医学院院长。贵阳医学院是全国第九所国立医学院，也是贵州的第一所高等学府。李宗恩与一批志同道合的医学精英一起白手起家，硬是在"天无三日晴，地无三尺平，人无三分银"的贵州，"从无中创造出有，在荒地上开发出新园地。[3]"国立贵阳医学院于 1938 年 6 月 1 日正式开学。此后，尽管敌机轰炸不断，物质匮乏，交通阻滞，通货膨胀，李宗恩始终坚持用高标准办学，他认为"一个合格的医师，至少在学识经验与技术上都要能符合起码的要求，但这个起码的要求，决不能在短期内做到。如果匆匆了事，训练马虎，结果所造就出来的医师，大多学识短浅，经验缺乏，技术低下，则其可能给予社会的危险，那真不堪想像。[4]" 他为贵医写下的校训——"诚于己，忠于群，敬往思来"——在 80 年

---

[1]《院长对首届毕业生临别赠书》，见《国立贵阳医学院院刊》，1939 年 2 月 7 日。

[2] 协和医学院由美国洛氏基金会创立，在珍珠港事变之前，日军不得进入校园。

[3]《欢迎词》，1938 年 6 月 1 日，贵州省档案馆，卷号 534。

[4]《医生业务的探讨》，见《贵州日报》1943 年 7 月 23 日。

后依然闪闪发光。李宗恩提倡“生理健全、心理健全和精神健全的健全生活”，他还认为“生活应该是有声有色的，是内容丰富、色彩浓厚的。[1]” 8 年战争中，国立贵阳医学院办的红红火火，为抗战建国培养了数百名合格的医生，被誉为大西南的“小协和”。

1947 年 3 月 12 日，以胡适为首的协和董事会一致选举李宗恩为协和医学院首任有实权的中国籍院长，主持恢复在太平洋战争爆发后被关闭了 5 年的协和医学院。此时国共内战一触即发，通货恶性膨胀，协和医学院的资金只有战前购买力的八分之一。李宗恩提出，“在最经济的条件之下来维持我们协和的特殊精神”，“这种精神就是‘不论任何一件事、一件工作，要么不做，要做的话就要达到一种标准。’绝不马虎，绝不苟且。[2]”他带领团队制定财政预算，修缮校舍，购置设备。5 个月后，22 名新生开始上课。复校初期，李宗恩放眼于协和的未来，邀请当时中国最优秀的医学专家到协和工作，张孝骞、林巧稚、邓家栋、裘祖源、吴英恺、张鋆、张锡均、胡正详、何观清、冯兰洲、谢少文等应招而来，为协和医学院在以后领先中国医学教育几十年奠定了坚实的基础。接着，李宗恩又组织了 12 次教授午餐会，讨论医学教育的目的——为中国培养什么样的医生。“（1）他应该身心健全。精神健康，我们是指社会适应能力，既对他人的同情和理解，对他人的需求寄予回应，个人的悟性包括对自己的了解、自信和随机应变的能力；（2）他必须有足够的综合的知识积累；（3）他必须具备专业知识，具有平衡而综合地运用预防医学、治疗方法、社会学等各方面知识的能力；（4）最后，他必须具备作为一个公民和医生的责任感。[3]”——这就是一代老协和人数十年来从事精英教育、在抗战的艰苦环境中坚持不懈以及亲手重建协和之后的集体智慧，也是李宗恩的医学教育理想。

李宗恩是一位坚定的理想主义者。他相信“为了人类的进步，团体尽可制裁个人反对团体的行动，却不能强制他变更自己的思想。而个人方面呢，自己有一种思想，也应该勇敢地发表，这不但是你的权利．也是你对人类文化的义务。[4]”1957年鸣放期间，李宗恩对中国的医学教育和医学院的管理提出了自己的

---

[1] 《为什么提倡健全生活》，见《国立贵阳医学院院刊》第 12 期，1939 年 7 月 1。
[2] 《任协和校长时的讲演》，1947 年 10 月 9 日，协和医学院档案室。
[3] 《非正式医学教授会议总结》，1949 年 5 月，协和医学院档案室。
[4] 《1938 年国庆讲演》，1938 年 10 月 10 日，贵州省档案馆，卷号 534。

意见，因此受到了从上到下的大批判，最后成了钦点的医药界头号右派，在垂暮之年被流放到西南边陲。不到四年，他心肾衰竭，住院抢救。临终前，李宗恩写下："我将心满意足地离去，无怨无悔。"，其诠释可见于他1939年写给贵医学生的文字："生活应该是有意义的。我们不能够醉生梦死的空活一辈子。我们活一天要有一天的成绩。我们要从自己的志愿由实现的当中取得满足。我们要让自己到了老年没有什么懊悔，临死都一点不觉得遗憾……。[1]"

2017年9月，北京协和医学院举办百年校庆；2018年10月，贵州医科大学（原贵阳医学院）校庆80周年，竖立李宗恩像，命名宗恩广场。今年是李宗恩诞辰125周年，我完成了李宗恩纪念文集的最后一册——《李宗恩先生文存》，以纪念我的祖父。

李维华

2019 年 5 月，美国印第安纳州

[1] 《为什么提倡健全生活》，见《国立贵阳医学院院刊》第 12 期，1939 年 7 月 1。

学术论文

以下是李宗恩在 1921 年至 1942 年期间发表的 30 篇学术论文中的 28 篇，有一篇缺失，最后一篇因太平洋战争爆发而未能发表。为保留原著的文体和杂志的学术风格，所有文章采用了原始书影。另外，每篇文章之前都加入题目的中文翻译和内容的翻译概要，以方便非医学专业的读者阅读。

1. **Bilharzia Infection in the New World**

Lee, C.U. and Khalil, M. Read at the West Indian Medical Conference, July 8, 1921, on behalf of the Filariasis Commission of the London School of Tropical Medicine.

李宗恩，Khalil M.《新大陆的丝虫病感染》，代表伦敦热带病学院考察团在西印度群岛医学会议上的发言，1921 年 7 月 8 日。

李宗恩发言《对乔治敦华裔、东印度裔、葡萄牙裔、非裔和混合族裔丝虫病发病率的初步考察》

翻译概要 丝虫病考察团一到达乔治敦就开始研究该地区的丝虫病发病率，并检测随机采集的血标本中丝虫卵阳性率（见附表）。因为不是所有丝虫病人的血样中都检测到了丝虫卵，实际感染率应高于这一结果。以种族而论，混合族裔的丝虫病感染率最高，依次为非裔、葡萄牙裔、东印度裔、华裔。以性别而论，华裔、非裔、混合族裔的男性比女性的感染率高；葡萄牙裔和东印度裔的女性感染率比男性高。

如利帕（Robert Leiper，1881-1969）[1]教授所言，中国人不存在种族的免疫力。虽然我们的调查表明所有族裔中华裔的丝虫病感染率最低，但丝虫病在中国也有发生，如厦门地区。我们认为华裔丝虫病发病率低的原因有三：1. 华裔是最近到来的移民；2. 由习惯和传统所致，华裔一般不与其他族裔自由融合；3.大部分乔治敦的华裔都是小商贩，习惯用蚊帐，穿衣也比较注意。

[1] Robert T. Leiper，1881-1969，寄生虫学创始人。李宗恩在 1921 年获得格拉斯哥大学医学院医学学位以后，到利帕教授在伦敦热带病学院的实验室工作，并参加该院丝虫病考察团赴西印度群岛考察。

The inhabitants of this block were Blacks, Mixed, Portuguese and East Indians.

Blacks	192	with microfilaria	66 or 34·3	per cent.
Mixed	74	,, ,,	28 or 37·7	do.
Portuguese	11	,, ,,	5 or 45·4	do.
East Indians... ...	9	,, ,,	4 or 44·4	do.

The survey was commenced on the 22nd instant. It is premature to draw any final conclusions from the figures cited above. We hope that they may be of interest to the Conference for comparison with those which may be submitted from other colonies.

Dr. C. U. LEE (London) read the following paper :—

A PRELIMINARY REPORT ON THE INCIDENCE OF FILARIAL INFECTION AMONGST CHINESE, EAST INDIANS, PORTUGUESE, BLACKS AND MIXED RACES IN GEORGETOWN.

Presented on behalf of the Filariasis Commission of the London School of Tropical Medicine.

Since its arrival the Filariasis Commission has been devoting part of its time to studying the incidence of filarial infection in this Colony. The following figures relate to the presence of filaria embryos in the blood of the general population of Georgetown. They are not from picked cases but taken at random in the Hospital, in Public Institutions and in certain areas of the town, and ought to bear more or less close relation to the general population of the town.

While the presence of microfilariae in the blood indicates positive infection, the reverse does not hold. In a number of cases of lymphangitis, elephantiasis and other clinical types usually attributed to filariasis, no microfilaria could be found in the blood. There are also cases, where microfilariae were absent from the blood at the time of our examination, but their presence had been detected on previous occasions. Therefore the actual percentage of filariasis would be higher than the figures shown in the following tables.

The tables are so constructed as to show the incidence of positive blood infections amongst the different races inhabiting this town.

Out of 150 Chinese	examined	7	were found infected	or	4.7	per cent.
,, ,, 104 East Indians	,,	14	,, ,, ,,	,,	13.5	do.
,, ,, 38 Portuguese	,,	7	,, ,, ,,	,,	18.4	do.
,, ,, 400 Blacks	,,	100	,, ,, ,,	,,	25.0	do.
,, ,, 116 Mixed	,,	32	,, ,, ,,	,,	27.6	do.
Total 808 persons	,,	160	,, ,, ,,	,,	19.7	do.

The Mixed Race is most heavily infected, next come the Blacks, Portuguese, East Indians, while the Chinese are least infected.

With regard to the frequency of positive blood infections the order in our series coincides with that published by DANIELS in 1896. It should, however, be mentioned that DANIELS did not include the Chinese in his series.

As to sex incidence, the males amongst the Chinese, Blacks and Mixed are more infected than the females, while amongst the East Indians and Portuguese, the females are more infected than the males, but taking the general population as a whole both sexes seem to be equally infected. DANIELS in 1896 gave a positive blood infection of 14.9 per cent. WISE in 1909 gave a percentage of 13.0. Our figure, namely, 19.7, is appreciably higher, but this may be explainable on the ground that at present Albert-town alone forms about a quarter of our total survey.

Out of 808 examined, 223 were taken from Albert-town and the proportion of infected individuals was 33.2%.

Excluding Albert-town the remaining 685 examined in Georgetown showed a percentage of 11.1.

Dr. LEE (London): Racial immunity does not exist among the Chinese, as Professor LEIPER has stated. Filariasis occurs in certain parts of China, of which Amoy is one. Some time ago a general survey of the Chinese inhabitants was instituted. The figures so far reached indicate that the Chinese show an appreciably lower rate of blood infection than is the case with the other races. It is yet premature to offer an explanation, but it might be interesting to the Conference to know the following points. The Chinese are, firstly, the most recent arrivals of all the immigrant races in this Colony; secondly, the Chinese, by reason of customs and traditions, like to keep to themselves and do not mix freely with the other races; thirdly, the majority of the Chinese in Georgetown belong to the class of shop-keepers, and being thus in a better position than the other classes usually provide themselves with things such as mosquito netting, proper clothing and other material comfort, which may have something to do with the low percentage of blood infection shown in the table.

The following table was presented to the Conference by Dr. LEE in connection with the paper read by him :—

The Presence of Filaria Embryos in the Blood of the General Population of Georgetown.

RACE.	MALES.			FEMALES.			TOTAL.		
	Number Examined.	Number Infected.	Per-centage.	Number Examined.	Number Infected.	Per-centage.	Number Examined	Number Infected.	Per-centage.
Chinese ...	70	5	7·1	80	2	2·5	150	7	4·7
East Indian ...	63	8	12·7	41	6	14·6	104	14	13·5
Portuguese ...	12	2	16·7	26	5	19·2	38	7	18·4
Black ...	142	40	28·3	258	60	13·3	400	100	25·0
Mixed ...	45	18	40·0	71	14	19·7	116	32	27·6
TOTAL ...	332	73	21·9	476	87	18.3	808	160	19·7

2. A Filarial Survey in British Guiana, 1921

Anderson, J. Khalil, M. Lee, C.U., and Leiper, R.T., *Journal of Helminthology*, 1:215-226, 1923; *London School of Tropical Medicine Research Memoir Series*, 5:105-116, 1924.

Anderson, J. Khalil, M. 李宗恩，罗伯特 · 利帕 《1921 年英属圭亚那丝虫病考察》，载于《寄生虫学杂志》1923 年，1:215-226；《伦敦热带病学院医学研究文集》，1924 年, 5:105-116 页。

翻译概要 丝虫病可能是由西非洲的奴隶带到英属圭亚那的。1877 年，Hillis 医生在当地搜集的血样中发现了微丝蚴。此后 40 年在英属圭亚那的 4 次考察显示，丝虫病的发病率似有逐渐上升的趋势。但这一趋势还没有被现代的实验技术证实过。1921 年，由英国、中国、伊斯兰团员组成的丝虫病考察团对英属圭亚那的丝虫病进行了首次考察。Khalil 医生应当地穆斯林社区邀请多次参加他们晚间的穆斯林礼仪，期间搜集了很多东印度移民的血液标本。李宗恩医生受到乔治敦华裔家庭的欢迎，搜集到了难得的统计数字。考察团群策群力，在英属圭亚那的医院、学校、监狱、难民所和家访中搜集并检测了 4,215 份血样（耳血），其中 835（19.8%）显示微丝蚴阳性。

根据 1921 年人口统计，乔治敦有华人 2,722，大部分是第一代移民。据传说，华人从不患丝虫病，但因为华人的丝虫病还未被考察过，考察团需要考证种族免疫性的可能。在 David Ewing-Chow 和乔治敦华人协会的帮助下，李宗恩医生家访了近 50%的华人。经过血液化验和对生活习性的调查，李医生认为中国人丝虫病患病率低不是种族原因，而是因为他们有日落而息和使用蚊帐的习惯。他提出中国人并没有对丝虫病的种族免疫性，患病率低是他们的卫生习惯和文化传统使然。

Journal of Helminthology, Vol. 1, 1923, pp. 215-226.

A Filarial Survey in British Guiana, 1921

By J. ANDERSON, M. KHALIL, C. U. LEE and R. T. LEIPER
(*Members of the Filariasis Commission of the London School of Tropical Medicine.*)

THE Filariasis Commission, composed as it was of British, Chinese, and Mohammedan members, was able to take a more extensive and a more representative survey of the incidence of filariasis than would have been possible in the case of a single investigator. Dr. Khalil had frequent invitations to local Mohammedan ceremonies, and as these were usually held at night, he was able to examine a large number of blood-films from East Indian immigrants. Dr. C. U. Lee was very hospitably received by the Chinese families of Georgetown, and collected statistics as to the filarial rate amongst them on a scale that was hitherto unattainable. The whole commission, working together, was able to undertake a survey of an institution such as Georgetown Prison, the Almshouse, or Christchurch Public School with little inconvenience to the children or inmates. Thus from hospitals, schools, prisons, asylums, and domiciliary visitations, the Commission collected details and examined blood-films from 4,215 inhabitants of British Guiana. The total number of examinations was made up as follows :—

Cases examined at random in Georgetown	2,434
" " " country districts	785
Patients attending the Night Clinic for Filariasis at Georgetown Public Hospital	865
Aboriginal Indians	131
Total	4,215

In the examination of these blood-films 835 or 19·8 per cent. showed microfilariæ of different types.

TECHNIQUE.

It was found most convenient to take specimens of blood from the lobe of the ear. The lobe was rubbed vigorously with spirit and allowed to dry. With a straight surgical needle a puncture was made, and a drop of blood was collected on a microscope slide. This drop was then spread in a thick film by the aid of the needle. Where accurate microfilarial counts were necessary, a hæmocytometer pipette was used, and 20 cubic millimetres of blood were placed on each slide. This quantity was taken as the standard in all the therapeutic tests.

As a routine practice in the examination of bloodfilms it was found unnecessary to use any stain. In many cases the fresh blood-film was examined on the spot, and the active movements of the microfilariæ seen under a 2/3 in. lens made an immediate diagnosis possible. Generally, however, the films were allowed to dry, and were then taken back to the laboratory for careful scrutiny. There the films were de-hæmoglobinised in a tray of distilled water, and examined microscopically while still wet. If the slide had been allowed to dry, the embryos could still be detected, but they did not stand out so clearly under the low power as in the wet state.

Filarial Survey.—British Guiana.

Historical.—Infection by *Filaria bancrofti* was probably introduced into British Guiana and the West Indies by slaves brought from West Africa. Some of the old inhabitants state that various manifestations such as elephantiasis and "rose" were not uncommon in the middle of last century, and they are convinced that in the last seventy years the infection has steadily become more widespread. The presence of microfilariæ in the blood was first recognised, it is believed, by a Dr. Hillis about the year 1877, shortly after Lewis and Manson had published similar observations in India and China.

In May, 1883, Dr. Grieve, when Medical Superintendent of the lunatic asylum, published a paper in the asylum journal showing the percentages of persons of different races in the institution who were suffering from elephantiasis. From a survey of 400 patients he found this disease in 21 or 5·2 per cent. He considered that as insanity could hardly affect the incidence of elephantiasis, his figures would give a fairly accurate indication of the proportion of the disease in the colony.

Interest in the subject was next stimulated by Dr. Daniels[1], who described in 1896 some specimens of adult worms found in the course of an operation for the removal of an inguinal cyst. These he identified as *Filaria bancrofti*. In the same periodical he published, in collaboration

[1] "British Guiana Medical Annual" for 1896, p. 62.

with Dr. Conyers[3], a filarial survey of the patients in Georgetown Hospital. In one group of 752 persons examined they found 9·1 per cent. suffering from elephantoid disease ; and 348 blood examinations showed microfilariæ in 14·9 per cent. of the cases.

In the following year Dr. A. T. Ozzard[3] announced his discovery of a new species prevalent amongst the aboriginal Indians on the Demerara River, which came to be known later as *Filaria ozzardi*. Dr. Daniels[4] at once confirmed the discovery, and described the parasite.

In 1902, Dr. G. C. Low[5], of the London School of Tropical Medicine, visited British Guiana during his researches in the West Indies, and wrote a very suggestive paper on "Filarial Lymphangitis." Dr. K. S. Wise[6] took up the quest from this point, and in 1907 he published his pathological and bacteriological observations on the grave septicæmic conditions which he called "Abdominal Filariasis." In the following year he drew up statistics[7] regarding the filarial rate amongst the patients in Georgetown Hospital, and in a total of 493 persons examined he found filarial embryos in the blood in 13·0 per cent.

Wise continued his work on the bacteriology of filariasis, and published several papers in the Reports of the Committee for the Tropical Diseases Research Fund. In 1915, Dr. F. G. Rose[8] described the first results of his treatment of filarial conditions by vaccines, a promising therapeutic agent which has been elaborated and employed up to the present day. Rose also made a more extensive survey of the filarial rate than had hitherto been attempted, and he published his results in a Report to the Committee of the Tropical Diseases Research Fund in 1920.

The four different surveys thus conducted over a period of 40 years pointed to a steady increase in the proportion of persons infected. To what extent this apparent increase might be discounted by the more modern methods of examination is an open question.

Tables I. to IV. summarise the findings in the total of 4,215 blood-films examined by the Filariasis Commission in 1921.

Tables I. and II. show a heavy infection with *Filaria bancrofti* throughout the Colony, but particularly in the city of Georgetown. They also

[2] "British Guiana Medical Annual" for 1896, p. 42.
[3] Ibid for 1897, p. 28. [4] Ibid, p. 24. [5] Ibid for 1902, p. 1.
[6] Ibid for 1907, p. 134. [7] Ibid for 1908, p. 35. [8] Ibid for 1915, p. 7.

show that while all races are liable to infection, the highest rates of incidence are found amongst the Blacks, the Mixed races and the Portuguese.

TABLE I.

INHABITANTS OF GEORGETOWN TAKEN AT RANDOM.

Race.	Males.			Females.		
	Number examined.	Number with Micro-filariæ.	Per-centage.	Number examined.	Number with Micro-filariæ.	Per-centage.
Blacks ...	614	189	30·78	397	119	30·0
Mixed Races ...	171	46	26·90	216	46	21·3
East Indians ...	275	34	12·36	140	13	9·3
Portuguese ...	63	15	23·81	61	13	21·3
Chinese ...	209	21	10·05	222	10	4·5
Europeans ...	53	5	9·43	13	1	7·7
Total ...	1,385	310	22·38%	1,049	202	19·26%

TABLE II.

COUNTRY DISTRICTS TAKEN AT RANDOM.

Race.	Males.			Females.		
	Number examined.	Number with Micro-filariæ.	Per-centage.	Number examined.	Number with Micro-filariæ.	Per-centage.
Blacks ...	273	41	15·0	80	12	15·0
Mixed	22	5	22·7	14	1	7·1
East Indians ...	295	35	11·9	31	2	6·5
Portuguese ...	4	—	—	3	—	—
Chinese ...	8	2	25·0	3	—	—
Europeans ...	48	4	8·3	4	—	—
Total ...	650	87	13·4%	135	15	11·1%

TABLE III.

NIGHT CLINIC FOR FILARIASIS, GEORGETOWN PUBLIC HOSPITAL.

	Number of Cases.	Number with Microfilariæ.	Percentage.
Elephantiasis	434	42	9·67
Other manifestations	275	120	43·63
Healthy relatives...	156	30	19·23
Total	865	192	22·8%

TABLE IV.

ABORIGINAL INDIANS.

	Number examined.	Number with *F. perstans*.	*F. ozzardi*.	*F. perstans* and *F. ozzardi*.	*F. bancrofti*.
Males	90	10	4	4	1
Females... ...	41	8	—	4	—
Total ...	131	18	4	8	1

It is interesting to compare the percentage of infection shown in Table I. with the findngs of previous observers in the same area. Table V. is divided into four columns to show the percentage of cases infected with *F. bancrofti* in four different surveys carried out during the past 25 years.

TABLE V.

GEORGETOWN AND DISTRICT.

		A. 1896.	B. 1908.	C. 1919–20.	D. 1921.
Numbers examined ...		—	—	351	2,434
		%	%	%	%
Blacks ...	...Male	13·0	10·2	24·8	30·8
	Female	24·0	16·8	26·0	30·0
Mixed ...	...Male	14·2	18·3	27·3	26·9
	Female	24·0	16·8	21·4	21·3
East Indians	...Male	6·4	5·4	14·2	12·4
	Female	6·6	6·2	—	9·3
Portuguese	...Male	16·6	16·4	15·4	23·8
	Female	25·0	24·8	16·7	21·3
Chinese ...	...Male	—	—	—	10·0
	Female	—	—	—	4·5
Europeans	...Male	—	—	—	9·4
	Female	—	—	—	7·7
All above	...Male	10·8	9·7	19·5	22·4
	Female	20·1	17·3	23·3	19·3

Column A gives the percentage found amongst the patients of Georgetown Hospital by Conyers and Daniels in 1896 ; column B gives the corresponding infection found by Wise in 1908 ; column C shows the percentage found by Rose in 1919-20 during a general survey of normal members of the population ; column D gives the percentage found in Georgetown by us

These figures show a considerable increase in the general filarial infection during the past quarter of a century, and as the rate amongst women has remained fairly constant, the increase is much more marked amongst the males. Modern methods of examination differ but slightly from those practised by the older observers, and could not account for such a striking variation.

Albert Town.—In order to get an accurate idea of the filarial rate in the heart of Georgetown, the Commission decided to make an intensive examination of the residents in a compact area. The most suitable area for this purpose was the municipal district of Albert Town because it was largely inhabited by typical working-class citizens, and it was situated in convenient proximity to the laboratory. In this district three blocks of residences were selected, and the Government Registrar kindly supplied a copy of the census returns made in April, 1921. The population of the three blocks given in the census register was 637. By regular domiciliary visits each night between 9 p.m. and 10 p.m. for about a fortnight the Commission, assisted by Drs. F. G. Rose and Ewing-Chow, examined altogether 515 individuals, or 81 per cent. of the population of the area. Table VI. gives the results of the blood examination in these cases. All infections were *F. bancrofti*.

TABLE VI.

ALBERT TOWN.

Races.	Males.			Females.		
	Number examined.	Number with Micro-filariæ.	Per-centage.	Number examined.	Number with Micro-filariæ.	Per-centage.
Blacks ...	128	45	35·2	210	58	27·5
Mixed	53	18	34·0	71	16	26·0
East Indians ...	6	4	—	7	2	—
Portuguese ...	15	6	—	20	7	—
Europeans ...	2	1	—	3	—	—
Total ...	204	74	36·3%	311	83	26·7%

Prisoners.—Through the kindness of the various authorities concerned, the Commission paid visits to H.M. Penal Settlement at Bartica and the prison in Georgetown. The prisoners in general were a healthy body of men and women drawn from all parts of the country, and the filarial survey might be taken as representative of the incidence of infection amongst the lower classes of the Colony. Altogether 424 prisoners were examined, and 115 or 27 per cent. were infected with *F. bancrofti*. One Aboriginal Indian showed embryos of *F. perstans*.

Table VII. gives the percentage of infection for males and females amongst those who had resided in Georgetown and those drawn from country districts.

TABLE VII.

	Former Residents in Georgetown.			Former Residents in Country Districts.		
	Number examined.	Number with Micro-filariæ.	Per-centage.	Number examined.	Number with Micro-filariæ.	Per-centage.
Males	152	70	46·1	230	33	14·4
Females ...	28	10	35·7	14	3	21·4
Total ...	180	80	44·4%	244	36	14·8%

Table VIII. shows the infection rate according to racial distribution.

TABLE VIII.

RACIAL DISTRIBUTION OF PRISONERS.

	Resident in Georgetown.			Resident in Country.		
	Number examined.	Number with Micro-filariæ.	Per-centage.	Number examined.	Number with Micro-filariæ.	Per-centage.
Blacks ...	143	68	47·5	134	23	17·2
Mixed	12	4	33·3	6	2	33·3
East Indians ...	17	4	23·5	99	12	12·1
Portuguese ...	3	1	—	2	—	—
Chinese ...	2	1	—	2	—	—
Europeans ...	3	2	—	—	—	—
Aboriginals ...	—	—	—	1	*F. perstans*	—

The figures in the above table point definitely to filariasis being largely an urban infection in British Guiana, and they again give premier position in the racial distribution to the Blacks. A survey of a number of cases in Berbice Lunatic Asylum gave similar results.

It is significant that in very few of the houses in Albert Town was there any mosquito netting used, and in practically all of them mosquitoes were plentiful. One of the sanitary inspectors kindly made a random collection of 1,660 mosquitoes from the houses visited by the Commission, and these were identified as follows :—

Culex fatigans, 1,429 ; *Ædes argenteus*, 187 ; *Mansonia titillans*, 3 ; *Ædes scapularis*, 41.

From the group of *Culex fatigans* 141 females were sectioned in celloidin, and 24·1 per cent. were found infected with filarial embryos.

New Amsterdam.—Next in importance to Georgetown, the town of New Amsterdam has a population of slightly over 8,000. A visit was paid one night to New Amsterdam Hospital, and the filarial infection was found to be 14 per cent. of the total blood examinations. The following table gives the racial distribution in the total of 100 cases examined :—

TABLE IX.
NEW AMSTERDAM.

	Males.			Females.		
	Number examined.	Number with Micro-filariæ.	Per-centage.	Number examined.	Number with Micro-filariæ.	Per-centage.
Blacks ...	38	6	—	29	7	—
Mixed	5	—	—	4	—	—
East Indians ...	18	1	—	6	—	—
Total ...	61	7	11·5%	39	7	18·2%

Chinese.—According to the census returns for 1921, the Chinese in British Guiana numbered 2,722, the majority of whom were native born. There was a tradition that none of the Chinese in the Colony had ever suffered from filariasis or elephantiasis, and the Commission was particularly anxious to ascertain whether there might be some racial immunity. For various reasons no previous survey of the filarial rate amongst the Chinese colonists had ever been undertaken, but through the great influence of Mr. David Ewing-Chow and the Chinese Association of Georgetown, Dr. C. U. Lee commenced a domiciliary visitation on extensive lines.

The survey embraced roughly 50 per cent. of the Chinese population in Georgetown, and showed at once that the theory of racial immunity was untenable. In Table X. the results of blood examination give a positive filarial infection by *F. bancrofti* of 7·4 per cent.

No frank case of elephantiasis was found amongst 442 individuals, and the incidence of lymphangitis, lymphadenitis, and other filarial manifestations was unusually low.

Dr. Lee discovered that the low incidence of filariasis amongst the Chinese could be accounted for by their careful attention to personal hygiene. Most of the women and a large proportion of the men retire to bed soon after dark, and practically all of them sleep under mosquito curtains. The infected cases were practically all found in the districts of Charlestown, Lacytown, and Werkenrust, neighbourhoods which are inhabited chiefly by the poorer classes.

TABLE X.

CHINESE.

	Males.			Females.		
	Number examined	Number with Micro-filariæ.	Per-centage.	Number examined.	Number with Micro-filariæ.	Per-centage.
Georgetown ...	209	21	10·0	222	10	4·5
Country districts	8	2	—	3	—	—
Totals ...	217	23	10·6%	225	10	4·4%

AGE INCIDENCE.

For a long time it was believed that the incubation period of filariasis extended into several years, as microfilariæ had not been found in the blood of very young children. The Commission made periodical examinations in the children's ward in Georgetown Public Hospital, and found positive infections under 5 years of age on several occasions. The youngest child with microfilariæ in the peripheral blood was 14 months old, and three infected children were under 2 years of age.

The education authorities kindly granted facilities for an examination of the children attending one of the large schools in Georgetown, and a considerable proportion of the scholars were induced to return to school one evening accompanied by their parents. In this way over 200 children ranging from 4 to 16 years of age were examined for physical signs of filariasis, and blood-films were taken from 196.

Tables XI. and XII. give the analyses of these 196 cases in age groups according to symptoms and according to race.

TABLE XI.

CHRISTCHURCH SCHOOL.

	Number examined.	Number with Enlarged Glands.	Number with Elephantiasis.	Number with Microfilariæ.
4 to 10 years of age	106	68 = 64%	1 = 0·9%	12 = 11·3%
11 to 16	90	50 = 55%	4 = 4·4%	11 = 12·2%
Totals	196	118 = 60·2%	5 = 2·6%	23 = 11·7%

TABLE XII.

CHRISTCHURCH SCHOOL.

Age	Males.				Females.			
	4 to 10 yrs.		11 to 16 yrs.		4 to 10 yrs.		11 to 16 yrs.	
	No. examined.	No. with Microfilariæ.	No. examined.	No. with Microfilariæ.	No. examined.	No. with Microfilariæ.	No. examined.	No. with Microfilariæ.
Blacks ...	35	4	39	5	40	5	18	2
Mixed ...	10	1	11	–	10	1	13	3
East Indians	4	–	2	–	1	–	3	–
Portuguese	3	–	3	1	1	1	–	–
Europeans	2	–	1	–	–	–	–	–

The above tables show a high rate of infection even amongst children under 10 years of age, and as in all previous tables, the Blacks again occupy the premier position. A true estimate of the age period showing the highest filarial rate might perhaps be obtained from an analysis of the survey conducted in Albert Town. The collective results of this survey have already been given in Table VI. In Table XIII. the 515 inhabitants examined in this compact area are divided into age periods of 10 years, and only those are marked positive who had microfilariæ in the peripheral blood. It will be observed that the highest incidence is found in young people from 10 to 20 years of age, but even up till 50 years the percentage of infection remains fairly uniform.

TABLE XIII.

ALBERT TOWN.

Age-Periods	Up to 10 yrs.		11 to 20 yrs.		21 to 30 yrs.		31 to 40 yrs.	
	No. examined.	Positive for Microfilariæ.	No. examined.	Positive for Microfilariæ.	No. examined.	Positive for Microfilariæ.	No. examined.	Positive for Microfilariæ.
Males ...	61	16	49	18	25	8	19	8
Females ...	72	10	66	22	55	19	45	16
Total ...	133	26	115	40	80	27	64	24
Percentage Infection	—	19·5%	—	37·4%	—	33·7%	—	37·5%

Age-Periods	41 to 50 yrs.		51 to 60 yrs.		Over 60 yrs.			
	No. examined.	Positive for Microfilariæ.	No. examined.	Positive for Microfilariæ.	No. examined.	Positive for Microfilariæ.		
Males ...	18	8	15	7	17	9		
Females ...	37	11	19	3	17	2		
Total ...	55	19	34	10	34	11		
Percentage Infection	—	34·5%	—	29·4%	—	32·3%		

ELEPHANTIASIS.

Elephantiasis.—The racial distribution of elephantiasis is a question which has been raised in the four previous surveys conducted between 1883 and 1920. In the report of the Government Bacteriologist for British Guiana, 1920, Rose states that " the Portuguese, especially the Portuguese women, retain their priority of place." The Filariasis Clinique conducted by the Commission in 1921, was attended by 352 cases of elephantiasis living in Georgetown, and the following table gives the number and percentage belonging to each of the different races, together with the percentage of these races living in the city at the last census.

TABLE XIV.
ELEPHANTIASIS IN GEORGETOWN.

	Number of cases of Elephantiasis who visited Clinic.	Percentage of all cases.	Percentage population of Georgetown. Census Records.
Blacks	205	58·2	49·9
Mixed	73	20·8	24·7
East Indians	26	7·4	10·8
Portuguese	39	11·0	9·4
Chinese	—	—	1·4
Europeans	9	2·6	3·7
Aboriginal Indians ...	—	—	0·1
Total	352	100·0	100·0

It is clear, therefore, that with the above criteria the priority of place seems now to rest with the Blacks.

3. **Two Cases of Schistosomiasis Japonica (Abstract)**
Lee, C.U. *Proceedings of Joint Conference of China Medical Association and China Branch of British Medical Association, Hong Kong*, P. 25, 1925.
李宗恩《两例日本血吸虫》，载于《中华医学会和英国医学会中国分会联合研讨会（香港）发言摘要汇编》，1925 年，25 页。

翻译概要 1924 年 7 月上旬，两个罗马尼亚吉普赛兄弟在九江（长江水灾地区）游泳，1 个月后同时开始发烧、胃肠道不适。经药物（一例用 Patassium Antimony 治疗，另一例又加了 Emetine）治疗后，两例均恢复健康，大便血吸虫卵呈阴性。

BRING THIS WITH YOU TO THE MEETINGS

JOINT CONFERENCE

OF THE

China Medical Missionary Association

AND THE

China Branch, British Medical Association

HONGKONG, JANUARY, 1925.

ABSTRACTS OF MEDICAL PAPERS TO BE PRESENTED AT THE SECTIONAL MEETINGS OF THE CONFERENCE.

dosage of 2 grams was administered in 6 cases, and 1.65 gram in one case, over a period covering from 33 to 62 days.

4. Fecal examinations showed that eggs of *Schistosoma japonicum* were absent from 9 to 33 days following the first administration, but that miracidia from washed feces samples were detected several days after the apparent disappearance of the eggs in the stool.

5. From the point of view of laboratory diagnosis the cases would be recorded as "cured" of the infection and clinical improvement was observed in each case. However, "follow up" examinations, which were not feasible, would be necessary to determine the permanent effect of the treatment.

Two Cases of Schistosomiasis Japonica.—C. U. LEE, M. B., Ph. B., D. T. M. AND H., Department of Medicine, Peking Union Medical College, Peking.

Two cases of schistosomiasis japonica in two Roumanian brothers are reported. The infection occurred simultaneously in the first half of July, 1924, from swimming in the water on the flooded bank of the Yang-tse River at Kiukiang. Symptoms of fever and gastro-intestinal disturbances developed about a mouth later. A course of treatment with potassium antimony tartrate in one case, and with emetine and potassium antimony tartrate in the other, apparently cured the condition in so far as all symptoms cleared up and the stools became repeatedly negative for ova.

Ova of *Ascaris* and *Fasciolopsis* as well as of *Giardia* and *Trichomonas*, which were incidentally found in the stools, also disappeared after treatment.

The practical aspect of Hookworm control in china.—N. Bercovitz, M.D., Kachek, Hainan.

The chronic disability caused by hookworm, and the means of dissemination of the infestation by the use of nightsoil as fertilizer and the absence of latrines make it desirable, in order to get the most lasting results, to aim at the treatment of communities as far as possible, with repetition of the treatment at intervals of six months to a year in order to reduce the ground infestation.

Carbon tetrachloride and oil of chenopodium mixture, in proportion of 10 to 1, dosage 1½ drops for each year of age of patient till maximum of 30 to 35 drops is reached, followed by magnesium sulphate purge seems to bring best results.

In order to secure community treatment preliminary educational work has to be done, and it is urged that evangelists, while itinerating, give as part of their message some information as to the ravages of the disease, and the ease of cure. As the public health service of China is built up, hookworm control will be done by the government.

4. The Treatment of Schistosomiasis Japonica

Lee, C.U., *The China Medical Journal* 39: 321-331, 1925.

李宗恩《血吸虫病的治疗》，载于《中华医学杂志》，1925 年，39:321-331 页。

翻译概要 作者回顾了血吸虫病的药物治疗，并详细报告了一个罗马尼亚吉普赛五口之家在九江感染血吸虫病的经过，及其中住院治疗的两兄弟（40 岁）的体检及治疗过程。结论如下：

a) 在长江水灾地区洗澡后感染血吸虫病的病例说明，若流行区域发生水灾，血吸虫病的感染率将增高。
b) 接触污水后的一过性丘疹值得注意。
c) 从感染到开始发烧之间的 4 周时间可能是寄生虫需要成熟的时间。
d) 本组病例没有典型的风疹和肺部临床体征。
e) 嗜伊红血球过多和无脾肿大可能是早期临床观察，也许有预后的价值。
f) Antimony 的副作用较小，至少在治疗早期。
g) 仍不能确立血吸虫病治愈的指标为粪便中不再有血吸虫卵（意味着成虫的死亡），但跟踪观察这两个病例会提供线索。
h) 虽然没有加大 Emetine 的剂量以确定其疗效，但它确实有治疗作用，值得继续研究，特别在幼儿和青少年人群，如 Cawston 所推荐。
i) 治疗后血吸虫卵和其它虫卵（Ascaris lumbricoides, Fasciolopsis buski, Giardia, and Trichomonas）从粪便中消失值得注意。

THE TREATMENT OF SCHISTOSOMIASIS JAPONICA*

C. U. LEE, M. B., Ch. B., D. T. M. and H., Peking.

Since Christopherson's publication on the successful treatment of Egyptian schistosomiasis with tartar emetic appeared in 1918, a number of authors have tried it out on the Oriental variety of the disease with equally good results.

In China, Tyau[1] claimed to have thus used the drug with success in 1920. In 1921, Sanders and Priston[2] reported a number of cases apparently cured by tartar emetic. More recently, Faust and Meleney, in their exhaustive monograph[3] gave an account of the case of an American naval officer, who, after an intensive course of antimony, made a complete recovery. Tootell[4], of Hunan, in a series of 24 cases treated with tartar emetic obtained cures in fifty per cent and improvement in twenty-nine per cent of the remainder. In the experience of Libby[5], of Wuhu, the drug proved effective in mild cases, though it did not stay the progress of the disease in severe cases in which the liver and spleen were extensively diseased. Kau[6], of Kashing, also had good results in three cases. These results seem to show fairly conclusively that antimony is a specific for schistosomiasis japonica as for the other types of schistosomiasis.

With regard to dosage, it varied considerably with different authors. Kau secured his results with a total dosage of 0.54 gm. the maximum single dose being 0.1 gm; while Libby used in one case as much as 2.31 gms. with a maximum single dose of 0.18 gm. This case, however, succumbed either from the disease or from the energetic treatment. None of the others gave more than 2.0 gms. Faust and Meleney recommend the intensive method of treatment, in which the drug is pushed rapidly up to the limit of the patient's tolerance and then kept up in doses just below it. A course of 2.0 gms can thus be completed in eighteen days.

While antimony is to be regarded as the drug of choice in all cases of schistosomiasis, the importance of having at our command

*From the Department of Medicine, Peking Union Medical College, Peking.

another drug approaching it in potency becomes apparent when individual susceptibility and tolerance to antimony are taken into consideration. In certain cases, e.g., children or fat women, where intravenous injection is a difficult procedure, emetine has the decided advantage of being more easily administered than antimony. Cawston[12], of Egypt, even prefers emetine to antimony in children and young adults but warns against its severe depressive action on the heart, which is said to occur during the second or third week of the treatment. It is interesting to note that emetine was first tried by Hutcheson[7] in schistosomiasis japonica in 1913, and then by Chastang[8] in 1914, before its therapeutic value became known in the Egyptian type of the disease. Within more recent years, however, it has been quite extensively tried in Egypt by Diamantis[9], Erian[10], Tsykalas[11], and Cawston[12]. All these authors concur in holding that emetine, either intravenously or intramuscularly, has a curative action on the disease.

Tyau[13] was recently quoted by Faust and Meleney as having used emetine in one case of schistosomiasis japonica with apparent success, and suggested giving two courses of 1.00 gm. each, separated by an interval of one week.

Cawston[14] referred to a verbal report made to him by a certain Japanese medical officer, who successfully treated three cases with emetine. These seem to be the only recent records of the use of this drug in Oriental schistosomiasis in the literature.

As the number of reported cases of schistosomiasis japonica successfully treated with antimony or emetine is still small, the following two typical cases so treated may be of some interest.

Owing to our patients speaking neither Chinese nor English, the data obtained were not as precise as could be desired, but were sufficiently accurate to determine the date of infection and duration of the disease.

History of Family Infection.

In about the middle of May, 1924, a party of Roumanian gypsies, including J.M., M.M., (the two brothers who later came under our care) their mother, and M.M.'s wife, started from Harbin in Manchuria on a wandering trip in inland China. After stopping for a few days in Tientsin, they spent a month in Peking, whence they journeyed to Shanghai by train. In the second week of July, they embarked at Shanghai for Hankow, breaking their journey at Nanking where they stayed for two days, and at Kiukiang for one night.

While at Kiukiang, on or round about the 11th of July, the above mentioned members of the party bathed in the water on the flooded banks of the Yangtse river. Upon their arrival in Hankow, five days after the bathing incident, the said members with the exception of M.M. developed a skin affection in the form of itchy red papules distributed over various parts of the body, unaccompanied by febrile reactions and lasting for one or two days. In the case of J. M. the eruption affected chiefly the back of the hands and forearms, and shortly after its subsidence he began to have looseness of the bowels which persisted but did not trouble him much.

After a month's stay at Hankow, the party left for Peking by train, making a short stay at Cheng-chow in the Province of Honan, on their way up. On about the 11th of August, while at Cheng-chow, the two brothers and their mother developed pain and discomfort in the epigastric region, radiating to the right flank and back, accompanied by daily attacks of fever, malaise and gradual loss of weight. Six days later, blood and mucus were noticed in the stools of M.M. and the mother. This mild dysenteric attack, however, lasted only two days and was followed by a tendency to constipation. J.M. had no history of dysentery but his diarrhoea continued. After a few days the mother apparently recovered but the condition of the two brothers gradually got worse. Neither the sister nor M.M.'s wife developed any symptoms apart from the transient skin eruption.

The party reached Peking on the 21st of August and the two brothers were seen in the Out-patient Department of the P.U.M.C. Hospital the next day. The illness of M.M., being more severe, he was immediately admitted into the hospital and a diagnosis of schistosomiasis japonica was made on discovering the characteristic ova in his stool. J.M. joined his brother in the hospital six days later and his stools also showed the presence of schistosoma ova. The stools of the mother, the sister, and M.M.'s wife, were then carefully searched but only in that of the mother were a few ova found. As she apparently suffered no inconvenience from her infection, she could not be induced to come into the hospital.

TABLE I. SHOWING SYMPTOMS OF FAMILY.

Member of party	Skin eruption	Fever	Epigastric pain	Intestinal symptoms.
Mother	+	+	+	Dysentery
J. M.	+	+	+	Diarrhoea
M. M.	—	+	+	Dysentery
Sister	+	—	—	—
M. M.'s wife	+	—	—	—

In the absence of evidence indicating possible contact with infected water at other points along the Yangtse River, our conclusion was that all the five were infected at Kiukiang, but to varying degrees. While the mother did show some reaction to her infection, she was not ill enough to demand treatment. It would have been interesting to follow her case, if it had been possible. The two younger women were apparently very lightly infected and suffered no more inconvenience than a transient skin rash.

CASE REPORTS.

The chief complaints of the two brothers at the time of admission were of daily attacks of fever, accompanied by pain and distension in epigastric region. Their past history was negative regarding syphilis, malaria and dysentery. They first visited China in 1922, having been to Shanghai and Hankow, but between that time and the onset of present condition they gave no history of any illness.

The history of their present illness having already been gone over it is only necessary here to recapitulate the important points. On about the 16th of July, five days after bathing at Kiukiang, J. M. developed a transient skin eruption, with a glove-like distribution. Shortly after, on or about the 20th of July, a mild diarrhoea set in, which persisted but caused little inconvenience. Daily attacks of fever with malaise, headache and, prostration dated from the 11th of August, about a month after infection. About this time, the patient also began to complain of epigastric pain, and as the condition progressed some loss of weight was noted.

His brother, M.M., apparently suffered from no symptom until the 11th of August, when he developed fever and epigastric pain, followed six days later by a mild attack of dysentery lasting two days. Fever continued and the patient became progressively weakened.

Upon admission, the clinical findings were as follows :—

J. M. was a well developed and well nourished adult of forty years of age with an earthy complexion and dark areolae round the eyes. He had an intermittent temperature with a daily afternoon rise of two or three degrees Centigrade above the normal. In the early part of the day, when his temperature was down, he appeared fairly comfortable, but looked pretty ill during the height of the fever in the afternoon. Physical examination revealed nothing abnormal in the chest. On examination of the abdomen there was a fullness in the epigastric region, and on palpation a soft, smooth mass was felt extending downwards to a distance of 11.5 cm. from the tip of xiphoid cartilage in the middle line. Pressure over this mass caused pain. This obviously was an enlarged left lobe of the liver. The spleen could not be felt. There was no evidence of ascites being present, nor was there oedema in any part of the body. The reflexes were present and equal on the two sides.

Examination of the blood showed haemoglobin 84 per cent; red cells, 4,800,000; and a leucocytosis of 18,500 with polymorphonuclears, 42 per cent; lymphocytes, 5 per cent; large mononuclears, 3 per cent; and eosinophiles 50 per cent. The Wassermann test was negative; the serum globulin test was negative on admission but faintly positive a few days later.

Faeces showed the presence of *Giardia*, *Trichomonas*, and ova of *Schistosoma japonicum*, and occasionally of *Fasciolopsis buski*. The urine was negative.

With reference to his Fasciolopsis infestation, the patient admitted having eaten one or two water chestnuts *(Eliocharis tuberosa)* on one occasion during his stay in Hankow in the month of July.

The clinical findings in M.M. were very similar. He was a man twenty-one years of age, of much slighter build and looked more worn out by his illness. He also showed a temperature of see-saw type with an evening rise to 40° C.

His chest was without any abnormal physical signs. Examination of the abdomen showed, as in the case of his brother, the presence of a mass in the epigastrium, extending downwards to a distance of 9 cm. from the tip of xiphoid process in the middle line. Pain and tenderness were marked over this area and for a little distance below. Neither ascites nor oedema was found. Reflexes were normal.

Blood showed hemoglobin 94 per cent; red blood cells 4,860,000; white blood cells 22,730, with polymorphonuclears 22 per cent; lymphocytes 6 per cent; large mononuclears 2 per cent and eosinophiles 70 per cent.

The Wassermann test was negative. Globulin test was definitely positive. Microscopic examination of the faeces revealed the presence of *Trichomonas*, and ova of *Ascaris* and *Schistosoma japonicum*.

Treatment and Progress of Cases Reported.

In the case of M.M., treatment with potassium antimony tartrate (Table 2) was instituted on the 27th of August. A daily, freshly prepared 2% solution of the drug in distilled water was used. At first, intravenous injections were given daily, beginning with 2 c.c. (0.04 gm.) gradually increasing up to 5 c.c. (0.10 gm.). On account of slight dizziness after a total amount of 1.35 gm. had been given, the treatment was continued on alternate days until the total dosage reached 2.00 gm. The whole course took thirty-four days. The patient tolerated the drug well.

Table 2.—Treatment and Progress of Case of M.M.

Days after beginning of antimony treatment	Total amount of drug used	Fever	Presence of eggs in faeces	Distance of lower border of liver from tip of xiphoid process	Leucocyte count	Degree of eosinophilia	Serum globulin test
On admission	—	39.8	* ++V	9 cm.	18,200	70%	++
8	0.35	39.4	* ++V	9 cm.	18,400	72%	++
16	0.95	37.5	** +V	9 cm.	34,000	—	+
22	1.45	37.8	** +V	9 cm.	22,800	—	+
32	1.95	37.4	** +D	9 cm.	10,600	57%	+
34 Treatment stopped	2.00	38.5	— ***	—	—	—	—
On discharge...	—	37.2	—	5 cm.	10,800	27%	±

* = eggs easily found V = Viable
** = eggs found with difficulty D = Dead
*** = subsequent examinations all negative

As a result of this treatment he made a slow but uneventful recovery. The fever gradually subsided and became normal after a total of 0.95 gm. of antimony had been given during a period of sixteen days. About this time, the ova in the stools also began to diminish in number, though still viable. The last few ova that hatched were recovered on the twentieth day of the treatment after a total dosage of 1.45 gm. Thereafter the stools became persistently negative except on one occasion just before the termination of the treatment when a few dead ova were found. Five repeated examinations after the completion of the course all proved negative not only for the ova of *Schistoma*, but also for the ova of *Ascaris* and for *Trichomonas*.

The leucocytosis and eosinophilia showed a continued rise during the first part of the treatment, but came down gradually to 10,800 and 27 per cent respectively.

At the time of his discharge, the patient felt perfectly well, the pain and tenderness in the epigastrium being entirely gone, and the lower border of the liver measuring 5 cm. from the tip of xiphoid cartilage.

In the treatment of J.M., (Table 3) it was thought worth while to try the effect of emetine on the course of the disease. Accordingly, a course of emetine hydrochloride was started on the 2nd of October, using Burroughs Wellcome's tablets. Daily intramuscular injections were given, beginning with 0.022 gm., gradually increasing the dose to 0.076 gm. After a total amount of 0.726 gm. had been given, it became apparent that the drug was exerting some depressing influence on the patient, though the condition showed slight improvement in that the eggs in the stools diminished in number and the swing of the temperature became less. On the other hand, there was a distinct drop in weight and blood pressure, with general depression. The patient became restive at not getting on so well as his brother, who, by this time, was making a good recovery.

From the patient's point of view and from our lack of previous experience with emetine in this disease, and the absence of animal experimentation, it did not seem justifiable to continue the experiment and we were compelled to resort to the standard treatment with antimony.

After a week's rest, daily intravenous injections of potassium antimony tartrate were begun. Beginning with 2.5 c.c. of the 2% solution (0.05 gm.), the dose was gradually increased to 4 c.c. (0.08) per day. A total amount of 2.00 gms. in twenty-six days completed the course.

TABLE 3. TREATMENT AND PROGRESS OF CASE OF J. M.

Days after beginning of emetine treatment	Days after beginning of antimony treatment	Total amount of drug used	Fever	Presence of eggs in faeces	Distance of lower border of liver from tip of xyphoid process	Leucocyte count	Degree of eosinophilia	Serum globulin test
On admission	—	—	38.9	* ++V	11.5 cm.	18,500	50%	—
1	—	0.022	39.9	* ++V	11.5 cm.	19,900	55%	+
10	—	0.422	38.7	** +V	11.5 cm.	29,000	—	±
14 Emetine stopped	—	0.726	38.0	** +V	—	—	—	—
21	—	—	37.3	** +V	—	—	—	—
22	1	0.05	37.6	** +V	—	—	—	—
26	5	0.32	37.4	** +V	11.5 cm.	20,000	71%	+
35	14	1.04	37.8	** +V	10 cm.	8,560	44%	+
47	26	2.00	37.5	—***	7 cm.	7,760	36%	+

* = eggs easily found.
** = eggs found with difficulty. V = Viable.
*** = subsequent examinations all negative.

Under the administration of antimony his condition gradually improved. The eggs disappeared from the stools on the fourteenth day of treatment after a total dosage of 1.00 gm. The leucocytosis, having shown a rise during emetine treatment, steadily declined under antimony. The eosinophilia from 71% shortly after the commencement of antimony therapy came down to 36% at the completion of the course.

At the time of discharge the patient was quite well, complaining no more of pain in the epigastric region. The lower border of the liver now measured 7 cm. from tip of xiphoid process. Repeated examinations of his stools were all negative for ova of *Schistosoma* and *Fasciolopsis*, as well as for *Giardia* and *Trichomonas*.

It may be noted that during treatment every stool was first examined by direct smear for the presence of ova. It was then placed in a large flask and stirred with tap water. After sedimentation the supernatant fluid was decanted off and more water was added. This process was repeated several times till the fluid became perfectly clear. The ova, being thus concentrated, could be found easily in the sediment, if present in any number. Whether ova were found or not, the treated specimen was allowed to stand over night at room temperature and examined with a hand lens for hatched out miracidia the next morning. This is the method described by Faust and Meleney [15] and I am indebted to Dr. Faust for reports on all the stools of these patients during their treatment.

Conclusions.

These two cases present several points of interest :—

(a) The fact that the infection occurred through bathing in the water on the flooded banks of the Yangtse River suggests that a flood in any endemic area tends to heighten the incidence of the disease among the general population.

(b) The development of a transient papular skin eruption occurring shortly after bathing in the infested water is noteworthy.

(c) The interval between infection and onset of febrile reaction was about four weeks, probably the time required by the parasites to attain maturity.

(d) Some of the typical clinical manifestations such as urticarial rash and pulmonary involvement were lacking in these cases.

(e) The remarkably high degree of eosinophilia and absence of splenic enlargement may be important features in the early stages of the disease and of prognostic value.

(f) Antimony is well tolerated, at least in the early stages of the disease as shown by these two cases.

(g) Whether or not the absence of Schistosoma ova in the stools is permanent, and, if permanent, whether it means death of the parasites and cure of the disease, remains to be seen. We hope to have an opportunity to ascertain these points in the two cases in the future.

(h) Although emetine was not pushed to a point to establish its therapeutic value in this disease, yet there are evidences to show that it does influence its course. It certainly deserves to be more extensively tried, especially in children and young adults, as recommended by Cawston.

(i) The disappearance from the stools after treatment of not only ova of *Schistosoma japonicum*, but also ova of *Ascaris lumbricoides* and of *Fasciolopsis buski*, *Giardia*, and *Trichomonas*, must be of some significance.

REFERENCES.

1. Tyau, E. S. 1922. "The Treatment of Asiatic Schistosomiasis." China Nat. Med. Jour., xiii : 83.

2. Sanders, A. A. and Priston, J. L. 1921. "Schistosomiasis in the Yangtse Valley." Jl. Roy. Nav. Med. Serv., Vol. 7 No. 3, pp. 187-199; and No. 4. pp. 290-292.

3. Faust, E. C. and Meleney, H. E. 1924. "Schistosomiasis japonica in an American Naval officer." Am. Jl. Hyg. Monograph, No. 3, p. 236.

4. Tootell, G. T. 1924. "Tartar emetic treatment for Schistosomiasis japonica." China Med. Jour., xxxviii : 276.

5. Libby, W. E. 1923. (a) "Tartar emetic in Schistosomiasis japonica: A Preliminary Report." China Med. Jour., xxxvii: 158. (b) "A further study in Schistosomiasis japonica." China Med. Jour., (1924) xxxviii : 376.

6. Kau, C. L. 1924. "Observations on Schistosomiasis." China Nat. Med. Jour., Vol. 10, p. 337. Chinese text.

7. Hutcheson, Allen C. 1913. "Results of Thirteen Cases of Dysentery treated with Emetine." China Med. Jour., xxvii : 243.

8. Chastang. 1914. "Schistosomum japonicum et Fievre du Yangtse." Arch. de Med. et Pharm. Naval, Vol. 101, p. 321.

9. Diamentis. 1918. "Sur un nouveau Traitment de l'Hematurie Bilharzienne en Egypte." Jour. d'Urol., vii : 17.

10. Erian, A. 1919. "The Treatment of Bilharziosis by massive Doses of Emetine." The Practitioner, Vol 103 pp. 391-393.

11. Tsykalas. 1921. "Neue Wage in der Behandlung der Bilharziakrankheit in Aegypten." Wien. Klin. Woch., xxxiv : 579.

12. Cawston, F. G. (a) "Antimony and Emetine in Bilharzia Disease." Lancet, 1921, Vol. ii. p. 1049 : (b) "The Emetine Treatment for Bilharzia Disease." Jour., Trop. Med. Hyg., 1922. Vol 25, p. 112.

13. Tyau, E. S. "Successful Treatment of one Case of Schistosomiasis japonica by Emetine" Quoted by Faust and Meleney in Amer. Jl. Hyg. Monograph No. 3. 1924. p. 231.

14. Cawston, F. G. 1921. "Emetine in Japanese Bilharzia Disease." Brit. Med. Jour., ii p. 1031.

15. Faust, E. C. and Meleney, H. E. 1924. "Method of Examination of the Faeces for the Eggs and Miracidia of Schistosoma japonicum." Amer. Jl. Hyg., Monograph No. 3 p. 218.

---

5. **Pellagra in China: Some Recent Views on Its Etiology**
Lee, C.U. *Nationtal Medical Journal of China*, 11: 65-74, 1925.
李宗恩《中国的糙皮病：糙皮病发病机制的新观点》，载于《中华医学杂志》[1]，1925年，11:65-74页。

翻译概要 糙皮病在世界很多地方已是常见疾病，如美国在1917年有16.5万个病例。可是在饮食蛋白质普遍偏低的中国，直到1923年才有两篇文章首次报告了在上海和芜湖发生7例糙皮病。目前对糙皮病的病因说法不一，如卫生条件差、蛋白质缺乏、细菌感染、肠道菌群失调等。作者根据中国罕有病例的事实，质疑笼统的蛋白质缺乏为糙皮病的发病机理，并通过分析中西饮食结构，提出豆类蛋白可能含有糙皮病患者缺失的氨基酸，如色氨酸和赖氨酸。

[1] 《中华医学杂志》1915年创刊，初为中、英文双语期刊，英文刊名为 *National Medical Journal of China*。1932年，期刊的英文部分与中国博医会的英文杂志 *China Medical Journal*（博医会报）合并，以 *Chinese Medical Journal* 为刊名出版；中文部分仍称《中华医学杂志》继续出版，并继续保留 *National Medical Journal of China* 的英文刊名。

THE

NATIONAL MEDICAL JOURNAL

OF CHINA

VOLUME XI APRIL 1925 NUMBER 2

"PELLAGRA IN CHINA: SOME RECENT VIEWS ON ITS ÆTIOLOGY"

C. U. LEE, M. B., CH. B., D. T. M. and H.
Peking

Prior to 1923, pellagra was not known to occur in this country. No mention was made of it in a well-known textbook on the diseases of China. The sudden occurrence in 1923 of 6 cases in Shanghai reported by Dr. E. S. Tyau and of 1 case at Wuhu reported by Dr. S. C. Wu seems to be worthy of more than a passing note.

Whether or not this was the first occurrence of the disease in China is a moot point. A careful search in ancient Chinese medical literature may reveal evidences of its earlier existence, though no reference to it is known in modern literature. This apparent absence may have been due to the fact that pellagra, owing to the protean nature of its symptoms, is one of the most difficult diseases to diagnose and no reliable laboratory method of detection is at present known. In many countries this disease had been missed till very recently. In the United States, for example, it only became generally recognized in 1907, and by 1917, 165,000 cases were said to exist. Hence its first recognition in a country has a significance and importance calling for the closest attention.

At the present state of our knowledge, it would be unwise to accept as final any theory on the ætiology of pellagra; but if we were to agree with the conclusions of Joseph Goldberger, a well-known authority on the subject, who insisted that pellagra is due to a protein deficiency in the diet, we should be rather surprised to find the disease to be such a rarity in China, that is to say, in a country where, to a casual observer, food deficiency, especially protein deficiency, seems to be a more or less chronic condition among the poor classes. Moreover, since the disease is known to exist in almost every part of the globe, including India, the Straits Settlements, and Siam, there is no reason to hope that China will be so fortunate as to escape its ravages. Could it be that its apparent rarity is really due to its nonrecognition?

Be that as it may, there is no doubt of the importance, which should be accorded to Dr. Tyau's and Dr. Wu's reports of the presence of this disease in Shanghai and Wuhu, respectively. While to Dr. Tyau probably goes the honor of being the first to report pellagra in China, it is much to be regretted that the account had to be so incomplete, and some of the cases are somewhat unconvincing. Dr. Wu's report was no less so. The photographs were so badly reproduced, that they offered no help to one in trying to establish the identity of the disease. No detailed reference was made to the diet these patients were on prior to the onset of the disease, and very little was said of the subsequent treatment.

The description of these cases is, however, highly suggestive that the disease dealt with was of a pellagrous nature. In all the seven cases, there was the occurrence on the exposed parts of the body of an erythematous eruption, followed by desquamation and pigmentation. This, accompanied by stomatitis with ulceration in some and gastro-intestinal disturbances in all cases, presents a striking picture in favor of pellagra. In none of Dr. Tyau's cases were there marked nervous or mental disturbances, but the absence of such symptoms may have been due to the acute course these cases apparently took. Nervous symptoms, however, did occur in Dr. Wu's case, a fact placing the diagnosis of his case on firmer ground.

If we agree with Drs. Tyau and Wu that these were true pellagrins, there arise several points that are of very great significance. In the first place, the sudden occurrence of 6 cases in Shanghai within a period of 5 months and the simultaneous appearance of another case at Wuhu, higher up the Yangtze River, pointed to the occurrence of an acute epidemic, a rather important fact from the point of view of ætiology and the future control. Unfortunately, neither of these authors made any careful study into the epidemiology of these cases.

The Shanghai cases were all males over 40, belonging to the poor working classes, and living in overcrowded and insanitary conditions. The only reference to diet was that they subsisted mainly on rice prior to onset of disease. The Wuhu case was a boatman, 36 years of age, living on rice and vegetables and rarely on fresh meat. From this, we gather that there had been a chronic deficiency in the supply of animal proteins. If this be an important factor in the causation of the disease, then pellagra ought to be one of the commonest instead of being the rarest of diseases in China. If, on the other hand, its occurrence in epidemic form makes infection as the more likely cause of the disease, are there any measures to be taken against its subsequent outbreaks ?

The second point of importance is the apparent acute course these cases took. All the cases had a sudden onset and a comparatively short duration, the longest being of 9 months. Some of the cases even showed pyrexia. Death occurred in three. No recurrence has so far been reported among those who survived.

Although pellagra is essentially a chronic disease, acute types such as these are not of infrequent occurrence during an epidemic. In 1907, when pellagra occurred in epidemic form in the Southern States of the United States, many cases of a fulminating type were reported, but since then the number of such cases has gradually decreased, so that at present the disease is regarded as being endemic and chronic in nature. In view of this fact, these cases may mark the beginning of a pellagrous invasion of this country. If so, a brief review of the prevailing views regarding the ætiology of this disease may not be out of place.

The problem of ætiology has puzzled and exercised many great minds and has been studied from as many angles. Facts thus brought out are many, but theories are more. Some of the latter are but random shots leading nowhere, while others represent results of painstaking experiments and scientific analysis.

One of the best-known authorities on this subject is Joseph Goldberger, of the United States Public Health Service. He and his associates began their study on pellagra ætiology in 1914. They set out with the idea that it is a food deficiency disease and their experimental production of pellagrous eruption in 6 out of 11 convicts on a diet deficient in animal protein has become classic. Their study of the preventability and control of pellagra by means of diet in institutions further substantiated their claim. Among 414 pellagrins, only one recurrent case was noted during a period of 3 years following the introduction of a diet rich in animal protein, including meat, milk, and legumes.

To exclude the possibility of a low or inadequate supply of any of the known vitamins or of the mineral elements in the diet playing a rôle in the production of pellagra, a number of pellagrins were put on a diet rich in all the known vitamins and mineral elements but poor in protein supply. A uniform failure to prevent a recurrence in these cases during a period of over 2½ months' observation was taken to mean that a deficiency of these factors, namely vitamins and mineral salts, is not essential in the causation of the disease. Similar experiments were carried out to exclude any curative value of cod-liver oil in pellagra.

On the other hand, milk and fresh meat were shown to be therapeutically efficient in preventing recurrences in pellagra cases, provided sufficient quantity has been supplied in the diet. It was brought out also that protein, *per se*, is not sufficient to explain its efficiency, for gelatin failed to prevent recurrences. While milk and fresh meat do seem to possess to a marked degree pellagra-preventing factors, it must be pointed out that proteins from other sources, animal or vegetable, may also contain them. Hence the present position regarding the ætiology of pellagra, taken up by Joseph Goldberger and his school, is that "the primary ætiological dietary factor in pellagra is a faulty protein mixture (or amino-acid mixture); a deficiency in some as yet unrecognized dietary complex possibly a vitamin, or some combination of these."

During the war, two epidemics of pellagra were carefully investigated in Egypt, one among the Armenian refugees and another among the Turkish and German war prisoners. The results agreed in the main with those of Goldberger's school. W. H. Wilson, in his studies of these epidemics, came to some important conclusions regarding the nutritive value of proteins in pellagra. Now it is a well-known fact that the nutritive value of protein varies according to its source. It has been shown by experiment that for a man of 70 kilos, to maintain his nitrogenous equilibrium, the minimal amount of protein required is 30 gms. in the case of animal proteins from meat or milk, but more when the proteins were from other sources. The biological value of proteins from various sources, taking animal protein as the standard, is as shown in the table.

TABLE SHOWING THE BIOLOGICAL VALUE OF VARIOUS PROTEINS

PROTEIN SOURCE	SMALLEST AMOUNT PROTECTING A MAN OF 70 KILOS FROM LOSS OF BODY PROTEIN	BIOLOGICAL VALUE
Meat	30 grams per diem	1.000
Milk	31 ,,	0.965
Rice	34 ,,	0 880
Potato	38 ,,	0.989
Beans*	50 ,,	0.600
Bread	76 ,,	0.395
Maize	102 ,,	0.293

Wilson, after analyzing a large number of diets, which were reputed to be pellagra-producing, came to the conclusion that pellagra is the ultimate result of a deficient supply of protein in the diet and the deficiency must be judged of by the biological value of the protein. He formulated that a minimum amount of protein, equivalent in biological value to 40 gm. of animal protein per diem, is necessary for a man at rest or on light labor and 45 gm. for a man on hard labor. Anything below this scale, pellagra is likely to occur. Boyd and Lelean, in their report regarding the prevalence of pellagra among Turkish war prisoners in Egypt, agreed with Wilson that the epidemic was traceable to a diet of low biological protein value and lowered its incidence considerably by supplementing the diet with proteins of high biological value.

Goldberger is, however, of opinion that the biological value of protein is not the only criterion. A protein of low biological value may be equally pellagra-preventing as one of high biological value. No definite instance, however, was given by him in support of this statement.

While the evidence brought forward by these authorities is in favor of a dietetic ætiology of pellagra, their conclusions by no means met with general agreement. It is important to note, in passing, the views held on

*Soy bean excepted.

this subject by E. V. McCollum, the undisputed authority on nutritional disorders. He states in his book on "The Newer Knowledge of Nutrition," 1922, that "from results of experiments on rats, he is inclined to regard pellagra as an infectious disease, the rôle or diet in its ætiology involving only increased susceptibility to infection due to lowered resistance caused by faulty diet."

As a matter of fact, strong evidences in favor of pellagra being an infectious disease were brought forward some years ago by the Thompson McFadden Pellagra Commission, which was organized by the New York Postgraduate Medical School for the express purpose of investigating the ætiology of pellagra as it existed in the United States. The directing members of this commission were J. F. Siler, P. E. Garrison, and W. J. McNeal.

After a most careful study of an enormous mass of epidemiological and clinical data, they became more or less convinced that pellagra is a gastrointestinal infection, and that the disease spreads from case to case. Although they failed to find the actual infective agent they threw out the suggestion that the stable fly may have something to do with its transmission, and this on purely epidemiological grounds. Absence of properly constructed privies and of effective screening for dwellings, has, in their opinion, direct bearing on the spread of the disease. They came to this conclusion upon the following considerations: (1) Pellagra morbidity was higher in congested communities using surface privies than in more sparsely settled districts, in which similar methods of disposal of excreta were employed. (2) In the city of Spartanburg, the endemic foci of pellagra were located in districts, in which surface privies were in use. (3) Since the installation of the sewer system at the Spartan Mills, the spread of pellagra has been decidedly restricted.

Though they admitted that the diets among the affected were deficient in protein, they regarded the deficiency merely as a predisposing factor of the same type as other weakening processes. Milk was found to possess a certain degree of protective value against recurrence in pellagra, but the protection is by no means complete. Upon these findings, they advocate the installation of the proper system for the disposal of human waste and the effective screening of dwelling houses as the principal prophylactic measures.

In this connection, the findings of W. H. Holmes are of some interest. This author found in investigating one of the epidemics in the southern part of the United States, that B. welchii was present with marked regularity in the stools of pellagrins in numbers greater than usual. He pointed out that B. welchii, though often a harmless inhabitant of the human intestine, may assume under certain conditions pathological importance. For example, an excess of carbohydrates with a lack of organisms of the lactic acid group in the intestinal tract, would furnish a favorable medium for its growth to the detriment of its host. The theory is that B. welchii alone or in symbiosis with another organism in the presence of an excess of carbohydrates produces a toxin, the absorption of which may produce pellagra.

The value of this observation seemed to be enhanced by the finding of a similar state of affairs among Turkish prisoners of war in Egypt during an epidemic of pellagra in 1919. P. J. Marett discovered that cultures taken from stools of definite pellagra cases showed 90 per cent positives for organisms indistinguishable from B. welchii, while stools from healthy Turks did not show these anaërobes.

This idea of pellagra being a gastrointestinal infection gained in more recent years further support from another quarter. Impressed with the effect of sunlight on this disease, a number of authors have been attacking this problem with this point in view. It was Raubistschek in Germany, who first brought forward the theory that pellagra is due to a prepondering maize or possibly other cereal dietary, which results in certain substances being introduced into the circulation, and these substances are capable of becoming toxic under the influence of sunlight. This photodynamic action, as it is called, has been demonstrated in certain fluorescent dyes, which are capable of killing protozoal organisms, such as Paramœcia, in the light, but are without action in the darkness. It is also known that the disease occurring in animals known as buckwheat poisoning is said to be due to the action of a photodynamic substance in the circulation. Raubistschek is said to have demonstrated the lethal effece of light on white mice, fed on maize.

Gay and McIver, of Boston, recently investigated this subject anew. They were able to extract from corn a fluorescent pigment, which possessed photodynamic action on microörganisms in test tubes, but no attempt was made to show this action on vertebrate animals. This photodynamic theory has still more recently been modified by the work of Jobling and Arnold, published in the *J. A. M. A.* in 1923. These authors worked on the possibility that pellagra may be due to a photodynamic substance, produced by an organism located in the intestinal tract, and it was assumed that this organism can only grow or only produce the photodynamic substance in a favorable medium, consisting of an excess of carbohydrates. Special technic was devised to isolate organisms from stools, which might answer to these requirements. In a number of stools from pellagrins, a fungus was discovered, which not only produced a fluorescent substance, but when that substance was injected into mice, it caused remarkably suggestive lesions. This interesting observation, however, awaits confirmation.

There are, of course, still many other theories and scattered observations, but the one given above is sufficient to show that opinions regarding the ætiology of pellagra are divided between two main schools — the one considering it a deficiency disease pure and simple, while the other favoring infection or toxæmia as the primary causative factor. The balance of evidence, however, seems to be on the side of the former. It is noteworthy that almost every adherent to the infection school admits that diet does play an important rôle in pellagra.

If an adequate supply of protein in the diet has such an important bearing on the incidence of pellagra, it becomes extremely puzzling why we apparently see so little of this disease in China. Since the diet, among the lower classes at least, is mainly vegetarian, the question naturally arises as to the source of the pellagra-preventing factor or factors, if these do exist in the diet. To those who are interested in the nutritive value of soy beans, this question may have some importance.

We know that the proteins from soy beans approach very closely to those of milk, which certainly possesses a high degree of protective value against pellagra. For many years it has been alleged and is still maintained in some quarters that prolonged use of maize produces pellagra, and according to Wilson this must be due to the low biological value of corn proteins. It is also known that corn proteins are deficient in the essential amino acids — tryptophane and lysine. Goldberger has made experiments, which showed tentatively that the amino acids — tryptophane exerts a favorable influence on certain symptoms of pellagra. Now both tryptophane and lysine are present in soy bean proteins. It is interesting to speculate on whether soy bean, in virtue of its proteins, has any preventive or curative property in pellagra, and whether the universal use of soy bean as an article of diet could explain the rarity of the disease in China.

Of course, at the present state of our knowledge, we cannot afford to disregard the possibility of an infection playing a rôle in this disease. The mere fact that pellagra could be prevented and even cured by judicious and generous feeding does not exclude such a possibility. For example, good feeding is an important item in the treatment of tuberculosis.

To conclude, may I quote Castellani and Chalmers on this subject of pellagra: "Firstly the observer must suspect its presence and be on the lookout for it in any and every country and secondly he must not be unduly swayed by any ætiological theory but be prepared to make a diagnosis of pellagra in a person of any age, any race, any social condition, living in any place, whether tropical, temperate or frigid, in any town or country."

REFERENCES

Tyau, E. S., "Pellagra in Shanghai," *Nat. Med. Jl. of China*, Dec., 1923, Vol. 9, No. 4, p. 272.

Wu, S. C., "A Case of Pellagra in Wuhu," *Nat. Med. Jl. of China*, Dec., 1923, Vol. 9, No. 4, p. 280.

Goldberger, J., "The Relation of Diet to Pellagra," *Jl. Am. Med. Assoc.*, June, 1922, Vol. 78, p. 1676.

Goldberger, J., Waring, C. H., and Tanner, W. F., "Pellagra Prevention by Diet Among Institutional Inmates," *Pub. Health Rep.*, Oct., 1923, Vol. 38, No. 41, p. 2361.

Goldberger, J., and Tanner, W. F., "Amino-Acid Deficiency Probably the Primary Etiological Factor in Pellagra," *Pub. Health Rep.*, March, 1922, Vol. 37, Part I, p. 462.

Goldberger, J., and Tanner, W. F., "A Study of Treatment and Prevention of Pellagra," *Pub. Health. Rep.*, Jan., 1924, Vol. 39, No. 3, p. 87.

Wilson, W. H., "The Diet Factor in Pellagra," *Jl. Hygiene*, July, 1921, Vol. 20, No. 1, p. 1.

Boyd, F. D., and Lelean, P. S., "Report of a Committee of Enquiry Regarding the Prevalence of Pellagra Among Turkish Prisoners of War," *Jl. Roy. Army Med. Corp.*, 1919, Vol. 33, p. 508.

Siler, J. F., Garrison, P. E., and McNeal, W. J., Reports of Thompson-McFadden Pellagra Commission, 1st Report — Summary, *Jl. Am. Med. Assoc.*, Jan., 1914, Vol. 62, No. 1, p. 8.

2d Report — Summary, *Jl. Am. Med. Assoc.*, Sept., 1914, Vol. 63, No. 13, p. 1090.

3d Report — Summary, *Trop. Dis. Bull.*, 1920, Vol. 15, p. 54.

Holmes, W. H., "Remarks on B. welchii (*B. aerogenes capsulatus*) in the Stools of Pellagrins," *Arch. Int. Med.*, March, 1916, Vol. 17, No. 3, p. 453.

McCollum, E. V., "Newer Knowledge of Nutrition," New York, 1922, p. 273.

Gay, D. M., and McIver, M., "Photodynamic Action of Extracts of Grains with Special Reference to Pellagra," *Am. J. Trop. Med.*, March, 1922, Vol. 2, p. 115.

Jobling, J. W., and Arnold, L. "Observations and Reflections on the Etiology of Pellagra," *Jl. Am. Med. Assoc.*, Feb., 1923, Vol. 80, No. 6, p. 365.

6. Filariasis Investigations in the Province of Kiangsu, China.

Lee, C.U. *Transactions of Royal Society of Tropical Medicine and Hygiene*, 20: 279-287, 1926.

李宗恩《中国江苏省丝虫病研究》，载于《皇家热带病和卫生协会学报》，1926 年，20:279-287 页。

翻译概要　作者总结了 1925 年江苏省丝虫病的发病率和分布的调查结果，及对所搜集的蚊子的显微镜观察。其结论如下：

1. 丝虫病和淋巴疾病在江苏省北部的发病率较高。
2. 证据表明，此病主要局限在该省的长江以北地区。
3. 作者在 Culex Pipiens 蚊的胸肌内确认了不同发育时期的丝虫卵，认为 Culex Pipiens 与 C. Fatigans 都可能是在中国传播丝虫病的媒介。
4. 应该大力宣传预防丝虫病和所有由蚊子传染的疾病。
5. 应该在流行地区的医院、机关和学校采取积极的预防措施。

FILARIASIS INVESTIGATIONS IN THE PROVINCE OF KIANG-SU, CHINA.

BY

C. U. LEE, M.B., Ch.B., D.T.M. & H.
From the Department of Medicine, Peking Union Medical College, Peking, China.

INTRODUCTION.

In the autumn of 1924, Dr. C. W. YOUNG brought back to Peking, from Hsüchowfu, a few specimens of *Filaria bancrofti*, recovered on the 9th May, 1924, from a female patient undergoing an operation for carcinoma of the breast. They were extracted from the subcutaneous tissue of the removed breast. The fact that the patient was a native of Hsüchowfu, coupled with the verbal report that elephantiasis of the lower limbs is occasionally met with in that part of the country, suggested the existence there of an endemic area of filariasis.

In the summer of 1925, permission was granted me to visit Hsüchowfu and other parts of Kiang Su Province, with a view to making a preliminary survey regarding the actual prevalence of filariasis in that province.

Only five days could be spent at each of the two districts visited, namely, Hsüchowfu and Tsing Kiang Pu. For the purpose of a survey, blood examination of local inhabitants at night was necessary, but, since the conditions were unfavourable for the development of night clinics of any size, I had to be content with those hospital in-patients and employees who could be persuaded to submit to the examination.

On my way to Tsing Kiang Pu, an enforced delay of two days at Chinkiang, on the Yangtse River, enabled me to make certain enquiries regarding elephantiasis.

The shortness of time at my disposal accounts for the incompleteness of some of my data, but it is hoped that the results obtained will encourage future research on more extensive lines.

In this work I am especially indebted to Dr. YOUNG and Dr. HERTIG of the Kalaazar Field Studies Unit of the Peking Union Medical College, Dr. McFADYEN of Hsüchowfu, and Dr. WOODS and Dr. BELL of Tsing Kiang Pu for their co-operation and hospitality, without which the trip would not have been worth while.

Incidence of Filariasis and Elephantiasis Arabum in Kiang Su Province.

Though it is well known that filariasis and elephantiasis are very common in China, scientific data are still lacking regarding their exact distribution. In the province of Kiang Su, JEFFERY and J. L. MAXWELL (1911) state that elephantiasis is said to be abundant in Chinkiang and Soochow, and present in Yangchow, Nanking and Shanghai, while filariasis has only been reported in Yangchow and Shanghai. J. P. MAXWELL (1921), states that " the infection does not spread north of the Yangtse Valley, though individual cases of the disease may be met with farther north. These individuals, however, have been infected in the southern regions and not in the northern." He referred, however, to a paper by BELL (1919), reporting elephantiasis in Tsing Kiang Pu. Therefore, with the exception of Yangchow and Tsing Kiang Pu, the part of Kiang Su Province north of the Yangste River has not been carefully explored, as far as filariasis is concerned.

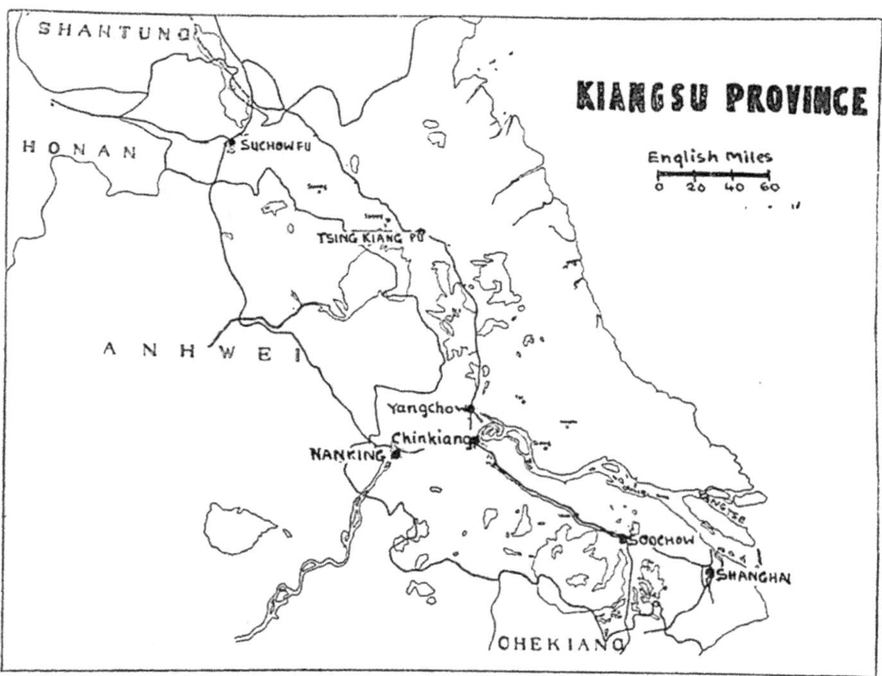

My enquiries at Chinkiang regarding elephantiasis elicited information which tends to throw doubt on certain impressions of previous authors. Inhabitants there maintain that elephantiasis does not occur on the south side of the river. Cases are seen in Chinkiang, but only among people who come from regions north of the river. On the other hand, natives from various districts north of the Yangtse River are quite familiar with this disease in their own towns or villages. Regarding my own native city, Soochow, my impression is that the disease is very rare, if it occurs at all, and cases which occur in Shanghai and Nanking may easily have been among immigrants from north of the river. I have no statistics to substantiate this observation but, if true, an explanation will have to be sought for this peculiar distribution. The patchy distribution of elephantiasis and filariasis has, of course, been frequently observed in other parts of the world, independent of the presence of possible vectors, but no satisfactory explanation is yet forthcoming.

Filariasis and elephantiasis occur fairly extensively north of the Yangtse River.

The results of the present survey are as follows : Persons numbering 363 were examined for the presence of microfilariæ. Of this number, 33 were not natives of the districts visited but were recent arrivals and need concern us no farther except to note that one of them, a soldier and a native of Shantung Province, showed microfilariæ in his blood, indicating the probable existence of filariasis in that province.* Sixteen were foreign missionaries and their families, who lived in screened houses and were all negative. Of the rest, 7 of 119 from Hsüchowfu and 31 of 195 from the Tsing Kiang Pu district showed infection.

The details concerning these are shown in Table I. The picked cases include all those individuals whose blood was examined on account of their being known to have some filarial disease or to have been in intimate contact with persons suffering from such disease. The rest, being taken at random,

TABLE I.

MICROFILARIA RATE AMONG INHABITANTS OF HSÜCHOWFU AND TSING KIANG PU DISTRICTS.

		Number of Persons Examined.			Number of Persons Positive for Microfilariæ.			Percentage infected.
		Male	Female	Total	Male	Female	Total	
Hsüchowfu district	Random Cases	73	32	105	4†	0	4	3·8
	Picked Cases	13	1	14	3	0	3	21·4
Tsing Kiang Pu district	Random Cases	121	61	182	20	9	29	15·9
	Picked Cases	9	4	13	2	0	2	15·4

* According to JEFFERY and MAXWELL, elephantiasis exists in Shantung.

† Two of these positives are uncle and nephew from Suining Hsien, about 60 miles south-east of Hsüchowfu.

ought to represent more or less the general population. The difference in percentage of those found infected in the two districts suggests that Tsing Kiang Pu is much more heavily infected than Hsüchowfu.

Table II shows that the microfilaria rate among persons showing signs of filarial infection is much higher than among those apparently free from filarial disease. I found also, in common with other observers elsewhere, that where the microfilaria rate is high, lymphatic diseases are much in evidence, and *vice versa*. Thus, in Hsüchowfu, with a microfilaria rate of 3·8 per cent.,

TABLE II.

MICROFILARIA RATE AMONG THOSE SHOWING SIGNS OF LYMPHATIC DISEASE AND AMONG THOSE NOT SHOWING SIGNS.

	Hsüchowfu District.			Tsing Kiang Pu District.		
	Number Examined	Number Positive	Percentage	Number Examined	Number Positive	Percentage
Cases with Lymphatic Disease	4	2	50	15*	4	26·6
Cases with no Lymphatic Distance.	115	5	4·3	180	27	15·0

* Two other cases were seen with marked elephantiasis but refused blood examination.

I saw only four cases of clinical filariasis, whereas in Tsing Kiang Pu, with a microfilaria rate of 15·9 per cent., seventeen cases were met with during the same period of time.

Representatives of all age periods were examined. Filarial infection was not confined to any particular period of life. The oldest and youngest were males of 63 and 9 years of age respectively.

The microfilaria rates of 3·8 per cent. and 15·9 per cent. for Hsüchowfu and Tsing Kiang Pu respectively, would certainly have been much higher had it been possible to examine each individual more thoroughly, by taking a larger amount of blood than 10 to 20 c.mm., at later hours of the night, and on repeated occasions. Also, it is to be remembered that the microfilaria rate of a district does not indicate the amount of actual filarial infection, as many cases with disease conditions of undoubtedly filarial origin fail to show microfilariæ in their blood, so that the rate of filarial infection of a particular district is actually much higher than its microfilaria rate.

That some of the inhabitants from Suining and Szeyang—districts between Hsüchowfu and Tsing Kiang Pu—also showed microfilariæ in their blood, and that elephantiasis exists along the north bank of the Yangtse River, make it safe to assume that filariasis and elephantiasis are extensively prevalent in the whole of that part of the Kiang Su Province lying north of the Yangtse River.

Clinical Aspects.

Though no definite case of acute lymphangitis was seen during my trip, quite a number of cases, especially those showing elephantiasis, gave a history of having had attacks of fever, accompanied by lymphatic inflammation resulting in hard and swollen groin glands. I saw three typical cases of varicose groin glands at Tsing Kiang Pu. Cases of abscess were very common there, and it is more than probable that a proportion of them were directly or indirectly due to filarial infection. Time did not permit me, however, to examine pus from any of these cases for the presence of dead filariæ.

I saw two cases of lymphuria at Tsing Kiang Pu and one of chylous ascites at Hsüchowfu. The last, in whose blood microfilariæ were found, also showed signs of hepatic cirrhosis, probably due to a different cause.

Numerous cases of elephantiasis involving the lower limbs and scrotum were met with in both localities. Dr. Bell was also kind enough to lend me a large number of photographs illustrating this condition. An early case of elephantiasis of the penis was seen at Dr. Bell's clinic, during my stay at Tsing Kiang Pu. It is interesting to note that all the cases of varicose groin glands, and those of chylous ascites and lymphuria, showed microfilariæ in the blood ; while all the cases of elephantiasis, except one in which the condition was just developing, were negative.

Morbid Anatomy.

The piece of elephantoid penile skin, surgically removed by Dr. Bell, was the only pathologiçal specimen brought back for study. In appearance it differs in no way from the text-book description of elephantoid tissue.

Mosquito Transmission.

The species of mosquito with which Manson's original work on the transmission of filariasis was performed was never absolutely determined. Edwards, of the British Museum (1922), believes it to have been *Culex fatigans* and not *C. pipiens*, as some suggested, on the ground that *C. pipiens* does not extend so far south in China as Amoy, where Manson did his work. Furthermore, while *C. fatigans* has been proved definitely to be a ready and efficient intermediate host to *Filaria bancrofti* in other parts of the world, there could be found, previous to 1924, no record in which *C. pipiens* was thus implicated. In May, 1924, however, Le Chuiton (1924), working under the direction of Guerin, in the Pasteur Institute of Saigon, Indo-China, claimed to have observed complete development of *F. bancrofti* in *C. pipiens*. The question naturally arises as to the correct identification of the species, for *C. pipiens*, which is a palæarctic mosquito, has not been known to occur in Indo-China

(EDWARDS, 1921), and LE CHUITON did not mention the authority by whom the species with which he worked was identified. Confirmation seems necessary before his claim can be accepted.*

As the subject of filarial transmission in China has not, so far as I am aware, been re-studied since MANSON'S time, it is safe, for the reasons stated above, to assert that hitherto *C. fatigans* is the only species of mosquito believed to transmit *F. bancrofti*, as far as China is concerned.

During the course of the present survey, I collected a large number of mosquitoes, chiefly from houses the inmates of which were known by me to harbour microfilariæ in their blood. These I sorted out into three groups, in the first of which I placed all the mosquitoes I took to be *C. pipiens* from Hsüchowfu ; in the second, similar mosquitoes from Tsing Kiang Pu ; and in the third, all those unfamiliar to me. When there was the least doubt regarding a *Culex* mosquito being *C. pipiens* I placed it in the last group. A number of male and female specimens from each of the first two groups, along with specimens from the third group, were sent on pins to Mr. F. W. EDWARDS, of the British Museum, for identification, and the rest were preserved in 70 per cent. alcohol for future study. All the specimens sent under the name of *C. pipiens* were identified by EDWARDS as such ; one specimen from the third group also turned out to be of the same species, while another of the same group was *C. sinensis*. The rest of the mosquitoes belonged to other genera. It seems clear that if *C. fatigans* exists in the districts investigated, which are within the limits of the palæarctic region, none was among my collection. This is of some interest in view of my findings given below.

TABLE III.

NATURAL FILARIAL INFECTION IN MOSQUITOES FROM INFECTED HOUSES.

	Mosquito	Number Examined	Number Positive	Percentage Positive
Hsüchowfu	*Culex pipiens*	8	1	12·5
Tsing Kiang Pu House A ...	*Culex pipiens*	17	2	11·7
	?	11	0	0
Tsing Kiang Pu House B	*Culex pipiens*	25	15	60

* In a recent communication to Dr. E. C. FAUST, Dr. GUÉRIN of Saigon gave as his opinion that " en ce qui concerne le *Culex pipiens*, que, dans son article ' Recherches sur l'épidémiologie de la filariose en Cochinchine,' F. le CHUITTON établit être le vecteur de *Filaria bancrofti* COBBOLD 1877, aucune prospection n'a pu permettre en 1925 d'établir sa présence en Indochine. L'auteur ne donne aucune caractéristique de l'espèce de moustique dont il s'est servi dans ses expériences, *mais il y a de fortes chances de présumer qu'il s'agit en l'occurrence de Culex fatigans*." (Italics mine, C.U.L.)

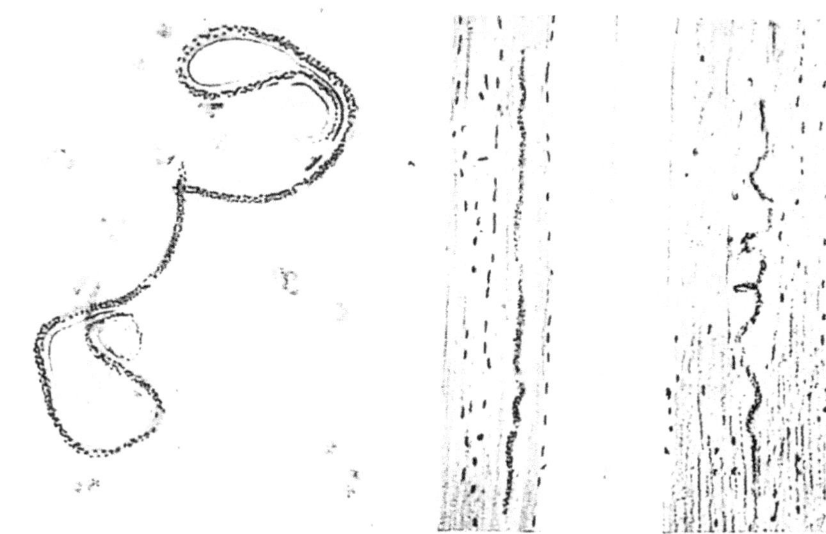

Fig. 1.
Microfilariæ from peripheral blood of an infected person.

Figs. 2 and 3.
Filarial larvæ in the thoracic muscle of *Culex pipiens*.

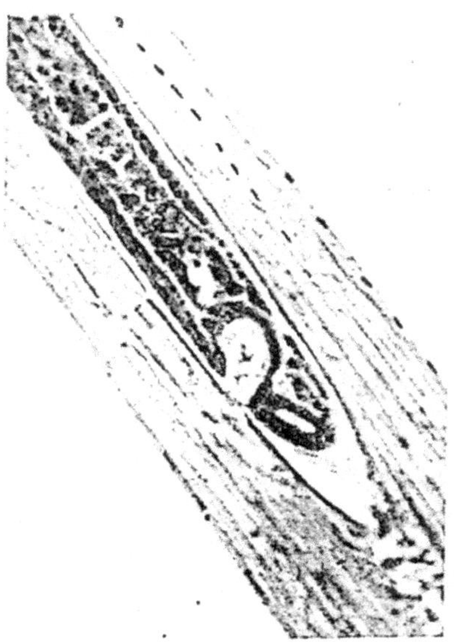

Fig. 4.
Enlarged tail end of larva, sausage stage, in the ... muscle of *C. pipiens*.

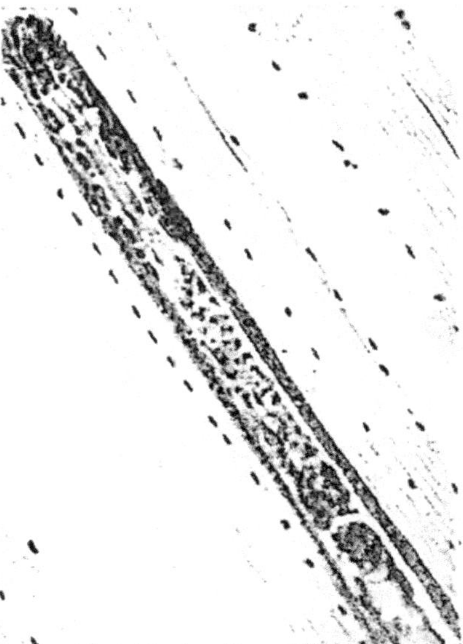

Fig. 5.
Head end of larva slightly more mature than that shown in Fig. 4.

On my return to Peking, serial sections of the mosquitoes collected at Hsüchowfu and Tsing Kiang Pu were cut in paraffin. It was found that quite a large proportion of the mosquitoes which I identified as *C. pipiens* showed in the thoracic muscles filaria larvæ in different stages of development (see photomicrographs), while mosquitoes of other species proved negative. The percentage of positives varied in different lots collected at different houses (Table III.). Regarding the identity of these larvæ, I believe they are those of *F. bancrofti*, many specimens showing all the characters depicted in Looss's well-known figures of this parasite (1905) as it is found in the muscles of infected mosquitoes. The presence of these larvæ in the thoracic muscles at once excludes their being those of *Dirofilaria immitis*, which develops in the Malpighian tubes. That these larvæ could be those of other species of filaria inhabiting mammals other than dogs, birds or lower vertebrates, is possible, but not probable on morphological* and epidemiological grounds.

Though no larvæ were encountered in the proboscis, the finding of larvæ at different stages of development in the thoracic muscles is strong evidence that in China *C. pipiens*, as well as *C. fatigans*, can act as an efficient intermediate host for *F. bancrofti*.

Filariasis, being carried by such a domestic mosquito as *C. pipiens*, is, as one would expect, largely a house infection. The results of a careful examination of one family at Tsing Kiang Pu are of interest in this connection. All three male members, occupying one part of the house, showed definite evidence of filarial infection (elephantiasis of right leg : varicose groin glands and microfilariæ in blood : microfilariæ in blood), while all the female members, living somewhat apart, escaped.

In another instance, a father and one of his sons harboured microfilariæ in their blood though otherwise healthy, while his other son was negative. I also came across two sisters, 20 and 18 years old respectively, living in the same room, who were both positive for microfilariæ but apparently enjoyed good health.

Since filariasis is a house infection, one would expect its incidence to be equal in the two sexes, but as a matter of fact the males were more frequently affected than the females (Table I.). At Hsüchowfu, no females were found infected, while at Tsing Kiang Pu, the incidence was also slightly higher among males than among females, 16·5 per cent. as against 14·7 per cent. I am inclined to attribute this to the custom among Chinese womenfolk of wearing more clothes while sleeping at night, thus exposing less body surface to the attack of mosquitoes.

* Dr. E. C. Faust has kindly compared the specimen shown in Fig. 4 with Looss's classical figure (1905) representing the same stage of development and found them to be identical. The relative proportions of (*a*) width to length and (*b*) the distances between important landmarks namely excretory pore, œsophageal bulbus, genital anlage and rectal anlage, are the same.

Filarial Periodicity.

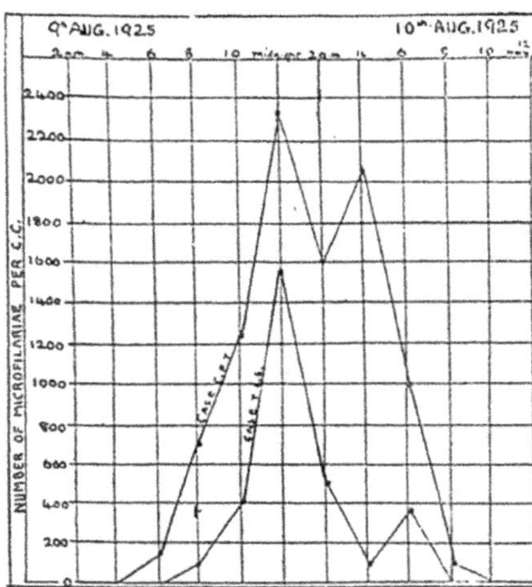

Since Manson's discovery of this interesting phenomenon, many careful studies have been made in search of an explanation, but so far it remains a mystery. I have nothing new to add to our knowledge on this subject. The accompanying chart merely records the results of a careful study of two cases at Hsüchowfu. It is interesting to note that in both cases the initial fall in the number of microfilariæ at 12 (midnight) was followed by a secondary rise before the occurrence of the final drop. I do not think, however, that this is a constant finding.

Prophylaxis.

The prevention of filarial infection, as Manson-Bahr (1925) tersely puts it, resolves itself into anti-mosquito measures and protection from mosquito bites. In China, under the present conditions, anti-mosquito measures involving land drainage, installation of pipe-borne water supplies, modern systems of sewage disposal, etc., are well nigh impossible; but the use of mosquito nets can be encouraged to good purpose. Mass education of at least the intelligent classes of the population, as to the danger of mosquito bites in the production of diseases, will go a long way toward lowering both malarial and filarial incidence in this country. The clinical manifestations of filariasis, especially elephantiasis, will impress the lay mind more forcibly than any other disease, and on this account ought to have a strong appeal to workers interested in health propaganda.

For hospitals and other well supervised institutions, situated in heavily infected areas such as Tsing Kiang Pu, the following specific measures are recommended :—

1. All water tanks in these institutions should be properly covered or screened and other possible mosquito-breeding places within the precincts should be eliminated.

2. All members of the staff and their families should sleep under mosquito nets unless living in houses efficiently screened, and should have their blood examined for the presence of microfilariæ once every year.

3. All employees should be required, as one of the conditions of employment, to undergo, on entrance and annually, an examination of the blood for filariasis, and those found infected should occupy sleeping quarters separate from the healthy and be required to sleep under mosquito nets.

4. Those infected should take special care in avoiding over-exertion, chills and injury to the feet.

5. In hospitals, if possible, all patients should be examined on the night of admission for microfilariæ in the blood, and those infected should be placed in a small ward apart from the other patients.

SUMMARY.

1. The incidence of filariasis and of lymphatic diseases in the northern part of Kiang Su Province is high.

2. Certain evidences adduced seem to suggest that the disease is largely confined to that portion of the province north of the Yangtse River.

3. Filaria larvæ, at different stages of development, were found in the thoracic muscles of *Culex pipiens*, indicating that this mosquito is probably as efficient a vector of *Filaria bancrofti* in China as *C. fatigans*.

4. Filarial diseases furnish excellent material for health propaganda, especially in connection with mosquito-borne diseases.

5. Certain prophylactic measures are recommended for hospitals and other institutions situated in heavily-infected areas in China.

REFERENCES.

BELL, L. NELSON (1919). Elephantiasis of the Scrotum. *Surg. Gyn. & Obstet.* xxix, 199.
EDWARDS, F. W. (1921). A Revision of the Mosquitoes of the Palæarctic Region. *Bull. Ent. Res.* xii, 263.
EDWARDS, F. W. (1922). The Carriers of *Filaria bancrofti*. *Jl. Trop. Med. & Hyg.* xxv, 168; June.
JEFFERY, W. H. and MAXWELL, J. L. (1911). *The Diseases of China*. Philadelphia. 142.
LE CHUITON, F. (1924). Recherches sur l'épidémiologie de la Filariose (*Filaria bancrofti* COBBOLD, 1877) en Cochinchine. *Bull. Soc. Path. Exot.* xvii, 405; May.
LOOSS, A. (1905). *Handbuch der Tropenkrankheiten*, Edited by CARL MENSE, Leipzig.
MANSON-BAHR, P. H. (1925). *Manson's Tropical Diseases*, 538. Eighth edition, London.
MAXWELL, J. P. (1921). Filariasis in China. *Philipp. Jl. Sc.* xix, 257; Sept.

7. A Preliminary Survey of The Anopheline Mosquitoes of the Peking Area
Meleney, H.E. Lee, C.U., and Chung, H.L. *China Medical Journal*, 41:509-512, 1927.

亨利·梅莱尼[1]，李宗恩，钟惠澜《对北京地区按蚊的考察》，载于《中华医学杂志》，1927 年，41:509-512 页。

翻译概要 作者希望用本文引起在中国研究蚊子的兴趣，特别是那些传播疟疾、丝虫病、甘草热的蚊子。1926 年 8-10 月，作者在北京郊区（香山、卧佛寺、丰台、燕京大学、海淀等地）采集了三种按蚊(Anopheles：A. hyrcanus, A. pattoni, A. lindesayi）的幼虫和其成虫，并研究了它们的形态特征、分布和繁殖习性。虽然这是研习蚊子繁殖地点和获取成虫的最佳办法，却无法研究与传染疾病关系密切的成虫的叮咬习性，后一项研究有望在下一个繁殖季节完成。结论如下：

1. 三种蚊子的幼虫和成虫都于 1926 年夏秋季节在北京附近郊被发现。
2. 三种蚊子的不同体征总结于附表。
3. A. hyrcanus 只在平原（海拔 50 米）和西山脚下（海拔 135 米）繁殖。
4. A. pattoni 主要在山上的流水中繁殖，但也可以和 A. hyrcanus 一样在山边的池塘里繁殖。
5. A. lindesayi 的成虫存在于 A. pattoni 繁殖的山泉中，但其幼虫却和 A. pattoni 的幼虫都在海拔 320 米高的山泉中生存。
6. A. hyrcanus 有可能是在北京传染疟疾的媒介。A. pattoni, A. lindesayi 是否有同样作用还有待研究。

[1] Frank L. Meleney（1889-1963），协和医学院内科襄教授（1920-1927）。

A PRELIMINARY SURVEY OF THE ANOPHELINE MOSQUITOES OF THE PEKING AREA*

HENRY E. MELENEY, M.D., C. U. LEE, M.B., CH.B., D.T.M. & H., AND H. L. CHANG,
Peking.

This report is made in the hope of stimulating others to study the mosquitoes of China, particularly in connection with their transmission of malaria, filariasis and dengue fever. Our observations were made during the summer and autumn of 1926 and consisted chiefly of the collection of larvae and the breeding out of adults. This is the simplest method of studying the breeding places of mosquitoes and of obtaining perfect specimens of adults, but it does not take into consideration the feeding habits of the adults, which are most important in connection with disease transmission. It is hoped that further observations on adult anophelines may be made in this region during the coming summer.

Three species of *Anopheles* were encountered, namely *A. hyrcanus*, variety *sinensis*, *A. pattoni* and *A. lindesayi*. The collection of these three species in Shantung Province by Major W. S. Patton has already been reported by Christophers (1). The simplest distinguishing features of the three species are given in Table 1. These features are not necessarily diagnostic of the species if considered among anopheline mosquitoes in general, but will probably be found to be accurate for North China anophelines.

The larvae of *A. hyrcanus* and of *A. pattoni* were found in considerable numbers, but only twice were specimens of *A. lindesayi* bred out from larvae. The larva of *A. hyrcanus* can be distinguished easily form those of *A. pattoni* and *A. lindesayi*, but the two latter species are much more difficult to distinguish. Since no complete description of the larvae of *A. pattoni* and *A. lindesayi* has yet been published, we prefer to postpone any statement of the distinguishing features of the anopheline larvae of this region.

BREEDING PLACES

The plain on which the city of Peking stands has an altitude of about fifty meters above sea level. To the eastward the plain extends uninterruptedly to the sea in the region of Tientsin. To the southward the plain is also practically level for hundreds of miles. To the north and west, however, are several ranges of hills, beginning at a distance of about fifteen kilometers from the city, and rising as high as 755 meters in the first range.

* From the Department of Medicine, Peking Union Medical College, Peking, China.

It may be stated in general that, typically, *A. hyrcanus* breeds in ponds, while *A. pattoni* and *A. lindesayi* breed in streams, the latter perhaps at higher altitudes than the former. However, larvae of *A. pattoni* were found in a few ponds on the plain where *A. hyrcanus* was also breeding, and *A. lindesayi* was found breeding in streams together with *A. pattoni*, but never with *A. hyrcanus*.

A detailed description of the types of breeding place used by *A. hyrcanus* has recently been published by one of us (2). In the Peking area, this mosquito was found breeding only in ponds, in rice fields and in slow-moving streams on the plain. *A. hyrcanus* was the only anopheline which was found breeding in and close to the city of Peking itself. It was also the only anopheline found breeding about Fengtai, a town on the plain eight kilometers south-west of Peking. At Haitien, which is on the plain north-west of Peking, eight kilometers from the foot of the hills, *A. hyrcanus* was found breeding with *A. pattoni* in ponds on and about the campus of Yenching University. These ponds form part of the course of streams which flow down from the "Western Hills". These two species were also found breeding together at Wo Fu Ssu, a temple at the foot of the Western Hills, in a large "tank" 25 meters square which was paved and bordered with flag-stones and in which neither water-plants nor fish were present. This temple has an altitude of 110 meters above sea level. *A. hyrcanus* was found breeding alone in a smaller artificial pond thickly overgrown with water-plants of the genera *Spirogyra* and *Ceratophyllum* at an altitude of 135 meters. Higher than this the larvae of *A. hyrcanus* were not found.

The breeding places of *A. pattoni* are typically running streams. Two such streams, one at Wo Fu Ssu and one at Pi Yun Ssu, altitude 150 meters, contained these larvae in large numbers, always in small pools and usually well protected by thick growths of alga-like plants attached to the rocks. Finally, *A. pattoni* was found breeding in a pool formed by a spring in the hunting park at Hsiang Shan, at an altitude of 320 meters.

The breeding places of *A. lindesayi* still require much investigation. While examining the breeding places of *A. pattoni* in the stream at Pi Yun Ssu in October, adults of *A. lindesayi* were found in damp crevices between rocks just above the stream. Adults of *A. pattoni* and *A. hyrcanus* were found here also, but in the stream only the larvae of *A. pattoni* were found. At the spring in the hunting park at Hsiang Shan, altitude 320 meters, a few adults of *A. lindesayi* were caught during August in a net which was placed over the entire pool for twenty-four hours. At that time no adults of this species were bred from the larvae found in this pool, although frequent collections were made over a period of two weeks. In October, however, two larvae, among about ten collected from the pool, bred out *A. lindesayi*. The remainder were *A. pattoni*. This pool contained very little algal growth and no large water plants. Larvae of *Aedes koreicus* and of *Culex pipiens* were also found in this pool.

RELATION TO MALARIA

There was more malaria than usual in the region of Peking during the summer and autumn of 1926. It was practically all of the benign tertian type, although a few cases of subtertian (aestivo-autumnal) malaria were reported. This was probably due to the fact that there were large numbers of soldiers camped about Peking, many of whom came from farther south. The rainfall for the months April to September was much less than usual. The records at the Peking Observatory show 345.7 millimeters for 1926, while those for 1924 and 1925 are 1006.7 and 968.5 millimeters respectively. The disease was much more prevalent in the villages outside of Peking than in the city itself, and villages at the foot of the Western Hills, where *A. pattoni* predominated in the breeding places, suffered apparently as much as villages where *A. hyrcanus* alone was found to breed. *A. hyrcanus* is known to transmit malaria under certain conditions, and is undoubtedly the vector of the disease in Central China where no other anopheline mosquito ahs yet been discovered. Whether *A. pattoni* is able to transmit the disease has not yet been demonstrated.

SUMMARY

1. Larvae and adults of three anopheline mosquitoes, *A. hyrcanus*, var. *sinensis*, *A. pattoni* and *A. lindesayi* were found in the neighborhood of Peking during the summer and autumn of 1926.
2. A table is given showing the distinguishing features of the adults of these three species.
3. *A. hyrcanus* was found to breed only on the plain (altitude 50 meters above sea level) and at the foot of the "Western Hills" up to an altitude of 135 meters. It was found in ponds, rice fields and slow moving streams.
4. *A. pattoni* was found to breed mostly in hill streams, but, close to the hills, was found breeding in ponds with *A. hyrcanus*.
5. Adults of *A. lindesayi* were found on rocks near the streams in which *A. pattoni* was breeding, and larvae were found in a spring together with larvae of *A. pattoni* at an altitude of 320 meters.
6. *A. hyrcanus* is probably the vector of malaria on the plain about Peking. The possible role of *A. pattoni* and *A. lindesayi* as vectors remains to be studied.

Table I

	Wing	Female Palpi	Hind leg
A. hyrcanus var. *sinensis*	Anterior margin (costa) dark except for the white spots, one at junction of middle and outer third, one close to tip.	Apical segment with white base and tip, but dark in middle. Two other white bands more proximal.	Femur dark. White bands at intertarsal joints. Distal (5th) tarsal segment dark.
A. pattoni	Costa has five white spots, the fifth almost at tip of wing.	Apical segment entirely white. Two other white bands more proximal.	Femur dark. White bands at intertarsal joints. Fifth tarsal segment white.
A. lindesayi	Costa dark except for one large yellowishwhite spot near tip of wing.	Entirely dark.	Femur with broad white band in middle. Knee joint white. Remainder of leg dark.

Literature Cited

1. Christophers, S. R. *A. (Myzomyia) pattoni*, a new Anopheles from Shantung, North China; with notes on some other species of Anopheles from the same locality. Ind. Jour. Med. Res., 1926, XIII, 871.

2. Meleney, H. E. The types of breeding place used by *Anopheles hyrcanus* in North and Central China. China Med. Jour. 1927, XLI, 347.

8. Malaria in A Village Near Peking

Lee, C.U. and Meleney, H.E. *China Medical Journal,* 41:989-993, 1927.

李宗恩，亨利 · 梅莱尼《北京郊区一个村庄的疟疾考察》，载于《中华医学杂志》，1927 年，41:989-993 页。

翻译概要 作者利用了灭蝇运动的机会，发给每个送死苍蝇来的孩子（均不到 20 岁）一个苍蝇拍，并对其进行体捡，以脾肿大作为疟疾的诊断标准。如此，作者检查了北京西郊城府村 276 位 20 岁以下居民（全体居民 3000），其间日虐发病率为 10.4%。

The

China Medical Journal.

Vol. XLI. DECEMBER, 1927 No. 12

MALARIA IN A VILLAGE NEAR PEKING

C. U. Lee, M.B., Ch.B., D.T.M. H. and H. E. Meleney, M.D.

Although in Peking and its vicinity a fair amount of tertian malaria exists endemically, and on rare occasions even epidemically, it is surprising how little attention and much less actual study it has hitherto received.

During the past few months, we have been able to secure some epidemiological data, relating to the malarial situation in a village near Peking which may serve to focus attention on this problem.

The following study was undertaken in conjunction with Yenching University and we are particularly indebted to Dr. C. F. Wu, whose generous cooperation and organizing skill have been indispensable to us, to Drs. Basil and Agnes Livingstone Learmonth for the clinical data, unreservedly placed at our disposal, and to several others on the staffs of Yenching University and the Peking Union Medical College who assisted in the work.

One of the recognised methods of measuring the extent to which malaria is endemic in a district is by estimating the percentage of children and young adults with enlarged spleens due to malaria, in other words by the spleen rate. A still more accurate gauge is the *spleen index*, by which is meant the percentage of children between the ages of 2 and 10 years with enlarged spleens due to malaria.

There are many ways of measuring and recording the size of an enlarged spleen. The method which we used is that recommended by Dr. L. W. Hackett of the Division of International Health of the Rockefeller Foundation in an unpublished report to the League of Nations on the organization and methods of the Experiment Station for Malaria Control, Portotorres, Sardinia. He designates spleens as "O" when not palpable; "P" when just palpable on inspiration; 1, 2 and 3 (Arabic numerals) in the upper abdomen and I, II, III (Roman numerals) below the level of the umbilicus. This dispenses with the use of correction tables for the size of the individual in calculating splenic enlargement.

The scene of our study is a little village, known as Ch'engfu, about four miles from Peking, and just east of the campus of Yenching University, with a population of a little over 3000. This population includes a considerable number of men employed in construction work at the university. In order to examine as large a number of children as possible, we organised, in conjunction with Yenching University and the Health Centre of the Peking Metropolitan Police Department, an anti-fly campaign, during the course of which we examined for enlarged spleens a large number of more or less healthy children and young adults below the age of 20. In most cases the examination was carried out with the subject lying on his right side with knees drawn up. Inquiries were made regarding past history of malarial attacks but the information so obtained was, in most cases, unreliable.

The result of our examination is shown on Table I. It is necessary to point out here that a spleen rate or a spleen index only tells us the degree of endemicity of malaria in the district examined. It does not represent the actual malarial morbidity at the time of examination. The question whether conditions other than malaria may account for some of the enlarged spleens, is difficult to settle absolutely, but by deliberate exclusion of cases of enlarged spleen due to causes obviously not malarial, such as secondary anaemia following severe rickets, we are tolerably certain that practically all the enlarged spleens recorded in the table are of malarial origin. We watched carefully for kala-azar but did not meet with a single case. Of the 27 enlarged spleens 19 were just palpable; 3 under category 1, 4 under category 2 and only one of them reached the level of the umbilicus.

One significant feature which stands out clearly in this table is the marked difference between the spleen rate for the age period of 4-10 and that for the period of 11-15. The explanation may be found in the increased acquired immunity in children falling into the latter age period but may be merely accidental. The number examined in the age period of 15-20 is too small to draw any definite inference. The sex did not seem to affect the spleen rate.

While the spleen rate gives us some information as to the occurrence of endemic malaria in Ch'engfu village, Dr. and Mrs. Learmonth have been kind enough to supply us with data showing the monthly distribution of actual malarial cases in their clinics throughout the spring and summer. This is shown in Table II and the accompanying Chart. The cases were all benign tertian infections.

The number of cases increased at first gradually in February, March and April, more rapidly in May and June and reached its highest peak in August. Since the first Anopheles larva was found on the 14th of June (indicated by an arrow on the Chart) we are inclined to think that most, if not all, of the cases recorded up to the end of June were relapses from previous infections, while many of the cases occurring after that date were undoubtedly due to fresh infections.

Of the cases seen in these clinics 160 came from Ch'engfu village and from the campus of Yenching University. It is probable that many other cases which occurred in Ch'engfu did not appear at either clinic for treatment. It is reasonable to estimate, therefore, that between five and seven per cent of the population of the village suffered from malaria during the present season. This indicates that the disease is of considerable importance in this region, and deserves more intensive study than has been given to it heretofore.

Table I

SPLEEN RATE

Age period	Total examined	Total positive	Per cent positive
4-10	108	15	13.8
11-15	135	10	7.4
15-20	17	2	11.8
Total	260	27	10.4

Table II

MONTHLY INCIDENCE OF MALARIA CASES

		Feb.	Mar.	April	May	June	July	Aug.	Sept.	Total
Dr. Learmonth's cases			1	3	5	14	11	31	26	91*
Mrs. Learmonth's cases	Diagnosed Microscopically			2	10	17	20	9	11	69
	Diagnosed Clinically	2	2	1	5	18	17	27	24	96
	Diagnosed Therapeutically		3	2	1	0	2	9	3	20
Total		2	6	8	21	49	59	76	64	276

*29 of these cases were proved by blood smears.

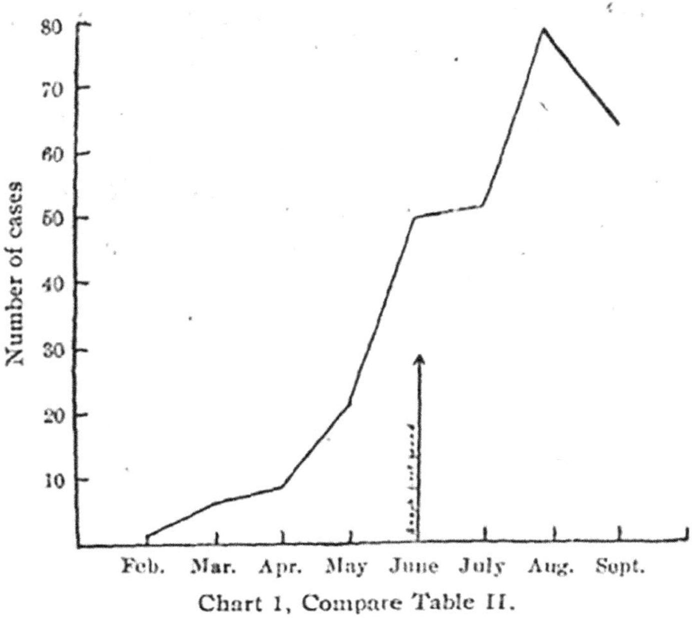

Chart 1, Compare Table II.

OBSERVATIONS ON THE FINDINGS IN 1602 EYE EXAMINATIONS FOR TRACHOMA

Y. P. Chan M.D. and Frank Oldt M.D.
Canton

During the period between Dec. 13 and 18, 1926, a child welfare exhibit was held at the Y. M. C. A. in Canton, as a memorial to the daughter of Mr. and Mrs. T. K. Jones. In addition to the demonstrations of the care of babies, the sale of literature, and showing of lantern slides and moving pictures, opportunity was given those visiting the exhibit to be vaccinated and to have their eyes examined for trachoma.

Of those coming 1602 had their eyes examined. There was no charge for examination. Appropriate advice and prescriptions, where indicated, were given. No medicine was dispensed nor was there any actual treatment of cases. In addition to the writers two other doctors, eye specialists, with large experience in trachoma, Dr. Wong Man of Hackett Medical College and Dr. Chan Ue Kim of Canton Hospital, took part in the examinations. An analysis of the data and report of the findings is the purpose of this paper.

In evaluating reports of examinations for trachoma diagnosis is important. Too often the incidence rate of trachoma in China has been greatly exaggerated because folliculosis and follicular conjunctivitis were called trachoma. Findings in some school examinations reported in the China Medical Journal[1] show conclusively that granulations do not necessarily indicate trachoma.—187 pupils were diagnosed as having follicular conjunctivitis. One year later, of 115 of these (all who had returned to school) not one was found to have trachoma on reexamination, 2 were suspected of having trachoma, 14 still had follicular conjunctivitis, 6 had simple conjunctivitis, and 93 were cured without treatment for trachoma and were free from granulations with no scar tissue. If these were trachoma there would have been no cure and scar tissue would have been present.

The points to be observed in diagnosis of trachoma are: obscuration of Meibomian ducts and subconjunctival vessels, thickening and scarring of palpebral conjunctiva, narrowing of palpebral fissure, irregular follicles and papillae in retrotarsal folds and on the ocular conjunctiva, superficial punctate keratitis of upper segment of cornea, pannus, infiltration of upper limbus, entropion, and trichiasis. Pain, photophobia, and history are suggestive.

In acute conjunctivitis many of the symptoms of trachoma are masked or simulated and it is impossible to make a correct diagnosis. When for this reason diagnosis was doubtful the case was put down as suspected trachoma. Treatment was recommended,—silvol or zinc sulphate,—and patients were told to go to certain hospitals after one month for reexamination.

On the record blanks were spaces for name, address, age, sex, trachoma, suspected trachoma, follicular conjunctivitis, simple conjunctivitis, and other eye diseases. The findings for each day's examinations are recorded in Table I.

After the first two or three days many came primarily because of eye disease and not as visitors to the exhibit. This tended to raise the percentage of eye disease and the trachoma rate also. The incidence of eye disease for the first three days is 38.1% and for the last three days is 46.6%. For the first three days, which are more nearly the normal cross section of the population, the trachoma rate is 12.7% while for the last three days which are affected by the special selection just mentioned, the rate is 18.2%. While this cause operates to make a difference in the trachoma rate it should not be so marked, as there is another factor causing a raise in the trachoma rate. On the fourth day the trachoma rate is very high 29.3% while the follicular conjunctivitis rate is but 5.8% a ratio of 5:1 while on other days it is about 3:1. It is probable that on this day a considerable number of follicular conjunctivitis cases were called trachoma. It is well again at this point to speak of the importance of making accurate diagnoses.

9. Experiments with Anti-Mosquito Measures at Yenching

Meleney, H.E. Lee, C.U., and Yang, C.P. Experiments with anti-mosquito measures at Yenching. *China Medical Journal*, Vol XLII (10) 725-735, 1928.

亨利 · 梅莱尼，李宗恩，杨静波 《燕京灭蚊的实验》，载于《中华医学杂志》，1928 年， XLII （10） ： 725-735 页。

翻译概要 1927 年暑假，作者与燕京大学生物系师生在燕京大学校园内（此项工作在校园外的城府村因村民不合作而无法开展）搜集了 17 种蚊虫标本，并将其进行分类。作者研究了其中两种疟蚊的繁殖期、分布，及与疟疾流行期的关系。经过比较几种灭蚊措施的效果，作者提出 9 项灭蚊建议，如填平与风景和农田无关的水洼，保留的小湖应除掉芦苇和沿岸的高草，小湖中放养土生食蚊鱼种或可食鱼，水表面植物需保留，Paris green 灭绝孑孓最经济有效（全校需 300 银元一年），学校建筑应加纱窗等。

The
China Medical Journal.

VOL. XLII. OCTOBER, 1928 No. 10

EXPERIMENTS WITH ANTI-MOSQUITO MEASURES AT YENCHING*

H. E. MELENEY, M.D., C. U. LEE, M.B., CH.B., D.T.M. & H.,
AND CHING-PO YANG.

The region included in the present study is the campus of Yenching University, situated about four miles northwest of Peking. The campus consists of an area of 58 acres, on which the new buildings of the University are still under construction. The fact that construction is still going on affects the value of the present study in two ways. In the first place it has presented certain conditions which will not be present when the construction is completed. In the second place it makes possible certain constructional recommendations which might be more difficult to carry out, if construction had been already completed.

The study was undertaken in the summer of 1927 with the cooperation of the Department of Biology and the medical staff of Yenching University, and we are particularly indebted to Dr. Chenfu F. Wu and Drs. Basil and Agnes Livingstone Learmonth, as well as to many others of the staff and student body of the University. Dr. K. F. Huang and his assistants on the staff of the Health Demonstration Center of the Peking Metropolitan Police Department also deserve thanks for assistance in an anti-fly campaign which was undertaken.

The region surrounding Yenching is a flat plain, well supplied with water from the Jade Fountain Spring about two miles to the west. The water runs in swiftly flowing streams about ten meters wide, whose main course is eastward. One of these feeds the ponds in the Yenching Campus from the west,

*From the Laboratory of Tropical Medicine, Department of Medicine, Peking Union Medical College, Peking.

and the outlet from these ponds on the east side finally joins the main stream again. These streams also furnish irrigation to rice fields on the east and north sides of the campus, and supply the ponds on the campus of Tsing Hua College. Beside this source of water there are many temporary or permanent ponds in the region which are dry or nearly dry in winter and spring but which fill up with water as a result of the summer rains. These are especially numerous in Yuan Ming Yuan, the old Summer Palace. Numerous ditches about Ch'engfu village, west of the campus, and between fields all over the region, contain water after heavy rains.

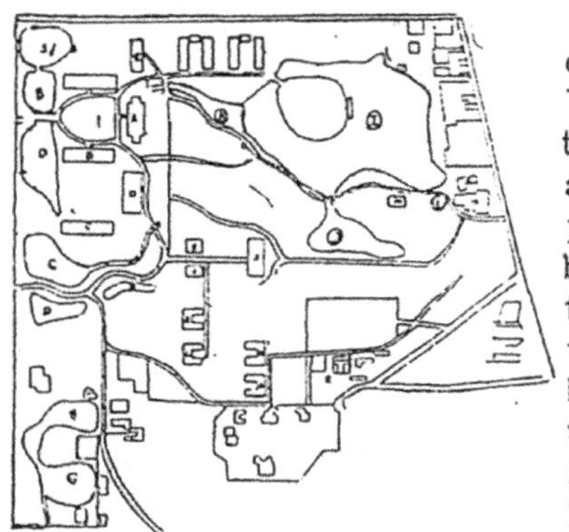

Map 1
Yenching Campus showing buildings and ponds.

Map 1 shows the distribution of buildings and water on the Yenching Campus itself. Certain of the ponds (C, H, I, and J) are part of the architectural plan of the campus and have been deepened and partly bunded to increase their beauty. A wide channel has been dug between them to assure a free, though sluggish, flow of water, and the inlets and outlets have been made permanent. Other ponds (A, D, F, and G) are to be filled in. All of these ponds develop early in the summer a heavy growth of reeds which, if uncut, grow to a height of six to ten feet above the surface, and must be recut several times during the summer in order to keep them below the surface. Beside this the permanent ponds develop a luxuriant growth of other water plants, particularly *Ceratophyllum,* which reaches the surface in June or July and by September covers practically the entire surface in a matted tangle. In this coarse growth, the fine algae like *Spirogyra* also grow luxuriantly. Ponds, A, D, E, F, and G have no permanent inlet or outlet. They start with underground seepage each spring and are deepened by the summer rains. Several species of fish exist in the permanent ponds and are sometimes carried to the other ponds by overflow after the rains.

It can readily be seen that any attempt to control the mosquitoes on the Yenching Campus would involve not only control measures on the campus itself, but also a similar

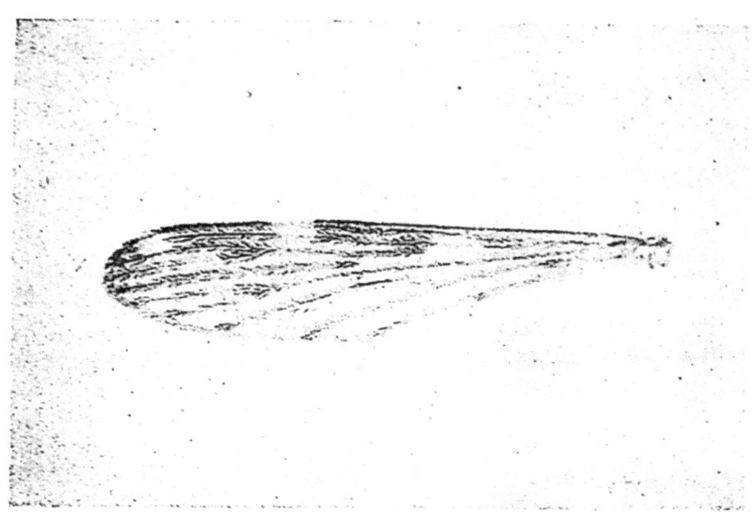

Fig. I.

Wing of *Anopheles hyrcanus*. Note two white areas on costa (anterior margin).

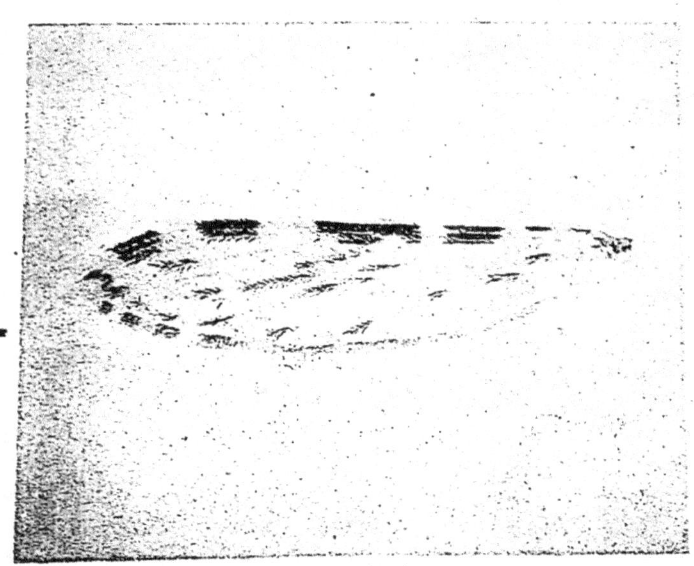

Fig. II.

Wing of *Anopheles pattoni*. Note five white areas on costa.

program for the entire neighborhood, including ponds, streams, rice fields and the courtyards of houses. This is obviously impossible without a large staff, a large sum of money, and police power over the entire area. The purpose of the present study was, therefore, merely to discover on the Yenching Campus what anti-mosquito measures would be most efficacious, to gain experience in applying various measures, and to interest a group of people in this important work. This paper attempts to demonstrate what measures were efficacious. That a large group of people were interested in the work is shown by the fact that five physicians, one biologist, one medical student, and several premedical students took active part in the work, and a number of other Yenching students were employed for collecting larvae and adult mosquitoes.

Seventeen different species of mosquitoes were encountered during the summer, of which two were *Anopheles*, seven *Culex*, six *Aedes*, one *Lutzia* and one *Taeniorrhynchus*. A list of these is given at the end of this paper. As our efforts were directed primarily against the *Anopheles*, special attention will be called only to these. The two species encountered were *A. hyrcanus*, var. *sinensis*, and *A. pattoni*. The simplest differential points between the adults of these two species have already been published (5). Figures 1 to 4 show the differences between the markings of the wings and the female palps of the two species, differences which are easily distinguishable with a hand lens.

The larva of *A. hyrcanus* is well known, but that of *A. pattoni* has not yet been described in detail. They are easily distinguished, however, by differences in the internal and external anterior clypeal hairs. Figures 5 and 6 show these differences.

Although *A. pattoni* was the first to appear in larval form in the neighborhood, it breeds mostly in the streams at the foot of the Western Hills, some three miles to the west of Yenching. It was first encountered on June 14th, 1927. Larvae of *A. hyrcanus* were first found on June 28th. They rapidly increased in numbers, and were almost exclusively found until September, when *A. pattoni* again appeared in almost equal numbers in certain ponds.

Collections of larvae were made more or less regularly, once a week or oftener, from ponds on the campus and in the

Fig. V.

Head of larva of *Anopheles hyrcanus*. Note that the internal anterior clypeal hairs (i) are close together, and that the external anterior clypeal hairs (e) are tufted.

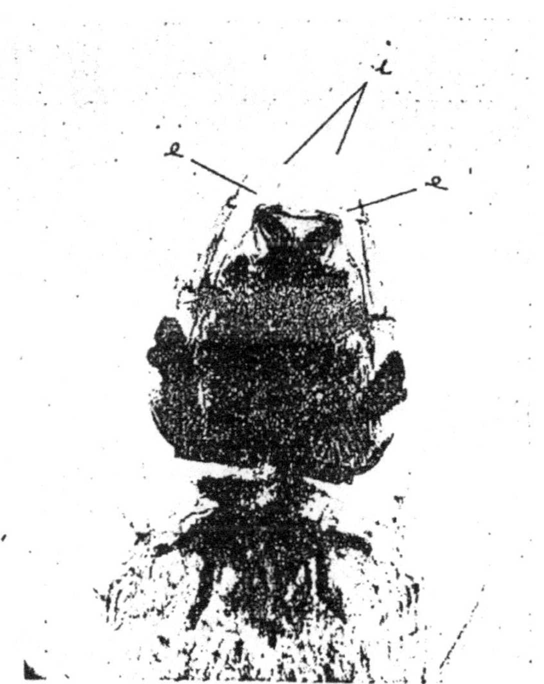

Fig. VI.

Head of larva of *Anopheles pattoni*. Note that the internal anterior clypeal hairs (i) are widely separated, and that the external anterior clypeal hairs (e) are simple.

surrounding neighborhood. In addition the students searched their dormitory rooms for adults, and collections were occasionally made in the stables of the University dairy and in houses in Ch'engfu village. The breeding of *Anopheles* was more abundant at first in rice fields along the Tsing Hua road and in ponds in Yuan Ming Yuan, but as the water plants increased in amount in the campus ponds, breeding became more abundant there, first in the shallow ponds (A, F, G, and H) and later in the deeper (permanent) ponds (C and I).

A hyrcanus and *A. pattoni* breed in almost any natural body of water in this region, even if there is practically no vegetation in it. For instance, larvae of both species have been found in the square pond at Wo Fo Ssu which is lined with flag stones and contains no water plants except minute algae clinging to the stones. The most favorable breeding places, however, are, for *A. hyrcanus,* ponds where there is considerable growth of *Ceratophyllum* and algae; and, for *A. pattoni,* the pools along hill streams, which contain abundant algae.

The first adults of *A. hyrcanus* were caught in dormitories on July 7th, at about the same time that larvae of this species were first discovered in ponds on the Campus. Thereafter specimens were brought in every few days from the dormitories. Since most of the dormitory windows were screened with netting, the number of adults was smaller than might have been obtained from unscreened houses. Unscreened huts used by construction laborers were occasionally searched without success, although *Culex pipiens* was found there in large numbers. In September after abundant breeding had been discovered in ditches filled with rain water close to the stables of the dairy, many adults of both *A. hyrcanus* and *A. pattoni* were found in the stables. A census of the mosquitoes in these stables in September showed in four catches, 458 *A. hyrcanus,* 258 *A. pattoni,* 226 *C. pipiens,* and 212 *Aedes koreicus.* Unfortunately parallel observations could not be made in the neighboring dwellings in Ch'engfu village, owing to the conservatism of the people. It is evident, however, that these two species of *Anopheles* prefer the environment of animals to that of man, since they seem to escape, if possible, from human habitations in the daytime, but remain in the stables of cattle.

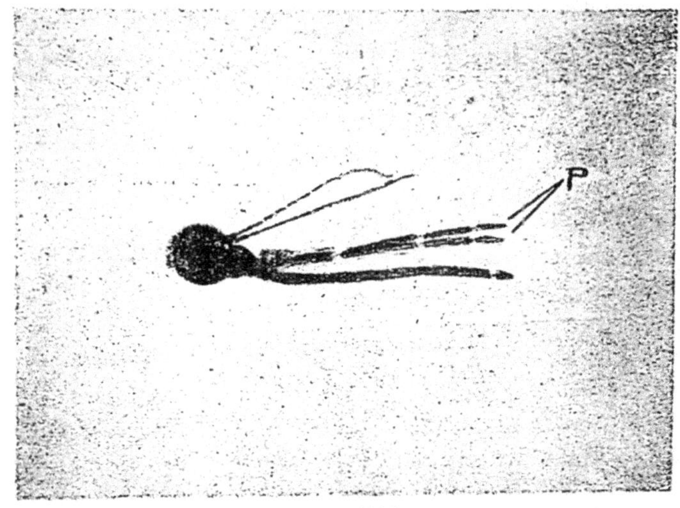

Fig. III.

Head and appendages of female *Anopheles hyrcanus.* Note that palps (p) are dark except for three narrow light bands.

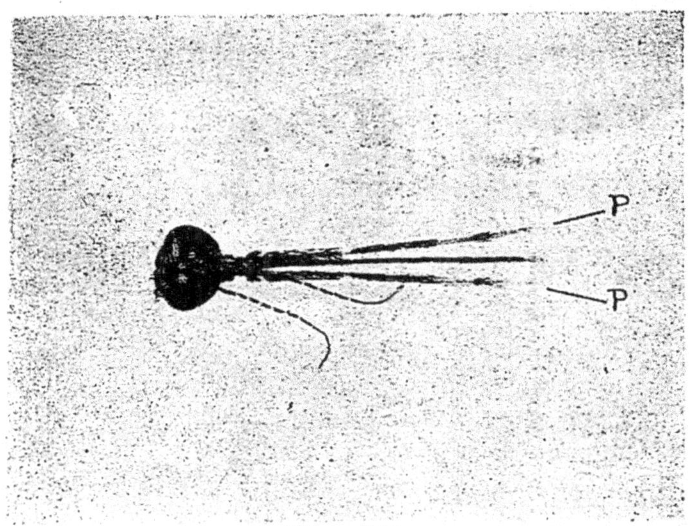

Fig. IV.

Head and appendages of female *Anopheles pattoni.* Note that palps (p) have white tips with two narrower proximal white bands.

The relation of these two species of *Anopheles* to the transmission of malaria in this region has not yet been definitely ascertained. Dr. E. Hindle at Tsinanfu was able last year to demonstrate the development of the malaria parasite in both species as far as the infective sporozoite stage in the salivary glands. *A. hyrcanus* is a very widely distributed mosquito, being found in practically all parts of Asia as well as in Europe. In most places it is not considered important in the transmission of malaria, although it has been incriminated in some epidemics in the Dutch East Indies. In Central China, however, it is the only known species of *Anopheles,* and is undoubtedly responsible for the malaria there. *A. pattoni* has been found thus far only in North China, and no studies have been made as to its actual participation in the transmission of malaria.

SURFACE VEGETATION AND FISH

In studying the ponds on the Yenching Campus, it was necessary, first of all, to have a fairly clear water surface. To secure this the reeds had to be cut in June and again in July. (In ponds F and G the reeds were not cut until August.) By the end of September there was again considerable growth of reeds in pond C, but the large lake (Pond 1) remained comparatively free. Regrowth was much slower after the second cutting than after the first. No measures of any kind could be taken against larvae without removing the reeds. On the other hand, this may have been an encouragement to the breeding of *Anopheles,* since they thrive better in the sunlight. After the reeds were cut there was still very little breeding of *Anopheles* in the campus ponds during July. Two factors were together responsible for this. First, the water plants had not yet grown up abundantly to the surface, and second, this had given the fish free access to the larvae. The only ponds where breeding was abundant in July were F and G, where *Anopheles, Culex* and *Aedes* were found abundantly. The reed growth was very heavy there and was uncut. The *Anopheles* larvae were most abundant where reeds had not grown up, but among the reeds *Culex* and *Aedes* were very plentiful. The most important reason for this heavy breeding, however, was the absence of fish from these ponds. Frogs and tadpoles were very abundant but did not touch the larvae.

The small fish in the campus ponds were studied from the point of view of their larva-eating habits. Two species of top minnows were found. Specimens of these fish have been sent for identification, but no report has yet been received.

Experiments in small aquaria were performed with these two species of fish to determine the speed with which they would devour mosquito larvae. Separate tests were carried out with *Anopheles* and *Culex* larvae. One specimen of each species of fish, recently caught, was placed in a separate aquarium, together with twenty *Anopheles* or *Culex* larvae, and the time required by each fish to devour the twenty larvae was noted. The following results were obtained:—

Species of Fish	Larvae	All devoured in
1	20 Anopheles	12 minutes
1	20 Culex	8 ,,
2	20 Anopheles	21 ,,
2	20 Culex	20 ,,
3	20 Anopheles	5 left after 24 hours.
3	20 Culex	1 ,, ,, ,, ,,

The slightly shorter time required to devour *Culex* larvae may be due to the fact that they lie at an angle with the surface and, when disturbed, descend to a deeper level, while the *Anopheles* lie flat at the surface and often move swiftly along the surface when disturbed.

It is evident that these fish do prey on mosquito larvae and may act as efficient larva-destroyers under natural conditions. As both species were present in large numbers in the ponds, it was undoubtedly due to their presence that breeding failed to develop early in the summer in most of the ponds, and their absence from ponds F and G, from the temporary ponds in Yuan Ming Yuan, from the rice fields and from the rain-water ditches, may be held responsible for the excessive breeding in those places. As an illustration of their influence the following instance may be given. Late in July we searched carefully for larvae all over the large lake (Pond 1). At a few places along the edges, where *Ceratophyllum* formed a thick surface growth, a few large *Anopheles* larvae were found. In the center of the lake, where the surface growth was scanty and composed mostly of a thin leafed grass, only first and second stage larvae were found. Where there was no surface grass there were no larvae. By August 1st the surface growth on this lake had become heavy, and spraying with Paris green was resorted to. Collections were made at frequent intervals thereafter and soon another application of Paris green was required. Later in August, however, heavy rains increased the depth of this pond about a foot, so that the water plants no longer reached the surface. After this no more larvae were found in the lake until the water had again receded to near its former level.

We conclude then that the top-minnows, native to the water of this region, comprise one of the most valuable weapons against mosquito larvae, and that in any anti-mosquito campaign they should be introduced into all bodies of water and permanent water containers. In order that they may work efficiently, however, surface water plants must be removed. Whether this can be done more economically than other measures can be carried out, must be determined by practice. The water plants are used to some extent for feeding fish and ducks, but this use is mostly in the early part of the summer. It might be possible for agriculturists to develop the use of the plants for fertilizer or for feeding other animals. The possibility of introducing commercial fish-raising in the large campus ponds should be considered also. Where this was done in one pond in Lang Jung Yuan, one of the residence compounds of the University, the large fish ate the water plants and no mosquito larvae were found during the entire summer.

PARIS GREEN

The use of Paris green (copper aceto-arsenite) to destroy *Anopheles* larvae was introduced by Barber in the United States in 1921 (1). It has since been used by many workers in the new world, by Hackett in Italy (2), by Kligler in Palestine (3) and by von D. Tiedeman in the Philippine Islands (6). It is considered to be the cheapest and most efficient chemical larvicide for anopheline larvae yet discovered. Its chief disadvantage is that it has practically no lethal effect on culicine larvae, for the reason that it floats on the surface of the water, whereas all larvae except the anophelines feed below the surface. It is used as a dry powder, mixed with 100 parts of finely screened road dust, and is applied by spraying or throwing it in a cloud over the surface of the water. To be of standard quality the Paris green must contain over fifty percent of arsenious oxide. When it is applied in the amount of one cubic centimeter (or 100 cc of the dust mixture) to 10 cubic meters of water surface or ten linear meters of the bank of a stream, all anopheline larvae are killed within a few hours.

The Paris green which was available for our use this summer was of two grades, one being manufactured by Merck and Company the other probably made in a Chinese drug shop in Peking. Merck's product was guaranteed to contain over fifty percent of arsenious oxide, whereas the Chinese product was found by Mr. Cameron, Pharmacist of the Peking Union Medical College Hospital, to contain about twenty-five percent. In September a third product, that of the Ansbacher Insecticide Co. of New York, was received, which was also guaranteed to contain more than fifty percent of arsenious oxide.

Tests performed in pans of water with dust mixtures of these three products showed that all *Anopheles* larvae were killed by a one percent mixture of the German and American products within two and a half hours after application. With the Chinese product concentrations of 1.2 and 1.4 percent required about four hours to kill all larvae, while higher concentrations (1.6, 1.8, 2.0%) killed them within two hours. Since the German and American products were not available in the early part of the summer, a two percent mixture of the Chinese product was used, and gave satisfactory results.

The relative cost of the three products makes the American product the one of choice. It was delivered in Peking by freight at a cost of Mex. $0.60 per pound, while the Merck product cost $1.80 per pound and the Chinese product $0.90. It is said, however, that a good quality of Paris green may be available shortly from Germany at a price about equal to that of the American product.

The kind of dust used is important. A fine sand which had been dusted on new roads on the Yenching campus was first used, but it sank quickly to the bottom, carrying some of the Paris green with it. Gray dust from the highway, however, proved to be satisfactory, and could be seen on the surface for a day or two after application.

Dusting was begun on July 29th, and all the campus ponds were covered by August 8th. After the dusting of each pond, watch was kept at intervals of a few days for the appearance of larvae. Usually no larvae were found for one or two days, then first-stage larvae appeared and the size increased until dusting was again necessary. A ten-day interval was used. This, we believe, is the limit of safety and is possibly too long an interval during the hottest weather when eight days is a safer interval. The area of the ponds was so large that judgment was used in the amount of dust applied to a pond. This was dependent upon the amount of surface vegetation. The large lake, for instance, required the use of only 10 liters of dust at the first application on August 5th, but on October 1st, 340 liters were required to dust the whole lake.

The total area of all the campus ponds is about 58,000 square meters. For one complete dusting of these ponds 5,800 cc. or about thirteen pounds of American Paris green are required, costing about Mex. $8.00. It requires the work of two coolies for ten days to prepare and apply this to the ponds, and their wages would amount to $6.00, making a total cost of $14.00 aside from the initial cost of equipment, including sprayers, mixer, etc., and the salary of a responsible technician to control the efficiency of the work by dipping for larvae. For the entire summer it is estimated that the cost of the work was about Mex. $300.00.

Experiments with Paris green were carried out also in rice fields near the campus. Water is led into these fields from the streams and an outlet is provided also, so that the water flows through the fields rather than standing on them. The speed of flow of the water affected the experiments somewhat, since new larvae may have been carried into the treated field and some of the Paris green may have escaped. In a field where the water was running rather swiftly no larvae were found on the first day after the spraying, but on the second day a few large ones were found together with very small ones, and by the fifth day many large ones were found. In a field where the flow of water was sluggish, only first stage larvae appeared on the second day after spraying, and the first large ones appeared on the fifth day. It was found that the Paris green could be efficiently applied when the rice plants were small, that is, not over one foot in height. At about this time, however, the breeding naturally diminished, and by the time the plants were two feet in height no more larvae could be found.

Oiling of one pond containing no surface vegetation or fish, using kerosene oil, was carried out under the direction of Dr. B. L. Learmonth. It was effective in destroying both anopheline and culicine larvae. Where surface vegetation is present, however, it is well known that oil will not spread well and does not prevent breeding.

MALARIA IN YENCHING AND CH'ENGFU

Our observations on this subject have been reported separately (4). A careful record of malaria cases was kept during the spring and summer by Drs. Basil and Agnes Learmonth in their clinics. The first cases appeared in February, and there was a slow increase in numbers in March and April, more in May and a much greater increase in June, July and August. Seventy-six cases were seen in August. All the cases were of the benign tertain type. As the first *Anopheles* larvae were found in this region on June 14th, it is evident that there was a large amount of endemic and latent malaria among the inhabitants, which had already declared itself in the form of spring relapses before the mosquitoes appeared. The field was well prepared, therefore, for the propagation of the disease when the new generation of mosquitoes developed to carry on its transmission.

The endemicity of the disease in Ch'engfu was also demonstrated by an estimate of the spleen rate, which was taken among the children of the village. An anti-fly campaign was instituted at the suggestion of Dr. C. F. Wu with the cooperation of Dr. K. F. Huang and his staff and several members of the Yenching community. Each child who brought in flies was examined for splenic enlargement before being presented with a fly-swatter. This did away with all opposition, and 260 boys and girls between four and twenty years of age were examined. An incidence of 10.4 per cent of enlarged spleens, not apparently due to other causes than malaria, was found. These facts emphasize the importance of malaria as an endemic disease in the neighborhood of Yenching University, and as a potential source of danger to the staff and students.

RECOMMENDATIONS

As a result of the summer's work certain suggestions can be made as to the direction which anti-mosquito, and particularly anti-Anopheles measures should take on the Yenching Campus.

1. All ponds not necessary for scenic or agricultural purposes should be filled in.

2. Ponds which remain should be kept free of reeds and their banks should be kept free of long grass.

3. Such ponds should be stocked with indigenous fish known to be of value as larva-destroyers, or should be used for commercial fish-raising.

4. If top-minnows are depended upon for the prevention of breeding, the ponds must be kept free of surface vegetation. A commercial use for water plants should be sought.

5. If the surface vegetation cannot be eliminated, Paris green is probably the cheapest and most efficient larvicide for *Anopheles* larvae. It should be used under intelligent supervision.

6. Temporary breeding places of *Anopheles* due to summer rains should be drained, if possible, or treated with Paris green.

7. For the prevention of breeding of *Culex* and *Aedes,* practical experiments with fish in rain-water receptables should be carried out. Unnecessary standing water about houses should be done away with under the supervision of an inspector.

8. The University buildings should be efficiently screened throughout.

9. It is realized that at present no anti-Anopheles program applied to the Yenching Campus alone will prevent malaria in the region or on the campus. Nevertheless, the university authorities can perform a valuable service by carrying out each year some such measures as have been outlined, first as a partial protection to the University and the neighboring villages, second as an educational project for students of biology and medicine, and third in order to lay a foundation for similar work on a large scale in the future.

SPECIES OF MOSQUITOES ENCOUNTERED

(These identifications were made by Mr. F. W. Edwards of the British Museum of Natural History.)

Anopheles

A. hyrcanus

A. pattoni

10. Some Notes on The Treatment and Diagnosis of Malaria

Lee, C.U. *National Med.ical Journal of China*, 15:38-45, 1929.

李宗恩《关于疟疾诊断和治疗的观察》，载于《中华医学杂志》，1929 年，15:38-45 页。

翻译概要：作者通过用 Plasmochin 治疗 8 例疟疾的临床观察，对其治疗效果给予肯定，但提请注意其副作用（发绀）。经过对三例疟疾患者的确诊，作者建议在常规体征和血液检查不能确定的情况下，采用脾穿刺的办法最后确诊。

National Medical Journal of China, 1929, XV, 38-45

SOME NOTES ON THE TREATMENT AND DIAGNOSIS OF MALARIA

C. U. LEE

Department of Medicine, Peking Union Medical College, Peping.

ON TREATMENT

The cure of an attack of tertian malarial fever through the use of what is now known as cinchona bark in the case of the Countess of Chinchon in Peru in 1638 marked an event of some significance in the history of modern medicine. Shortly after, on her return to Spain, the bark was introduced into Europe. It was, however, not until 1820 that the alkaloid, quinine, was isolated from the bark by Pelletier and Caventou. Since that this alkaloid has been regarded as the only effective drug in the treatment of malaria. Recent investigations have, however, shown that its value among the alkaloids derived from cinchona bark is by no means unique. Quinidine possesses in the same doses an equal value as an anti-malarial agent and cinchonine is also equally effective, though it requires larger doses and a longer course.

While the value of quinine (and its companion alkaloids) in the treatment of malaria is beyond question, it nevertheless falls short in many respects of being an ideal specific drug. It is true that the symptoms of an acute attack of benign tertian or quartan malaria yield readily to quinine but it is equally certain that a proportion of the treated cases relapse, no matter how efficiently the drug is used; in other words, quinine is never certain to bring about an actual cure in mild malarial infections. In this respect quinine is more specific for the aestivo-autumnal form of malaria, for a much higher percentage of actual cures can be obtained with it. It has, however, little or no effect in removing the gametocytes of *Plasmodium falciparum* or crescents from the blood. This is an annoying drawback of quinine from the point of view of malarial prevention, for the spread of this malignant form of malaria is necessarily dependent on the presence in the community of crescent carriers.

The intensely bitter taste of quinine and its liability to cause toxic symptoms, especially in susceptible individuals, also detract not a little from its value as an anti-malarial agent. Furthermore the fact that the cultivation of cinchona trees is limited to certain parts of the world and the production of quinine is monopolised by private agencies, is apt to keep the price at an unreasonably high level.

It is for these considerations that the introduction of plasmochin, a new synthetic product, by workers in the pharmaceutical laboratories at Elberfeld in 1925 merits special attention. The exact formula has not yet been published but Horlein (2) in a paper dealing with its chemistry states that it is of the same class of bodies as quinine, which he considers to be a complicated alkylamino-6-methoxyquinoline. It is a tasteless, light yellow powder, put up in tablet form. Experiments with it on Proteosoma infection in canaries by Roehl (3) showed that it possesses a parasitotropic action sixty times greater than quinine. Its therapeutic value in tertian and quartan infections is said to equal to that of quinine, but the most important observation has been with regard to its destructive action on the crescents in subtertian infections, although it is less efficient than quinine in sterilising the blood of ring forms. Hence for this latter type of malaria a combination of quinine and plasmochin is advocated.

After extensive trials in various parts of the world, the following dosage and plan of treatment has generally been recommended. In tertian and quartan malaria, 0.02 gm. (1/3 grain) may be given three or four times a day continued for four or five days after the temperature has become normal and then for three days weekly for the subsequent four to six weeks. For aestivo-autumnal malaria, plasmochin compound may be used, each tablet of which contains 0.005 gm. (1/12 grain) of plasmochin and 0.0625 gm. (1 grain) of quinine, in dosage of twelve tablets daily for fourteen days without break and then for four days weekly for the subsequent five weeks. Children bear big doses remarkably well and for those above the age of ten, the adult dosage may be tried.

Through the kindness of the manufacturers, we have been favored with a small supply of this new drug for experimental trial. Unfortunately, malaria occurs very irregularly in Peking and only eight cases, of which six were benign tertian and two aestivo-autumnal, have so far been treated with it. Small as the series is, the results obtained seem to confirm those of previous workers. The plan of treatment recommended above has been in the main followed but as it was impracticable to keep the patients in the hospital more than two or three weeks, the duration of treatment in some cases was cases unavoidably curtailed. The effect of the treatment on the parasites was checked in most of the cases by daily blood examinations.

These cases show that in benign tertian malaria, the acute symptoms are easily controlled and the parasites quickly disappear from the peripheral blood following the use of plasmochin. The amount of plasmochin required to prevent the onset of a paroxysm or to "sterilise" the blood of parasites necessarily varies according to the degree of infection. While 0.14 gm. prevented a paroxysm from occurring in Case 5, the same amount only succeed in modifying it severity in Case 2. The dosage, which caused the disappearance of parasites from the peripheral blood ranged from 0.14 gm. in Case 1 and to 0.20 gm. in Case 6. With regard to relapse, 1, 3, 4 and 5 had none within an observation period of four and half to six months. In Cases 2 and 6 the patients failed to report after their discharge from hospital. In the two cases of aestivo-autumnal infection plasmochin compound was equally effective. Rings as well as crescents promptly disappeared from the peripheral blood.

The great disadvantage in the use of this drug has been its liability to cause certain toxic symptoms. Six of the eight cases treated showed some degrees of cyanosis, slight in Cases 1, 2 and 8, but rather marked in Cases 3, 6, and 7. This symptom is said to be due to the formation of methaemoglobin in the blood and, though it is not considered by the German authors to be of serious import, it nevertheless constitutes a distinct disadvantage. During treatment Cases 2 and 8 also complained of abdominal pain which could not be attributed to any definite cause. These and other even more alarming symptoms recorded by other authors make it necessary to emphasize that at present plasmochin should be used with great care.

With regard to the cost of treatment there is at present no choice between plasmochin and quinine but when plasmochin is produced on a large scale, it can probably be considerably cheapened and will no doubt bring the price of quinine down with it.

Benign tertian infection. Case 1.—A Chinese male nurse (Hosp. No. 9356) aged 25, was admitted on September 3rd., 1927 with daily chill and fever for three days. Blood film showed presence of benign tertian parasites. Spleen was enlarged and tender. No history of similar attack previously. Plasmochin treatment was instituted on September 4th. A daily amount of 0.08 gm. was at first given, which was later reduced to 0.06 gm. per day. During a period of seven weeks he had six courses of three days each representing a total dosage of 1.24 gm. of plasmochin. A mild febrile paroxysm occurred on second day of treatment after 0.1 gm. of plasmochin. Blood was negative for parasites on third day of treatment with a total of 0.14 gm. of plasmochin. No relapse occurred up to February 1928. On September 14th at end of the second course slight cyanosis developed unaccompanied by subjective distress, passing off in a few days. On September 9th the patient complained of vague abdominal pain, which continued off and on for several weeks. He was operated upon on October 14th for chronic appendicitis, a diagnosis which was confirmed by pathological examination.

Case 2.—A Chinese male (Hosp. No. 18084) of 18, was admitted on January 3rd. 1928 with history of chill and fever every other day for a week. No previous history of malaria. Infection probably occurred in the autumn months in the West City of Peking with long latent period. Benign tertian parasites were found in blood on admission. No enlargement of spleen. Plasmochin 0.06 gm. daily was started on January 5th just before a febrile paroxysm was due. A mild attack occurred on 7th January after 0.14 gm. of the drug. Parasites could still be found after 0.14 gm. but were not found after January 8th when 0.18 gm. had been administered. Three courses were given. A slight degree of cyanosis was noted and vague abdominal pain and dizziness were complained of after 0.30 gm. of plasmochin. No relapse took place up to the day of discharge, January 31st.

Case 3.—A Chinese woman student (Hosp. No. 11670), aged 25, was admitted on August 30th, 1927 with fever and sweating on August 28th and again on day of admission. History of malaria in childhood. Tertian parasites found in blood. Spleen not enlarged. Plasmochin treatment began on August 31st with 0.02 gm. thrice daily on first day, increased to four times a day the next day. A febrile paroxysm occurred on September 1st after 0.08 gm. of plasmochin. Blood film was positive for parasites after 0.1 gm. but negative after 0.16 gm. of the drug. After 1.4 gm. marked cyanosis developed, which disappeared a few days after discontinuance of the drug. Subsequently treatment was continued with quinine at the patient's request. No relapse up to February 1928.

Case 4.—A Chinese boy (Hosp. No. 17622) aged 12, was admitted on August 5th, 1917 with history of five attacks of chill and fever every other day, dating back five weeks prior to admission. These symptoms had been controlled by five "white powders" taken prior to admission. A low continuous fever was present at the time of admission, probably associated with pleurisy with effusion which was also found to be present. Blood was positive for tertian parasites. Spleen enlarged. Plasmochin, 0.08 gm. daily, was started on August 12th, and four courses of three days each were given. Blood examination gave negative results on the second day of treatment. No untoward symptoms noted. No relapse up to December 26th, 1927 when the patient showed marked improvement in general condition, with gain in weight.

Case 5.—A Chinese male (Hosp. No. 17596) aged 38, was first admitted on August 1st, 1927 with sudden onset of chill and fever five hours previously. Tertian parasites found in blood on August 5th. Spleen enlarged. Course of quinine given for two weeks with disappearance of symptoms. Relapse occurred and the patient was admitted for the second time on August 29th. Tertian parasites again found in blood. Plasmochin started on August 31st, 0.08 gm. per day. Five courses of three days each were given. No paroxysm occurred after institution of this treatment. Plasmochin 0.14 gm. seems to have prevented the onset of a paroxysm. Parasites disappeared from blood after 0.14 gm. No untoward symptoms noted. No relapse up to February 1928.

Case 6.—A Chinese boy (Hosp. No. 18085) aged 19, was admitted on September 21st 1927 with history of chill and fever on alternate days for five days. No previous history of malaria. Tertian parasites found in blood on admission. Spleen enlarged. Plasmochin, 0.08 gm. daily, was started on September 24th and continued for six days. Mild paroxysm on September 25th when 0.08 gm. had been given. Temperature normal from that time on. Blood negative for parasites after September 26th after 0.20 gm. of plasmochin. During treatment marked cyanosis occurred without subjective distress, and passed off a few days after discontinuance of the drug. Patient left hospital on October 6th against advice. No later date obtained.

Aestivo-autumnal infection. Case 7.—A Chinese boy (Hosp. No. 18192) of 17, was admitted on October 3rd, 1927 with history of chill and fever for three days. Subtertian parasites found in blood. Spleen just palpable at costal margin. Blood films showed presence of not only numerous subtertian rings, few crescents but also many schizonts on August 7th. On the 8th, rings were still numerous but schizonts were few and on the 9th, only rings were found. Plasmochin compound, each tablet containing 0.005 gm. of plasmochin and 0.0625 gm. of quinine, was given, at first 12 tablets daily and later 8 tablets. Plasmochin 0.1 gm. and quinine 1.25 gm. did not reduce the temperature but after 0.2 gm. of plasmochin and 2.5 gm. of quinine the temperature fell to normal. The same dose also freed the peripheral blood of parasites. On the third day of treatment gradually deepening cyanosis began. On October 14th the first course was finished. Cyanosis disappeared by the 18th. A second three day course with a daily dosage of 0.04 gm. plasmochin and 0.5 gm. of quinine was given beginning on October 21st, without causing cyanosis. No relapse up to November 17th, 1927.

Case 8.—A Chinese male (Hosp. No. 18530) aged 30, was admitted on November 5th, 1927 with history of daily chill and fever for three weeks. Subtertian rings and crescents were found in blood on admission. Spleen enlarged. No history of previous malaria. Plasmochin compound was begun on November 8th, 1927, at first 6 tablets, but later 12 tablets a day. Treatment was continued for fifteen days. During the last six days of treatment only 4 tablets a day were given. Plasmochin 0.155 gm. and quinine 1.938 gm. brought the temperature down to normal. The blood showed no rings or crescents after the fourth day of treatment. Some degree of cyanosis and occasional attacks of abdominal pain were noted though the patient felt on the whole comfortable. He was discharged on November 23rd. No later data are available.

ON DIAGNOSIS

Effective control of acute symptoms of malaria often means no more than a reduction in the number of parasites below a level necessary for symptom production. It seems as though the organs involved, such as the spleen and bone marrow, exert a protective influence over the parasites from the destructive action of the anti-malarial drug used and thereby allow them to multiply later under favourable conditions and cause a relapse. Thus in a patient with a past history of malaria but without demonstrable parasites in the peripheral blood, a diagnosis for or against malaria is extremely difficult, unless the case be observed over a long period. Various methods with the aim of increasing the number of parasites so that they may be detected in the peripheral blood, have been devised. These include the injection of foreign proteins or other substances acting on the circulation such as adrenalin and strychnine, and physical agents such as X-rays and quartz lamp radiation. Such provocative procedures occasionally succeed in producing a parasitic relapse but more often meet with failure.

Spleen puncture, as far as the author is aware, has not been seriously recommended either as a provocative method or as a diagnostic aid. While it is admittedly a heroic procedure, yet with certain precautions there is no reason why it should be attended with undue risk. If spleen puncture is regarded as an essential step in the management of cases of kala-azar, it seems unreasonable to deny its benefit to certain cases of malaria, in which suspense may do more harm than a spleen puncture. Opinions still differ in regard to the relative danger involved in the puncture of a malarial spleen as compared with that of a kala-azar spleen. The fact that the spleen in kala-azar is softer, more vascular and more friable argues that puncture is more dangerous in the case of kala-azar than it is in chronic malaria.

The following illustrative cases are intended to show that at least in some cases spleen puncture is of definite help in establishing a diagnosis and in one case (Case 9) it was of great moment to the patient. This case and one other (Case 11) also show that spleen puncture may be followed by a clinical and parasitic relapse. Case 10 is of interest in that certain provocative measure were of no avail in inducing a relapse and a diagnosis was made possible only by a spleen puncture.

In recommending spleen puncture not for general adoption but as a last resort in certain exceptional cases of malaria, we include certain necessary precautions. Apart from asepsis, and a certain amount of tech nical skill, it is necessary to ascertain patient's bleeding time. If this is unusually prolonged, it should be regarded as a serious contraindication because of the possibility of dangerous haemorrhage. It is unwise to puncture the spleen unless its lower pole extends well beyond the costal margin. Lastly the patient should be enjoined to rest in bed for at least 24 hours following the operation.

CASE REPORTS

Case 9.—A Chinese soldier (Hosp. No. 15000) aged 30, was admitted on October 4th, 1926. He gave a history of attacks of fever a year previously, from which he recovered without treatment. The present illness began six weeks prior to admission with chill and fever accompanied by certain neurological symptoms* pointing to definite brain lesions. After admission patient had a low fluctuating fever of about 38°C. Spleen was enlarged, extending 1 cm. below costal margin. Blood examination showed 8600 leucocytes, 4,120,000 erythrocytes, and 85 per cent haemoglobin, the differential count gave 68 per cent neutrophiles, 23 per cent lymphocytes, 8 per cent large mononuclear leucocytes and 1 per cent eosinophiles. Careful examination of thin blood films was repeatedly negative for malarial parasites. A spleen puncture was done on October 22nd and in smears of the splenic juice thus obtained a few crescents were found. Following the spleen puncture the patient's temperature rose above 38°C. and on October 24th, to 39.3°C., with the appearance of a few crescents in the peripheral blood. Under quinine therapy and occasional doses of neosalvarsan, the fever promptly subsided and parasites disappeared form blood. The patient was discharged on November 26th with marked improvement of his neurological symptoms.

Case 10.—A Chinese girl (Hosp. No. 17700) of 16, was first admitted to the surgical service on August 15th, 1927 for chronic suppurative osteomyelitis of the right scapula with a discharging sinus of one years duration. She also gave a history of chill and fever on alternate days during the months of June and July 1927 and of a gradually enlarging mass in left upper abdomen. She took a few tablets of quinine which reduced the temperature somewhat. On admission she had a fever of 39.3°C. which fell to within normal limits on the following day. The spleen was enlarged to the level of umbilicus. Blood examination showed 8200 leucocytes, 2,984,000 erythrocytes and 53 per cent haemoglobin; the differential count was 65 per cent neutrophiles, 33 per cent lymphocytes and 2 per cent large mononuclear leucocytes. Benign tertian schizonts were found on the day following admission. Under quinine treatment the temperature remained normal, parasites disappeared from the perhiperal blood and the spleen diminished slightly in size. The patient was discharged on August 29th with her surgical condition untreated.

Patient was well up to October 17th when she had a chill followed by fever. On October 20th she had another chill and was admitted for the second time. On examination she a nasal discharge, a congested throat and a slight cough. The spleen was smaller than on first admission. Blood was negative for malarial parasites. The temperature became normal the day following admission. In order to ascertain whether or not her malarial infection has really been cured, various provocative procedures were adopted. Hypodermic injection of 1 cc. of 1: 100 solution of adrenalin was tried on October 25th. The caused marked temporatory contraction of the spleen but neither clinical nor parasitic relapse followed. On November 5th 0.002 gm. of strychnine nitrate was given hypodermically without result. On November 8th spleen puncture was performed and benign tertain parasites were demonstrated in the spleen smear. The puncture, however, was not followed by clinical relapse or,

* The neurological aspects of this case have been fully reported on by De. Vries (1).

by the appearance of parasites in peripheral blood. Three days later the patient was exposed over the upper part of her abdomen to the mercury-vapour quartz lamp for 15 minutes at a distance of 40 cm. A slight degree of erythema over the exposed part occurred but no relapes followed. On December 12th she was operated upon under gas, oxygen and ether for her surgical condition. No relapse occurred after the operation and patient has enjoyed normal health up to the time of writing.

Case 11.—A Chinese boy (Hosp. No. 16827) of six, was admitted on May 5th 1927 for splenomegaly, fever and emaciation of one month's duration. A diagnosis of kala-azar was made by spleen puncture and the condition was effectively treated with stiburea (an organic antimony compound). Because of his anaemia 300 cc. of citrated blood were given intraperitoneally on May 17th. On June 4th the patient developed an intermittent fever with the appearance of benign tertain malarial parasites in peripheral blood. It was impossible to be certain whether this was a relapse or an accidental infection from the transfusion. On quinine therapy the fever subsided and blood became negative for parasites. The patient remained afebrile and treatment was continued for his kala-azar. On July 8th another spleen puncture was wone in search of Leishmania parasites which were not found, but in the splenic pulp tertian parasites were demonstrated. Following the puncture, the patient had a chill followed by a sharp rise of temperature to 40.6°C. On July 10th a similar attack occurred with the appearance of parasites in peripheral blood. No further attack took place after quinine treatment was resumed.

SUMMARY

1. The value of plasmochin as an anti-malarial agent is confirmed. The histories of eight cases of malaria, six benign tertain and two aestivo-autumnal, treated with it in Peking are given in detail. The rather frequent occurrence of cyanosis following its use is a distinct disadvantage.

2. Spleen puncture as a means of diagnosis is advocated in certain cases of malaria, in which a prompt decision is desirable but repeated blood examinations fail to reveal the parasites even after the application of some of the so-called provocative measures. In certain cases, spleen puncture is followed by febrile reactions and appearance of parasites in the peripheral blood. The details of three cases are given.

REFERENCES

1. De Vries, Ernst. Nervous complications in pernicious malaria. China Med Jour., 1927, *41*, 503-508.

2. Horlein, H. Ueber die chemischen Grundlagen und die Entwicklungageschichte des Plasmochins. Beihefte z. Arch. f. Schiffs-u. Trop.-Hyg., 1926, *30*, 305-310.

3. Roehl, W. Die Wirkung des Plasmochins auf die Vogel-malaria. Ibid., 1926, *30*, 311-318.

11. New Technique for Feeding Sandflies (Phlebotomus) for Experimental Transmission of Kala-Azar

Hu, C.H. and Lee, C.U. *Proceedings of the Society for Experimental Biology and Medicine*, 26:227-280, 1929.

胡正详, 李宗恩《用于研究黑热病传播的白玲喂养新技术》，载于《实验生物医学学会会议记录》，1929 年，26:227-280 页。

翻译概要 作者报告了一种人工喂养白蛉的实验装置。该装置可同时喂养数十只白蛉。用此装置饲养的白蛉，在食用了患有黑热病的仓鼠的脾脏后，也感染了黑热病。所以，此装置为证实白蛉通过叮咬传染黑热病提供了条件。

4257

New Technique for Feeding Sandflies (Phlebotomus) for Experimental Transmission of Kala-Azar.

C. H. HU AND C. U. LEE. (Introduced by Hsien Wu.)

From the Departments of Pathology and Medicine, Peking Union Medical College.

In the experimental attempts to transmit kala-azar by the bites of sandflies, it has been found desirable to substitute an artificial feeding on blood rich in Leishmann-Donovan bodies for the natural feeding upon infected animals, in order to obtain an abundant growth of flagellates within the flies. This blood is obtained by mixing the blood of a normal animal with the crushed spleen of a hamster heavily infected with kala-azar.

For such artificial feeding we used the technique of Hertig and Hertig.[1] This technique was learned in a few days and in the course of 2 months during the summer of 1928, 565 flies were fed. During this work it became clear that this technique had a number of limitations. The flies had to be fed one by one, making the procedure tedious. During the etherization and handling of the flies, many were injured. A satisfactory engorgement was obtained with *P. sergenti,* while *P. major* only in rare instances could be fully engorged. In order to feed a larger number of flies with a minimum of injury and a maximum of engorgement, the following technique has been devised.

Technique. Etherize a hamster heavily infected with kala-azar, pin its feet on a wooden board, and place its head and neck between the arms of a U-shaped wooden block. Remove the hair over the anterior surface of the neck and chest by pulling and sterilize the skin with alcohol and ether. With aseptic precautions, make a median incision through the skin extending from the anterior end of the lower jaw to the middle of the sternum. Pull apart the skin flaps and pin them to the arms of the U-shaped block, the upper surface of which is slightly raised above the level of the head and neck. Cut the carotid artery on one side and, as the blood wells up, quickly draw it into a sterile pipette. Practically all the blood that is obtained by bleeding can be drawn into the pipette. Defibrinate and centrifuge the blood.

Remove the spleen aseptically, cut the whole or a part of it in small pieces, and place it in a small test-tube 3 inches long and 1/3 inch in diameter. Crush it thoroughly with a glass rod. Into this crushed material stir the blood plasma and centrifuge the mixture to throw the cell clumps to the bottom. Add enough red cells to the supernatant fluid to give the resultant mixture the approximate concentration of normal blood.

Place a piece of flannel in the shallow dish on the upper surface of an aluminum feeding stage (Figs. 1 and 2B) and add the blood-parasite mixture. In order thoroughly to saturate the flannel piece, work the mixture into the flannel by repeated pressing. This flannel represents the subcutaneous tissue of the animal. Cover with a piece of skin from the hamster, removed during the centrifuging of the spleen-plasma mixture. The skin most suitable for this purpose is that of the back. Before applying the skin to the stage, remove the hair on the external surface and also the thin layer of muscle attached to the inside. Do not sterilize the external skin surface, as the flies do not bite as well on sterilized skin. Place the

[1] Hertig, Arthur T., and Hertig, Marshall, 1927, lxv, 328.

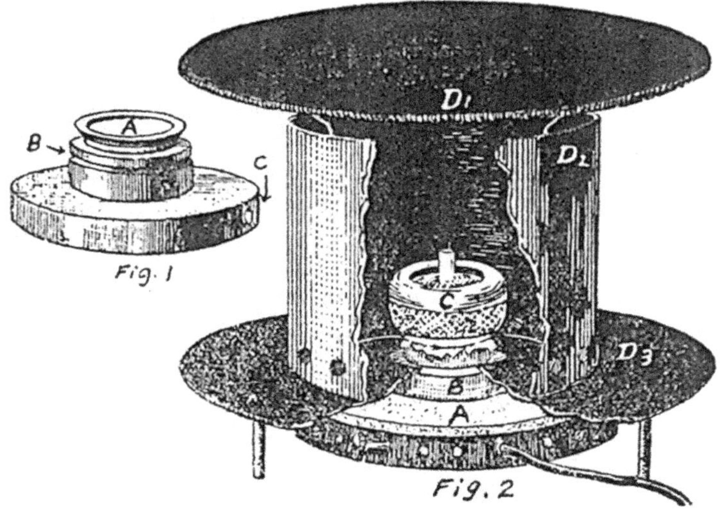

FIG. 1. *Feeding Stage.*

(A) Dish, about ¾ inch in diameter, for the holding of flannel. (B) the groove for the tying of the skin which covers the flannel. (C) a hole for the insertion of a thermometer to register the temperature of the feeding stage.

FIG. 2. *Feeding Outfit.*

(A) The electric heater (this heater is manufactured by Chicago Surgical and Electrical Co.) (B) the feeding stage covered with hamster skin. (C) the cage containing flies. (D1), (D2), (D3) 3 separate parts of cover, all painted black.

stage thus prepared on an electric heater (Fig. 2A) at a steady temperature of 35° C., and put on the skin surface a cage (Fig. 2C) containing the flies hatched in the laboratory during the last 24 hours. Arrange a set of covers (Fig. 2, D1, D2, D3) to keep the cage dark and to prevent the rising of heat from the heater.

Many flies may be put into one cage for feeding, but the best result is obtained when the number is not too large. In 30 minutes, 95% of the flies may be fully engorged if the number of flies in the cage does not exceed 20, whereas the percentage drops to 50 or 60 when the number of flies is 60 or more. There are always a number of flies which will not feed until they are 24 hours old. The feeding is best done in the evening, but is sometimes successful in day time, if the covers are properly set.

Flies fed by this method almost never die within the first 3 or 4 days of life. During the months of July and August, with an average temperature in the laboratory of 27° C. and a humidity of approximately 60%, the average span of life of these flies, unless refed on the fourth or fifth day, was 5 or 6 days. In order to lengthen this period to give the parasites longer time to develop, the flies were kept in an ice box at a temperature of approximately 21°

C. With refeeding some of the flies at this temperature lived for 18 days, and an abundant growth of flagellates in the flies were obtained.

For breeding purposes flies are fed on the whole blood of a normal hamster, on the same stage.

From July 16th to August 31st, 1928, 2131 female sandflies (1918 *Phlebotomus major* and 213 *Phlebotomus sergenti*), practically all that were hatched in our laboratory, were fed so satisfactorily that we feel justified in suggesting the adoption of this technique for the artificial feeding of sandflies. The method described is an attempt to imitate the natural conditions under which the flies feed, but the artificial conditions are better than the direct feeding on animals. The immobility of the feeding stage is a decided advantage, as the biting insects are frequently disturbed by the movements of the live animal. The ease with which the insect gets blood, practically every time the stylets pierce the skin, is another distinct advantage of this feeding stage.

The principle of this method might be used in experiments on transmission of diseases in which biting insects play a rôle. The skin preparation of the feeding stage might serve either as the source of infection, or as a medium for transmission.[2]

[2] Hu, C. H., Huie, Dorothy, and Lee, C. U., PROC. SOC. EXP. BIOL. AND MED., 1928, xxvi.

12. Slapping as Factor in Transmission of Kala-Azar by Sandflies (Phlebotomus)

Lee, C.U., Hu, C.H. and Huie, D. *Proceedings of the Society for Experimental Biology and Medicine*, 280-284, 1929.

李宗恩，胡正详，许德兰《拍打是感染黑热病的途径》，载于《实验生物医学学会会议记录》，1929 年，26:280-284 页。

翻译概要 作者利用上文描述的实验装置和另一拍打白蛉的装置，试图求证拍打白蛉是传染黑热病的一个途径。在 27 次尝试中，有一例在拍打后培养出利什曼原虫，剩余的 26 例中有 23 例被鞭毛虫污染。根据这一例的阳性结果，作者认为拍打有可能是白蛉传染黑热病的途径之一。

4258

Slapping as a Factor in Transmission of Kala-Azar by Sandflies (Phlebotomus).

C. H. HU, DOROTHY HUIE, AND C. U. LEE. (Introduced by Hsien Wu.)

From the Departments of Pathology and Medicine, Peking Union Medical College.

The results in the experimental transmission of kala-azar thus far have been uniformly negative.[1, 2] Shortt, attempting transmission by means of sandflies, attributes his negative results to insufficient susceptibility of the experimental animals rather than to inability of the fly to expel the flagellates from its buccal cavity into the wound while feeding. We are inclined to believe that the negative results

[1] Shortt, H. E., Barraud, P. J., and Craighead, A. C., *Indian J. Med. Res.*, 1927, xiv, 589.

[2] Young, C. W., and Hertig, Marshall, PROC. SOC. EXP. BIOL. AND MED., 1927, xxiv, 823.

might have been due to the overlooking of one natural factor not previously considered, namely, the crushing of the fly by slapping the itching skin, where the fly is feeding. To ascertain the importance of this factor in the transmission of kala-azar, a method has been worked out, imitating as far as possible the natural conditions under which the flies feed and are crushed.

The sandflies, *P. major*, are fed with the blood-parasite mixture on the feeding stage within 24 hours after hatching,[3] and are then kept in the ice box at 21° C. After 6 to 10 days, they are allowed to refeed and, while feeding, are crushed by slapping. This is occasionally done as late as the 18th day, if the flies have had a second feeding.

1. *The feeding stage.* This stage is like the one for the blood-parasite mixture, except that the dish is only ½ inch in diameter. The flannel is cut a little smaller than the dish and is cut in 2 equal halves. It is then pressed and saturated with defibrinated rabbit blood, and covered with a piece of skin from a normal hamster. Strictest asepsis is necessary in these preparations, but the heavily contaminated external surface of the skin is not sterilized for reasons which are given below. The prepared feeding stage is placed on the electric heater set at 35° C., and the slapper is adjusted to the skin surface.

2. *Feeding and slapping.* After the slapper is set with the lower end of the piston lifted by the magnet to a level ½ inch above the skin surface, a fly is introduced through the side-tube which is then plugged with cotton. With a bright electric light the fly is closely watched. When its abdomen is being engorged the switch for the electric magnet is turned off, the piston instantly drops, and crushes the fly while its biting parts are still in the skin. The fly is then immediately fixed for serial sections. The skin is removed from the stage and each of the two pieces of flannel is put into a separate tube of NNN media for the cultivation of flagellates. The cultures are examined at the end of 3 weeks. (Table I.)

The process described is time-consuming, for the flies must be fed and slapped one by one. Most of them do not feed, probably due to the sudden change in surroundings, and to the presence of a bright light. Those which do feed are not as fully engorged as when fed in the dark, usually stopping to suck when they show blood in the thorax or in the anterior abdomen.

In a second series of experiments the flies were allowed to with-

[3] Hu, C. H., and Lee, C. U., PROC. SOC. EXP. BIOL. AND MED., 1928, xxvi.

draw their stylets after feeding without being slapped, after which the flannels bitten by them were cultured. (See Table II.)

TABLE I.

A record of the flies slapped in the act of feeding and the result of cultures made from the flannels.

Culture No.	Date of hatching and first feeding	Interval between 1st feeding and slapping	Flagellates in serial sections	Culture of flannel A.	Culture of flannel B.	Remarks
15	Aug. 18	9 days	+	—	—	
16	,, 18	9 ,,	+	—	—	
17	,, 19	8 ,,	+	—	Cont.	
18	,, 19	8 ,,	+	—	—	
20	,, 18	10 ,,	+	—	—	
22	,, 19	10 ,,	+	—	—	
23	,, 19	10 ,,	+	—	Cont.	
24	,, 17	12 ,,	+	—	,,	
26	,, 22	8 ,,	+	—	,,	
28	,, 25	6 ,,	+	—	+	
29	,, 14	18 ,,	+	—	Cont.	Refed with rabbit blood on August 22.
30	,, 18	14 ,,	+	—	—	Refed with rabbit blood on August 27.
32	,, 26	7 ,,	+	—	—	
33	,, 26	7 ,,	—	—	—	
34	,, 27	7 ,,	+	—	—	
36	,, 28	7 ,,	+	—	—	
37	,, 28	7 ,,	—	—	Cont.	
39	,, 29	7 ,,	+	—	—	
39a	,, 29	7 ,,	+	—	—	
40	,, 30	7 ,,	+	—	—	
41	,, 30	7 ,,	+	—	—	
42	,, 30	7 ,,	+	—	Cont.	
43	,, 30	7 ,,	+	—	—	
44	,, 31	8 ,,	+	—	—	
46	Sept. 2	8 ,,	+	—	—	
47	,, 6	7 ,,	—	—	—	
48	,, 6	7 ,,	+	—	—	

Cont. = Contamination by bacteria.

TABLE II.

A record of the flies not slapped and the results of cultures of the flannels.

Culture No.	Date of hatching and first feeding	Interval between first feeding and slapping	Date of death of fly	Flagellates in serial sections	Culture of flannel A.	Culture of flannel B.
19	Aug. 14	8 days	Aug. 27	+	—	—
27	,, 22	9 ,,	,, 31	+	—	—
35a	,, 27	7 ,,	Sept. 8?	+	—	—
38	,, 28	7 ,,	,, 8	+	—	—
38a	,, 28	7 ,,	,, 8	—	—	—
38b	,, 28	7 ,,	,, 8	—	—	—
44	,, 31	8 ,,	,, 10	+	—	—
45	,, 31	8 ,,	,, 12	+	—	Cont.
49	Sept. 6	7 ,,	,, 13	+	—	—

Cont. = Contaminated by bacteria.

FIG. 1. *The Slapper.*

The upper end of the copper piston is screwed to an iron cap (A), the lower end is expanded, a little less than 3/8 inch in diameter, and projects 3/16 inch below the bottom of the glass tube. The glass tube is 2.5 inches long and 3/8 inch in its inner diameter. 1/4 inch above the lower edge of the tube is a short side-tube for the introduction of the fly. Around the piston is a steel-wire spring which pushes down when the current in the magnet (B) is broken.

Table I shows one positive experiment out of 27. Here a positive, non-contaminated culture of flagellates morphologically typical of Leishmann-Donovan bodies was obtained from one of the 2 flannel pieces on the feeding stage. Of the remaining 26 flies 23 contained flagellates, but failed to infect the flannel. Seven flannel pieces showed contamination by bacteria. Table II shows 9 experiments without slapping, all negative. Two of the 9 flies proved microscopically negative for flagellates. One flannel piece was contaminated by bacteria. All contaminations were due to direct introduction of bacteria through the hamster skin by the stylets. This statement is based upon the fact that in every case only one of the 2 flannel pieces was contaminated.

From the one positive culture (Table I) subcultures were made. We believe this positive finding to be significant, as demonstrating a means through which transmission of kala-azar might take place. As to the minute mechanism in play in our experiment we believe that the slapping, when undertaken at the right moment, causes a back flow of blood through the stylet all the way from the midgut. During the feeding there certainly are moments of relaxation of the crinkly posterior portion of the pharynx, making such a back flow possible.

Slapping does occur in nature as all know. If slapping is a necessary factor, explanation for the apparent high immunity to kala-azar among infants might be found in as simple a fact as their inability to slap when bitten.

4259

Antipneumococcus Protective Substances in Normal Pig Serum.

RICHARD H. P. SIA.

From the Department of Medicine, Peking Union Medical College.

It has been generally held that natural immunity to the Pneumococcus, in common with other pathogenic micro-organisms, depends on a fundamental cellular difference of the host rather than on circulating antibodies.[1, 2] Bull and McKee,[3] however, showed that normal chicken serum was capable of protecting mice and guinea pigs against many times the fatal dose of virulent pneumococci. Furthermore, in a recent publication,[4] evidence was presented to indicate that a high concentration of antipneumococcus opsonins in the blood of naturally resistant mammals forms a common means of defense against pneumococcus infection. These findings would suggest that humoral defensive elements may play a much more important rôle in the mechanism of natural immunity than has hitherto been believed. This report presents further evidence in support of this view.

In the present study, serum from pigs, a naturally pneumococcus-resistant species, has been employed. Table I represents the protocol of an experiment in which white mice weighing about 20 gm. were each given intraperitoneal injections of 1 cc. of pig serum and 4 hours later varying amounts of an actively growing culture of a virulent Type I pneumococcus. Sera from susceptible animals, the rabbit and the guinea pig, were used as controls. It is clearly shown that normal pig serum protected mice against 10,000 times the minimum fatal dose while rabbit or guinea pig serum conferred no protection on mice against pneumococcus infection. Mice receiving less than 0.01 cc. of culture were protected by the pig serum, whereas 0.000,000,1 cc. of the same culture alone killed mice regularly.

1 Zinsser, H., "Infection and Resistance," New York, 3rd edition, 1923, 68.

2 Eastwood, A., *Rep. Pub. Health and Med. Subj.*, Ministry of Health, No. 22, 1923, 15.

3 Bull, C. G., and McKee, C. M., *Am. J. Hyg.*, 1921, i, 284.

4 Robertson, O. H., and Sia, R. H. P., *J. Exp. Med.*, 1927, xlvi, 239.

13. Preliminary Note of the Artificial Feeding of Mosquitoes

Macgregor, M.E. and Lee, C.U. *Transactions of Royal Society of Tropical Medicine and Hygiene*, 23: 203-204, 1929.

Macgregor, M.E. 李宗恩 《人工喂蚊的初步改进》，载于《皇家热带病和卫生协会学报》，1929 年 23:203-204 页。

翻译概要 英国蚊子因不愿叮咬感染疟疾的鸟，而不易感染疟疾。作者发现在加入柠檬酸的血液中再加少量蜂蜜后，不仅雌蚊子，而且雄蚊子也用力吸食。因为柠檬酸和蜂蜜对红血球的形状并无影响，这一喂养方法可以用于研究蚊子传染的疾病。

TRANSACTIONS OF THE ROYAL SOCIETY OF
TROPICAL MEDICINE AND HYGIENE.
Vol. XXIII. No. 2. August, 1929.

PRELIMINARY NOTE ON THE ARTIFICIAL FEEDING OF MOSQUITOES.

BY

MALCOLM E. MACGREGOR
(*Wellcome Entomological Field Laboratory, Wisley, Surrey*),
AND
CHUNG UN LEE,
(*Wellcome Entomological Field Laboratory and Peking Union Medical College, Peking, China*).

During the course of investigations on the possibility of infecting British mosquitoes with the malaria parasite of birds, an unforeseen difficulty arose in that only a very small proportion of the mosquitoes (*Anopheles maculipennis*, *Culex pipiens* and *Aëdes argenteus*) could be induced to feed on the birds. Various procedures including starvation were tried in order to overcome this, but without success. Finally it was decided to experiment with citrated blood, and a preliminary test with human blood was made. Again the mosquitoes refused to feed. The citrated blood was then mixed with a little honey and this simple change had a surprising effect, for immediately it was presented to the mosquitoes they became agitated, and within half a minute were feeding vivaciously. Furthermore, it was found that not only the females, but also the males fed upon the mixture, so that in a very short time all that had an opportunity of feeding had red distended abdomens. It appears that this is the first occasion in which male mosquitoes have been induced to ingest blood in the laboratory.

As regards the position in the body of the ingested blood mixture, it was found by dissection that this was almost entirely in the œsophageal diverticula, the ventral diverticulum being most distended. When the mosquitoes had fed to their utmost capacity, all the diverticula were fully distended; but when the intake of food was less extreme, and perhaps more normal in quantity, the ventral diverticulum alone contained the mixture, though in this case it was fully distended. It has been demonstrated in this laboratory that when a mosquito feeds by puncturing the skin, the blood it withdraws passes directly into the stomach and not into the diverticula. To determine whether the difference is due to the artificial method, further experiments including the feeding of mosquitoes through membranes are in progress.

As the addition of honey to the citrated blood appears to have no deleterious effect on the red blood corpuscles; and as mosquitoes feed upon the mixture at all times, it is evident that this simple method of inducing mosquitoes to ingest blood opens a field for the investigation of many interesting problems connected with the food requirements of mosquitoes, the behaviour in them of parasites and the effect of drugs on those parasites and on the insects themselves.

14. Sublura Malayensis N. Sp., A New Nematode from Two Malayan Monkeys

C.U. Lee, Zentralblatt für Bakteriologie, Parasitenkunde u. Infectionskrakheiten, 116: 169-173, 1930.

李宗恩《从两只马来西亚猴子分离的新线虫类》，载于《细菌、寄生虫、传染病研究》，1930年，116: 169-173页。

翻译概要 作者在德国汉堡的两只猴子(Pithecus fascicularis Raffl., & Cynopithecus maurus F. Cuv.)的肠道中发现了一类新的线虫。此线虫的外形与S. otolicni相似，但咽部的牙齿和生殖乳头的排列有所不同。本文对其形态，性别、特征进行了详细描述，并将其命名为 Subulura malayensis。

[Aus dem Institut für Schiffs- und Tropenkrankheiten zu Hamburg (Direktor: Obermed.-Rat Prof. Dr. Nocht). Helminthologische Abteilung (Vorsteher: Prof. Dr. F. Fülleborn).]

Subulura malayensis n. sp. a new Nematode from two Malayian Monkeys.

By C. U. Lee,

Department of Medicine, Peiping Union Medical College, Peiping (China).

With 6 figures in the text.

The following description applies to a species of nematodes collected at Hamburg from two monkeys, one Pithecus fascicularis Raffl., a laboratory monkey imported from Java and the other Cynopithecus maurus F. Cuv., obtained from an animal dealer who imported it probably from the Malay Archipelago. Seven females and one male specimens were from the large and small intestines of Pithecus fascicularis Raffl., and nine female and two male specimens from the small intestine of Cynopithecus maurus F. Cuv.

Diagnosis: Subulura malayensis n. sp. resembles S. otolicni but for the character of its pharyngeal teeth and the number and arrangements of its genital papillae.

Description: Body slender, yellowish white. Cuticle with fine transverse striations. Female almost straight with a sharply pointed tail. Male tail ventrally curved terminating in a fine point. Anterior end truncated. No lateral alae. Head provided with 6 papillae, two lateral and four submedian. Mouth terminal and triangular with three inconspicuous lips, whose edges are not thickened. Buccal cavity fairly spacious and clearly divided into two parts. Guarding the entrance of the oesophagus are three teeth with sharp free edges. Oesophagus long, slightly sinuous and club-shaped followed by a cuboidal oesophageal bulb separated by a constriction from the first.

Male. Total length 15.4—15.9 mm.
greatest width 0.500—0.525 mm.

Length of oesophagus including the bulb 2.54—2.65 mm. Nerve ring from anterior end 0.403 mm. Excretory pore from anterior end 0.528—0.692 mm. Tail (from anus to tip of tail) 0.333—0.372 mm. Genital sucker 1.154—1.200 from tail end, ellipsoidal, without chitinous armature, surrounded by radiating muscular fibres. 10 pairs of genital papillae thus arranged: 3 preanal, the first at the side of the upper third of the sucker, the second between the anus and the sucker, slightly nearer to the anus, the third more laterally situated and immediately in front of the anus; one adanal and 6 postanal, four ventral, two near the anus, two near the tip of the tail, two lateral between these two groupes, the one in front being much larger than the one behind. Two spicules of equal length with sharply pointed distal ends measuring 1.795—1.859 mm in length. Gubernaculum is triangular in shape with a blunt distal end measuring 0.211—0.220 mm.

Table showing specific differences among

	Size		Lateral cephalic alae
	Male	Female	
S. distans	14.7—25.4 mm (Diesing) 27 mm (Duj.) 25 mm (Schneider)	25.4—40 mm (Diesing) 40 mm (Duj.)	—
S. jacchi	10.2—14.2 mm	13.4—17.9 mm	present
S. pararmata	6—7 mm	8—10 mm	—
S. otolicni	8 mm (v. Ben.) 19 mm (Baylis)	12.5—16.6 mm (v. Ben.) 29.7 mm (Baylis)	absent
S. sarasinorum	7.5 mm	10—11.24 mm	well developed
S. malayensis	15.4—15.9 mm	21.5—26.7 mm	absent

Female. 21.5—26.7 mm. Greatest width 0.550—0.700 mm, length of oesophagus 2.5—2.8 mm. Nerve ring from anterior end 0.432—0.489 mm. Excretory pore from anterior end 0.653—0.690 mm. Vulva not salient and situated in front of the middle of the body 9.54—12.00 mm from head end. From the vulva, the genital tube runs in a forward direction for a distance of 1.27 mm and then turns backwards. The ovejector (from vulva to sphincter) measures 0.87 mm long. Its vulvar end is somewhat bulbous and at a distance of 0.47 mm from the vulva it expands into a piriform vestibule, which measures 0.23 mm in length and usually contains one or two eggs. It leaves the vestibule by an opening at its antero-lateral aspect and proceeds for a distance approximately equal to the length of the vestibule, until it reaches a short sphincter, which is only about 0.036 mm in length and beyond which it becomes the uterine tube. In serial cross sections it is found that the wall of the ovejector from the vulva to a short distance above the vestibule consists of three coats, a thick outer muscular coat composed of circular fibres, next a cuticular coat and an inner thick coat, which stains blue with haematoxylin and eosin and is devoid of nuclei. Its apparently homogenous and structureless character suggests a secretory product and probably serves as a sort of cushion, preventing the too rapid passage of the eggs through this part of the genital tube. The cuticular and inner coats disappear a short distance above the vestibule and beyond this the wall of the ovijector and of the uterus consists of an outer coat of circular muscles and an inner coat of longitudinal muscles.

Anus from tip of tail: 1.41—1.77 mm.

Ova ellipsoidal in shape, contain embryos when laid. 64.3 $\mu \times 50.8$ μ.

Subulura species fond in primates.

Character of pharyngeal teeth	Oesophagus	Genital papillae	Spicules	Gubernaculum
—	—	11 pairs	Unequal	—
Three subquadrangular (Barreto)	Short. $^1/_{10}$ of total length. Oesophageal bulb spherical	11 pairs, 3 preanal	Equal 1.694 mm	0.194 mm
Buccal cavity with an organ formed by 6 chitinous plates, 3 large and curved ones and 3 lesser ones (Barreto)	$^1/_8$ of total length	—	Equal 2.5 mm, anterior extremity dilated	0.150 mm
Three with rounded free edges	$^1/_{10}$ of total length	11 pairs, 3 preanal	Equal 1.8 mm (v. Ben.) 1.55 mm (Baylis)	0.230 mm
4 in number badly outlined (Barreto)	$^1/_6$ of total length	10 pairs, 4 preanal	Equal 2.5 mm	—
Three with sharp edges	Long ♂ $^1/_6$, ♀ $^1/_9$ of total length. Oesophageal bulb cuboidal	10 pairs, 3 preanal	Equal 1.8 mm	0.211 mm —0.220 ,,

Habitat: intestine.
Hosts: Pithecus fascicularis, Raffl. Cynopithecus maurus, F. Cuv.
Locality: Malay. Archipelago.
Type specimens: Institut für Schiffs- und Tropenkrankheiten, Hamburg, Germany.

There are at present 44 species included in the genus Subulura, the majority of which are from birds and only 5 are reported from primates namely S. distans, S. jacchi, S. perarmata, S. otolicni and S. sarasinorum. The existing descriptions, as summarised by Barreto (1919) of S. distans: S. jacchi, S. perarmata and S. sarasinorum do not agree with the present species (see table). It however resembles closely with a species of Subulura, which Baylis (1920) first described as S. loveridgei but which has since been regarded by Boulenger (1923) as a larger form of S. otolicni. The present writer has had an opportunity of examining some of Baylis's specimens and found them to be different from the present species in the character of the pharyngeal teeth and the arrangement of the genital papillae. The postanal papillae of the present species are arranged in a fashion somewhat similar to those in S. jacchi, from which, however, it differs in bodily size, in the relative length of the oesophagus and in the characters of the pharyngeal teeth.

Summary.

A new species of Subulura from two malayian monkeys is described and named Subulura malayensis.

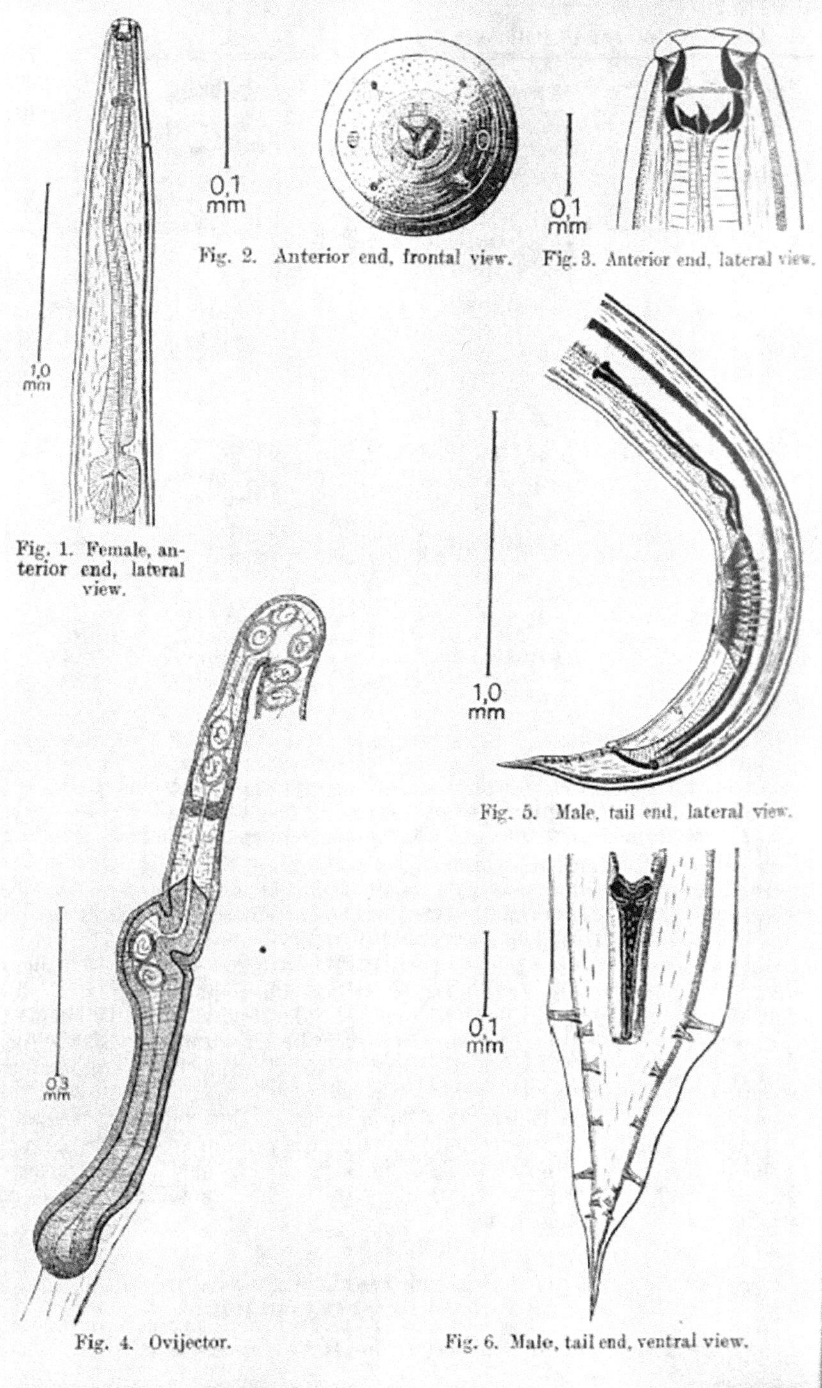

Fig. 1. Female, anterior end, lateral view.

Fig. 2. Anterior end, frontal view.

Fig. 3. Anterior end, lateral view.

Fig. 4. Ovijector.

Fig. 5. Male, tail end, lateral view.

Fig. 6. Male, tail end, ventral view.

Acknowledgement.

The writer is indebted to Dr. H. Vogel for kindly providing the material for the study; to Dr. H. A. Baylis of the British Museum, London, for the gift of several specimens of Subulura, which he described under the name of S. loveridgei and to Prof. L. Travassos, for the opportunity of examining some of his specimens of S. jacchi.

References.

Barreto, A. L. de B., Mem. Inst. Cruz (port.) **11**, 6 (1919). — Baylis, H. A., Ann. and Mag. Nat. Hist., IX. s. **6**, 283 (1920). — Boulenger, C. L., Parasitology **15**, 117 (1923).

15. Some Observations on Strongyloides Stercoralis

C.U. Lee, *Archive Fűr Schiffs- und Tropenhygiene*, 34: 262-274, 1930.

李宗恩《粪类圆线虫研究》，载于《海洋与热带卫生资料》， 1930 年，34: 262-274 页。

翻译概要 作者用体外模型来查证粪类圆线虫是否可在体内自感染——从杆状圆线虫发育成为有感染力的丝状圆线虫。因其结果为阴性，所以对此线虫在体内成熟的论点，既不能加以否认，也不能提供支持。总结如下：

1. 本文描述了没有被污染的、各发育期的粪类圆线虫的幼虫。
2. 曾有报道称可在新鲜粪便中找到线性幼虫。尽管我们仔细查找，但没有在正常或便秘的人和狗的粪便里找到线性幼虫。
3. 一条狗在食入很多直接杆状幼虫后没有发生感染。
4. 狗在食入直接和间接微丝幼虫后亦无异样。
5. 因为直接杆状幼虫还不能在无氧的条件下培养，目前对体内自感染的可能仍无定论。
6. 间接丝状幼虫比直接幼虫体积大。四种幼虫的未成熟生殖器大小不同，但细胞数没有相应差异。

(Aus dem Institut für Schiffs- und Tropenkrankheiten zu Hamburg.
Direktor: Obermed.-Rat Prof. Dr. Nocht.
Helminthologische Abteilung, Leiter: Prof. F. Fülleborn)

Some observations on Strongyloides stercoralis

By

C. U. Lee, Department of Medicine, Peiping Union Medical College, Peiping, China

With nine Text figures

In spite of the extensive studies on Strongyloides stercoralis, certain aspects of its life history still evade final explanation and the manner in which auto-infection takes place remains an experimental problem.

With regard to the two different modes of development of the rhabditiform larvae from the parasitic adults the opinion has been that they are determined either by factors inherent in the individual larvae or as Sandground (1926) believes, by the chromosomal constitution of the eggs and in both cases independent of external influences. Nishigori (1928), however, claims to have shown that the direction of development depends largely on environmental conditions and maintains that when conditions for development are favourable, free-living sexual forms predominate, while otherwise direct filariform larvae result. It is unfortunate that Nishigori's paper is in the Japanese language, making it difficult to examine critically his experimental techniques, which gave results so entirely different from those of previous authors.

On the question of autoinfection, much evidence, chiefly from clinical observations, is in favour of its occurrence. The finding of infective filariform larvae in freshly evacuated faeces has been reported from many quarters; Gabe (1910—1911), Thira (1919), Sandground (1926), Nishigori (1928) and Schuurmans Stekhoven (1928). Sandground also found active filariform larvae in the intestinal mucosa of a rat examined immediately after sacrifice and summed up his attitude on the question thus: „Yet it is only upon the same presumption (of the occurrence of autoinfection) that it would be possible to account for the periodicity of larval production that is so frequently encountered in the daily examination of infections with S. stercoralis and S. ratti" and „autoinfection, in addition, makes it possible to account for the extreme duration of infections with S. stercoralis". Nishigori goes a step further and produces experimental proofs in support of its occurrence. Some of his results are of such a character that, if confirmed, they should be of the greatest significance. The following study was made primarily in an effort to confirm, if possible some of Nishigori's claims. Our results are, however, of a negative character and as such do not refute the actual occurrence of autoinfection in the manner indicated by Nishigori. They are published merely to indicate an urgent necessity for further inquiry, which owing to exigencies of other work we are unable to undertake at present.

Our material for study was derived from a German male adult, who after having been in East Africa and Cairo, returned to Germany in 1919 and in whose stools were always to be found a fair number of rhabditiform strongyloides larvae. He had an attack of amoebic dysentery, for which he was treated in the hospital of the Institute, but otherwise he complained of no gastro-intestinal disturbances attributable to his strongyloides infection.

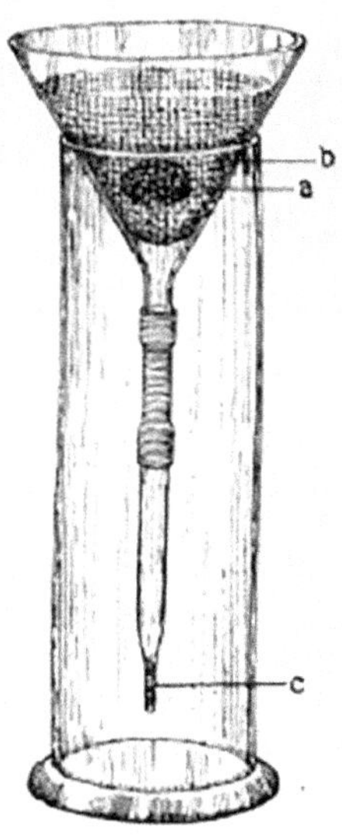

Fig. 1. Baermann's apparatus with a receiving tube for the collection of direct rhabditiform larvae from freshly evacuated faeces. (a) Mass of faeces mixed with sand. (b) Sterile sand. (c) Collection of living larvae

I. Methods of collecting different stages of strongyloides larvae

At the outset of our study it was found necessary to perfect our techniques for collecting the various stages of larvae in large numbers free from particulate foreign matter. After repeated trials, the following methods are found satisfactory.

a) Direct rhabditiform larvae from fresh faeces.

These can be collected in large numbers in a small glass tube attached to a Baermann's apparatus. A quantity of faeces, mixed with coarse sterile sand, is deposited on a layer of similar sand spread over the gauze lining the funnel so that there is no direct contact between the faecal mass and the gauze. This prevents the collection of any faecal debris in the receiving tube. The apparatus is then carefully filled with water just to cover the faecal mass. After standing for $1^1/_2$ hour in an incubator at 37° C, a seething white mass will appear at the bottom of the receiving tube consisting of hundreds or thousands of direct rhabditiform larvae (Fig. 1).

b) Direct filariform larvae from 24 hours old agar culture.

The method used by Looss (1911) for collecting ancylostome larvae is also applicable here. The washings from culture plates, containing sexual adults, direct filariform larvae, faecal debris and carbon particles used in the culture, are allowed to pass through a filter. After most of the water is passed through, the funnel with the moist filter paper is placed in an incubator at 37° C for 1/2 hour, by which time most of the filariforme larvae will have migrated through the filter paper and can be collected by again passing some warm water through the filter.

c) Indirect rhabditiform larvae. — These can be obtained for study by allowing faecal cultures to remain in the incubator for 48 hours. By this time all the rhabditiform larvae are derived from sexual adults. It is, however, difficult to separate these indirect rhabditiform larvae at different stages of development from the sexual adults and direct filariform larvae.

d) Indirect filariform larvae. — If a pure collection of indirect filariform larvae is required, they can be cultured from isolated sexual adults in sterile carbon and faeces mixture on agar plates and collected in the same way as for the direct filariform larvae. For infection purpose those from a „trichter" culture described by Fülleborn (1924) serves admirably well.

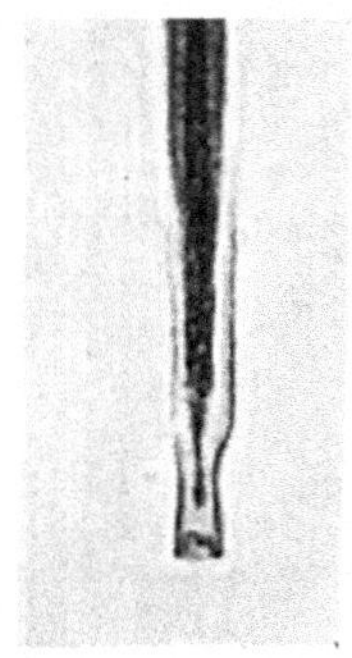

Fig. 2
Tail end of filariform larva

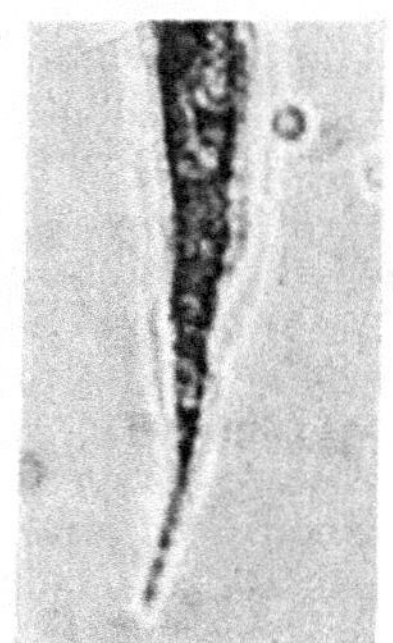

Fig. 3.
Tail end of rhabditiform larva

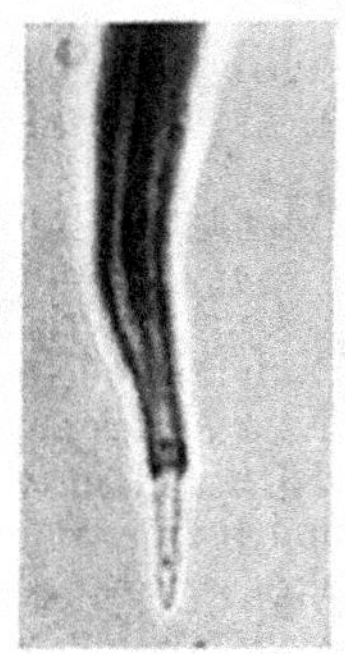

Fig. 4.
Tail end of direct filariform larva showing presence of a sheath

II. Observations and experiments on autoinfection

In face of the different reports on the finding of filariform larvae in freshly passed faeces, the fact would seem to be well established, yet during the course of our study we never once noted undoubted examples of such larvae in fresh faeces. The size of the direct rhabditiform larvae as well as the relative length of their oesophagus vary somewhat but the variation, while indicating some degree of growth during their residence within the intestine of the host, can hardly be regarded as definite evidence of their ability to develop into filariform larvae as Nishigori suggests. A filariform larva has a characteristic tip to its tail (Fig. 2), by which it can be at once distinguished from a rhabditiform larvae (Fig. 3). Some direct filariform larvae from a 24 hour faecal culture also possess a sheath showing the occurrence of a moult (Fig. 4). Our failure to find these larvae in freshly evacuated faeces suggests that some extraordinary condition, which we have not been able to ascertain and reproduce, must be present in the intestine to cause their appearance.

On the other hand, we have constantly observed that in the fresh faeces of our subject and of our experimentally infected dog a certain percentage of the direct rhabditiform larvae are dead and show evidence of degeneration. Whether their premature death is due to the presence of some letal influences in the intestinal tract (e. g. bacterial decomposition or to a prolonged absence of conditions necessary for development) is a question requiring elucidation.

In order to prove the ability of the direct rhabditiform larvae to develop into infective filariform larvae within the intestinal tract of the host, Nishigori apparently succeeded in establishing infection in dogs with direct rhabditiform larvae introduced into either the appendix or the rectum or the stomach, measures being at the same time taken to ensure a period of constipation. Infection may even result from an intravenous injection of such larvae.

It may be recalled that Fülleborn reported similar but negative experiments in 1914 and the following experiment was again negative.

Experiment I. Dog No. 3.

4th April 1929. — This dog, 2½ years old, was given per os about 30.000 direct rhabditiform larvae in 2 gelatine capsules. No food was given for 3 hours prior to the time of experiment and its stool was negative to culture. For 44 hours after the experimental feeding, it was spontaneously constipated. Subsequently for 2 weeks, its stools were repeatedly searched for evidence of infection by Baermann's method as well as by cultures, but with persistently negative results. The dog remained healthy.

A second experiment was undertaken to see if constipation would cause in an infected dog the appearance of filariform larvae in its stools.

Experiment II. Dog No. 4. 6850 gm.

13th April 1929, infected over an area of shaved skin with a large number of indirect filariform larvae from a fresh „trichter" culture.

15th. The area of skin, over which larvae were applied was inflamed, thickened and upon pressure showed drops of thin exudate.

19th. Stools were diarrhoeic, but no larvae found.

20th. Stool cultured with negative result.

23rd—24th. No stool.

25th. Faeces well formed. Positive for rhabditiform larvae, 96% of which were, however, dead. Strings of eggs were also found indicating a heavy infection. No filariform larvae found.

26th. Stool hard. 6% of the larvae were alive. No filariform larvae noted. At 12 noon 14 mgm. of Pantopon were given subcutaneously to indice constipation and the animal put on a diet of boiled meat and milk. Drowsy after Pantopon.

27th at 10 a.m. A well formed stool was passed with 30% living larvae. No filariform larvae found. At 1,45 p.m. another stool rather diarrhoeic was collected, in which 35% of the larvae were alive. No filariform larvae noted.

29th. Stool hard with 6% living larvae. At p.m. a diarrhoeic stool with 27% living larvae.

4th may. Stool still positive.

6th. Formed stool found in cage. At 2 p.m. 12 drops of tincture of opium given per os.

7th—8th. No stool.

9th. At 9.15 a.m. a well formed chalky stool found in cage (constipation lasted at least 52 hours). On smear examination no larvae were found. With Baermann's method a single specimen of young sexual form was noted, which, however, appeared dead. Culture proved negative. At 3 p.m. 15 drops of tincture of opium were given per os.

10th. Two stools collected from cage, one well formed and one rather soft. In neither were larvae found. No more opium was given after this day and the dog was observed for possible reappearance of larvae.

13th. Stool showed negative culture.

23rd. Stool still negative to culture.

The outstanding feature in this experiment is that no filariform larvae were ever found in the stools including one passed after a period of spontaneous constipation lasting at least 48 hours. Pantopon failed to produce constipation. The first dose of opium did induce constipation but unfortunately at a time when the animal was recovering from his infection. The second dose of opium had no constipating effect. A further point, which has already been referred to, is that the percentage of living larvae in the stool was never above 35.

Among Nishigori's positive statements is one, which arrested our attention rather forcibly, namely that the direct and indirect filariform larvae can be distinguished by a difference in size as well as in the number of genital cells. Although we have not been able to substantiate the observation regarding the number of genital cells, to which we shall return later, we thought of the possibility that a difference in behaviour between these two forms of filariform larvae may well exist. To test out whether or not the direct filariform larvae, when introduced into the alimentary tract, can develop into parasitic adults without migration through the body of the host, the following experiments were made.

Experiment III. Dog No. 1.

12th February 1929. — This dog was fed by means of gelatine capsules with about 2000 direct filariform larvae. Autopsied 3 days later. Trachea and intestine were searched for larvae without result. The lungs which showed extensive haemorrhagic lesions due to distemper, yielded one slightly developed larvae with the „Gaze-Anreicherung"-method (Fülleborn 1925).

Dog No. 2.

15th March 1929. This dog, probably 5 years old, was fed with 8000 direct filariform larvae. Autopsied 4 days later. Lungs and intestine were negative but in the peritoneal cavity 20 slightly developed larvae were found.

These results make improbable the direct development of filariform larvae without migration through the body of the host and indicate that they probably behave in the same manner as the indirect forms.

III. Attempts to cultivate rhabditiform larvae in the absence of oxygen

The development of strongyloides larvae depends on the presence of a number of factors, the chief of which are: 1) a sufficiency of nutriment, 2) certain degree of humidity, 3) a suitable temperature and 4) a supply of oxygen. With the exception of oxygen, these factors are present within the intestinal canal of the host. Hence the question of auto-infection hangs largely on the ability of some of the direct rhabditiform larvae to develop into filariform larvae in the absence of oxygen. This Nishigori claims to have proved by recovering filariform larvae from cultures made in atmospheres of Co_2, H_2 and CH_4. Our results are, however, not quite so conclusive.

At the outset we realised that, apart from an absence of oxygen, the conditions that obtain in a mass of faeces within the intestinal canal, are not quite the same as in evacuated specimens. For one thing, the bacterial growth is much more rapid and intense in the evacuated faecal mass kept at body temperature and inhibits the normal development of the larvae and in time kills them. It is possible that within the intestine the removal of excessive fluid by the intestinal mucous membrane and the absence of oxygen limit to a large extent the bacterial growth in the faeces and that the mucous membrane also provides for the absorption of a certain amount of gaseous products of bacterial decomposition. The success attending the use of animal charcoal in faecal cultures of nematode larvae is principally duo to its absorptive power. When the supply of oxygen is plentiful, the effect of bacterial overgrowth on the development of larvae in cultures is not so evident as when it is poor or absent. This can be shown by making two cultures without admixture with charcoal, one in ordinary atmosphere and the other in an atmosphere mainly of hydrogen. After 24 hours at 37° C, in the former many larvae will show good development, while in the latter only few will be found alive.

One of the greatest difficulties we experienced in studying the effect of oxygen absence on the development of the direct rhabditiform larvae is to be absolutely certain that all sources of oxygen have been excluded in any of our experiments. This difficulty seems unsurmountable when one tries to cultivate the larvae in an atmosphere of hydrogen.

a) Cultures under indian rubber membrane.

As it is impossible to exclude air from a faecal culture by hermatically sealing it in a solid watch glass on account of the evolved gases invariably forcing the lid open, it was thought that rubber membrane might obviate this difficulty; its elasticity would accommodate the accumulated gases. Such cultures, however, show that the development of rhabditiform larvae into sexual and filarial forms goes on unimpended over the surface of the faecal mass immediately in contact with the rubber membrane. It was then realised that oxygen diffuses through even comparatively thick rubber membrane on account of its colloidal nature. Same results were obtained, when the culture is placed under water, which, of course, also contains a certain amount of oxygen in solution even after boiling.

b) Cultures in Hydrogen, Nitrogen and Carbon dioxide.

Hydrogen gas generated from a Kipp's apparatus is first washed in 2% potassium permanganate and then in 5% silver nitrate before it is collected under water in a jar, into which a smaller vessel, containing the faeces mixed with animal charcoal to be cultured, is brought through water and by means of a metal spring fixed to its bottom. Then still under water the lid is placed in position and the jar taken out of the water bath. By means of two tubes on the lid of the jar, more hydrogen is passed through until on applying a light to the exit tube no explosion occurs but a faint flame burns. Then the two tubes are securely clamped and the lid of the jar sealed all round with a thick layer of hard paraffin (Fig. 5). As an additional safeguard the sealed jar is placed under water in a larger jar so as to exclude air from direct contact. This precaution is not necessary in the case of nitrogen or carbon dioxide. It needs to be emphasized that hydrogen gas is most difficult to work with, as it being lighter than air tends to escape through the minutest crevices.

In one experiment, the culture was examined after 24 hours at 37° C resulting in the finding that the majority of the rhabditiform larvae were active and show a slight increase in size and 2% of the larvae examined were of the filariform type. From the results of this experiment alone, we might have concluded that some of the larvae at least are capable of developing into direct filariform larvae in the absence of oxygen. That this is probably not the case is shown by another experiment, in which the culture was not examined till it had been for 48 hours at 37° C, when a large number of filariform larvae as well as sexual forms were found, indicating that oxygen must have been present. There are two possible sources for this oxygen. Firstly it may have come from the water, through which the hydrogen was passed into the jar or from the small amount of water, which is necessarily present at the bottom of the jar. Secondly it is possible that the animal charcoal used in the culture may have provided the required oxygen as it is known that charcoal is capable of absorbing a large amount of oxygen from the air.

These experiments do, however, show that the development is retarded when the oxygen supply is insufficient, for in an ordinary 24 hour culture, the development would have advanced much further than what was found in the first experiment and that this oxygen insufficiency affects the development of filariform larvae less than the sexual forms. Further than this we can not go.

Similar results were obtained in another series of experiments with nitrogen supplied from a „bomb“. Here in addition to the possible sources of oxygen already mentioned the fact that nitrogen gas from a „bomb“ is seldom entirely free from oxygen must also be considered. Passing it through pyrogallol does not guaranted

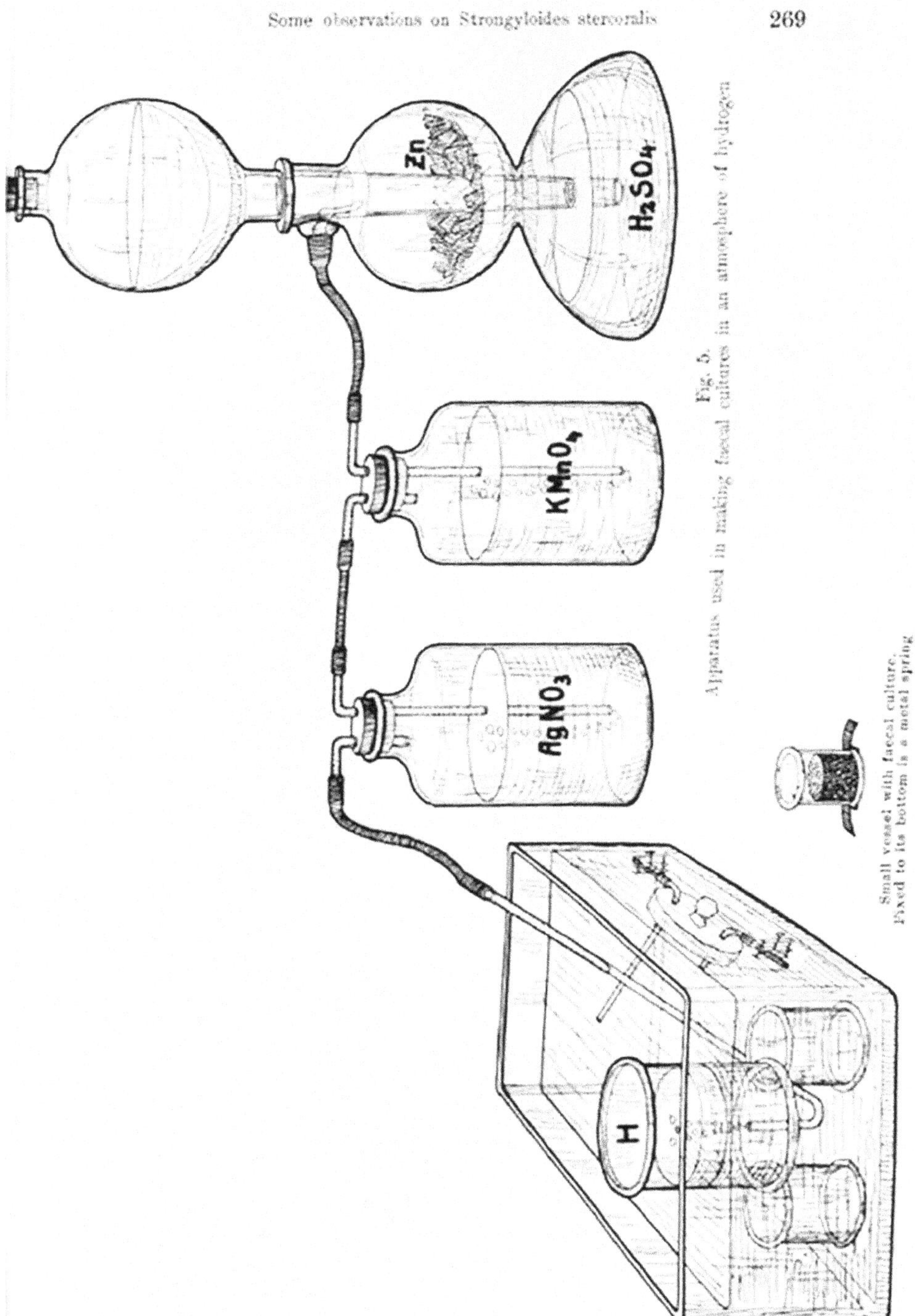

Fig. 5.
Apparatus used in making faecal cultures in an atmosphere of hydrogen

Small vessel with faecal culture.
Fixed to its bottom is a metal spring

its purity for pyrogallol absorbs oxygen very slowly and not completely.

Cultures made in an atmosphere of carbon dioxide yielded more definite results. This gas, generated from a Kipp's apparatus, is first passed through a strong solution of $Na_2 CO_3$ and then collected in the jar, in which the culture is to be made, in the same way as hydrogen or nitrogen. Carbon dioxide being heavier than air excludes oxygen from contact with the culture. After 24 hours many of the rhabditiform larvae were alive but show no development and after 48 hours all larvae were dead. It would thus appear that carbon dioxide not only prevents development of the larvae, but in time kills them. These experiments tend to emphasize the difficulties attending attempts to cultivate faeces containing nematode larvae in the absence of oxygen with a view to providing an experimental basis for the question of autoinfection and the risk in drawing hasty conclusions from experiments of this nature.

IV. On the genital primordium of the different stages of strongyloides larvae

In most morphological descriptions of the different stages of strongyloides larvae, no distinction is made between the direct rhabditiform and filariform larvae derived from the parasitic „females" and those indirect forms from the free living sexual parents. Nishigori, however, states that „morphologically the direct and indirect filariform larvae can easily be distinguished. The latter are about 0,016 mm longer than the former and their genital primordium is smaller than in the former, consisting of only 3 to 4 cells against the former's 12 to 22 cells". More recently Schuurmans Stekhoven restudied most carefully the morphology of Strongyloides stercoralis and points out that the genital primordium of the filariform larvae (wheter direct or indirect not stated) consists of about 8 cells and that of the larva of the indirect mode of development, preceeding the free living sexes, 14 cells. Through personal communication, we understand that by „larvae of the indirect mode of development, preceeding the free living sexes" he means the rhabditiform larvae from faeces, which are on the way to become sexual forms to the exclusion of those, which are to develop into direct filariform larvae. Though he did not state the number of genital cells in the latter form of rhabditiform larvae, we presume it could not be more than the number he gave for both forms of filariform larvae, namely 8. The number of genital cells for the indirect rhabditiform larvae is not given but the statement is made that the direct and indirect forms of rhabditiform larvae can be distinguished by the size of the genital primordium and this is shown in the drawings.

In our study, we attempted to compare the genital primordii of the different stages of larvae by measuring their size and enumerating the component cells. These studies are rather difficult on account of the fact that the genital cells cannot be seen all in one plane since they are grouped round the convexity of the intestinal tube in a somewhat diamand shaped or quadrilateral mass, whose longest diameter does not always lie antero-posteriorly and whose apparent lenticular shape is merely an optical effect. Therefore it is impossible to be certain of the exact number of cells composing the genital primordium in every case but after studying a large number of haematoxylin stained specimens we came to the conclusion that there is no difference in the number of cells in the four different forms of larvae and the number varies probably from 12—18 (Fig. 6, 7, 8 and 9).

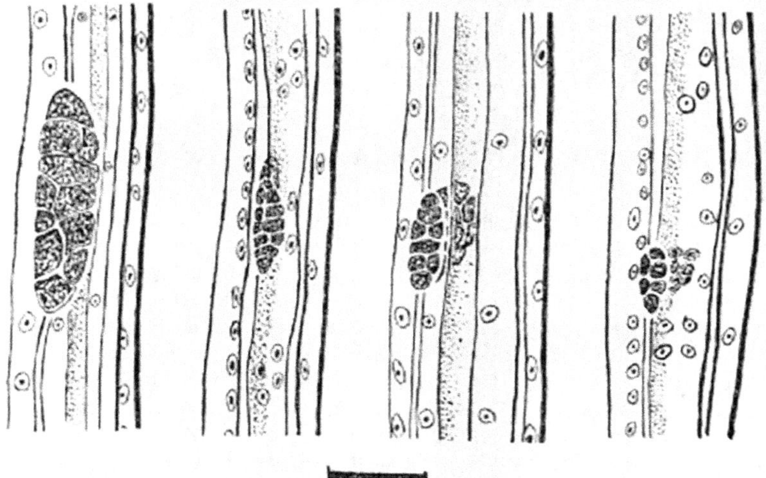

Fig. 6. Genital primordium of direct rhabditiform larva

Fig. 7. Genital primordium of direct filariform larva

Fig. 8. Genital primordium of indirect rhabditiform larva

Fig. 9. Genital primordium of indirect filariform larva

Measurements were then made as far as possible of the longest diameter of the genital primordium in the four different forms of larvae as well as the length and breadth of the two forms of filariform larvae. The genital primordium of the direct rhabditiform larvae has its longest diameter varying from 0,020 to 0,032 among 19 larvae measured, while that of the indirect rhabditiform larvae has its longest diameter varying from 0,010—0,013 among 25 larvae measured. The measurements in the case of filariform larvae are presented in table I and II.

It is clear that the direct rhabditiform larvae have the largest genital primordium among all the forms and as they develop into the direct filariform larvae, the genital mass gradually shrinks in size as evidenced by the fact that the smaller of the direct filariform larvae have actually larger genital primordii (see Nos. 7, 8, 17, 19, 20, 22, 24 and 26 in Table I; no. 23 being an exception). Be it noted, however, that a diminution in the size of the genital primordium does not imply a reduction in the number of its component cells. The size of the genital primordium of the indirect rhabditiform larvae is the same as that of the indirect filariform larvae. Finally our results confirm Nishigori's statement that a difference in size exists between the two forms of filariform larvae.

Table I. Direct filariform larvae

Number of larvae	Total length	Breadth	G. P. Longest diameter
1	0,472	0,014	0,014
2	0,468	0,016	0,012
3	0,444	0,014	0,012
4	0,472	0,014	0,012
5	0,468	0,016	0,014
6	0,472	0,014	0,012
7	0,424	0,016	0,024
8	0,416	0,016	0,020
9	0,440	0,016	0,013
10	0,448	0,015	0,013
11	0,448	0,014	0,012
12	0,476	0,016	0,012
13	0,472	0,014	0,012
14	0,444	0,016	0,013
15	0,476	0,016	0,011
16	0,484	0,015	0,016
17	0,428	0,016	0,024
18	0,476	0,014	0,012
19	0,420	0,016	0,016
20	0,444	0,016	0,020
21	0,464	0,015	0,012
22	0,428	0,013	0,024
23	0,416	0,016	0,012
24	0,396	0,016	0,020
25	0,460	0,013	0,010
26	0,424	0,016	0,024
27	0,468	0,015	0,012
28	0,464	0,014	0,012
29	0,448	0,014	0,012
30	0,460	0,016	0,014
Mean value	0,451	0,015	0,015

Summary

A series of observations were undertaken with the object of testing out some of the statements made recently by Nishigori on the question of autoinfection in Strongyloides stercoralis. Its occurrence may be inferred from certain clinical evidences but confirmation of Nishigoris results would place it on an experimental basis. Our own results, being negative, neither refute nor support Nishigori's claims but indicate that further inquiries are necessary before the question can be considered as settled. Our observations may be summarised as follows: —

Table II. Indirect filariform larvae

Number of larvae	Total length	Breadth	G. P. longest diameter
1	0,520	0,016	0,016
2	0,552	0,016	0,012
3	0,524	0,016	0,012
4	0,532	0,016	0,012
5	0,524	0,016	0,012
6	0,492	0,016	0,012
7	0,532	0,016	0,014
8	0,536	0,016	0,016
9	0,528	0,016	0,014
10	0,528	0,016	0,012
11	0,536	0,016	0,012
12	0,544	0,016	0,014
13	0,544	0,016	0,012
14	0,524	0,016	0,014
15	0,516	0,016	0,014
16	0,532	0,016	0,016
17	0,528	0,016	0,012
18	0,516	0,016	0,012
19	0,496	0,016	0,012
20	0,548	0,016	0,012
21	0,536	0,016	0,016
22	0,532	0,016	0,012
23	0,496	0,016	0,012
24	0,532	0,016	0,012
25	0,532	0,016	0,014
26	0,528	0,016	0,012
27	0,496	0,016	0,014
28	0,520	0,016	0,012
29	0,496	0,016	0,012
30	0,460	0,016	0,013
Mean value	0,523	0,016	0,013

1) Methods are described for the collection of various stages of strongyloides larvae in large numbers free from particulate foreign matter.

2) The finding of filariform larvae in freshly evacuated faeces have been reported by different authors but in spite of careful search we never once noted undoubted examples of such larvae in either normal or constipated stools from infected man or dog.

3) A dog, experimentally fed with a large number of direct rhabditiform larvae, failed to show infection.

4) The results of experiments, in which dogs were fed with direct filariform larvae seem to exclude any possibility of a difference in behaviour between the direct and indirect filariform larvae.

5) In attempts to cultivate faeces containing direct rhabditiform larvae in the absence of oxygen, considerable difficulty was experienced in excluding all possible sources of oxygen. Hence great care needs to be exercised in drawing conclusions from experiments of this nature.

6) Measurements showed that the indirect filariform larvae are larger than the direct forms. Among the four forms of larvae, a difference in the size of the genital primordium exists but no corresponding difference in the number of its component cells was observed.

References

Gage, J. G., 1910. Larvae of S. intestinalis in human lungs. Journ. Med. Res., XXIII, pp. 177—183.

Gage, J. G., 1911, A case of S. intestinalis with larvae in the sputum. Arch. Int. Med., VII, pp. 560—579.

Thira, Tokuzo, 1919, Studien über Strongyloides stercoralis. Mitt. d. med. Ges. zu Tokio, XXXIII, pp. 2—3. Abstract in Trop. Dis. Bull., 1924, XXI, p. 210.

Sandground, J. H., 1926, Biological studies on the life-cycle in the Genus Strongyloides, Grassi, 1879. Americ. Journ. Hyg., VI, pp. 337—388.

Fülleborn, F., 1914, Untersuchungen über den Infektionsweg bei Strongyloides und Ankylostomum und die Biologie dieser Parasiten. Arch. f. Schiffs- u. Tropenhyg., XVIII, Beiheft 5, pp. 26—80.

Fülleborn, F., 1924, Über „Taxis" (Tropismus) bei Strongyloides- und Ankylostomenlarven. Arch. f. Schiffs- u. Tropenhyg., XXVIII. pp. 144—165.

Fülleborn, F., 1925, Über die Durchlässigkeit der Blutkapillaren für Nematodenlarven bzw. für unbewegliche Körper von ähnlicher Dicke, sowie über den Transport solcher Gebilde durch das Flimmerepithel der Luftwege. Arch. f. Schiffs- u. Tropenhyg., Beiheft 3.

Nishigori, M., 1928, The factors which influence the external development of Strongyloides stercoralis and on Autoinfection with this parasite. Journ. Med. Ass. Formosa, No. 276.

Schuurmans Stekhoven, Jr. J. H., 1928, Researches on nemas and their larvae. III. Strongyloides stercoralis Bavay. Zeitschr. f. Parasitenkunde, I, pp. 231—261.

Looss, A., 1911, The Anatomy and Life-History of Agchylostoma duodenale Dub. A monograph. Part. II. Records of School of Medicine. Cairo Egypt., Vol. IV, pp 306—307.

---

16. Certain Biological and Pathological Aspects of Schistosomiasis Japonica as Studied in Hamsters (Cricetulus Griseus)

Lee, C.U. *D'hygiene, Cairo*, December 1928. Published 1932, p. 373-386.

李宗恩《使用仓鼠研究血吸虫的生理和病理观察》，载于《热带病卫生组织百年庆典论文集》，1932 年（1928 年宣读），373-386 页。

翻译概要　作者于 1925 年夏在血吸虫病多发区（苏州）搜集钉螺，后保存于潮湿、低温的沙子中。次年 3 月，这些钉螺不仅存活，而且一些已被血吸虫尾蚴感染。这些血吸虫尾蚴可用人工传代，并可致仓鼠患血吸虫病。这一观察说明，钉螺是血吸虫尾蚴在冬天寒冷、干燥的条件下存活的寄生宿主。作者通过比较单性（25）和双性感染（2）仓鼠之后的病理观察，认为虫卵所造成的组织伤害较大，而血吸虫本身释放的毒素引起的组织损伤较轻，不能导致组织坏死。作者对双性感染（96）和单性感染（18）后血吸虫的计量显示，两性交媾对成虫，特别是雌性，起重要作用。

Certain Biological and Pathological Aspects of Schistosomiasis Japonica as Studied in Hamsters (*Cricetulus griseus*).

BY

C. U. LEE., M.B., CH.B., D.T.M. & H.

Extensive studies on the pathology of Schistosomiasis have been made in man and animals by many Japanese workers, by Ferguson(1), Fairley (2), Dew (3), Faust and Meleney (4), Hutchison (5) and others.

Since the animal hosts in these studies were infected with both male and female schistosomes, it is, of course, difficult to separate the effects on the tissues of the host produced by the parasites themselves from those due to the presence of their ova. Among authors whose publications are in English, there seems to be a consensus of opinion that some of the late effects of Schistosomiasis, such as cir-

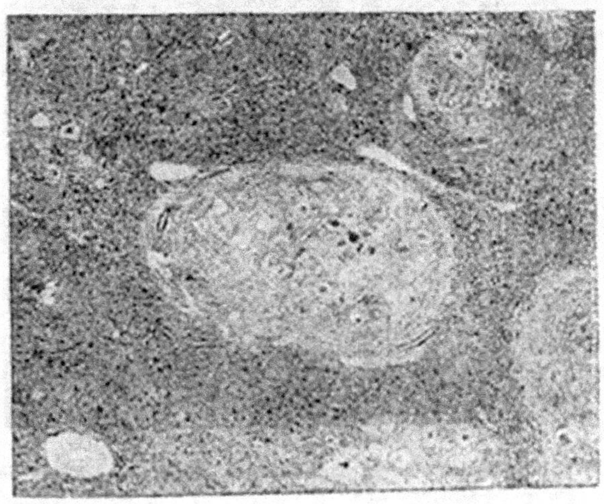

FIG. 1.—Section of liver from a hamster infected with schistosomes of both sexes, showing fibrotic nodules formed round egg deposits. ×40.

rhosis of the liver, are due in part to the mechanical and chemical irritation set up by the presence of ova in the tissues and in part to some kind of toxin produced by the parasites themselves.

As it is possible to infect animals with schistosomes of one sex, it was thought worth while to study the pathological effects induced in experimental animals by the parasites in the absence of egg deposition, particular attention being paid to lesions in the liver.

Incidentally, the development of schistosomes in unisexually infected animals is studied.

Technique and Material.

In the summer of 1925, a collection of snails (*Oncomelania hupensis* Gredler) were received from Soochow, a well-known infected area in South China. As it was not convenient to make use of them at the time, they were kept in trays of moist sand in the ice-chest. The majority of them were still alive in March 1926, when they were crushed one by one and examined for the presence of cercariæ. In all, nineteen snails were found infected with actively living cercariæ. Two or three hamsters (*Cricetulus griseus*) were subjected to infection by being placed for an hour or so in water charged with cercariæ from a single snail. Nineteen groups of hamsters were thus infected.

FIG. 2.—Section of liver from a hamster infected with schistosomes of one sex, showing worms in a portal vein with some cellular infiltration in portal space and marked pigmentation. The surrounding liver tissue is apparently normal. × 80.

The hamsters, either upon death or being killed with ether, were autopsied and examined for the presence of schistosomes by laying open the portal veins at the hilum of the liver with the aid of a dissecting microscope. The worms recovered were fixed either in 10 per cent. formalin or in hot saturated solution of corrosive sublimate, containing 2 per cent. acetic acid. Some of these were stained with dilute hæmatoxylin and mounted for study and measurement.

The organs of infected hamsters were fixed in Zenker's fluid, paraffin-blocked and sectioned. The sections were stained with hæmatoxylin and eosin and some with Mallory's connective tissue stain. A number of hamsters, in which post mortem changes upon autopsy were marked and the worms were already dead, were discarded. In all, schistosomes from twenty hamsters were studied and organs from 25 unisexually and two bisexually infected hamsters were examined.

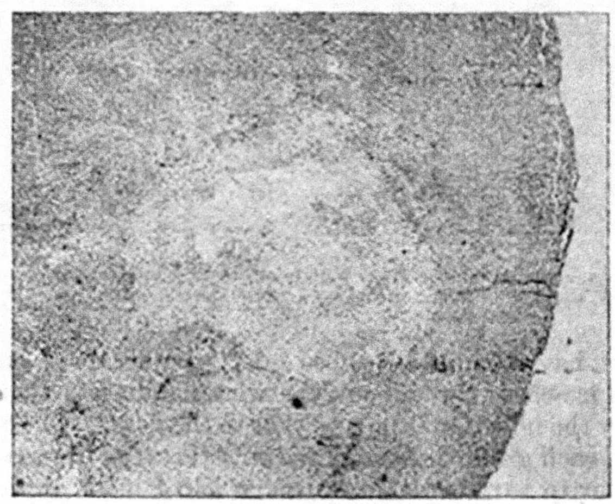

FIG 3.—Section of liver from a hamster infected with schistosomes of one sex, showing an abscess containing dead worms. ×40.

Epidemiological Observations.

It has long been known to Japanese workers that the cercariæ of *Schistosoma japonicum*, derived from a single infected snail, usually developed in experimental animals into adult schistosomes of one sex. This gave rise to the theory in the words of Cort (6), that "sex in the schistosomes is differentiated in the miracidium stage and that all cercariæ which develop from a single miracidium are of the same sex." Recently, Faust (7) reported that from a number of rabbits and dogs, infected with cercariæ from fifteen infected snails out of a batch of 10,000 collected in the region of Soochow in 1926, only male schistosomes were obtained. Faust suggests that the dry conditions prevailing during the season in which the collections were made, may have been more severe on the female than on the male parthenitæ within the snails and natural human infections acquired under such conditions would probably have consisted only of male worms. The practical importance of such an occurrence lies in the fact that in the light of the present study, the pathological lesions produced by worms of one sex can not be compared in severity with those due to a bisexual infection resulting in egg production.

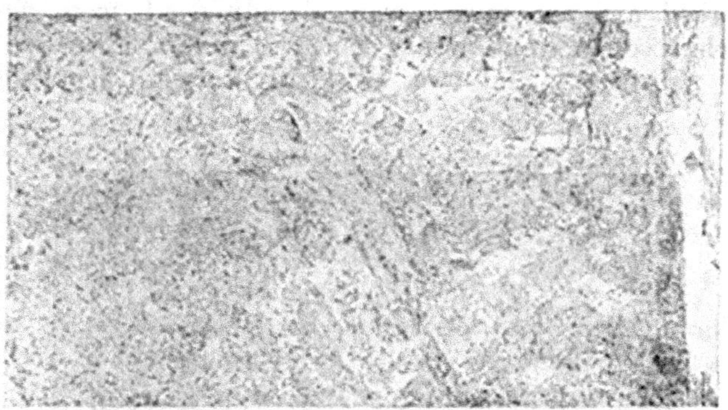

Fig. 4.—Section of liver from a hamster infected with schistosomes of one sex, showing an infarct caused by a worm blocking an end artery. ×80.

That we have been able to find infected individuals among snails kept in the ice-chest throughout the winter indicates that snails are able to carry the infection from one year to the next. Out of 19 groups of hamsters, each group being infected with cercariæ from a single snail, 13 turned out to harbour male worms, 5 had female worms and only one had worms of both sexes. While in this case the winter conditions may have something to do with the smaller number of snails carrying female producing cercariæ, they did not eliminate them altogether. The possibility must also be borne in mind that there is at all times a preponderance of snails with male producing cercariæ.

Pathology of Schistosomiasis in Hamsters.

In our two hamsters infected with both male and female schistosomes and dying on the 72nd and 86th day, respectively, after infection, the pathological changes are definite and characteristic, as they do not differ essentially from those described for other experimental animals, it is only necessary to state that the liver, spleen and intestine are everywhere studded with egg deposits, each surrounded by a considerable amount of fibrous tissue. The lesions in the liver (Plate I, Fig. 1) are, however, much more marked than those found in the dogs by Faust and Meleney (4). Much of the liver tissue is squeezed out of existence by fibrous nodules of varying sizes resulting from extensive egg deposition. There is, however, no evidence of diffuse cirrhosis independent of these lesions, nor is there any thickening of the portal vessels, such as is found in human Schistosomiasis.

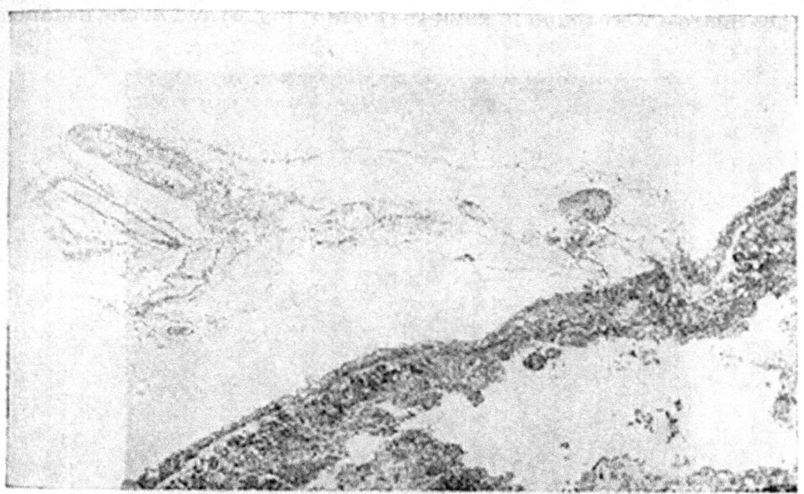

FIG. 5.—Section of mesentery and wall of intestine of a hamster infected with shcistosomes of one sex, showing worms in mesenteric vessel. × 40.

In the unisexually infected hamsters worms were found in the portal and splenic veins, as well as in the mesenteric veins as far down as the peritoneal coat of the intestine. (Plate II, Fig. 5). Few mononuclear and polymorphonuclear leucocytes were noted in the neighbourhood of some of the mesenteric veins with worms in their lumina. In the liver, all the hamsters with one exception showed some degree of lymphocytic infiltration in the periportal spaces (Plate I, Fig. 2, Plate II, Figs. 6 and 7) and occasionally between the column of liver cells, but as they are frequently found in hamsters uninfected with schistosomes, they cannot be regarded as specific for this infection. They probably represent a non-specific reaction to some toxic substance in the portal circulation and it is possible that schistosomes do produce some kind of toxin, perhaps metabolic in origin. It is to be noted, however, that no evidence of fibrosis, diffuse or localized, was ever met with in the liver even after the infection has lasted nearly three years. The only constant feature, which is characteristic of Schistosomiasis is the presence of hæmatin pigment, not only in cells of the reticulo-endothelial system but also in liver cells (Plate I, Fig. 2, Plate II. Figs. 6, 7, 8 and 9) and cells lining the kidney tubules. In the spleen there is apparently no increase in the fibrous tissue framework but there is in some cases a definite increase in the clasmatocytic tissue, especially where pigmentation is heavy. The more serious lesions found in these hamsters are due to individual worms, which in their migration got caught in small arterioles or capillaries in various organs, thereby causing circulatory obstruction. Thus infarcts were found in kidneys (Plate I, Fig. 4) and in one instance

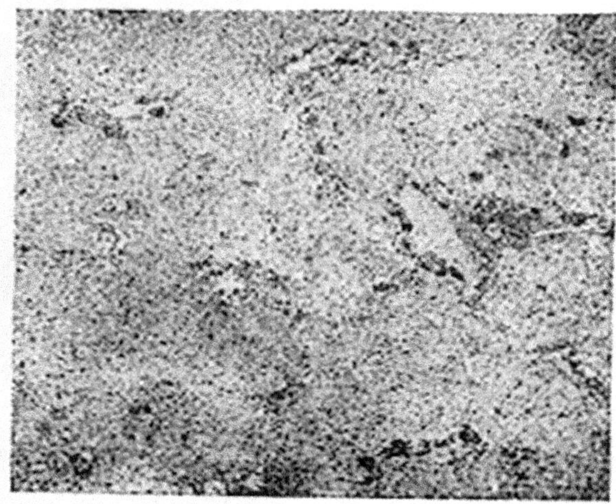

FIG. 6.—Section of liver from a hamster infected with schistosomes of one sex showing cellular infiltration in portal spaces and pigmentation. × 80.

gangrene of a section of the intestine was evidently due to the blocking of a small artery. Sometimes, instead of merely acting as emboli, the worms actually cause rupture of the vessels and break out into the tissues accompanied by hæmorrhages. Should these fail to regain entrance to other blood vessels, they are apt upon their death to give rise to tissue reactions, which may lead to abscess formation. In one of the animals, the liver was the seat of two large abscesses containing degenerated worms (Plate I, Fig. 3). The above findings seem to point to the conclusion that in hamsters the most serious tissue damage resulting from schistosome infection is due to the presence of eggs and that though a toxin probably exists as evidenced by the frequent finding of periportal cellular infiltrations, it does not give rise to diffuse cirrhotic changes in the liver. Nor does the periportal cellular infiltration give place to fibroblastic reaction and the pigmentation, however heavy, never causes more than some pressure atrophy of liver cells. In this connection, it is interesting to recall that Faust and Meleney (4) working with dogs, were also unable to obtain any definite evidence of diffuse cirrhosis of the liver independent of lesions produced by eggs. These findings are not in accord with those reported for man or for monkeys infected with Schistosomiasis. In these cases, all authorities seem to be agreed that the diffuse cirrhotic changes with thickening of the portal vessels found in the liver are due in part to the action of a specific toxin associated with schistosome infection. The source of this toxin is difficult to ascertain. On the one hand it may come from

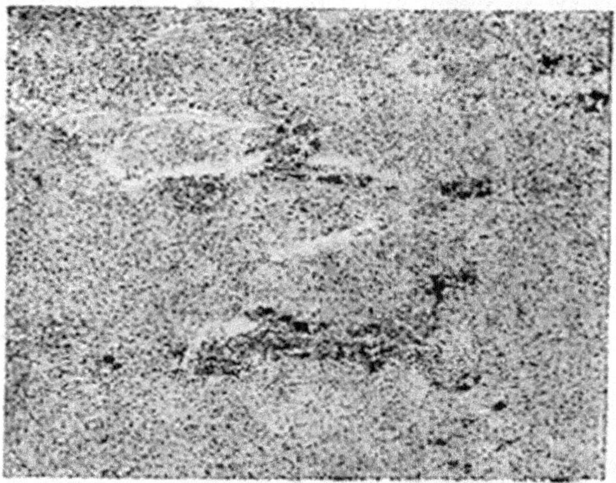

Fig. 7.—Section of liver from a hamster infected with schistosomes of one sex showing cellular infiltration in portal spaces and pigmentation. × 80.

adult parasites, as such, or only from those that are sexually united. On the other hand, eggs may be solely responsible for its production. It was, perhaps, unfortunate that hamsters were used in the present study, as no diffuse cirrhosis was ever found, even in those animals heavily infected with schistosomes of both sexes, accompanied by heavy egg deposition.

Two explanations seem possible for this difference of tissue reaction in different animal hosts : one is that a specific toxin exists but that hamsters and dogs do not react to it in the same way as do monkeys and man, and the other is that the hepatic lesions of the diffuse type in man and monkeys are produced by a toxin independent of the schistosome infection but acting on an organ extensively demaged by schistosomes and their eggs.

This question could be settled by studying the effect of unisexual infection in monkeys with rigid exclusion of other sources of toxin.

The Development of Schistosomes in Unisexually infected Hamsters.

It has been found by Yokogawa according to Cort (6) that schistosomes in unisexually infected animals do not develop to maturity. In their monograph on Schistosomiasis japonica, Faust and Meleney (4) indicated that one of the factors affecting the growth and maturity rate of the worms is what they term the maturity stimulus of one sex upon the other. No data based on actual measurements were, however, given by any of these authors. During the course of the present study an opportunity offered itself for studying this sex factor in the development of schistosomes. Careful measurements were made of 96 worms from a series of hamsters dying or being

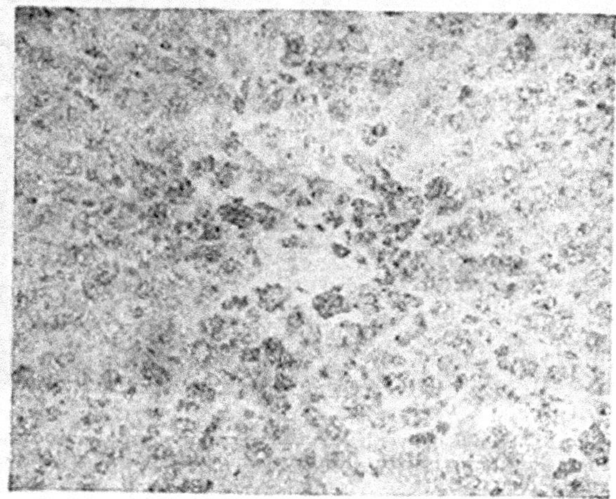

FIG. 8.—A more highly magnified portion of Fig. 6, showing haematin pigment in Kupffers' cells and liver cells, round the centre of a lobule. × 350.

sacrificed at varying periods after infection. It has been found that the measurements depend to some extent on the way the worms are fixed. Those fixed in 10 per cent formalin are in a more relaxed state than those fixed in hot saturated solution of corrosive sublimate. Thus, in the accompanying table, the male worms from unisexually infected hamsters are presented in two groups for better comparison.

An examination of the table will show that the unmated males in the bisexually infected hamsters only develop to about a third of the size of the largest mated ones in the same period of time and the males in the unisexually infected hamsters take about five or six times the period to grow to the size of the mated ones in the bisexually infected hamsters.

The fact that the percentage of total length taken up by the pre-acetabular region is never less than 9 among either unmated

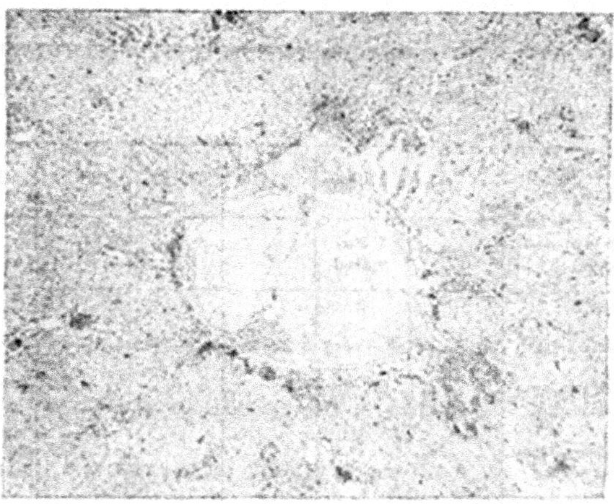

FIG. 9.—Section of spleen from a hamster infected with schistosomes of one sex, showing pigmentation. × 80.

males from bisexually infected hamsters or males from unisexually infected hamsters, seems to indicate that when the males are mated the growth is chiefly with the post-acetabular region. Mating, however, has no appreciable effect either on the width of the parasites or on the size of their suckers.

It is also interesting to note that there is no definite relation between the size of the worm and the ratio of the bifurcated to the united part of the intestine.

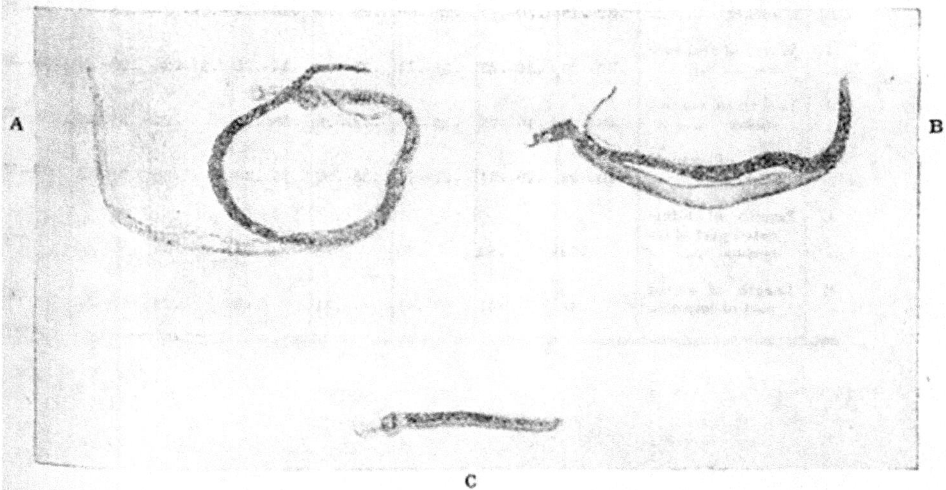

FIG. 10.—A—Male and female schistosomes in copula from a hamster 67 days after infection. B—Male and female schistosomes in copula from a hamster 86 days after infection. C—An unmated male schistosome from the same hamster in which the worms in B were found. × 10.

TABLE I. THE SEX FACTOR IN THE DEVELOP[...]

		Males from Bisexually infected hamsters		Males from [illegible]						
Period of Residence in Hamsters in Days		67–86 D		23 D	36 D	193 D	251 D	252 D	316 D	[illegible]
Number of Worms measured		8 mated	7 un-mated	5	5	4	6	4	4	[illegible]
A	Total body length	10.8–5.6	3.7–3.1	3.78–2.5	3.53–2.05	4.4–3.6	4.0–2.9	4.4–3.8	6.5–4.3	[illegible]
B	Length of pre-acetabular region	.95–.5	.77–.37	.53–.38	.51–.31	.63–.55	75–44	.63–.52	.88–.7	[illegible]
C	Length of post-acetabular region	9.9–5	2.96–2.48	3.3–2.1	3.22–2.44	3.78–3.1	3.41–2.46	3.98–3.19	5.62–3.6	[illegible]
D	Length of pre-acetabular region per cent. of total length ...	12.5	24–11	16–10	17–9	16–14	21–14	17–13	16–13	[illegible]
E	Width at middle of post-acetabular region	.83–.43	.72–.43	.36–.28	.59–.54	.68–.52	.76–.73	.83–.64	.89–.57	[illegible]
F	Width at ventral suker	.47–.32	.46–.34	.27–.17	.36–.34	.44–.34	.41–.30	.41–.34	.64–.38	[illegible]
G	Width at middle of pre-acetabular region	.3–.2	.25–.17	.17–.09	.28–.21	.28–.19	.34–.22	.26–.22	.35–.31	[illegible]
H	Length of oral sucker	.32–.18	.30–.21	.25–.09	.29–.25	.36–.27	.29–.21	.33–.21	.35–.29	[illegible]
I	Width of oral sucker	.32–.20	.36–.23	.31–.11	.33–.28	.34–.21	.31–.26	.29–.23	.33–.30	[illegible]
J	Length of ventral sucker	.40–.23	.40–.22	.20–.18	.43–.29	.38–.22	.27	.31–.26	.38–.37	[illegible]
K	Width of ventral sucker	.40–.28	.40–.31	.27–.14	.35–.22	.35–.30	.30	.31–.25	.37–.30	[illegible]
L	Length of bifurcated part of intestine	.73	.82	.68	.8	.74	.58	.55	1.0	
M	Length of united part of intestine	.48	.41	.41	.31	.08	.22	.35	.61	

…*Schistosoma japonicum* IN HAMSTERS

	…ally infected hamsters						Females from bisexually infected hamsters	Females from unisexually infected hamsters			
…0 D	318 K	320 K	322 K	389 K	821 K	851 K	67 86 D	322 D	326 K	389K	851 K
4	4	2	3	3	4	4	10	3	5	1	6
…-7.5	4.16-3.8	3.7-3.4	3.0-2.6	5.4-4.8	7.9-3.9	6.4-3.6	10.7-5.3	2.0-1.78	1.71-1.4	1.46	2.96-2.38
…-.83	.61-.49	.53-.41	.56-.51	.75-.57	.57-.4	.76-.5	.4-.18	.27-.17	.18-.15	.16	.28-.20
…-6.67	2.51-3.31	3.29-2.87	2.44-2.06	4.65-4.2	7.5-3.37	5.64-2.94	9.3-5.12	1.84-1.6	1.53-1.22	1.29	2.71-2.177
…2-11	15-13	16-11	20-19	14-11	14-6	18-12	4.3-2.7	14-10	13-10	11	10-9
…-.54	.8-.56	.43	.75-.64	.87-.68	.53-.42	.65-.43	.27-.17	.22-.19	.14-.09	.15	.20-.15
.4-.38	.41-.4	.27	.41-.35	.56-.5	.4-.35	.45-.36	.12	—	.09-.08	.10	—
…-.22	.32-.28	.2	.31-.26	.42-.37	.27	.33-.28	.16-.06	—	.08-.05	.08	—
…-.24	.25	.19	.25	.28	.24	.28-.25	.11-.09	.08-.07	.05-.04	.05	.08-.05
…-.26	.38-.30	.19	.28-.27	.36-.30	.26-.24	.32-.28	.09	—	.07-.04	.07	.07
.37-.31	.31-.26	.17	.09	.36	.29-.24	.28-.24	.08	[illegible].13	.07-.04	.07	.10-.06
.36	.39-.26	.20	.16	.38	.31-.27	.27-.24	.09	—	.03	.05	.05
—	.8	—	.52	.59	.57	.83	.78	—	.82	—	.58
.24	.63	—	.43	.4	.25	.41	.48	—	.69	.39	.45

The under development of female schistosomes in unisexually infected hamsters is even more remarkable; while the males by themselves will develop to their adult size if sufficient time is allowed, the females probably never attain to more than a fraction of their adult size in the absence of the males. Moreover, the unmated females do not become cylindrical, as they do when sexually mated. Thus, these underdeveloped females are easily mistaken for immature males, unless one takes care to examine their reproductive organs. Though unmated and under-developed in bodily size the component parts of genitalia in both males and females can be easily made out except that no eggs are found in the uteri of the females.

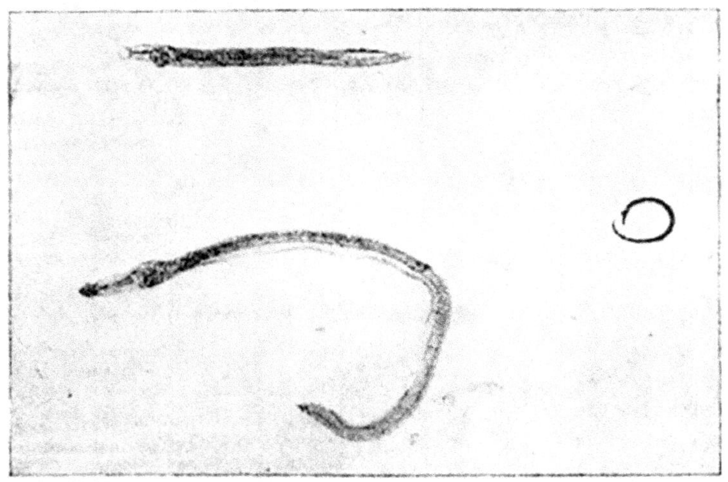

Fig. 11.—A Male schistosme from a unisexually infected hamster 252 days after infection. B. Male schistosome from a unisexually infected hamster 487 days after infection. C. Female schistosome from a unisexually infected hamster 851 days after infection. × 10.

We may thus conclude that the mating of the two sexes is a most important factor in the bodily development of *Schistosoma japonicum* and that the females are more dependent on this factor than the males in this respect (Plate III).

Summary and Conclusions.

1. Snails, *Oncomelania hupensis,* collected in summer of 1925, in an endemic region of Schistosomiasis in South China, were kept in trays of moist sand in ice-chest through the winter months. In March 1926 the majority of them were still alive and some were found infected with active schistosome cercariæ. Both male and

female worms were later recovered from hamsters subjected to infection with these cercariæ. It is, therefore, reasonable to presume that snails of this species are able to carry the infection from one year to the next, and that winter conditions are not as effective in eliminating the female parthenitæ within the snails or the snails containing them as a period of draught sometimes is in the light of Faust's recent observation.

2. From a study of the histopathology in two hamsters infected with schistosomes of both sexes and 25 infected with one sex only, it is concluded that the most serious lesions are caused by the presence of eggs in the tissues and that though a toxin is probably produced by the worms themselves, it does not give rise to cirrhotic changes in the liver, such as are found in man and monkeys.

3. Careful measurements were made of 96 worms recovered from 2 bisexually infected hamsters and 18 unisexually infected ones. It is shown that in their bodily development, the mating of the two sexes is a most important factor and that the females are more dependent on this factor than the males.

ACKNOWLEDGMENT.

The author is indebted to Dr. Henry E. Meleney for originally suggesting the problem and to Dr. C. H. Hu for valuable help and suggestions.

LITERATURE CITED.

1. FERGUSON, A. R.—The lesion of bilharzial disease. Glasgow Med. Journ. 1913, Vol. LXXIX, 14.

2. FAIRLEY, N. H.—A comparative study of experimental Bilharziasis in monkeys, contrasted with the hitherto described lesions in man. Journ. Path. and Bact. 1920, Vol. XXIII, 289.

3. DEW, H. R.—Observations on the pathology of Schistosomiasis in the human subject. Journ. Path. and Bact. 1923, Vol. XXVI, 27.

4. FAUST, C. F. and MELENY, H. E.—Studies on Schistosomiasis japonica. Amer. Journ. Hyg., Monograph No. 3, 1924, Baltimore.

5. HUTCHISON, H. S.—The pathology of Bilharziasis. Amer. Journ. Path. 1928, Vol. IV, 1.

6. CORT, W. W.—The development of the Japanese blood-fluke, *Schistosoma japonicum* Katsurada, in its final host. Amer. Journ. Hyg. 1921, Vol. I, 1.

7. FAUST, C. F.—The possible presence of male schistosomes alone in experimental and natural infections. Journ. Parasit. 1927, Vol, XIV, 62.

DISCUSSIONS.

DR. M. F. SOROUR.

I mentioned my experiment injecting powdered *Bilharzia*-worms, washed and sterile, subcutaneously in guinea-pigs. It produced eosinophilic and endothelial proliferation. This excited my interest in another experiment, namely, injecting tubercle bacilli mixed with *Bilharzia* worms pulp and after 6 weeks killing the animal. We found only a local caseation but well fibrosed lesion whereas guinea pig injected with same strain of T. B. with no Bilharzia worms, fully developed local and generalized Tuberculosis. These experiments support very much the post-mortem findings where the association of Tuberculosis and *Bilharzia* in natural infections in man is accompanied by very good fibrosis of the tuberculous lesion.

DR. DOLLFUS.

Dollfus demande si, dans les cas de Schistosomiase où des femelles seulement sont présentes, on a observé quelquefois des oeufs parthénogénétiques ?

Dr. Lee répond que on a jamais observé d'oeufs parthénogénétiques.

17. A Survey of the Mosquitoes and Their Breeding Habits in the Amoy Region

Lee, C.U. *Marine Biology Association of China*, 1st Annual Report, Oct. 1932.

李宗恩 《厦门地区蚊子及其习性的考察》. 载于《中国海洋生物协会第一次年度报告》, 1932 年 10 月。

18. Treatment of Schistosomiasis Japonica with Fouadin in Experimental Infected Rabbits

Lee, C.U. *Chinese Medical Journal,* 46:1169-1178, 1932.

李宗恩 《Fouadin 治疗血吸虫病兔的效果》，载于《中华医学杂志》，1932 年，46:1169-1178 页。

翻译概要 Fouadin 是德国化学公司 Bayer 最近生产的治疗血吸虫病的锑剂。虽然报道称该药对治疗埃及型血吸虫病有效，但对治疗日本型血吸虫病的效果还不明了。36 只血吸虫病兔中，用 Fouadin 治疗的 15 只的结果显示，Fouadin 有暂时的缓解作用，肌肉注射比静脉注射的效果稍好，但总体治疗效果不是最佳治疗药物。主要结论如下：

1. 15 只病兔子在经过 Fouadin 治疗（7 肌肉注射，8 只静脉注射）不同时间后，大便中的虫卵消失。有的兔子完全治愈，有的只是抑制了雌性血吸虫的排卵能力，因为 4 只静脉注射的兔子在停药一段时间后又在粪便中查到虫卵。所以此药物不能满足治愈药物的标准。6 只对照病兔中，5 只直到死亡都可在粪便中查到虫卵，另一只自愈。
2. Fouadin 肌肉注射比静脉注射的疗效好。
3. 以上结果表明，Fouadin 对日本血吸虫病有治疗作用，但不是最佳选择。

Chinese Medical Journal, 1932, XLVI, 1169-1178.

TREATMENT OF SCHISTOSOMIASIS JAPONICA WITH FOUADIN IN EXPERIMENTALLY INFECTED RABBITS

C. U. Lee

Laboratory of Parasitic Diseases, Department of Medicine, Peiping Union Medical College, Peiping

Fouadin, the trade name of a new organic antimony compound, was recently introduced by the German Chemical firm, Bayer and Company, for the treatment of the Egyptian forms of schistosomiasis. Reports by Khalil and his co-workers (1, 2, 3, 4) indicate its superiority over tartar emetic and other organic antimony compounds. Apart from the small series of successfully treated cases reported by Kastien (5) and Low and Franklin (6), its value in schistosomiasis japonica has not been seriously studied. The present report embodies results of a study on the therapeutic value of fouadin in rabbits experimentally infected with *Schistosoma japonicum*.

Fouadin is a 6.3 per cent solution of a trivalent organic antimony compound expressed by Schmidt (7) as Antimony—III—pyrocatechin-disulphonate of sodium with the following structural formula:

NaO_3S SO_3Na
O O
Sb $.7\ H_2O$
O O
NaO_3S Na SO_3Na

Each cc of fouadin contains 0.0085 gm of trivalent antimony.

Before proceeding with the examination of the details of the experiment, it is necessary to direct attention to certain pertinent considerations. In the first place it is technically difficult to standardize the intensity of infection in all animals. The numerical estimation of the actively motile cercariae does not always yield accurate results on account of the difficulty of securing their uniform distribution in a volume of water and their tendency to stick to the wall of the measuring pipette used for the counting. Attempts might be made to pool the cercariae from a large number of infected snails and inoculate animals with equal quantities of the infected water but the same lack of uniform distribution of the cercariae in the infected water and the necessity of infecting a large number of animals at one time render this method equally unpractical. Further even if it is possible to place equal quantities of cercariae on the skin of a number of animals, there is no way of ensuring that equal numbers of cercariae will succeed in penetrating the skin and reach their destination in the portal field. In this study, with the exception of three rabbits, Nos. 201, 202 and 203, each infected with cercariae from a single snail, all the rabbits were each infected with cercariae from two more or less heavily infected snails. The intensity of infection is roughly estimated from the number of macroscopic lesions present in the organs upon autopsy and for reasons stated below not from the number of worms recovered.

Secondly in evaluating the therapeutic potency of a drug it must be remembered that in rabbits with light infection spontaneous cure sometimes results. For example, in one of the untreated rabbits No. 212 (Table 3) this occurred and whether the absence of parasites in some of the treated rabbits, for example, Nos. 204 and 207 (Table 2) is actually due to the effect of the treatment is difficult to decide without further investigation.

Finally it remains to be pointed out that the number of worms recovered at autopsy is not necessarily a measure of the intensity of infection because the thorough search of all the portal and mesenteric veins and venules is often difficult and if the autopsy is performed some hours after the death of the animal, the worms are often very difficult to find in the presence of post-mortem changes especially if they are already dead.

EXPERIMENTAL METHODS

Snails of the species *Oncomelania hupensis* were collected in the Autumn of 1930 in a village just outside of the city of Soochow and forwarded to Peiping through the post. On arrival they were, if not immediately utilised, kept in the ice-chest.

For experimental infection a number of snails were crushed each in a small glass dish containing some water and examined under a dissecting microscope for the presence of fork-tailed cercariae. Rabbits immobilized on wooden racks were infected by transferring the cercariae in drops of water by means of glass pipettes onto a shaved area of the abdomen. They were released after about an hour, when the drops of water containing the cercariae were more or less completely evaporated. During the period September 24 to October 2, 1930, thirty-six rabbits were thus infected. Equal numbers of male and female rabbits were employed and their weights at the time of infection varied from 893 to 2172 grams. After infection the animals were kept in individual cages and fed with the same kind of ration. Their weights were recorded three or four times a week. The faeces of each animal were examined by the ordinary smear method for schistosome ova. Within one to three days of their appearance treatment with fouadin was instituted in a number of the rabbits, one series intramuscularly, another intravenously. The dosage and duration of the treatment were standardized, consisting of 0.25 cc daily for first two days, then 0.5 cc every other day up to a total dosage of 6 cc given in the course of 24 days.

All the 36 rabbits, whether died or killed, were autopsied. At autopsy the portal and mesenteric veins and venules were searched for adult parasites and the organs for macroscopic lesions.

DISCUSSION OF RESULTS

Out of the 36 rabbits, 28 showed ova in the stools after varying periods following infection. In a number of these chosen at random the infection was treated with fouadin either intramuscularly or intravenously, while in others it was allowed to run its course. The eight rabbits whose stools were persistently negative for ova, turned out upon autopsy to be either non-infected or infected with only schistosomes of one sex.

In the presentation of results, the rabbits are grouped in five series as follows:

Series A. Unisexually infected and non-infected (Table 1)........ 8
,, B. Bisexually infected and treated intramuscularly (Table 2). 7
,, C. Bisexually infected and treated intravenously (Table 2).. 8
,, D. Bisexually infected but short-lived (Table 3)............ 7
,, E. Bisexually infected and untreated (Control) (Table 3).... 6

Total.. 36

TABLE 1.

Series A. Unisexually injected and non-infected rabbits (♂ means male)

Rabbit no.	Died (D) or Killed (K)	Days after infection	Autopsy findings: Worms found	Autopsy findings: Condition of organs	Remarks
201	D	233	None	Grossly normal	No evidence of infection
202	D	135	Numerous ♂ alive	Death due to perforated stomach from excess of food	
203	D	324	A few ♂ alive	Grossly normal	
205	K	161	None	Grossly normal	No evidence of infection
213	K	159	Numerous ♂ alive	Grossly normal	
221	D	15	None	Grossly normal	No evidence of infection
223	K	162	Numerous ♂ alive	Grossly normal	
225	K	164	Numerous ♂ alive	Grossly normal	

Of the eight rabbits of Series A, five were infected with only schistosomes of the male sex and three showed no evidence of infection. As two of these three rabbits were autopsied some hours after death from accidental causes, the possibility of their being unisexually infected with female schistosomes cannot be entirely excluded in view of the fact that in such infected animals the female schistosomes are always very small and usually few in number (8, 9) and in the presence of post-mortem changes are extremely hard to find.

In the seven rabbits of Series B, fouadin given intramuscularly did seem to possess definite therapeutic value. Rabbit 204 probably had a light infection to begin with, for its stool was positive for ova only on one occasion just before treatment was instituted and no gross lesions were found in the organs at autopsy. The treatment may have prevented the further appearance of ova in the stool, though this happened rather too promptly. The stools of the other six rabbits of the series became negative for ova after an interval varying from 3 to 26 days from the commencement of treatment and remained so after treatment for periods of three and a half to four and a half months.

Upon autopsy, with the exception of two, Nos. 209, 214, the rabbits yielded no schistosomes. In Rabbit 209, only male schistosomes, many of which were immature, were recovered. The female parasites, which must have been present to account for the ova in the stools at one stage were probably all eliminated by the treatment. In Rabbit 214, however, living males and females were found. It is difficult to explain in this case the absence of ova in the stool unless it is assumed that the treatment in some way affected the egg producing capacity of the female schistosomes.

Thus fouadin given intramuscularly cleared the stools of all seven rabbits of ova, cured the infection in five, eliminated the female parasites in one and possibly affected their egg producing capacity in another.

The therapeutic affect of fouadin given intravenously to the eight animals in Series C is not so striking. It did, however, render the stool of all the rabbits free of ova temporarily in some but permanently in others. This phenomenon of relapse is of considerable interest. It may mean a temporary depressing effect of the treatment on the egg producing capacity of the female schistosomes; on the other hand, it may be due to ova produced by a separate set of female worms, which matured after the therapeutic effect of the treatment has already worn off, the assumption being that the mature females are more susceptible to antimony therapy than the immature ones.

Therefore of the eight rabbits of Series C only two, Nos. 231 and 235, seem to be permanently benefited by the intravenous use of fouadin; the female worms in one and both male and female worms in another were eliminated.

Though the results from two such small series of animals can not afford a basis for any general conclusion, it might be argued that the better therapeutic effect in the intramuscular series may be due to the more prolonged and continued action of fouadin and its less rapid excretion than when the drug is given intravenously. The average body weight dose in the intramuscular series is actually less than that in the intravenous series. The size of the dosage is, however, not the only factor in bringing about a cure, since the only rabbit in the intramuscular series that was definitely not cured had actually the next highest dosage of fouadin in the series. As compared with the therapeutic dosage advocated for man by Khalil, namely, 40 cc for an adult of average weight of 60 kilograms, the dosage in rabbits is considerably higher, in some cases as much as six times, yet results do not show that the optimum effective dose has been reached.

No comment is needed on the data for Series D and E presented in Table 3.

Appended is also a chart of compound curves showing the changes in body weight of the four series of rabbits, A, B, C, and E. Averages of the weights of each animal in each consecutive period of four days from the time of infection were first taken and each compound curve was constructed from the average of the weights of the four day periods of all the animals in the particular series. The weights of animals of series A showed a steady rise without interruption from the time of infection. The unisexual infection in some of

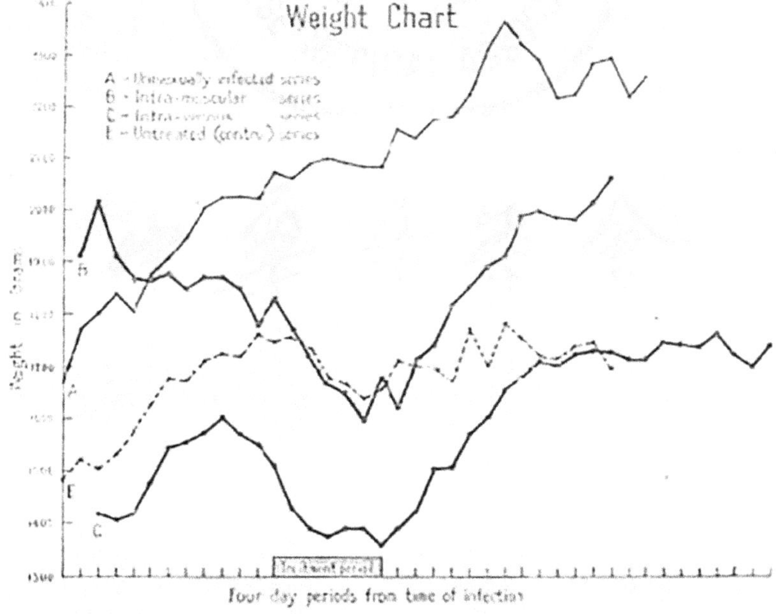

Chart showing weight curves of different series of animals.

TABLE 2.

Series B and C. Bisexually infected rabbits treated with fouadin

(♂ means male and ♀ means female)

Series	Rabb. No.	Days ova appeared after infection	Days ova disappeared after commencement of treatment	Total cc. of fouadin per kilo. body wt.	Ova reappeared after interval in days	Died (D) or Killed (K)				Autopsy findings		Remarks
							Days after infection	Days after appearance of ova	Days after treatment	Worms found	Condition of organs	
B. Intramuscular treatment	201	50	immediately (see text)	2.43		K	175	123	99	None	Grossly normal	Light infection, probably cured
	207	50	15	2.84		D	188	158	114	None	Grossly normal	Light infection, probably cured
	209	52	3	3.45		K	178	126	100	132 ♂ alive, many immature	Liver grossly normal. Egg deposits in intestinal wall	Lightly infected with ♀, which treatment probably cured
	211	51	22	3.11		K	213	162	137	None	Liver markedly cirrhosed	Cured
	214	50	24	5.45		K	201	151	126	28 ♂ 10 ♂ alive	Liver cirrhosed	Not cured
	216	45	26	5.85		K	185	159	116	None	Liver slightly cirrhosed	Cured
	218	48	16	4.30		K	182	154	109	None	Liver slightly cirrhosed	Cured
C. Intravenous treatment	226	44	18	4.09	93	K	174	130	106	16 couples alive	Liver cirrhosed, egg tumors in intestinal wal	Relapsed
	227	48	25	3.27		D	177	129	106	1 ♀ 187 ♂ (many immature) alive	Liver slightly cirrhosed	Not cured
	229	51	36	4.34	20	D	166	175	92	18 ♀ 52 ♂ alive	Liver markedly cirrhosed; egg deposits in intestinal wall	Relapsed
	231	43	28	4.54		K	182	139	115	About 100 ♂ alive Many immature	Liver slightly cirrhosed	Lightly infected with ♀, which treatment probably cured
	233	48	22	4.05		K	104	136	123	1 ♀ 13 ♂ alive	Liver cirrhosed	Not cured
	234	50	19	4.45	79	K	180	130	107	None	Grossly normal	No eggs in stool 2 days before autopsy. Relapse followed by spontaneous cure
	235	44	29	4.68		K	195	151	126	None	Grossly normal	Cured
	236	12	97	5.80	25	K	218	175	152	Numerous ♂+♀ alive	Liver markedly cirrhosed egg tumors in intestinal wall	Relapsed

TABLE 3.

Series D and E. Bisexually infected rabbits which died during treatment or were not treated

(♂ means male and ♀ means female)

Series	Rabbit No.	Days ova appeared after infection	Total cc. of fouadin received	Ova in stool	Died (D) or Killed (K)			Autopsy findings		Remarks
						Days after infection	Days after appearance of ova	Worms found	Condition of organs	
D. Short-lived	206	50	3.6	Negative 7 days after commencement of treatment	D	65	15	3 ♂ 1 ♀ alive	Liver markedly cirrhosed. Death due to intussusception of large intestine	Heavy infection
	208	52	3.5	Positive till death	D	68	16	13 ♂ alive	Liver cirrhosed, egg deposits in intestinal wall. Death due to peritonitis	Moderate infection
	210	45	3.0	.. .. ..	D	59	14	1 ♀ dead	Liver markedly cirrhosed egg deposits in intestinal wall	Heavy infection
	220	42	None	.. .. ..	D	45	3	Numerous ♂ and ♀	Liver markedly cirrhosed	.. ..
	222	39	None	.. .. ..	D	42	3	..	Liver cirrhosed	.. ..
	224	48	0.25	.. .. ..	D	48	Less than 1	..	Liver cirrhosed, egg deposits in intestinal wall	.. ..
	228	40	0.25	.. .. ..	D	45	5	..	Liver cirrhosed	.. ..
E. Control	210	47	None	Positive till death	D	73	26	None	Liver markedly cirrhosed egg deposits in intestinal wall. Death due to pneumonia	Heavy infection, failure to find worms due to delay in autopsy
	212	61	None	Positive for 62 days	K	173	112	None	Grossly normal	Light infection. Probably spontaneous cure
	217	42	None	Positive till death	K	212	170	Numerous ♂ and ♀	Liver markedly cirrhosed egg deposits in intestinal wall	Heavy infection
	219	58	None	.. .. ..	K	231	173	..	.. .. ..	.. ..
	220	52	None	.. .. ..	D	129	77	..	.. .. ..	.. ..
	232	59	None	.. .. ..	D	133	74	..	.. .. ..	.. ..

the animals did not seem to affect their general health. On the other hand, the animals of the two treated as well as the control series show after an initial period of one and a half months a drop in weight especially marked in the two treated series, to be followed by a rise also more pronounced in the treated animals. This constant drop in weight in the course of infection was probably due to the depressing effect of the infection at its height and treatment with fouadin accentuated it to some extent.

SUMMARY AND CONCLUSIONS

1. The results of a study of the therapeutic value of a new antimony compound, fouadin, in experimental schistosomiasis japonica in rabbits are reported.

2. In fifteen rabbits treated with fouadin seven intramuscularly and eight intravenously, ova disappeared from the stools after a varying interval. In some apparent cure resulted while in others the treatment only succeeded in depressing the egg producing capacity of the female schistosomes. In four rabbits treated with fouadin intravenously, ova reappeared in the stool after a period of freedom. The temporary disappearance of ova from the stool following specific treatment is, therefore, never a safe criterion of cure. Of the six untreated controls five were ova positive till death and only one showed evidence of spontaneous cure.

3. In these animals fouadin given intramuscularly seems more efficient than the same administered intravenously.

4. Fouadin does, therefore, possess therapeutic value in the treatment of schistosomiasis japonica in rabbits, though in many respects it falls short of an ideal specific.

Acknowledgment. The author is indebted to the Shanghai agents of Messrs. Bayer and Co. for the supply of snails and of fouadin for this study.

19. Relative Value of Urea-Stibamine and Neostibosan in Treatment of Kala-Azar

Lee, C.U. and Chu, C.F. *Chinese Medical Journal*, 49:328-339, 1935.

李宗恩，瞿承方《尿素斯锑巴民（urea-stibamine）与新斯锑波山（neostibosan）对于黑热病治疗效力之比较》，载于《中华医学杂志》，1935年，49:328-339页。

中文摘要（见1934年《中华医学杂志》第20卷第4期554页） 据考察九十五病例经过 neostibosan 治疗，六十三例经过 urea-stibamine 治疗，及十八例经过以上二种药剂先后治疗，所得结论如下：urea-stibamine 之效力强于 neostibosan，然其毒性亦较猛，肾之刺激及流血偏向均较常见；类似过敏反应状及带状疱疹亦只见于此药治疗中。惟经此药治疗者咸获愈。反之，经 neostibosan 治疗而不获愈者，凡十一例。

翻译概要

1. urea-stibamine的治疗剂量应为儿童1.00-1.50克，成人1.50-2.50克。neostibosan 的治疗剂量应为儿童1.50-2.50克，成人4.00-5.00克。
2. urea-stibamine 由不同的锑剂合成，而 neostibosan 是标准的单一锑剂。对于黑热病的治疗，urea-stibamine 的疗效优于 neostibosan。
3. 凡用此两种药物治疗的病人，尤其对 neostibosan 治疗的病人，需跟踪至少7个月甚至一年才可确认治愈。在药物治疗完成一个月后，如脾或肝穿刺发现寄生虫者，应继续治疗。
4. 改进黑热病的化疗有赖于五价锑剂的生产、标准化和无毒性的 neostibosan 及保持 urea-stibamine 的治疗效果。

Chinese Medical Journal, **49**: *328-339, 1935.*

RELATIVE VALUE OF UREA STIBAMINE AND NEOSTIBOSAN IN THE TREATMENT OF KALA-AZAR*

C. U. LEE AND C. F. CHU

Department of Medicine, Peiping Union Medical College, Peiping.

The introduction of pentavalent organic antimony compounds in the treatment of kala-azar was undoubtedly an advance in chemotherapy. It must, however, be admitted that an ideal specific for kala-azar has not yet been found and search for such must continue. Of the various organic antimony compounds introduced within recent years, two, namely urea-stibamine and neostibosan, have been given a thorough trial in the Peiping Union Medical College Hospital, and it is for the purpose of showing their respective merits as well as their shortcomings and of indicating the direction in which improvements must be sought that the following report is submitted.

Urea-stibamine was introduced by Brahmachari of India in 1922 (1). Its principal constituents are, according to Gray and Trevan (2), a substance corresponding in composition to the di-substituted urea (Symdiphenyl-carbamide-4:4'-distibinic acid) and antimonic acid. This drug has been extensively used in the treatment of kala-azar in Assam, India. Shortt, Craighead and Swaminath (3) maintained that urea-stibamine is as good a therapeutic agent in the treatment of kala-azar as any of the organic preparations of antimony subsequently put on the market. Shortt (4) in his introduction to the Second Report of the Indian Kala-azar Commission stated that the Commission used throughout the seven years of its existence one drug only in the routine treatment of kala-azar, viz., urea-stibamine and found it to be an eminently safe and reliable drug and among thousands of cases treated with it the members of the Commission personally came across no cases of death directly attributable to it. Napier (5) in an experience of 70 cases concluded that urea-stibamine is a drug of very considerable value in the treatment of kala-azar and is well tolerated by man in comparatively large doses. D'Oelsnitz and Carcopino (6) (7) in France recommend it in cases of kala-azar which have proved resistant to other antimony compounds. Urea-stibamine is, however, not a constant chemical compound and its antimony content has been reported by Ghosh, Chopra and Chatterjee (8) to vary from 20 to 43 per cent in different samples. Our supply comes directly from Brahmachari Research Institute, Calcutta.

*Paper read at the Chinese Medical Association General Conference held at Nanking March 31—April 7, 1934.

Neostibosan is made by Bayer & Co., Leverkusen, Germany, and is a well standardized chemical compound, diethylamine p-aminophenyl-stibinate, with an antimony content of 42 per cent. Ever since his first publication on neostibosan in its present improved form in 1928 (9), Napier has steadfastly advocated its superiority over all other pentavalent antimony compounds. In a recent publication (10) he stated that for future investigations into the question of the most suitable amount, strength and spacing of the injections, and of optimum total dosage, one drug, namely, neostibosan should be used. This drug has also been used in many Mediterranean centers of kala-azar. The results obtained by Zahra-Neumann (11) in Malta are not so striking as those of Napier in India and he concluded that neostibosan is not as efficacious in Mediterranean as it is in Indian kala azar, higher doses than those recommended by Napier having to be employed. In China neostibosan much more than urea-stibamine has been tried in various kala-azar districts apparently with uniformly good results.

In the Peiping Union Medical College Hospital during a period of a little over 6 years between March 1, 1927 and June 30, 1933, 95 proven cases of kala-azar were treated with neostibosan, 63 with urea-stibamine and 18 with more than one drug at different times on account of intolerance to one drug, absence of response or shortage of supply - a total of 176 cases. Since there is no conscious selection in the use of urea-stibamine or neostibosan as shown in Table 1, comparison of their therapeutic value is permissible.

TABLE 1. *Annual distribution of cases treated with Urea-stibamine or Neostibosan alone showing absence of conscious selection in the use of the two Drugs.*

Urea-stibamine	1927	1928	1929	1930	1931	1932	1933		Total	Grand Total
Children	0	5	1	15	0	2	1	=	24	
Adults	1	10	9	14	3	2	0	=	39	63
Neostibosan										
Children	0	0	4	2	17	19	8	=	50	
Adults	0	0	0	4	16	17	8	=	45	95

With a few exceptions in the urea-stibamine group all patients were treated in the hospital. Patients under 12 (Chinese reckoning) are considered as children.

Dosage and duration of treatment. The dosage and duration of treatment were left to the judgment of the physician in charge without any rigid routine. Table 2 shows the distribution of cases according to dosage, the average dosage and the average duration of treatment. The urea-stibamine was given intravenously in most of the cases every other day or every three or four days, the maximum single dose being 0.2 gm, while neostibosan was given either intramuscularly or intravenously more intensively, once every other day or daily, the maximum single dose being 0.3 gm. This accounts for the longer average duration of treatment in the urea-stibamine series in spite of its smaller average total dose.

TABLE 2. *Dosage and duration of treatment in patients treated with Urea-stibamine or Neostibosan alone excluding dead patients.*

	Urea-stibamine		Neostibosan	
	Children	Adults	Children	Adults
0.01-0.54 gm	3	2	2	0
0.55-1.00	4	4	2	1
1.05-1.50	7	4	2	1
1.55-2.00	2	7	12	2
2.05-2.50	1	7	18	2
2.55-3.00	1	9	2	2
3.05-3.50	0	1	2	17
3.55-4.00	2	0	0	10
4.05-5.50	0	0	1	4
Number of cases	20	34	41	39
Average dosage	1.39 gm	1.92 gm	2.15 gm	3.26 gm
Average duration	37 days	34 days	24 days	23 days

As the total effective dose can only be judged by cases that were known to be cured after a prolonged period of observation Table 3 is presented to show the maximum and minimum curative dose in 26 cases of the urea-stibamine group and 22 cases of the neostibosan group, in which cure is reasonably certain. That in certain cases a total dose below 1.0 gm of either drug may bring about a cure emphasizes the difficulty of deciding upon the total dose required at the time of treatment in any particular case. We have not been able to discover any reliable criterion which would assist in such a decision.

Our average total dose of urea-stibamine for children is about the same as that recommended by Indian workers (12, 13, 14), while that for adults is somewhat below it. But as we had no relapses among the cases treated with urea-stibamine we feel that a dosage of 1.00-1.50 gm for children and 1.50-2.50 gm for adults would be sufficient to cure the large majority of cases of kala-azar. In regard to neostibosan the total therapeutic dose varies in different hands. The manufacturers following Napier's suggestion originally recommended dosages of 0.75-2.00 gm for children and 2.30 gm for adults. The mean total dose given by

TABLE 3. *The maximum and minimum total dosage of Urea-stibamine and Neostibosan in cases which were known to be cured following a period of observation longer than seven months.*

	Urea-stibamine		Neostibosan	
	Children	Adults	Children	Adults
Number of cases	7	19	11	11
Max. dose	*3.85 gm	3.00 gm	2.30 gm	5.00 gm
Min. dose	0.95 gm	0.71 gm	0.70 gm	1.55 gm

*The patient that received this dosage was a child of 10 admitted with cancrum oris. The dosage was probably unnecessarily large as later experience indicates.

Napier (15) to 175 previously untreated patients who were cured was 2.064 gm. In treating Chinese children suffering from kala-azar Scott (16) used an average total dose of 1.6 gm, while Struthers (17) gave 1.6-2.0 gm to children and 2.6-3.0 gm to adults. Compared with these, our average total dose of neostibosan for both children and adults is slightly higher. But in view of the number of relapses in our series, we recommend 1.50-2.50 gm for children and 4.00-5.00 gm as more effective dosages. Independently the manufacturers have recently advised to the same effect.

Response to treatment. One of the first signs of clinical improvement in kala-azar under treatment is the subsidence of fever. Table 4 shows the more marked effect in this respect with urea-stibamine. Cases which were afebrile at the time of treatment and cases in which the temperature was distorted by intercurrent complications are of course not included for this study. The rapid fall of temperature under urea-stibamine therapy is sometimes very striking even after one or two doses. The white count (Table 5) in the peripheral blood tends to rise under treatment in the absence of complications. In some cases there may be a moderate drop during the early part of the treatment but as a rule the counts will approach normal by the end of three months from the commencement of treatment. Marked drop in the white count occasionally occurs under treatment but as it happens without treatment and is usually associated with marked fall in the percentage of granulocytes it should be regarded as a complication of kala-azar, though treatment may precipitate its onset. This will be referred to later.

TABLE 4. *Effects of treatment on fever.*

	Urea-stibamine	Neostibosan
Number of cases	22	41
1-3 days	5	1
4-7 ,,	7	6
8-14 ,,	7	16
15-21 ,,	2	9
21-31 ,,	1	6
Over 31 ,,	0	3

The rate of reduction in the size of spleen under treatment is more rapid as is shown by the index of reduction in Table 5.

TABLE 5. *Effects of treatment on the white count and the size of spleen at end of 3 months from the commencement of treatment.*

	Urea-stibamine	Neostibosan
Number of cases	29	26
White count above 5000	28	23
White count below 4500	1	3
*Index of reduction of spleen	1.28	0.81

*Enlargements of spleen are classified into 4 categories.

O = Not palpable.

I = Palpable at costal margin to 2.5 cm in children and 3.5 cm in adults below costal margin.

II = From 2.5 cm in children and 3.5 cm in adults below costal margin down to level of umbilicus.

III = Beyond level of umbilicus.

Index of reduction is the remainder obtained by subtracting from the figure indicating the initial category, the figure indicating the category after 3 months from the commencement of treatment. For example, if the initial category was III which became I after treatment, the index will be 2.

The question of cure in kala-azar is always a problem. Patients must be followed for many months after the completion of treatment without any evidence of recurrence of infection before a cure can be pronounced. There is no other reliable criterion of cure. On the other hand the recovery of a few parasites from a spleen or liver puncture within a short period (arbitrarily this period may be fixed at one month) after treatment does not necessarily mean failure to cure. We can point to 5 cases in which parasites were found as long as 19 days after a course of treatment with neostibosan but which were later proved to be cured by repeated negative spleen punctures. When, however, parasites are still present in smears from a spleen or liver puncture one month after treatment especially accompanied by other signs of activity of kala-azar, further treatment must be promptly instituted. The number of such cases in the neostibosan series is surprisingly large as shown in Table 8. In some of these cases, Hosp. Nos. 33980, 27894, and 30551, reinfection cannot be excluded but the others must be regarded as therapeutic failures.

Failures with urea-stibamine have been reported from India (18) but in our series none was observed.

Out of a total of 158 patients treated with urea-stibamine or neostibosan alone, 24, 13 children and 11 adults, died. In 13 of these patients the total dose administered was so small that it could not have possibly contributed to their death. Some of them died of severe complications shortly after admission while others were removed from the hospital against advice and later died at home. One of them, an infant of 5 months, was treated with small doses of urea-stibamine intraperitoneally and later developed symptoms of intestinal obstruction due to extensive peritoneal adhesions apparently the result of irritation from urea-stibamine. This patient thus died from a therapeutic misadventure and illustrates the danger of giving urea-stibamine by the intraperitoneal route. In 11 cases, Table 9, the patients, 7 children and 4 adults, received a fair amount of drug which may have in some way contributed to their death. The mortality rate, calculated upon this basis, would work out to be 6.4 per cent for urea-stibamine and 7.4 per cent for neostibosan. The difference is hardly appreciable. It is interesting to note that in case 31865 cancrum oris developed under treatment and in case 31464 a cancrum oris which showed signs of healing, broke down again under treatment. From these data one may draw the general conclusion that urea-stibamine is a more potent therapeutic agent than neostibosan in the treatment of kala-azar.

Toxic reactions. Table 6 shows the various toxic reactions met with in patients under treatment with urea-stibamine or neostibosan. The points to be noted are, first, that the tendency to bleeding is 10 times more frequent in the urea-stibamine series, sometimes necessitating the suspension of treatment, second, abdominal pain is 5 times more frequent with urea-stibamine, third, renal irritation is 2.5 times more frequent with urea-stibamine, fourth, herpes zoster occurred only with urea-stibamine, and finally one case treated with urea-stibamine showed alarming shock-like symptoms. Whether by giving urea-stibamine as intensively and in as large single doses as neostibosan was given, the incidence of toxic reaction would not be even higher is difficult to say. As it is, the conclusion is justified that the toxicity of urea-stibamine is considerably higher than neostibosan.

TABLE 6. *Toxic reactions including all cases treated with one or more than one drug.*

	Urea-stibamine	Neostibosan
Number of patients treated	80*	109
Immediate cough	5	12
Dizziness	4	3
Nausea	5	13
Vomiting	10	13
Abdominal pain	4	1
Muscular pain	1	2
Febrile reaction	4	4
Increase of bleeding	8	1
Urticaria	4	3
Herpes zoster	4	0
Renal irritation	4	2
Shock-like reaction	1	0
Total incidences of reactions	54	54

*This figure does not include a child of 5 months treated with urea-stibamine intraperitoneally (0.62 gm) which caused extensive peritoneal adhesions and later intestinal obstruction with fatal result.

Serious complications under treatment. Table 7 shows the important complications which occurred during or shortly after treatment. There does not seem to be any difference between the two drugs in the incidence of severe complications. The feeling prevails that with the exception of cancrum oris treatment is better suspended for a while in the presence of any serious complication. Cancrum oris is, however, a desperate condition and justifies desperate measures. It is interesting to note that a few cases of cancrum oris did actually recover (Table 7) with the continuance of specific treatment.

TABLE 7. *Important complications during or shortly after treatment, excluding dead patients.*

	Urea-stibamine	Neostibosan
Number of patients treated	70	93
Agranulocytosis	3	2
Marked granulocytopenia	4	6
Lobar pneumonia	2	1
Bronchopneumonia	0	1
Cancrum oris	2	1
Septic infections*	11	18
Active tuberculosis	1	4
Dysentery	5	5
Scarlet fever	0	1
Diphtheria	0	1
Epidemic parotitis	1	1
Total incidences of complications	29	41

*Septic infections include cellulitis about face, cervical lymphadenitis, ulcerative stomatitis, otitis media, mastoiditis and severe upper respiratory infections.

Relative cost. For mass treatment the cost of a drug is always an important consideration. Calculated upon the basis of above recommended dosages and on the assumption that the drugs are obtained in large quantities directly from the manufacturers and free of import duties, neostibosan is about one and half times for children and twice for adults the cost of urea-stibamine.

TABLE 8. *Cases in which one and even two courses of Neostibosan failed to cure. In cases 33980, 27894 and 30551 reinfection is possible.*

Hosp. No.	Age	Duration	1st. Course	Spleen* positive after	2nd. Course	Spleen* positive after	3rd. Course	Period* of observation	End result
33980	5 mos.	½ mos.	1.45 N	332	0.55 N	—	—	1	Died
30082	6	5 mos.	1.00 N	142	2.10 N	—	—	53	Unknown
27894	2½	2 mos.	2.00 N	350	1.03 U	—	—	21	Unknown
37283	9	2 yrs.	2.00 N	166	1.90 N	75	1.475 U	77	Unknown
35419	7	1 mos.	2.50 N	47	1.00 N 1.75 U	—	—	23	Unknown
38640	4	3 mos.	2.05 N	60	2.00 N	—	—	157	Cure
30551	27	½ mos.	2.50 N	30	2.50 N	265	2.00 U	401	Cure
31709	32	2 mos.	3.45 N	113	2.45 U	—	—	647	Cure
39623	22	½ mos.	3.40 N	54	2.50 U	—	—	203	Cure
36289	8	12 mos.	2.75 N	31	—	—	—	60	Unknown
30138	18	6 mos.	2.50 N	37	2.50 N	—	—	403	Cure

*Figures in these columns are in days after completion of course of treatment.
U denotes urea-stibamine and N, neostibosan.

TABLE 9. *Cases in which death occurred during treatment with Neostibosan or Urea-stibamine.*

Hosp. No.	Age	Duration	Complications before treatment	Dosage at which fatal complications occurred	Total dosage	Nature of fatal complications
21041	13 yrs.	3 yrs.	Furunculosis Diarrhoea	1.00 U	1.00 U	Lobar pneumonia Increase of furunculosis Increase of oedema
26323	15 ,,	3 ,,	Diarrhoea	1.55 U	1.55 U	Serofibrinous pleurisy Furunculosis Diarrhoea increased
29131	29 ,,	1 yr.	None	0.75 U	0.90 U	Lobar pneumonia
22287	9 ,,	4 yrs.	Severe anemia Chronic parotitis	2.025 U	2.025 U	Broncho-pneumonia
23775	5 ,,	3 mos.	Oedema Chronic otitis media	0.90 N	1.20 N	Cancrum oris
31865	8 ,,	5 ,,	Bacillary dysentery	1.70 N	1.70 N	Agranulocytosis Cancrum oris
33043	4 ,,	9 ,,	None	0.70 N	0.80 N	Broncho-pneumonia Ulcerative stomatitis
35137	1 yr.	3 ,,	Diarrhoea	1.05 N	1.95 N	Broncho-pneumonia
38325	2 yrs.	7 ,,	Oedema	2.00 N	2.00 N	Granulocytopenia Broncho-pneumonia 3 wks. after treatment
33980	5 mos.	½ mo.	None	1.45 N	2.00 N	Relapse Broncho-pneumonia
31461	14 yrs.	4 yrs.	Adv. Pulm. Tb. Cancrum oris healing	1.05 N	1.25 N	Recurrence of cancrum oris Broncho-pneumonia

U denotes urea-stibamine and N, neostibosan.

SUMMARY AND CONCLUSIONS

From a study of 63 cases treated with urea-stibamine, 95 cases with neostibosan and 18 cases with more than one drug at different times the following conclusions are reached:—

1. An adequate course of treatment with urea-stibamine should consist of 1.00-1.50 gm for children and 1.50-2.50 gm for adults. With neostibosan the dosage should be 1.50-2.50 gm for children and 4.00-5.00 gm for adults.

2. Urea-stibamine is not a pure chemical compound and has a varying antimony content while neostibosan is a well standardized single chemical compound. In their therapeutic value in kala-azar, urea-stibamine is definitely more potent but at the same time more toxic than neostibosan.

3. Patients treated with either of these drugs must be followed for at least 7 months, a year if possible before cure can be pronounced. This is more important with patients treated with neostibosan than with those with urea-stibamine. Recovery of parasites from a spleen or liver puncture one month after the completion of a course necessitates prompt institution of further treatment.

4. Future improvement in the chemotherapy of kala-azar lies in the production of an organic pentavalent antimony compound as well standardized and non-toxic as neostibosan but possessing the high therapeutic potency of urea-stibamine.

LITERATURE

1. *Brahmachari, U. N.* Chemotherapy of antimonial compounds in kala-azar infection. Part I. Ind. J. Med. Res. **10**: 492, 1922.
2. *Gray, W. H. and Trevan, J. W.* Experiments on antimony compounds used in Bilharzia disease and kala-azar. Trans. Roy. Soc. Trop. Med. and Hyg. **25**: 147, 1931.
3. *Shortt, H. E., Craighead, A. C., and Swaminath, C. S.* A brief resume of recent kala-azar research with special reference to India. Ind. J. Med. Res. **16**: 221, 1928.
4. *Shortt, H. E. et al.* Reports of the Kala-azar Commission. India, (Report No. II 1926-1930). Ind. Med. Research Mem. No. 25. Aug. 1932.
5. *Napier, L. E.* Pentavalent compounds of antimony; urea-stibamine; analysis of treatment in 70 cases. Ind. J. Med. Res. **16**: 901, 1929.

6. *D'Oelsnitz and Carcopino, E.* Un cas de kala-azar autochtone de l'adulte avec production d'ascite au cours du traitement stibie. Guerison par l'urea stibamine. Bull. et Mem. Soc. Med. Hopit. de Paris, 1933 3rd ser. No. 26, 1165.

7. *D'Oelsnitz and Carcopino, E.* Effets favorables de l'urea stibamine dans le traitment des formes stibio-resistantes du kala-azar. Ibid. p. 1171.

8. *Ghosh, S., Chopra, R. N., and Chatterjee, N. R.* Urea-stibamine: Its preparation and composition. Ind. J. Med. Res. **16**: 461, 1928.

9. *Napier, L. E. and Mullick, M. N.* The intensive treatment of kala-azar by neostibosan. Ind. Med. Gaz. **63**: 445, 1928.

10. *Napier, L. E.* The pentavalent compounds of antimony in the treatment of kala-azar. Part VI. A comparison of results with different compounds. Ind. J. Med. Res. **19**: 705, 1932.

11. *Zahra-Neumann, C.* A report on the treatment of infantile kala-azar. Trans. Roy. Soc. Trop. Med. and Hyg. **26**: 383, 1933.

12. *Shortt, H. E. and Sen.* Final report on the use of urea-stibamine in kala-azar. Ind. J. Med. Res. **12**: 335, 1924.

13. *Kapur, N. C.* Observations on the treatment of kala-azar with urea stibamine in the medical outpatient department of the Medical College Hospital, Calcutta. Ind. Med. Gaz. **60**: 206, 1925.

14. *Brahmachari, U., Majumder, A. R. and De, R. B.* The intensive antimonial treatment of Kala-azar Urea-stibamine. Part II. J. Trop Med. and Hyg. **36**: 1, 1933.

15. *Napier, L. E.* The pentavalent compounds of antimony in the treatment of Kala-azar. Part VII. Neostibosan: Diethyl-amine Para-aminophenyl stibiate; 254 cases. Ind. J. Med. Res. **19**: 719, 1932.

16. *Scott, A. V.* The treatment of Kala-azar in children. Arch. of Dis. in Childhood **7**: 213, 1932.

17. *Struthers, E. B.* Neostibosan in the treatment of Kala-azar. China Med. J. **45**: 1, 1931.

18. *Greig, E. D. W. and Kundu, S.* Observations on two cases of Kala-azar resistant to treatment. Ind. J. Med. Res. **12**: 689, 1925.

20. A Clinical Study of The Early Manifestations of Chinese Kala-Azar

Lee, C.U. and Chung, H.L. *Chinese Medical Journal*, 49: 1281-1300, 1935.

李宗恩, 钟惠澜 《黑热病初期之临诊现象》，载于《中华医学杂志》，1935年，49:1281-1300 页。

中文摘要（见 1934 年《中华医学杂志》第 20 卷第 4 期 555 页） 据考察五十例初期黑热病所得之结论如下：黑热病之初起为潜伏，逐渐，或忽然而生。其最普通之病征为发热、软弱、畏寒、盗汗、厌食、头痛、咳嗽、便秘、体量减轻、腹泻、鼻衄、腹胀、及流鼻涕等。初期患者，有时除感觉软弱不适，或厌食腹泻外，并无异常之处，故诊断实不可能，甚至发热及其他病征已显然时，验血及身体检查恒无变态。势须屡经刺脾及肝之检查，以及取验骨髓与淋巴腺，然后其诊断始可定。一经诊定，其治疗则甚易焉。

翻译概要 协和医院内科在过去 14 年（至 1934 年 6 月）收治了 394 位黑热病患者。作者总结了其中 51 位黑热病初期患者（两个月内、受过教育且表达清楚）的临床观察：（1）患黑热病与年龄无关，也没有明显的诱发因素，如疟疾和伤寒；（2）初期临床症状不明显，有的疑似伤寒，也有突发症状的；（一般症状见上）（3）早期症状一般为发烧，儿童会有淋巴结肿大，也许有呼吸道感染； （4）黑热病的典型症状为：肝脾肿大、淋巴细胞减少和蛋白沉淀异常，这些指征在发病初期均不明显，因此很难确诊。（5）需鉴别的疾病包括：结核、疟疾、伤寒和不规则发烧。因此，如果病人间歇发热，进行性淋巴细胞减少，就有患黑热病的可能；（6）如能早期诊断，病人一般对治疗反应良好。

THE
CHINESE MEDICAL JOURNAL

VOLUME 49 December, 1935 NUMBER 12

A CLINICAL STUDY OF THE EARLY MANIFESTATIONS OF CHINESE KALA-AZAR

C. U. LEE AND H. L. CHUNG

Department of Medicine, Peiping Union Medical College, Peiping

Volumes have been written on kala-azar during the past three decades. Investigators in both India and the Mediterranean region have published clinical descriptions of the disease in its more or less fully developed stage. There is, however, scanty reference in the literature to its early manifestations. Standard text-books on tropical diseases as well as monographs on kala-azar (1 and 2) contain no detailed description of the salient features of the disease in its early stage apart from mentioning the various possible modes of onset. Rogers (3) referred to three cases of early kala-azar which simulated typhoid fever. Low (4) described a similar case which presented considerable difficulty in diagnosis as it showed so few of the ordinary symptoms of kala-azar. One of us (5) recently reported an early case in which tuberculosis and undulant fever were at first suspected.

During a period of fourteen years up to the end of June 1934, 394 etiologically proven cases of kala-azar were admitted to the Peiping Union Medical College Hospital. In 51 of these when the patients first presented themselves the disease was considered to be in its early stage on account of the short duration of their illness, which varied from a few days to two months, and the absence of many of the diagnostic features of kala-azar. Cases in which though the subjective complaints have been of relatively short duration, the enlarged spleen and liver, the changes in the blood and nutrition and other findings indicate that the disease process must have been active for many months, are excluded. The latter being as a rule either children or uneducated and unobservant adults are not always reliable in their history, while the large majority or those selected for this study are either teachers, professional men or students themselves or the dependents of such.

One of the main reasons which prompted this study is the difficulty of diagnosis in connection with early kala-azar. We have had many instances in which repeated efforts had to be made before the parasites could be discovered. It is hoped that this study will be of assistance to clinicians in kala-azar endemic regions from the point of view of differential diagnosis of obscure fevers.

Predisposing conditions. In North China kala-azar is mainly a disease of children and young adults of either sex. In general children are relatively more susceptible and among them the disease is apt to run a more severe and alarming course. It may be here noted that the majority of the thirty-one adults included in this study are natives of South China which is outside of the kala-azar endemic area and developed the disease after a shorter or longer residence in or around Peiping. This is possibly due to an accidental social selection.

Indian investigators (2, 6, 7,) emphasize the importance of malaria and typhoid fever as predisposing factors from the point of view either of actual infection, or of development of clinical symptoms of kala-azar. This apparently does not hold true in North China. There were only four out of 51 patients that gave a history of tertian malaria within two years of the onset of symptoms of kala-azar. Only in one of our patients were we able to elicit a history of typhoid fever. As the diagnosis of kala-azar in its early stage is always a matter of difficulty, blood cultures and Widal reactions were performed as a diagnostic routine in 41 patients and these were all negative except in three patients who were recently vaccinated against typhoid. One of our children, however, developed typhoid fever in the course of kala-azar and another shortly after a complete course of specific treatment. In consideration of the high intelligence of the majority of our patients and the fact that statements of patients relating to past illnesses in these early cases of kala-azar are more reliable than in chronic cases, these findings seem significant.

Since the majority of our patients are well-to-do, we cannot satisfy ourselves that nutritional deficiency played any important role as a predisposing factor. Five of our adult patients showed evidence of active pulmonary tuberculosis, three had chronic maxillary sinusitis at time of onset of kala-azar and five of our children developed symptoms of kala-azar following an attack of measles. These are probably accidental associations. In short we fail to discover any constant factor which might predispose a person to infection, or development of clinical symptoms of kala-azar.

Incubation period. The incubation period in human kala-azar is difficult to determine as it is as a rule impossible to ascertain the date of infection. In Manson's text-book on Tropical Diseases a case is on record in which an Englishman developed symptoms of kala-azar after a residence of ten days or more correctly twenty days* in an endemic area. Muir (8) referred to a patient who fell sick after living in an infected house for fourteen days. Brahmachari (1) stated that in one of his cases the incubation period was not longer than a month. In the case reported by one of us (5), vague symptoms developed three and half months after what is thought to be a laboratory infection. Napier (2), however, mentioned of a case in which the patient had lived for eighteen months away from an endemic area before the first symptoms appeared. Thus the incubation period of kala-azar may vary from several weeks to many months.

Since all the adult patients and nearly all the children in the present study had been residents in the endemic area for at least one year before the onset of kala-azar, it is not possible to determine the incubation period. There are, however, two infants, one born in April and the other in June, who developed early symptoms of kala-azar in the following September and November respectively, that is when they were about four and half months old. With apparently healthy parents there was no question of intrauterine infection. The incubation period in these two instances must be within four and half months.

The onset and course. The clinical onset of kala-azar may be very insidious or may simulate closely that of typhoid fever but occasionally may be quite sudden.

When it is insidious different groups of symptoms may present themselves. Illness may begin with vague symptoms referable to the

*Low believes twenty days was the correct time in this case (B.M.J. 2: 758, 1919).

respiratory tract. Many patients date their illness to an attack of coryza or of a mild cough accompanied by slight feverishness, headache, dizziness and perhaps aches in the muscles or joints. Epistaxis rarely occurs as the first symptom but may be frequent later in the course of the disease. In a few patients a purulent infection of one or several of the paranasal sinuses was present at time of onset of kala-azar. Other patients complain chiefly of a general feeling of lassitude, slight feverishness in the afternoon and a tendency to night sweats and if they have also a cough present a picture of early tuberculosis. Some of these patients show a mental anxiety over their illness and sleep badly at night. In children it may be night cries, fretfulness and general irritability, that first engage the attention of the parents. In some cases gastro-intestinal complaints are the presenting symptoms, a mild diarrhoea with or without mucus in the stools or constipation. In children complaints of abdominal pain are rather frequent in the early days of their illness. Anorexia is not a prominent symptom among adults but in infants refusal or regurgitation of feedings may be the first sign that led the parents to suspect something amiss. In a few cases children were brought in by parents merely on account of an undue pallor and upon examination were found to have a moderate degree of anemia which later turned out to be due to kala-azar.

One-third of our patients ran a febrile course almost typical of typhoid fever. They complain of a slight chilliness and feverishness accompanied by headache, general malaise, lassitude and some impairment of appetite. For the first few days they manage to keep on their feet but by the fourth or fifth day with the fever mounting up to 40° C they are compelled to take to their bed. The fever in such cases is of a high continuous type, lasts several weeks and subsides by lysis. During this period there is usually some abdominal distension, constipation and epistaxis. There are, of course, no typical rose spots. Nor is the degree of prostration so marked as it is in typhoid fever and the patients do not tend to sink into the so-called typhoid state. The discrepancy between the degree of temperature and the pulse rate may be present but is usually not so striking as it is in typhoid fever. A tendency to profuse perspiration is, however, more in keeping with early kala-azar than with typhoid fever. The differential diagnosis of such cases of early kala-azar is sometimes extremely difficult and will be again referred to.

In addition we have records of a number of patients who took ill quite suddenly. Some of these patients are college students who declared that they never missed one day's tennis or football until the day they came down suddenly with chill, fever and sweating, so like a typical malarial paroxysm that they are usually treated as such. The paroxysm may occur like malaria once daily or every other day usually in the afternoon. But it may also occur twice in twenty-four hours, once in the early morning and again in the afternoon or evening.

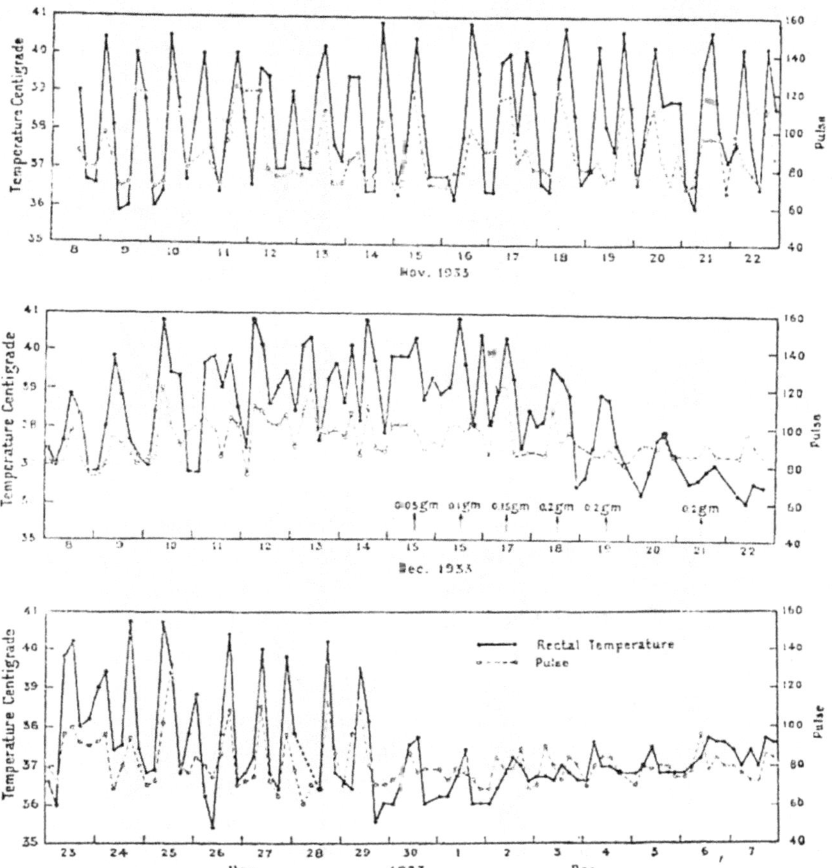

Chart I. A case (a man of 22) of one months's duration at time of admission, November 8, 1933 showing high intermittent fever with at times double rises in 24 hours, a short period of remission and response to urea-stibamine

This so-called double remittent fever was observed in about one-third of our cases. It may appear on only two or three successive days or may last for several weeks. Now and then triple rises may occur daily for several days but are uncommon. In such cases chills and profuse sweating may be very marked.

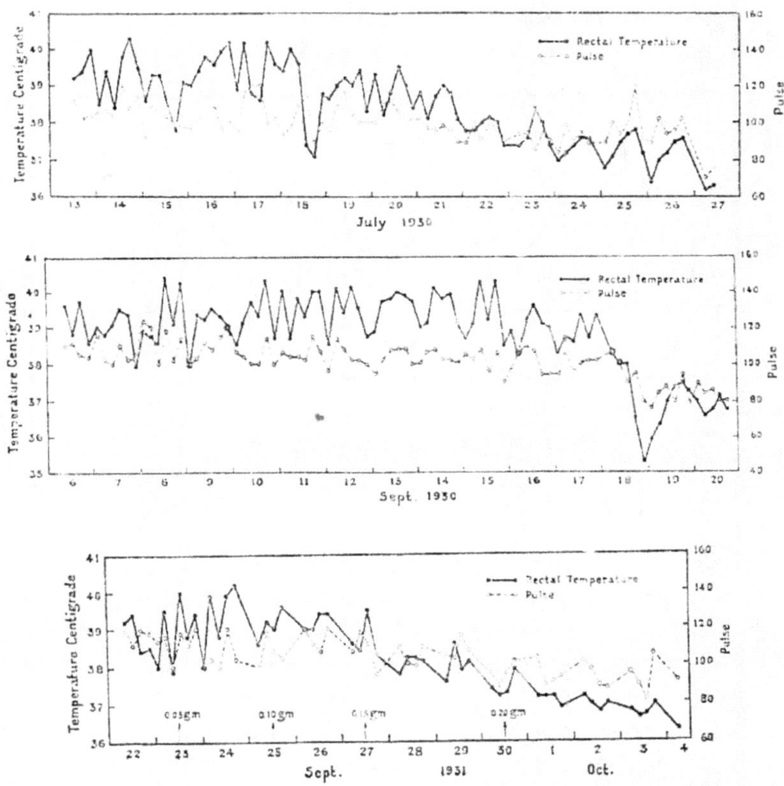

Chart II. A case (a woman of 23) of two weeks' duration at time of admission on July 13, 1930 showing high irregular fever, two spontaneous remissions and response a year later to urea-stibamine

In some cases there may be a history of sudden onset of high and sustained fever, which later breaks up into a regular or irregular intermittent or remittent type. The accompanying temperature charts (Charts I, II, and III) illustrate the various types of fever met with in early cases of kala-azar. The same case may show different temperature curves at different periods. When the disease is more advanced a prolonged course of daily remittent fever is the rule.

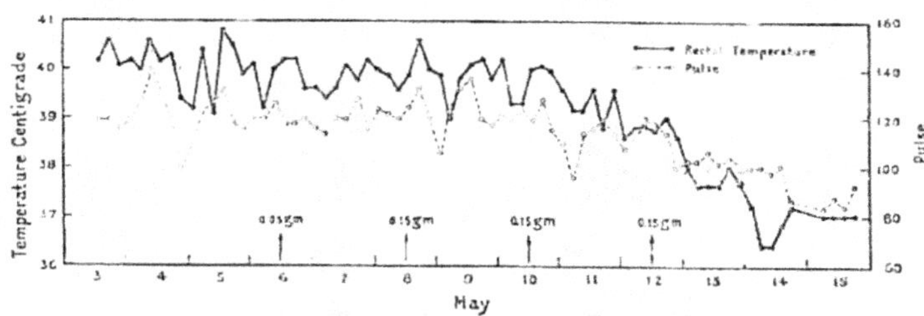

Chart III. A case (a woman of 28) of one month's duration showing typhoid-like temperature curve and response to neostibosan

Another type of explosive onset is exemplified by patients in whom kala-azar is ushered in by an attack of abdominal pain or of convulsion especially in children. In the case of one woman patient, the convulsive fits were mistaken for hysteria. The presence of fever and subsequent developments, however, clarified the diagnosis eventually. One child was brought in on account of sudden convulsion associated with fever, cough and diarrhoea. Another child had sudden abdominal pain with fever. Both proved to be cases of early kala-azar.

Chart VI shows the relative frequency of symptoms in early kala-azar in general. We only need to refer to certain symptoms which occur exclusively in women and children. In women menorrhagia or amenorrhoea may be among the early symptoms of kala-azar. In one patient each menstrual period would aggravate her symptoms of kala-azar or bring on a relapse. In children chronic kala-azar of one or two years' duration has a definite effect in retarding their growth, so that a boy of twelve years sick with kala-azar would look like one of seven or eight years. In the early stage, this interference with growth is not obvious but observant parents may remark a failure to gain in both weight and height in these children.

Remissions. The course of kala-azar is not continuous but frequently interrupted at least in its early stage by remissions simulating undulant fever. When the disease is allowed to run its natural course sooner or later a remission occurs. In most of our cases the first remission came within two or three weeks of the onset or within four to six weeks in some cases. The period of remission usually lasts from a few days to several weeks but sometimes longer. As time goes on the relapses become more and more prolonged until finally the patient may go for months without a remission. On the other hand we have had two cases in which relapses and remissions alternated for periods of eleven and twenty-six months respectively and each relapse never lasted beyond five weeks.

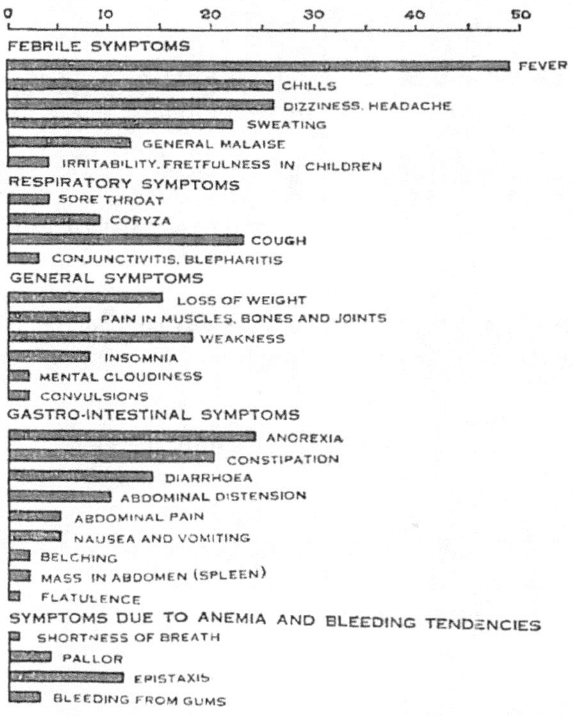

Chart IV. Relative frequency of symptoms in early cases of kala-azar.

During a remission all symptoms may subside so that the patient feels well enough to resume his work. He may regain his lost weight. The spleen may be reduced in size and the blood picture may become normal and a previously weakly positive globulin test may become negative (Charts V, VI, VII).

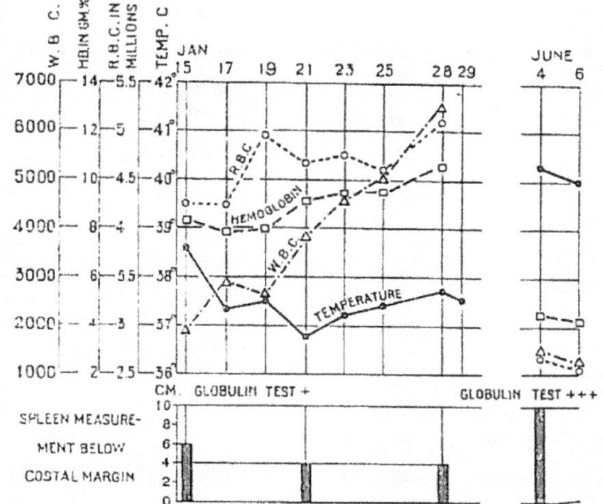

Chart V. Case showing clinical improvement during a remission.

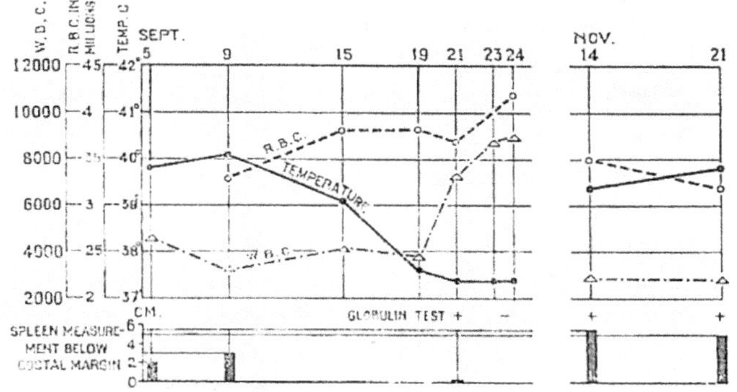

Chart VI. Case showing clinical improvement during a remission.

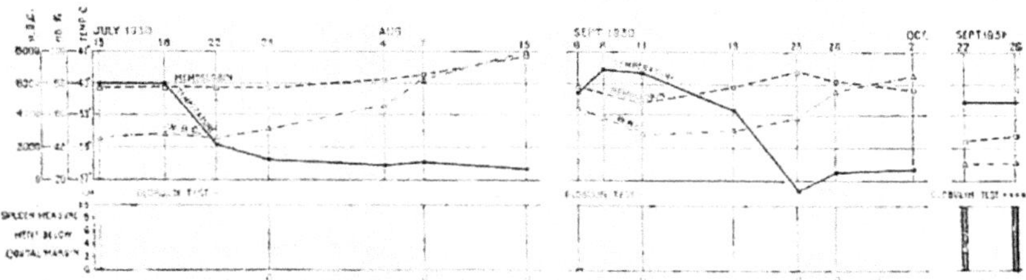

Chart VII. Case showing clinical improvement during two periods of remissions.

Physical findings. Within the first few weeks of onset a physical examination often reveals nothing characteristic apart from the fever. There may be some congestion of the throat and the tonsils and perhaps a mild degree of conjunctivitis. In some cases there may exist a rhinitis or maxillary sinusitis. The superficial lymph glands may be palpably enlarged especially in children. Hyperpigmentation of the skin, to which the disease owes its name, does not occur in early kala-azar. In children a degree of pallor is often evident shortly after onset of the disease.

An examination of the chest may show some evidence of mild bronchitis in the form of scattered rhonchi or rales and perhaps a systolic murmur over the precordium. There is often some tachycardia, which may even persist for some time after a complete course of treatment. Exceptionally the pulse may be dicrotic. The abdomen usual feels normal. In two of our cases there was, however, marked gaseous distension. The spleen is often not palpable in the early days of the illness. In the present series there were eleven cases in which the spleen was at first not palpable. In three of these it was not palpable even by the end of two months after onset. In two, it never became palpable at any time before, during or after treatment. As a rule the spleen becomes enlarged sooner than the liver. Yet in two of our cases the spleen was not palpable while the liver was demonstrably enlarged. Table 1 also shows that an enlargement of the spleen is usually associated with a fairly marked degree of leucopenia, below 4000 per c. mm. It occurs more readily among children than among adults. There is no definite correlation between the degree of enlargement of the liver or spleen and the duration of the disease; a patient with a relatively short history may have a larger spleen and liver than another patient with a much longer history of illness. We have seen an infant of six and half months who had symptoms for only one and half month but whose spleen and liver were as much enlarged as those of another child of four years, who had been sick for eleven months.

Blood picture. In the early stage of kala-azar the blood picture may be quite normal or slightly below the normal. In the present series there were three cases with neither anaemia nor leucopenia, six cases with slight anemia and moderate leucopenia and three cases with slight anemia but a normal leucocyte count. In the rest the anemia and leucopenia were both fairly marked. In general we find that the reduction in the number of leucocytes occurs more readily than the red blood cells or the hemoglobin. A severe anemia usually indicates a moderately advanced stage of the disease.

A differential count of the leucocytes often shows greater reduction in the percentage of granulocytes than the other types of cells. In twenty of our fifty-one cases the granulocytes were below 50 per cent at the time of admission. They may rarely drop to below twenty per cent. In two of our cases a state of acute agranulocytosis developed under observation. These have already been included as cases 1 and 3 in the paper on acute agranulocytosis by Zia and Forkner (9). It is only necessary to note here that this serious complication may occur quite early in the course of kala-azar. The reticulocytes were estimated in a few cases and were found to be within normal limits. In one case there was a definite rise following treatment with neostibosan.

Yang and Chen (10) have shown that in kala-azar the platelets are invariably decreased. They were, however, dealing with well advanced cases. In the present series of early cases the platelets were estimated in 21 patients. The counts were between 200,000 and 300,000 per cmm in two cases, between 100,000 and 200,000 in sixteen cases and below 100,000 in three cases. Thus it seems that a tendency to reduction of the platelets occurs quite early in the course of kala-azar though seldom to a severe degree. In the three cases in which they were markedly reduced to below 100,000, the bleeding time was considerably prolonged.

Globulin precipitation test and plasma proteins. The globulin precipitation test described by Sia (11) has been adopted as a routine procedure in all cases in which kala-azar is suspected or to be excluded. It is not specific for kala-azar as a positive reaction sometimes occurs in Banti's disease, schistosomiasis, chronic malaria, and rarely even in typhoid fever, but in these latter conditions it is seldom so strongly positive as in a well developed case of kala-azar. In the early stages of kala-azar, however, it is often negative. In Table 1, for instance, there are recorded 19 cases in which the test was negative. In addition there are two other cases which showed a negative globulin precipitation test over six months after the onset of symptoms. As a rule it becomes definitely positive when the disease has been of more than three months' duration. In twelve of these twenty-one cases the test remained negative throughout the course of treatment, while the rest became positive subsequently. Exceptionally a weakly positive test may become strongly positive during or shortly after a course of treatment.

TABLE I. *Blood picture, globulin test and the size of spleen and liver on admission in early cases of kala-azar presenting difficulty in diagnosis*

Case No.	Sex	Age in years	Duration in days	R.B.C. in million	Hgb. %	W.B.C.	Globulin test	Spleen°	Liver°
1	F	35	1	4.0	85	5,300	—	0	0
2	F	25	4	5.0	98	7,200	—	0	0
3	M	21	5	4.4	87	4,200	—	0	0
4	M	20	7	4.7	90	5,100	+	P	0
5	M	20	7	4.7	87	2,300	—	2.5	0
9	M	35	14	3.6	55	3,000	Not done	0	0
10	F	23	14	4.0	72	4,100	—	0	0
12	M	27	21	3.1	58	4,800	—	0	0
13	M	21	21	4.4	84	2,900	—	2.0	0
14	M	19	21	3.1	64	3,200	—	4.0	0
16	M	23	23	4.7	95	3,900	—	2.5	4.0
17	M	18	25	3.8	60	3,200	—	P	0
18	M	22	30	3.9	67	2,400	—	3.0	P
21	M	21	56	5.6	120	4,800	—	0	0
22	F	32	60	4.2	63	6,850	Not done	0	1.5
24	M	29	60	4.4	68	2,150	—	0	0
				Children					
6	M	7	7	4.5	67	4,100	—	6.0	2.5
7	M	4	9	3.3	63	3,200	—	2.5	P
8	M	3	11	4.4	93	5,850	Not done	0	0
11	M	9.5/12	14	3.6	60	2,600	—	5.0	5.0
19	M	5/12	35	4.2	76	3,500	—	4.5	2.0
23	M	12	60	4.2	65	5,800	—	P	0
25	F	1	60	2.8	46	3,900	—	0	3.0

\+ = weakly positive. ° O = not palpable.
P = just palpable at costal margin.
Figures = number of cm. below costal margin.

Sia and Wu (12), Ling (13) and others have shown that in kala-azar there is an increase in the globulin and euglobulin fractions of the blood plasma. These results were, however, from studies on well established cases of kala-azar. In our series of early cases plasma proteins were determined in thirteen cases within two months of the onset of symptoms. In the majority of these the albumen fraction is low, while the globulin and euglobulin fractions are slightly above the normal value, in many cases before the globulin precipitation test becomes positive.

Urinary findings. Of forty-three cases in which the urine was repeatedly examined, twenty-five showed a trace or one plus albumen in the urine. In seven of these twenty-five cases hyaline or granular casts were found in the sediments. These findings were transient and disappeared with the subsidence of fever or with the progress of treatment. There was, however, one case which had marked albuminuria with red blood cells and casts in the sediments of the urine and definitely lowered renal function. The nephritis, however, cleared up under treatment with neostibosan.

Complications. Respiratory infections such as acute rhinitis, pharyngitis and bronchitis are common events in early as well as in advanced cases of kala-azar. More serious complications also occur in the early course of kala-azar as is shown in Table 2.

TABLE 2. *Complications in early kala-azar*

Lobar or broncho-pneumonia	4	cases
Active pulmonary tuberculosis	3	,,
Typhoid fever	1	case
Bacillary dysentery	1	,,
Scarlet fever	1	,,
Acute agranulocytosis	2	cases
Septic infections*	6	,,
Miscarriage	1	case

*Septic infections include otitis media, pelvic infections, cystitis due to B. coli, cellulitis about the face, metastatic ophthalmia and furunculosis.

Diagnosis. The diagnosis of kala-azar in its early stage when fever is the only manifestation is frequently a matter of great difficulty inasmuch as such cardinal findings as splenomegaly, anemia, leucopenia and globulin precipitation test are absent or negative. In such cases the first few attempts to recover the causative organism by organ puncture or blood culture often fail. Table 3 illustrates the difficulty of establishing a diagnosis encountered in five cases. In such early cases we depended upon spleen puncture or liver puncture when the spleen was not accessible or blood culture according to the technique of Young and Van Sant (14). In a few cases the diagnosis was established by biopsy of the marrow of the sternum. Biopsy of an enlarged superficial lymph gland advocated by Cochrane (15) is another useful procedure but was not resorted to in the present series of cases. In

TABLE 3. *Difficulty in establishing a diagnosis*

Case No.	Date		Procedure	Results	
				smear*	culture*
1	Mar.	24	Spleen puncture	—	—
		26	Blood culture	o	—
		29	Spleen puncture	—	—
	April	9	Liver puncture	—	—
	May	21	Spleen puncture	+	+
9	Oct.	14	Spleen puncture	—	o
		16	Liver puncture	—	—
			Blood culture	o	+ (Reported on Nov. 1)
		30	Spleen puncture	—	o
14	Aug.	27	Spleen puncture	—	o
			Blood culture	o	Contaminated
	Sept.	25	Blood culture	o	+ (Reported Oct. 11)
	Oct.	2	Spleen puncture	+	o
18	Nov.	11	Spleen puncture	—	—
		25	Spleen puncture	—	—
			Blood culture	o	—
	Dec.	12	Spleen puncture	+	—
46	Mar.	9	Liver puncture	—	—
		15	Liver puncture	—	—
		17	Liver puncture	—	—
		20	Spleen puncture	+	—

* O = Not done. — = Negative.

more advanced cases of kala-azar the parasites may be found by carefully examining a blood smear (16) or a smear of nasal discharge as shown by Forkner and Zia (17) recently. Material obtained from a liver or spleen puncture is routinely examined by direct smear as well as cultured. The results in Table 4 show that the chances of finding the parasites are much better in a smear than by culture. This is fortumate because culture takes much longer time thereby causing delay in starting the treatment and may fail through bacterial contamination of the medium.

TABLE 4. *Summary of results of examination by direct smear, and by culture of material from spleen and liver punctures in 46 patients**

Procedure	Smear and culture both positive	Smear positive		Smear negative but culture positive
		Culture negative	Culture contaminated	
Spleen puncture	14	12	2	2
Liver puncture	10	3	3	0
Total	24	20		2

*The diagnosis of the remaining five cases of the present study was made by blood culture or bone marrow biopsy.

Differential diagnosis. The conditions from which a case of early kala-azar have to be differentiated are tuberculosis, malaria, typhoid fever, and undulant fever. The afternoon fever, nightsweats, respiratory symptoms and perhaps slight loss of weight naturally suggest pulmonary tuberculosis. Absence of definite physical signs in the chest and a negative x-ray examination of the lungs will be evidence against it. Abdominal tuberculosis is, however, not so easy to exclude. One patient went through an exploratory laparotomy on account of the presence of a soft tender mass in the left upper quadrant of the abdomen which at the operation was found to be an enlarged and hemorrhagic spleen, so soft that it felt like a sponge. There was also a considerable amount of bloody effusion in the peritoneal cavity. This case was later proved to be one of kala-azar.

Many cases of early kala-azar are treated with quinine as cases of malaria. As a rule the fever in kala-azar is not so regularly intermittent and periodic and repeated search for malaria parasites in blood smears will be of course negative.

The differential diagnosis between typhoid fever and kala-azar is most difficult. Time and again cases of early kala-azar have been mistaken for typhoid fever because of the high continuous fever, palpable spleen, leucopenia, and perhaps a dicrotic pulse. The Widal test may even be positive though the titre is usually low. The cultures of blood, urine and stool are of course negative for organisms of the typhoid group. The reverse is also true. Typhoid fever has been mistaken for early kala-azar because of the relative non-toxic appearance of the patient, the absence of skin rash and the negative serological and bacteriological evidences during the early weeks of illness. In such cases patients have even been subjected to a liver puncture in an attempt to establish the diagnosis.

Finally the remittent fever, the profuse sweating, the blood picture, palpable spleen and the tendency to remission make kala-azar clinically sometimes indistinguishable from undulant fever, we had one case in which the patient's serum agglutinated B. abortus in titres from 1/40 to 1/160 on different occasions. Time usually clears up the diagnosis. Experience has taught us always to think of kala-azar in the presence of an obscure fever accompanied by a definite and progressive leucopenia. A definitely positive globulin precipitation test affords some aid in differential diagnosis but a negative reaction does not exclude kala-azar.

Specific treatment. In discussing the specific treatment of kala-azar in its early stage we need only refer to those patients of this series who received treatment within three months of the onset of their symptoms and whose fate is known; of these there were 38 cases. Since those treated with tartar emetic, neostam or fouadin are so few, conclusions can only be drawn from cases treated with either neostibosan or urea-stibamine. Patients are considered cured only after a follow-up period of at least nine months; the majority of them having been followed for many years. From Table 5 it will be seen that among the patients (Categories 1, 2, 4, and 5) treated with neostibosan one of the children relapsed after 2.10 gm and died of complications and three of the adults relapsed after dosages ranging from 3.40 gm to 5.0 gm and were subsequently cured by urea-stibamine. Patients treated with urea-stibamine on the other hand all recovered except one child (Category 7) who died of complications resulting from urea-stibamine given intra-peritoneally. In regard to the curative dose it seems that in general a relatively larger quantity of neostibosan than urea-stibamine should be given though as has been pointed out by Lee and Chu (18), it is difficult to decide the total dose required to effect a cure at the time of beginning or during treatment in any particular case. Thus in the case of neostibosan a total dose as small as 0.70 gm brought about a cure in one child, while a total dose of 2.10 gm failed in another and in the case of urea-stibamine a total dose of 0.71 gm effected a cure in an adult but in the majority of cases a bigger dose was necessary and would be advisable.

TABLE 5. *38 patients who received specific treatment within three months of the onset of symptoms of kala-azar and whose fate is known*

Category	Adults or children	Antimony compounds*	Max. & min. dosage in gm.	Results	No. of cases
1	Children	Neostibosan	0.70-2.45	Cure	6
2	Children	Neostibosan	2.10	Relapsed and died of complications	1
3	Children	Neostibosan	0.175	Taken home during treatment and died at home	1
4	Adults	Neostibosan	2.75-3.65	Cure	11
5	Adults		Neostibosan 3.4 -5.0	Relapsed and cured by urea-stibamine 2.00-2.54	3
6	Children	Urea-stibamine	0.95-1 10	Cure	2
7	Children	Urea-stibamine intraperitoneally	0.62	Died of peritonitis and intestinal obstruction	1
8	Adults	Urea-stibamine	0.71-3.00	Cure	10
9	Adults	Neostam + urea-stibamine	Neostam 2.075 Urea-stibamine 1.25	Cure	1
10	Adults	Fouadin	60 cc. of 6.3% solution	Cure	1
11	Adults	Potassium antimonyl tartrate	1.698	Cure	1

*Antimony compounds are usually given intravenously; occasionally given intramuscularly in children when veins are not available. It was given to one infant intraperitoneally with disastrous result (Category 7).

Under specific treatment subsidence of fever and improvement in the blood picture constitute the early signs of beneficial effect. In these respects urea-stibamine seems to be more potent. Comparing the group of adults treated with neostibosan (Category 4) with those treated with urea-stibamine (Category 8) one finds that the average amount of neostibosan to bring the temperature down to normal is 1.25 gm and that of urea-stibamine is 0.47 gm. Again the average amount of neostibosan given before the blood picture becomes normal or practically normal, is 2.95 and that of urea-stibamine is 1.71 gm. The number of children treated with these two drugs is too small to serve as a basis for comparison.

In these early cases the reduction in the size of the spleen and liver is fairly rapid under specific treatment. When the spleen is just palpable at the costal margin or extends not more than 3 cm. beyond it at the commencement of treatment, it will be no longer palpable at the end of or shortly after a course of antimony therapy and when it extends 4-9 cm beyond the costal margin before treatment, it will be as a rule just palpable after the treatment. It may of course again increase in size should a relapse occur at a subsequent date. The change of the globulin precipitation test from a positive to a negative reaction is also fairly rapid under antimony therapy.

From above we gain the impression that kala-azar in its early stage responds to specific treatment fairly promptly. Many patients show entirely normal findings at the end of fourth or fifth week from the commencement of treatment. As compared with more advanced cases included in the study by Lee and Chu (18) the rate of improvement seems more rapid.

Napier (19) suggests that early cases do not respond best to treatment but that the contrary is actually the case. We are not in a position to refute or endorse this suggestion on account of the small number of patients dealt with. It is true that four out of 21 patients treated with neostibosan relapsed after doses which may be considered fairly adequate, but more advanced cases are also liable to relapses with neostibosan. At the same time all the thirteen early cases treated with urea-stibamine, including those which relapsed after a course of neostibosan, responded satisfactorily.

SUMMARY AND CONCLUSIONS

From a study of 51 proved cases of kala-azar seen within two months of the onset of symptoms, the following conclusions are obtained.

1. Apart from the general observation that children are relatively more susceptible and among them the disease is apt to run a more severe course, there is no discoverable factor which may predispose a person to infection or development of clinical symptom of kala-azar. Malaria and typhoid fever do not play an important role as predisposing factors, as seems to be the case in India.

2. The clinical onset of kala-azar may be very insidious or may simulate closely that of typhoid fever, but occasionally may be quite sudden. The common early symptoms in order of their relative frequency are fever, chills, dizziness, headache, anorexia, cough and sweating. The temperature curve may simulate that of malaria, typhoid fever, tuberculosis or undulant fever, but may be quite irregular and bizzare. Daily double rises of temperature occur frequently but not in every case. Remissions and relapses of symptoms are characteristic features in the early course of kala-azar. During remissions not only the fever and other symptoms subside, but the blood picture tends to improve, and enlarged spleen or liver shows reduction in size and a previously weakly positive globulin precipitation test becomes negative.

3 Within the first few weeks of onset the clinical and laboratory findings often reveal nothing characteristic apart from the fever. The superficial lymph glands may be palpably enlarged especially in children.

There may be evidences of mild upper respiratory infection. The spleen and liver may or may not be palpable at the costal margin. The blood picture may be entirely normal, but as a rule a degree or leucopenia appears relatively early with a greater reduction in the percentage of granulocytes than other types of cells. The globulin precipitation test is often negative though a study of the plasma proteins may show the globulin and euglobulin fractions to be slightly above the normal values.

4. Serious complications may occur in the early course of kala-azar. Of special interest are the two cases of acute agranulocytosis.

5. The diagnosis of kala-azar in its early stage is frequently a matter of great difficulty inasmuch as such cardinal signs as splenomegaly, leucopenia and globulin precipitation test are absent or negative. Repeated efforts to recover the causative organism are often necessary. The conditions from which a case of early kala-azar must be differentiated are tuberculosis, malaria, typhoid fever and undulant fever. Experience teaches that in the presence of an obscure fever accompanied by a definite and progressive leucopenia the possibility of early kala-azar must be borne in mind.

6. Early cases of kala-azar respond satisfactorily and readily to specific treatment. Many patients show entirely normal findings at the end of fourth or fifth week from the commencement of treatment. Com-

pared with more advanced cases the rate of improvement seems more rapid.

LITERATURE

1. *Brahmachari, U.* A Treatise on Kala-azar. John Bale, Sons and Danielsson, Ltd., London, 1928.
2. *Napier, L. E.* Kala-azar—A Handbook for Students and Practitioners. Second Edition, Oxford University Press, London, 1927.
3. *Rogers, L.* Fevers in the Tropics. Third edition Oxford University Press, London, 1919, pp. 25-28.
4. *Low, G. C.* An interesting case of kala-azar from the point of view of diagnosis. Trans. Roy. Soc. Trop. Med. & Hyg. **23**: 305, 1929.
5. *Chung, H. L.* An early case of kala-azar, possibly a laboratory infection. Nat. Med. J. China, **17**: 617, 1931.
6. *Lloyd, R. B., Napier, L. E. and Paul, S. N.* The serological control of treatment of kala-azar with observations on the significance of hypoprotein-anemia. Ind. J. Med. Res. **16**: 1065, 1929.
7. *Napier, L. E. and Krishnan, K. V.* A study of the aetiology and epidemiology of kala-azar in India. Ind. Med. Gaz. **66**: 603, 1931.
8. *Napier, L. E. and Muir, E.* Kala-azar—A Handbook for Students and Practitioners. Oxford University Press, London, 1923.
9. *Zia, L. S. and Forkner, C. E.* The syndrome of acute agranulocytosis and its occurrence as a complication of kala-azar. Am. J. Med. Sci. **188**: 624, 1934.
10. *Yang, C. S. and Chen, K. T.* The blood platelets in kala-azar. Nat. Med. J. China, **16**: 34, 1930.
11. *Sia, R. H. P.* A simple method for estimating quantitative differences in the globulin precipitation test in kala-azar. China Med. J. **38**: 35, 1924.
12. *Sia, R. H. P. and Wu, H.* Serum globulin in kala-azar. China Med. J. **35**: 527, 1921.
13. *Ling, S. M.* Distribution of protein fractions in the serum of kala-azar patients. Proc. Soc. Exp. Biol. & Med. **27**: 247, 1930.
14. *Young, C. W. and Van Sant, H. M.* The diagnosis of kala-azar by blood culture. Proc. Soc. Exp. Biol. & Med. **19**: 299, 1922.
15. *Cochran, S.* The superficial lymph nodes as a source of Leishmania for diagnosis in cases of kala-azar. J. Trop. Med. & Hyg. **15**: 9, 1912.
16. *Young, C. W. and Van Sant, H. M.* Leishmania donovani in the peripheral blood. Proc. Soc. Exp. Biol. & Med. **20**: 219, 1923.
17. *Forkner, C. E. and Zia, L. S.* Viable Leishmania donovani in nasal and oral secretions of patients with kala-azar and the bearing of this finding on the transmission of the disease. J. Exp. Med. **59**: 491, 1934.
18. *Lee, C. U. and Chu, C. F.* Relative value of urea-stibamine and neostibosan in the treatment of kala-azar. Chinese Med. J. **49**: 328, 1935.
19. *Napier, L. E.* The pentavalent compounds of antimony in the treatment of kala-azar. Part VII. Neostibosan: Diethyl-amine para-amino-phenyl-stibiate; 254 cases. Ind. J. Med. Res. **19**: 719, 1932.

21. Simple Technique for Studying Schistocome Worms In Vitro

Lee, C.U. and Chu, H.J. *Proceedings of the Society for Experimental Biology and Medicine*, 32: 1397-1400, 1935.

李宗恩、朱宪彝《一项在体外培养血吸虫的简单技术》，载于《实验生物医学学会会议记录》，1935 年，32:1397-1400 页。

翻译概要　长期在体外培养血吸虫是研究其生长过程和药物研究必须的技术，但此前最长只能体外培养 21 天。我们发明了一种密封的玻璃培养皿，可延长血吸虫在体外存活时间至 75 天，而且可以随时进行显微镜观察。

8106 C

Simple Technique for Studying Schistosome Worms in Vitro.

C. U. LEE AND H. J. CHU.

From the Department of Medicine, Peiping Union Medical College, Peiping.

The study of adult parasitic helminths is often handicapped by difficulties in keeping them alive for prolonged observation outside the body of their host. According to Coutelen[1] the first attempts at artificially rearing helminth parasites were made by Lönnberg in 1892 and Tower in 1900, using cestodes. Reichenow and Wülker[2] referred to the use of artificial media by Meggit in preserving the life of cestodes for several days and by Meier, who through frequent changes of media kept alive certain trematodes and cestodes from fish for as long as 21 days.

In metabolic studies of helminth parasites such as undertaken by Alt and Tischer[3] and Brand[4] observations must be made on living parasites *in vitro*. Such studies might have been more exhaustive if the life of the parasites could be maintained for several days instead of a few hours. In testing the anthelmintic value of a drug preliminary *in vitro* experiments seem an essential step and for such purposes intestinal helminths are usually used. Ryoji,[5] however, studied the action of certain organic antimony compounds on *Clonorchis sinensis in vitro* and Oesterlin and Krainick[6] tested the action of about 80 organic substances on many kinds of parasites including adult schistosomes. The latter authors remarked that the adult schistosomes recovered from experimentally infected mice do not remain alive in serum for long, probably as a result of bacterial growth in the medium.

In the course of chemotherapeutic studies in experimental schistosomiasis japonica the present authors devised a simple technique by which it was possible to keep adult schistosomes alive in artificial medium for weeks and if necessary for months without difficulty. This technique may prove useful in future studies in which it is

---

[1] Coutelen, F., *Ann. de Parasit.*, 1927, **5**, 1.

[2] Reichenow, Ed., und Wülker, G., Leipzig, 1929, p. 125.

[3] Alt, H. L., and Tischer, O. A., PROC. SOC. EXP. BIOL. AND MED., 1931, **29**, 222.

[4] Brand, Th., von., *Z. f. Vergleichende Physiol.*, 1933, **18**, 562.

[5] Ryoji, S., *Okayama Igakkai Zasshi*, 1927, **39**, 1809 (Abstract) *Trop. Dis. Bull.*, 1930, **27**, 959.

[6] Oesterlin, M., und Krainick, H., *Zentralb. f. Bakt., Parasit. u. Infekt.*, 1934, **132**, 222.

desired to keep adult schistosomes or allied parasites alive for prolonged observation *in vitro*.

The difficulties in maintaining in artificial medium the life of such adult helminths as the schistosomes obtainable in an aseptic condition are mainly 2, accidental bacterial contamination and inspissation through evaporation of the medium. These difficulties can be surmounted by the use of a flask of the type employed in tissue culture work but smaller in size, which any competent glass blower can make to order (Fig. 1, A). The body of the flask is about 4 cm. in diameter and not more than 0.7 cm. in depth to permit observation under an ordinary low power objective (*e. g.*, Leitz No. 3) of the microscope without disturbing the contents. The mouth of the flask should be relatively wide, about 1.2 cm. in diameter, so as to allow easy introduction of the parasites and should be provided with a tight fitting rubber cap, which can be extemporized from the severed bulbous end of an ordinary rubber teat (Fig. 1, B, C). The flasks plugged with cotton wool and wrapped up in paper should be sterilized in the hot air sterilizer while the rubber caps placed in a petri dish are sterilized by steam under atmospheric pressure.

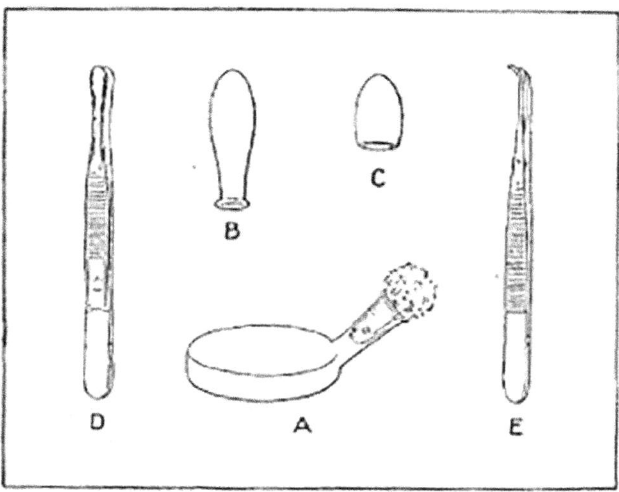

FIG. 1. For explanation of lettering see text.

The schistosomes are obtained from the large portal veins of an animal, preferably a rabbit on account of its large size, which has been infected 8 to 10 weeks previously with cercariae from snails. Rigid aseptic technique must be practiced in laying open the main portal veins entering the hilum of the liver. In extracting the worms from the lumen of the veins a pair of forceps with round and smooth tips (Fig. 1, D) should be used to avoid injury to the parasites. They are then first transferred to a small covered petri dish containing warm sterile Locke's or saline solution and later distributed in a number of culture flasks into each of which exactly 2 cc. of the medium to be used have been previously introduced by means of a 10 cc. pipette under bacteriological technique. In carrying the worms over the neck of the flask a pair of fine, curved forceps (Fig. 1, E) are of advantage. The culture flasks with their mouths covered by rubber caps are then placed in an incubator at 37°C. to simulate the natural environment of the schistosomes.

Daily or, when indicated, hourly observations should be made of the culture to ascertain the condition of the worms. Any culture, in which there is evidence of bacterial contamination by a cloudy appearance of the medium should be discarded. The condition of the worms may be judged by their movements. Those showing no movements can be induced to do so by gently heating the flask over an electric hot plate unless they are actually dead. No worm should be regarded as dead without passing this test. Worms becoming sluggish after a few days will show renewed activity upon a change of fresh medium.

Almost any animal blood sera will serve as satisfactory media. We have tried horse, sheep and rabbit serum and ascitic fluid from cases of cirrhosis of liver with success. The addition of Locke's solution or dextrose does not improve the efficiency of the media. The duration of life of the worms in different media varies somewhat depending probably more upon the inherent vitality of the parasites rather than upon the nature of the medium.

Table I shows the results of a typical experiment. In this experiment it would seem that ascitic fluid and sheep's serum are more efficient than horse or rabbit serum but in another experiment some worms lived for 21 days in rabbit serum. With changes of fresh

TABLE I.

Duration of Life in Days of Schistosomes in Different Media without Change.

	Horse serum	Sheep serum	Rabbit serum	Ascitic fluid
Copulating pairs—Males	(2) 13-14	(2) 18	—	(2) 13-14
Females	(2) 9-11	(2) 14-15	—	(2) 19-20
Mature males	(6) 9-22	(7) 13-19	(9) 7-10	(4) 14-16
Mature or almost mature females	(2) 8-17	(3) 8-9	—	—
Immature females	(5) 8-16	(5) 10-14	(8) 7-9	(5) 17-20
Aver.	13.4	14.4	8.2	16.3

Figures in parentheses indicate number of worms studied.

medium at intervals it is possible to prolong the life of the schistosomes for 2-3 months. In one experiment in which the medium (in this case rabbit serum) was renewed at intervals of 1-2 weeks 2 schistosomes lived for 82 days.

It was also found that not more than 4 or 5 worms should be placed in each flask. Overcrowding shortens the duration of life of the parasites as shown by the experiment recorded in Table II.

TABLE II.
The Effects of Overcrowding. The Worms Were All Mature Males Uniform in Size. Plain Ascitic Fluid Was the Medium Used. No Change of Medium.

No. of flasks	No. of worms in each flask	Aver. duration of life in days
3	3	16
3	6	13
3	9	11
3	12	10
1	30	8

Summary. A simple technique is described for maintaining the life of adult schistosomes *in vitro* over a period of several weeks which, with frequent changes of medium, may be extended to 2½ months. This is made possible by the use of small tissue culture flasks, which prevent bacterial contamination and desiccation of the media. The latter may be either horse, sheep or rabbit sera or human ascitic fluid.

8107 C

Action of Various Organic Antimony Compounds on Schistosoma Japonicum in Vitro.

C. U. LEE AND H. L. CHUNG.

From the Department of Medicine, Peiping Union Medical College, Peiping.

By using the technique described by Lee and Chu[1] studies were made of the lethal action of the following 4 antimony compounds on adult *Schistosoma japonicum in vitro.*

Trivalent Antimony Compounds

Sodium antimonyl tartrate; chemically pure, supplied by E. Merck, Germany.

Fouadin. This is a 6.3% solution of a colorless powder, antimony III-pyrocatechin-disulphonate of sodium, supplied by Bayer and Company, Leverkusen, Germany.

[1] Lee, C. U., and Chu, H. J., in press.

22. Cysticercus Cellulosae in Man with Special Reference to Involvement of Central Nervous System

Chung, H.L. and Lee, C.U. *Chinese Medical Journal*, 49:429-445, 1935.

钟惠澜、李宗恩《囊虫病的中枢神经系统症状》，载于《中华医学杂志》，1935 年，49:429-445 页。

翻译概要 在协和医院收治的 22 例囊虫病人中，10 例有中枢症状，如癫痫、昏迷、视力下降、头痛、失眠、抑郁、幻觉、嗜睡、歇斯底里等。本文详录了 10 个病例并回顾了文献中囊虫病的中枢症状（其中一例由于甲状腺肿大而显示甲亢症状），并对诊断、治疗和预防做了简单的讨论。

Chinese Medical Journal, 1935, Vol. 49: 429-445.

CYSTICERCOSIS CELLULOSAE IN MAN WITH SPECIAL REFERENCE TO INVOLVEMENT OF CENTRAL NERVOUS SYSTEM

H. L. Chung and C. U. Lee

Department of Medicine, Peiping Union Medical College, Peiping.

In China human tapeworm infestation was known in ancient times, since the famous *Pen Ts'ao*, the Chinese Classical Herbal, written about 1,500 B.C., contains records of tapeworms and their treatment.

In modern times a Report of the Research Committee of the China Missionary Medical Association published in 1910 (1) states that a medical officer in Tsingtao saw during a period of eight years between 1899 and 1907 thirteen cases of *Taenia solium* and twenty-eight cases of *T. saginata* among European residents. It is difficult to be certain that these cases were of local origin. The same report contains records of tapeworms (species not specified) from other parts of China, one case from each of the provinces of Chihli (Hopei), Hunan and Chekiang, three cases from Peking (Peiping) and three cases from Hankow, and also the entry "tapeworms not common; variety *T. solium*" for Manchuria. In 1912 Clark (2) reported a case of *T. solium* in the province of Yunnan and remarked that taenia infestation was common in that province.

The first case of human infestation with *Cysticercus cellulosae* in China was reported by Barnes in 1922 (3). The patient, a native of Weihaiwei, developed generalized cysticercosis after his return from India. Numbness of the legs and arms preceded the appearance of subcutaneous nodules, in some of which pain was felt. Diagnosis was made on biopsy of cysts from the right biceps muscle. No mention was made of intestinal taeniasis. Here the possibility of patient being infected outside of China exists. Faust in 1923 (4) stated in reference to somatic taeniasis that it was diagnosed once from Soochow. Mills reported in 1924 (5) a case of cysticercus in a Chinese youth from Manchuria seen in the Peiping Union Medical College. A nodule removed from the right pectoral muscle 12 years after its first appearance was identified to be *Cysticercus cellulosae*. In this case there was no evidence of intestinal taeniasis. In 1930 Hu, Khaw and Frazier (6) reported five cases in one of which cysts were present in the brain. Chin in 1933 (7) studied the histopathology of these cases as well as five other cases from the P.U.M.C. clinics and two cases referred from other clinics. Feng in 1934 (8) added another case of cysticercosis cellulosae under the conjunctiva.

Since Mills first drew attention to the condition, cysticercosis cellulosae has been unequivocally diagnosed in the P.U.M.C. Hospital in 22 patients, 12 of which have already been recorded in the literature as stated above. Of these 22 patients ten showed symptoms of involvement of the central nervous system. Although Chin (7) has discussed briefly the neurological symptoms in his pathological study, a detailed analysis of these ten cases, five of which are recorded for the first time, may serve to emphasize further the causal relationship of this parasite to certain nervous disorders, - epileptiform fits with or without psychosis, dementia, etc.

SUMMARY OF FINDINGS IN TEN CASES OF CYSTICERCOSIS OF CENTRAL NERVOUS SYSTEM

The ten patients, all residents of North China, included seven men and three women, whose ages ranged from 17 to 44 years. Their symptoms and findings are summarized in Table 1. In six of the ten patients the results of studies of the cerebro-spinal fluid are presented in Table 2.

TABLE 1

Epileptiform or convulsive fits (Case Nos. 1,2,3,4,6,8,9,10)	8
Stupor or coma without convulsions (Case No. 5)	1
Permanent paresis and atrophy of muscles of limbs (Case No. 7)	1
Temporary numbness, weakness or paresis of muscles of tongue, of face or of limbs (Case Nos. 2,3,4,6,8)	5
Transient motor aphasia (Case Nos. 1, 4, 6)	3
"Rheumatic" pains; shooting pains down legs (Case Nos. 5, 7)	2
Formication under the skin (Case No. 7)	1
Blurred vision (Case Nos, 2, 8, 9)	3

Headache (Case Nos. 1, 2, 3, 4, 5, 8) 6
Dizziness (Case Nos. 1, 3, 8) 3
Nausea and vomiting (Case Nos. 1, 2, 6, 8) 4
Insomnia (Case No. 1) 1
Irritability of temper (Case Nos. 2, 8) 2
Depression with defective memory (Case Nos. 2, 8) 2
Drowsiness (Case Nos. 2, 3, 4) 3
Hallucinations (Case Nos. 2, 5) 2
Delusions (Case No. 2) 1
Dementia (Case Nos. 2, 5) 2
Temporary psychosis (Case Nos. 5, 10) 2
Fever (Case Nos. 2, 4, 5, 7, 8) 5
Urticaria (Case No. 3) 1
Jaundice and abdominal pain (Case No. 6) 1
Hyperthyroidism, evidenced by bilateral exophthalmos, tachycardia, cardiac enlargement and raised basal metabolic rate (Case No. 2) 1
Presence of palpable subcutaneous nodules (Case Nos. 2, 3, 4, 6, 7, 8, 9, 10) 8
Intestinal taeniasis (Case Nos. 1, 2, 4, 10) 4
Leucocytosis (Case Nos. 1, 2, 4, 5, 7, 10) 6
Eosinophilia (Case Nos. 2, 6, 7) 3
Bilateral papillitis (Case No. 4) 1
Bilateral papillitis with choked discs (Case No. 1) 1
Bilateral papillitis with choked discs and retinal hemorrhages (Case No. 2) 1

DISCUSSION

Human infection with *Cysticercus cellulosae* usually follows oral ingestion of viable ova of *T. solium*. Thus a person harbouring an adult *T. solium* in his small intestine may constitute a source of infection to others from the presence of infective ova in his stools (cross infection) or to himself (external auto-infection). Occasionally it is said that such a person may suffer from cysticercosis through regurgitation of viable ova from his own small intestine back into the stomach, where the larvae are set free and find their way into the body (internal auto-infection). But Yoshino's recent experiments (9) show that the cysticercus larvae

TABLE 2. *Cerebro-spinal fluid findings*

Case No.	Appearance	Pressure in mm of water	Leucocytes per c mm			Sugar mgm per 100 cc	Chlorides as NaCl mgm per 100 cc	Pandy's test	Wassermann reaction	Colloidal gold reaction	Gum mastic reaction
			Total	Neutrophiles per cent	Lymphocytes per cent						
1	Normal	350	60	44	56	—	—	—	Negative	Negative	Negative
2	,,	250	15	—	—	57	698	Positive	,,	Paretic	Paretic
4	,,	100	440 (Aug. 9)	47	53	45	695	Positive	,,	Negative	Negative
			130 (Aug. 13)	0	100	—	—				
			24 (Sept. 3)	0	100	49	547				
7	,,	120	7	—	—	65	720	Negative	,,	Negative	?
8	,,	80	7	0	100	84	731	Positive	—	—	—
10	,,	120	2	0	100	55	729	Negative	Negative	Negative	Negative

are actually freed in the small intestine by the action of alkaline intestinal juice, which means that a person harbouring adult *T. solium* runs the constant risk of internal auto-infection. This seems to be the case in Case 2 of the present series, in which fresh crops of palpable cysts continued to appear under observation. One might reason, of course, with MacArthur (10) that these cysts have existed for a long time and became palpable as a result of changes occurring after the death of the embryos in the cysts. But judging from their morphology after excision, these palpable cysts do not appear to be all dead. That auto-infection occurs perhaps more frequently than it is generally believed is indicated by the fact that four of our ten patients had intestinal taeniasis at one time or another.

In passing it may be of interest to refer to certain symptoms which may occur at the time of invasion of the body by the young cysticerci. The presence or absence of these symptoms probably depends upon the number of cysticerci invading the body at any one time and the reactivity of the individual. In Case 2 the patient had a period of fever accompanied by leucocytosis and eosinophilia several months before the onset of manifest symptoms of cysticercosis, even before the detection of intestinal taeniasis. Case 3 had a history of urticaria which may or may not be of significance, but in Case 5 the fever, headache and muscle tenderness which occurred a year after the onset of cerebral symptoms of cysticercosis were probably related to a fresh invasion of the body by young cysticerci. In Case 8, the patient had a period of fever two months before the convulsive fits.

A perusal of the literature indicates that cysticercosis cellulosae may involve any organ or tissue of the human body. Vosgien (11) has described cases involving the visual apparatus (retina, vitreous body, lens, anterior chamber, iris, cornea, subconjunctiva, orbit, etc.), the central nervous system (brain, meninges, ventricles, pons, optic thalamus, basoganglia, spinal cord, etc.), the subcutaneous tissue, the skeletal muscles, the larynx, the lungs, the heart, the digestive tract, the pancreas, the liver, the peritoneum, the mesentery, the genito-urinary tract, the mammary glands and the bones. This wide distribution and the experimental work of Yoshino (12) leave no room to doubt that the route of dissemination of the young cysticerci is by the blood stream.

The brain appears to be the site of greatest predilection. Of the 807 cases collected by Vosgien (12), 330 (41 per cent) showed involvement of different parts of the brain, 120 (14.9 per cent) of the retina and 252 (31.1 per cent) of parts of the eye other than the retina. In discussing MacArthur's paper (10) on cysticercosis Blacklock referred to a series of cases investigated by Stephens in which there were 105 brain cases, 30 muscle cases and only two skin cases. The incidence of cysticercosis of the brain is, therefore, very high, especially if ocular cases are included. Cases of cerebral cysticercosis causing convulsions, epilepsy, paralysis, mental changes, loss of memory, etc. are not uncommon as pointed out by Vosgien (12), yet such are often regarded as mere medical rarities. Recently, however, MacArthur (10) stimulated renewed interest in cysticercosis as a cause of certain cerebral conditions, especially epilepsy. About one hundred persons are discharged annually from the British Army on account of epilepsy and after extensive study he was able to demonstrate that in many of these cases epilepsy was due to cysticercosis of the brain. He concluded with the statement that if an inquisitorial commission was to search in the lunatic asylums, institutions for epilepsy and general hospitals and fails to bring to light hundreds of unsuspected cases of cysticercosis, it would be the greatest miracle since Moses smote the rock.

When the brain is the seat of cysticerci, the most spectacular manifestations take the form of convulsive or epileptic fits. Eight of our ten patients had them. Except in Case 1, the first seizure occurred shortly after puberty or later in adult life. The attack is often preceded by numbness or twitching of the muscles of the face or arms, or transient motor aphasia. One patient complained of blurred vision before losing consciousness. The severity, frequency and character of the actual fit vary from patient to patient and from time to time in the same patient. The minor fits take the form of momentary spells of motor aphasia, attacks of dizziness, in one case accompanied by blurred vision, flushing of the skin, increased lacrymation and salivation, nausea, transient twitching or clumpsiness of muscles of the tongue, of the face or of the extremities, or a mere numbness or tingling in the legs. One patient went into a flight of uncontrollable temper following a lumbar puncture. In a major fit the patient falls unconscious showing all the features of true epilepsy, but the loss of consciousness may last from a few minutes to several hours and death may take place in status epilepticus. Following the fit there is often some confusion of the mind and a residual motor aphasia. In such cases sooner or later the mind deteriorates and a whole train of psychic symptoms manifest themselves; hallucinations, delusions, change of personality, dementia, and suicidal tendencies. Vosgien (12) in his monograph referred to cases of cysticercosis of the brain diagnosed during life as hydrophobia, general paresis or insanity. Recently MacArthur (10) also directed attention to the wide range of psychical disturbances in proved cases of cerebral cysticercosis.

Another type of case exists which presents a clinical picture suggesting some form of acute encephalitis. This is illustrated by Case 4 of the present series, in which the onset was sudden with fever and chills followed by stupor and hemiplegia, from which she recovered very slowly. Vosgien (12) referred to an exactly similar case reported by Bitot. Such cases often terminate in sudden death. [Tull and Subrahmanyan (13), Africa and Cruz (14) and Broughton-Alcock, Stevenson and Worster-Drought (15)]. Cases showing evidences of increased intracranial pressure are frequently mistaken for tumor of the brain and in Case 1 the patient was operated upon under such a diagnosis.

Very few patients having once developed brain symptoms recover. Dixon and Smithers (16) found among 71 cases of epilepsy due to cerebral cysticercosis only five ceasing to have fits. Our patient in Case 6 had been free from cerebral symptoms for two years when last seen. The patient in Case 1 came from a family in which the father, and five of his children (including the patient) had had fits during childhood. With the exception of the patient, the others had no more fits after the age of five. This probably indicates a strong element of nervous instability in the family rather than multiple cysticercus infections followed by recovery in all except the patient. The same may also be true in Case 9, in which one of patient's cousins had fits since childhood. The question arises as to whether symptoms attributable to cerebral cysticercosis are more prone to occur in subjects of certain nervous constitution. Cysticercosis in more than one member of the family, of course, occurs. Morrison (17) recently reported it in twin brothers.

Cases of cysticercosis involving the spinal cord are rarely encountered but there is some ground for regarding Case 7 as an example of it. The neurological findings in this patient suggest some such diagnosis as chronic anterior poliomyelitis or amyotrophic lateral sclerosis but in the presence of numerous cysticercus nodules in various parts of the body, cysticercosis of the spinal cord is a distinct possibility. Vosgien (12) gave 6 references on this condition. Some of the cases suggested the diagnosis of tabes dorsalis or amyotrophic lateral sclerosis. Recently Guillain, Bertrand and Thurel (18) reported an interesting case in which extensive basal and spinal meningitis and arachnoiditis from cysticercosis were found at autopsy.

Apart from the involvement of the central nervous system as a part of generalized cysticercosis, Case 2 is of interest in that the thyroid function was disturbed presumably from a mild degree of thyroiditis set up by the presence of cysts in the substance of the gland. In this patient there was moderate enlargement of the heart possibly as a result of hyperfunction of the thyroid, but the heart may also be the seat of cysticercus cysts such as was found in Case 5. In the case reported by Pulgram (19) the total cardiac arrhythmia was attributed to the presence of cysts in the myocardium and the bundle of His.

In regard to diagnosis, the cysticercus nodule when it appears under the skin has a characteristic feel which once acquired is diagnostic and its true nature is easily proved by biopsy. The presence of a number of these nodules in a patient presenting nervous symptoms is presumptive evidence of involvement of the central nervous system. But their absence under the skin does not exclude their presence in other parts of the body. Cases 1 and 5 illustrate this point. In the latter no subcutaneous nodules were detected either during life or on autopsy though numerous cysts were found in the brain and muscles. In such cases the diagnosis often remains obscure. Intestinal taeniasis past or present, if proven to be due to *T. solium* may provide a clue, but a very indirect one. Besides the ten cases reported in this paper we can point to several other cases in the P.U.M.C. clinic in which cerebral symptoms associated with intestinal taeniasis, but with no discoverable cysts, were suspected to be due to the progeny of *T. solium*. Cysts when calcified throw tell-tale shadows on x-ray films. In our limited experience roentgenological studies did not offer much help. Such studies were made in four of our cases with negative results. Dixon and Smithers (16) state that out of 179 cases of cysticercosis investigated by means of x-ray only 39 showed definite calcified cysticerci. It would thus seem that the value of x-ray examination is limited to only a small percentage of cases. Skin sensitization test was made only in two patients (Cases 3 and 4); one showed an immediate reaction while the other gave a negative result. According to MacArthur (10) it may be negative with heavy infections.

An eye ground examination is sometimes of value in establishing the presence of organic lesions in the brain. Three of our cases showed bilateral papillitis with or without choked discs or retinal haemorrhages. Such findings at once exclude idiopathic epilepsy as an explanation for the convulsive fits in these patients.

The blood picture shows some special features. A slight leucocytosis sometimes follows a fit or may be found in cases presenting cerebral symptoms accompanied by fever. Eosinophilia is not so constant a feature as might be expected. A marked leucocytosis with a high eosinophilia, up to 60 per cent probably indicates active invasion of the body by cysticerci such as may have occurred in Case 2.

As for cerebro-spinal fluid findings an examination of Table 2 will show that there is no distinctive feature. In certain cases there is evidence of increased intracranial pressure or of meningeal irritation. Pandy's test was frequently positive. In Case 2, the colloidal gold as well as the gum mastic reaction showed a distinct paretic curve without any evidence of syphilis.

The treatment of cysticercosis is symptomatic. No specific is known. If one takes MacArthur's view (10) that symptoms particularly those of the brain are more often due to tissue reactions about dead cysts, then a specific, if such exists, may do more harm than good. Certain symptoms, however, demand therapeutic measures. Simple decompression operation may be resorted to relieve increased intracranial tension such as was done in Cases 1 and 2. Severe headaches may be temporarily relieved by lumbar puncture as in Case 2. Large doses of sedatives may be given for frequent convulsive fits.

Prophylaxis consists of avoiding foods contaminated with viable ova of *T. solium*. Uncooked vegetables are particularly dangerous. Persons known to be harbouring *T. solium* should not be allowed to handle foods. Furthermore, it is important to avoid infection with the adult *T. solium* through eating improperly cooked measly pork for fear of subsequent internal and external auto-infection. For this reason also persons harbouring *T. solium* should be promptly and energetically treated. Aspidium is, however, a rather unsatisfactory drug against *T. solium*, as shown by Case 2. Recently Sokolovski (20) recommended giving of quinine through a duodenal tube. We have no experience with it.

SUMMARY

A short historical résumé is given of the reported cases of human cysticercosis in China.

An analysis of 10 cases of cysticercosis presenting symptoms of involvement of the central nervous system is made. One of these cases also showed hyperfunction of the thyroid apparently due to the presence of cysts in that gland. The diagnosis, treatment and prophylaxis of cysticercosis particularly of the brain are briefly discussed.

CASE PROTOCOL

CASE 1. A male Chinese medical student of 22, first admitted to the P.U.M.C. Hospital on Nov. 22, 1926 following a typical epileptic fit. His father, four of his brothers and sisters and he himself all had fits during childhood up to the age of five. The other members of the family ceased to have fits after childhood. Patient himself had a typical epileptic fit at the age of sixteen but was then free from symptoms until the present attack.

Examination after the fit yielded normal findings except for a small bitten wound on the inner surface of the left cheek, and a leucocytosis of 12,600 per cu. mm. No eosinophilia. Stool was negative for parasitic ova. Patient was discharged two days after admission with the diagnosis of idiopathic epilepsy. Soon afterwards patient complained of insomnia, vertigo and headache accompanied by nausea and vomiting and was found to have lateral nystagmus. Another seizure occurred on Dec. 2, 1926. During the same month he had five momentary spells of motor aphasia. At this time taenia ova of undetermined species were found in the stool on four different occasions. Treatment was attempted without apparent success, though stool was negative on subsequent examinations.

In Jan. 1927 patient had frequent frontal headaches associated with dizziness. On Feb. 18 headache became very severe with pain in the eyes. Bilateral neuroretinitis with retinal hemorrhages was demonstrated. On Feb. 25 presence of bilateral choked discs led to the suspicion of brain abscess. The cerebro-spinal fluid showed a pressure of 350 millimetres of water, 80 mg protein per 100 cc with a cell count of two erythrocytes and 60 leucocytes per cu. mm. of which 56 per cent were lymphocytes and 44 per cent neutrophiles. Wassermann, colloidal gold and gum mastic tests were negative.

On March 4 a right subtemporal decompression was done. As patient failed to improve, an exploratory craniotomy was performed on March 8. The cortex of the brain was very edematous and scattered over the temporo-sphenoidal lobes were a number of discrete nodules. One of these upon section established the diagnosis of *Cysticercus cellulosae*.

Following the operation headache and eye symptoms improved. Subsequently the patient continued to have at varying intervals seizures of a Jacksonian type often followed by transient motor aphasia. Patient died in the spring of 1934 in status epilepticus at his native home.

CASE 2. A girl of 20 was first admitted to the P.U.M.C. Hospital on Dec. 6, 1933, with fever of 14 days' duration. Nothing significant was found except a leucocytosis of 11,600 per cu. mm. and an eosinophilia of 3-15 per cent. An undue prominence of the eyes was noted with no apparent explanation. The stool examination was negative. The fever subsided in six days and patient was discharged with no definite diagnosis.

In Feb. 1934 patient visited the outpatient department complaining of general weakness, irritable disposition, palpitation of heart, loss of hair, puffiness of face and eye-lids and blurring of vision. In view of the prominence of the eyes with, lidlag a study of the basal metabolic rate was made showing 17.3 per cent above normal. There was, however, no other objective evidence of thyroid dysfunction.

In March, 1934 patient was readmitted with history of attacks of numbness and clumsiness of the tongue and the right hand two weeks previously. She had some fever, headache, sweating and nausea in the early mornings, and there appeared several subcutaneous nodules about the forehead.

Examination showed bilateral exophthalmus, localized swelling of both temporal regions (4 x 3 cm in size) and numerous subcutaneous nodules of 1.0 cm in diameter about the head and neck. Nodules were also palpable in the substance of the tongue and of the thyroid gland which, however, was not enlarged. Heart about 28 sq cm over-size by teleoroentgenography with a pulse rate of 90-100 per minute. Basal metabolic rate studied on four different occasions averaged 15.5 per cent above normal. The leucocyte counts were persistently high, ranging from 14,000 to 27,000 per cu mm with 25-61 per cent eosinophiles. Stools now positive for ova of taenia. Lumbar puncture yielded a clear fluid under slightly increased pressure. Pandy's test was positive. Colloidal gold and gum mastic tests showed typical paretic curves. Blood and spinal fluid Wassermann reactions were negative. Neurological examination was at the time negative except a bitemporal contraction of visual field for red color.

Mentally she was depressed with defective memory for recent events. During her three months' stay in the hospital, her condition went progressively downhill. Fresh subcutaneous nodules continued to appear about the head and upper part of the body. Headache became more severe and lumbar puncture afforded only temporary relief. Her vision became more blurred and fundi examination showed bilateral papillitis, retinal hemorrhages, and choked discs. On May 4 a right subtemporal decompression was performed to relieve the increasing intracranial pressure. Numerous cysts were found in the substance of the temporal muscle, over the dura and in the substance of the brain. These cysts on section proved to be *Cysticercus cellulosae*. No marked improvement followed the operation. Mentally she became more dull and answered questions very slowly. She was often found wandering about the ward aimlessly after midnight and unable to account for it. She had hallucinations and delusions. She had attacks of clonic convulsions of extremities with drowsiness. Mental deterioration progressed until she was unequal to the simplest arithmetic calculations.

In view of the continued formation of new cysts repeated attempts to expel the adult taenia resulted only in the passage of some segments of *Taenia solium*. Treatments were either by aspidium or by carbon tetrachloride. The patient was discharged on June 25, 1934 unimproved.

CASE 3. A male Chinese of 27 was admitted to the P.U.M.C. Hospital on April 1, 1929 for painless subcutaneous nodules. The first nodule was noticed in the right subclavicular area four years previously. Later more appeared over other parts of the trunk and the legs, the most recent ones being on the arms and the lower lip. The nodules grew slowly without symptoms. Four years previous to the appearance of the first nodule, he had one attack of urticaria lasting seven or eight days. In the same year he had two attacks of unconsciousness with twitchings of the extremities followed by a period of headache, dizziness and drowsiness. One year after the first nodule was felt, he experienced a weakness of the right facial muscles for 3 weeks. In the year previous to his admission he again had two attacks of convulsions and unconsciousness, milder in nature than previous ones.

Family history was negative for any nervous disorders. Patient was born and brought up in Honan province but had been to Shanghai, Nanking, Hankow and Tientsin. He was healthy up to the age of 19. He gave no history of eating raw or partially cooked pork or of passing segments of worms in stools.

Examination showed normal findings except for the presence of the subcutaneous nodules scattered over different parts of the body. The nodule is firm, non-tender and movable beneath the skin, having the size and shape of a shelled peanut.

Ophthalmoscopic and neurological examinations yielded normal findings. The blood picture was normal except for an eosinophilia of 3 per cent. Stools were repeatedly negative for taenia ova or segments. Blood Wassermann was negative. Skin reaction tested with fresh fluid from a cyst was negative. The diagnosis of *Cysticercus cellulosae* was established by biopsy of one of these nodules. Patient was last seen in May 1933 in apparent good health.

CASE 4. A girl of 23 was admitted to the P.U.M.C. Hospital on Aug. 9, 1934 in a stuporous state. For two or three weeks before admission patient complained of headache and was rather sleepy. In the evening of Aug. 7 chill and fever set in rather suddenly which intensified the headache. The next morning while attending a school examination she felt such a weakness of her right hand that she could hardly hold her pen. The next day she sank into a stupor.

Five years ago she passed segments of tapeworm in stools and two years ago was treated for taeniasis. During the past three years subcutaneous nodules appeared in successive crops in different parts of the body. In September 1933 she had a sudden attack of convulsions with loss of consciousness and incontinence of urine. She recovered completely the next day and since then she suffered from frequent headaches.

Patient, a native of Mukden, came to Peiping a month ago. She enjoyed good health in the past. Family history was negative for nervous or constitutional disorders.

On admission patient had a temperature of 40°C. She was semi-comatose with tightly clenched jaws and slightly rigid neck. There was suggestive deviation of the left eye ball to the nasal side, but pupils were reactive and equal in size. Eye ground examination showed moderate papillitis. Other cranial nerves were normal. Arms and legs were flaccid. Reflex movements of the left arm and leg could be induced with pricks of a pin but not of the right arm and leg. Abdominal reflexes were absent but deep tendon reflexes, particularly those on the right side were definitely exaggerated with suggestive Babinski on the right; Kernig's sign was negative. About a dozen cystic nodules were found over the trunk mostly in the subcutaneous tissue but a few seemed to be imbedded in the muscles. Biopsy proved these to be *Cysticerci cellulosae*.

Urine contained a trace of albumen. Stool was positive for taenia ova. Treatment later recovered segments of *Taenia solium*. Blood study showed a moderate anaemia and a leucocytosis of 17,600 with 83 per cent neutrophiles and the rest lymphocytes. A lumbar puncture yielded a clear fluid with a pressure of 100 mm of water and a cell count of 440 per c. mm of which 47 per cent were neutrophiles and 53 per cent lymphocytes. Its sugar and chloride contents were normal. Pandy's test was positive. Wassermann test of both blood and spinal fluid was negative. X-ray examination of the skull, chest, soft tissues of the neck and of the limbs revealed no abnormal findings.

Two days after admission with the fall of temperature to 38°C. patient became much clearer mentally though she still had motor aphasia. She could now move her left arm and both legs but the right arm and hand remained paralysed. The white count also fell to 10,400. Two days later temperature was normal and patient could answer questions though slowly. The spinal fluid now had a cell count of 130, all lymphocytes, which dropped to 24 a few weeks later. Eye-ground examination showed persistence of papillitis, though less marked. A chart of the visual field made at this time showed contraction of the red field on the nasal side of both eyes. Skin test with 0.2 cc of the fluid from patient's own cyst gave strong immediate reaction. A similar reaction also occurred with carbolised hydatid fluid from a case of ecchynococcus cyst of the liver. The normal controls were all negative.

Patient showed continued improvement. At the time of discharge at the end of September, 1934 she could move her right arm in all directions but still not the fingers and thumb, the use of which was only slowly regained some weeks after discharge.

CASE 5. A Chinese woman of 33, a native of Manchuria, was admitted to the P.U.M.C. Hospital on Mar. 7, 1934 for acute opium poisoning. Within ten minutes of her arrival, she became comatose and died ten hours later. Her brother stated that the patient was healthy and mentally normal until sometime in 1930 when she had frequent hallucinations. In 1931 she had a period of high fever with severe headache, pain and tenderness all over the body. In the summer of 1932 she had four or five attacks of complete unconsciousness, each lasting for about one hour. Since then her attitude towards her family members showed a lack of former sincerity. She took to opium smoking since 1931. There was no history of insanity or epilepsy in the family.

As patient had to be kept in a Drinker's respirator all the time to maintain artificial respiration, no routine physical examination was possible during life. A blood count showed moderate anaemia and a leucocytosis of 18,050 with no eosinophiles.

At autopsy, what might be termed a miliary cysticercosis was found with nodules, in the cerebrum, cerebellum, meninges, lungs, pleura, epicardium, tongue, muscles of the neck, chest, arms and legs and diaphragm.

* The pathological findings of this case will be reported in full by Dr. H. J. K'ang and Dr. Y. L. Ch'eng, in the Chinese Medical Journal.

CASE 6. A male Chinese of 23 was first seen in the outpatient department of the P.U.M.C.Hospital in Jan. 1928 for subcutaneous nodules of one year's duration. These were found under the skin of the neck, left arm and the abdomen. Biopsy of five of them showed typical *Cysticerci cellulosae*. Four consecutive stool examinations failed to show taenia ova or segments. In 1930, he had the first attack of convulsions, the details of which were not available. The second attack occurred in Mar. 1932. It was ushered in by a numbness of the right hand, spreading rapidly upwards to involve the mouth. Loss of consciousness soon followed lasting 20 min. Very shortly afterwards another attack occurred during sleep but patient was only informed of it by an eye witness. In April of the same year, he developed jaundice with abdominal pain and occasional vomiting for which he was admitted on May 25, 1932 for observation. During the two weeks preceding his admission he had many abortive epileptic fits during which he had clonic twitching of the facial muscles on the right side and difficulty of speech, or a numbness in the right hand spreading up the arm and to the face. Each attack lasted two or three minutes without loss of consciousness.

Examination on admission showed intense jaundice with enlarged liver besides the subcutaneous nodules referred to above. There was an eosinophilia of six per cent, otherwise the blood picture was normal. Urine was positive for bile. Icterus index was 75 with positive direct Van den Bergh reaction. Liver function test with bromsulphalein showed 20 per cent retention at the end of one hour. Blood Wassermann was negative. Stools were negative for taenia ova or segments. X-ray of chest and skull and eye ground examination showed nothing abnormal.

Patient stayed in the hospital for two weeks during which he had no seizures but became more jaundiced. According to later reports this jaundice persisted until the early part of 1933 and disappeared entirely by the end of March. About the same time he also ceased to have any more convulsions. When he was last seen on February 9, 1935 he looked in perfect health and a careful search for subcutaneous nodules failed to reveal any. Patient stated that the nodules disappeared one and half years previously. A differential count of the white blood cells at this time was normal.

CASE 7. A Chinese male of 32, a native of Hopei province, was admitted to the P.U.M.C. Hospital on Nov. 15, 1933 complaining of weakness and wasting of the arms for eight months, and weakness of the legs for two months. In May 1932 many small nodules appeared over the trunk and arms. In Mar. 1933 he first noticed some uneasiness in moving the right shoulder and a month later a weakness and clumsiness of the right hand and fingers with occasional twitching of the muscles of the right arm, which later showed signs of wasting. In June his left hand became similarly involved. By September he felt weakness in his legs and was slightly unsteady of gait. He had occasionally formication in different parts of the body and shooting pain down the legs. Never had he any convulsive fits. He admits many venereal exposures during past ten years and had urethritis in 1927 and bubo in 1929.

Examination showed marked atrophy of the extensors of both forearms as well as flexer carpi radialis more marked on the right side. Extensors of both hands were also weak. Coordination, sensation and reflexes were normal. Pupils showed a sluggish reaction to light. Mental rating gave an intelligence quotient of 59. Besides the above findings, there were many subcutaneous nodules, four on each arm, six on the chest, two on the left side of neck and one over the left temple.

During his hospital stay he ran an irregular fever for ten days. Blood picture during the fever showed a leucocyte count of 12,000 to 13,000 with eight per cent eosinophiles. Blood Wassermann reaction was strongly positive. Stools were negative and urine normal. Lumbar puncture yielded a clear and colorless fluid under normal pressure and with a cell count of seven, 65 mgm. of sugar and 720 mgm. of chlorides, negative Wassermann and colloidal gold reaction, and negative Pandy's and Nonne's tests for protein. Biopsy of one of the subcutaneous nodules proved it to be *Cysticercus cellulosae*.

The neurological changes were thought to be due to a chronic anterior poliomyelitis or myotrophic lateral sclerosis, but the possibility of cysticercosis cellulosae of the spinal cord and of the brain is difficult to exclude. The negative Wassermann reaction of the spinal fluid speaks against syphilis of the spinal cord.

CASE 8. A Chinese male of 29, native of Manchuria, was admitted to the P.U.M.C. Hospital on Feb. 24, 1933 for recurrent attacks of convulsions and unconsciousness for five years. In Jan. 1928 patient had fever for two weeks without apparent cause. One morning in March of the same year he suddenly felt twitching of the muscles of the right side of the face and of the limbs followed by loss of consciousness, cyanosis and foaming at the mouth. The attack was over in ten minutes. Three months later he had in a period of two hours five successive attacks of convulsion with mental confusion. Since then he has had many minor attacks manifested by twitching of the muscles of right side of face or of the hands or merely a numbness and tingling in the legs without loss of consciousness. In November 1932, however, another major attack occurred during which convulsions and unconsciousness were preceded by a numb feeling spreading from the left foot towards the head. His other complaints included headache sometimes accompanied by vomiting, poor memory, irritability and recently some blurring of vision with dilated pupils. Patient noticed for the first time in Aug. 1930 some nodules underneath the skin of the chest and arms which were at first slightly tender. He gave no history of partaking raw or undercooked pork, or of passing segments of worms in the stools. There was no familial taint of insanity or epilepsy.

The physical findings on admission were normal except for the presence of nineteen nodules, each the size of a shelled peanut, underneath the skin of the neck, arms, trunk and the right thigh. A biopsy of one of these showed a typical *Cysticercus cellulosae*.

Blood picture was entirely normal. Wassermann reaction was negative. Stool examination on four different occasions was negative for taenia ova or segments.

During his hospital stay patient had two attacks of "petit mal" which began with dizziness followed by blurring of vision of the right eye, generalized flushing of the skin, nausea, increased lacrimation and salivation. A lumbar puncture done on the morning after the second attack yielded a clear fluid under a pressure of 80 mm of water, with a cell count of seven 84 mg of sugar, 731 mg of chlorides and a positive Pandy's reaction. Patient was discharged on March 6, 1933. After discharge he had on an average two epileptiform fits each month and died in status epilepticus in Spring of 1934.

CASE 9. A Chinese male of 32, native of Manchuria, was first seen in the outpatient clinic of the P.U.M.C. Hospital on Oct. 28, 1929 complaining of recurrent convulsive fits for three and half years. During an attack he complains blurring of vision followed by loss of consciousness with upturned eyes and foaming at the mouth and recovery in about twenty minutes. After each attack his mind is confused for many hours. During the year prior to being seen the attacks have been less frequent and shorter in duration than formerly. Patient first noticed the presence of a nodule under the skin of the forehead twelve years ago and two years ago he could count 70-80 nodules over his body but since then the majority of these have disappeared. There was no past history of intestinal taeniasis. One of his cousins is said to have epileptic fits since childhood.

Examination was negative except for the presence of three nodules of 2-3 cm in diameter two under the skin of the left chest wall and one over the right deltoid muscle. One of these upon biopsy proved to be *Cysticercus cellulosae*. Two stool examinations were negative. Blood Wassermann reaction was negative. Patient disappeared from the clinic after a few visits and has not been heard of since.

CASE 10. A Chinese army officer of 44 was admitted to the P.U.M.C. Hospital on Sept. 9, 1934 following a convulsive fit. It was ushered in rather suddenly by twitchings of the hands. Unconsciousness lasted five hours, during which the tongue was bitten. He had a similar attack two years previously. Ten years ago he had many injections for a penile sore. Between 1926 and 1930 he frequently passed tapeworm segments per rectum. The family history was negative for nervous diseases.

Examination on admission showed normal findings except for the presence of three subcutaneous nodules, one below the right nipple, one on the left upper arm and one in the abdominal wall. There was a leucocytosis of 12,600 with 81 per cent neutrophiles. Cerebral spinal fluid was normal in every respect. Blood Wassermann was negative. X-ray of the skull showed no calcified nodules in the soft tissues. A biopsy of one of the nodules established the diagnosis of *Cysticercus cellulosae*. Patient became excited and irrational following the lumbar puncture and left the hospital against advice.

LITERATURE

1. Report of Research Committee, China Missionary Medical Association. China Med. J. **24**: 85, 1910.
2. *Clark, W. T.* A case of tenia solium in Yunnan Province. China Med. J. **26**: 11, 1912.
3. *Barnes, J. E.* Chinese patient with cysticercus cellulosae. China Med. J. **36**: 546, 1922.
4. *Faust, E. C.* The distribution and differentiation of human helminths in China and adjacent territory. Supplement to the China Med. J., Feb. 1923.
5. *Mills, R. G.* Notes on the occurrence of tenia solium and cysticercus cellulosae in North China. China Med. J. **38**: 465, 1924.
6. *Hu, C. K., Khaw, O. K., and Frazier, C. N.* Subcutaneous cysticercosis cellulosae in man. Arch. Derm. and Syph. **21**: 777, 1930.
7. *Ch'in, K. Y.* Nodules or tumors in subcutaneous and other tissues due to cysticercus cellulosae. Chinese Med. J. **47**: 1181, 1933.
8. *Feng, H. H.* Cysticercus cellulosae subconjunctivalis. Chinese Med. J. **48**: 863, 1934.
9. *Yoshino, K.* Studies on the post-embryonal development of taenia solium. I. On the hatching of the eggs of taenia solium. Taiwan Igakkai Zasshi, **32**: 1392, 1933.

10. *MacArthur, W. P.* Cysticercosis as seen in the British Army, with special reference to the production of epilepsy. Trans. Roy. Soc. Trop. Med. and Hyg. **27**: 343, 1934. Also in Roy. Army Med. Corps **62**: 241, 1934.

11. *Vosgien, Y.* Le cysticercus cellulosae chez l'homme & chez les animaux (a monograph). Imprimerie de la Faculte de Medecine, Paris, 1911.

12. *Yoshino, K.* Studies on the post-embryonal development of taenia solium. II. On the youngest form of cysticercus cellulosae and on the migratory course of the onchosphaera of taenia solium within the intermediate host. Taiwan Igakkai Zasshi, **32**: 1569, 1933.

13. *Tull, J. C., and Subrahmanyan, C.* A case of cysticercosis cellulosae of the brain. Trans. Roy. Trop. Med. and Hyg. **28**: 165, 1934.

14. *Africa, C. M., and Cruz, J. Z. S.* Cysticercus cellulosae in man. Philippine Islands Med. Assoc. **7**: 209, 1927.

15. *Broughton-Alcock, Stevenson, W. E. and Worster-Drought, C.* Cysticercosis of the brain. Brit. Med. J. **2**: 980, 1928.

16. *Dixon, H. B. F., and Smithers, D. W.* Epilepsy in cysticercosis (Taenia solium). A study of seventy-one cases. Quart. J. Med., New Series, **3**: 603, 1934.

17. *Morrison, W. K.* Cysticercosis in twin brothers aged thirteen years, with a radiological study of the calcified cysticercus in two cases. Brit. Med. J. **1**: 13, 1934.

18. *Guillain, G., Bertrand, I., et Thurel, R.* Etude anatomique et clinique d'une méningite basilaire et spinale-a cysticercus racemosus. Revue Neurologique **2**: 114, 1933.

19. *Pulgram, Fritz.* Ueber einen Fall von Cysticercosis cerebri et cordis. Wien Klin. Wochenschr. **41**: 1088, 1928.

20. *Sokolovski, W.* Transduodenal expulsion of cestodes with quinine. Milit. Ztschr. Leningrad., **4**: 274, 1933. Abstract Trop. Dis. Bull. **31**: 781, 1934.

23. Malaria and Relapsing Fever Following Blood Transfusion Including the Report of a Case of Congenital Transmission of Relapsing Fever

Wang, C.W. and Lee, C.U. *Chinese Medical Journal*, 50: 241, 1936.

王季午、李宗恩《输血后的疟疾与回归热》，载于《中华医学杂志》，1936 年，50:241-248 页。

翻译概要 在过去的 10 年里（1925–1935 年），协和医院有 3700 位病人接受输血治疗，其中 54 位感染了良性间日疟，6 位感染回归热。一位接受输血的孕妇，其胎儿因感染回归热在出生不久便死亡。尽管很难，但对献血者应该仔细筛选，尽可能避免悲剧的发生。如病人在输血后有发热症状，应该检查是否有感染疟疾和回归热的可能。

Chinese Medical Journal, **50**: *241-248, 1936.*

MALARIA AND RELAPSING FEVER FOLLOWING BLOOD TRANSFUSION

INCLUDING THE REPORT OF A CASE OF CONGENITAL TRANSMISSION OF RELAPSING FEVER

C. W. Wang, and C. U. Lee

Department of Medicine, Peiping Union Medical College, Peiping

Blood transfusion as a therapeutic measure is gaining recognition in China. In the Peiping Union Medical College Hospital it has been performed approximately 3,700 times in the ten year period from July 1925 to June 1935 inclusive. Apart from the well known dangers resulting from incompatibility of blood-groups the possibility of transmission of disease to the recipient is an ever present consideration. The present paper deals with two infections, namely, malaria and relapsing fever, which have developed subsequent to blood transfusions in this hospital during the stated period.

Chue and Wang (1) in their report on the system for enlisting blood-donors in force in this hospital made the following statement: "The possibility of chronic malaria in blood donors is difficult to guard against. Besides enlargement of spleen which may make one suspect the possible presence of malaria, there is no other method that we can use to exclude malarial infection. Even repeated blood smears may not show the presence of the parasites. Fortunately malaria is not very common in Peiping, so that it is not so important a question here as it may be elsewhere. Careful questioning has also to be made in each case to exclude relapsing fever which is not uncommon here." They did not, however, refer to actual cases.

In a recent report on the transmission of malaria by transfusion Stein (2) gave eleven references but as far as the present authors are aware none exists in regard to relapsing fever.

MALARIA

In the past ten years there have been 54 patients, who developed benign tertian malaria following blood transfusions. Of these, thirteen got infected after a single transfusion, the rest after one of a series of transfusions. Only data concerning the former group of patients are presented in Table 1 because of the definite relationship of donor and recipient and of the time interval between the transfusion and onset of malaria. The ages of these thirteen patients ranged from one month and a half to 66 years. In six, a negative history of malaria is given in the records, but in the other seven there is no evidence of enquiry into the past history regarding malaria. The interval between the blood transfusion and the first pyrexial attack varied from three to 60 days. All the infections were easily controlled by a short course of quinine and with the exception of one showed no tendency to relapse.

A word or two may be here added as to the clinical symptoms observed in the whole group of 54 patients. The typical malarial attack was preceded by a period of normal temperature or remittent fever in patients whose primary conditions for which the transfusions were given, were not accompanied by fever, while in patients who were suffering from a primary febrile disease at time of transfusion it was difficult to determine the exact onset of malaria. There were 34 patients in the former group, of whom fifteen had a normal temperature when a typical malarial paroxysm occurred; nineteen showed a preliminary period of remittent fever of one to sixteen days' duration before a regular malaria paroxysm occurred.

The periodicity of malarial attacks may be either tertian or quotidian. In twelve patients the fever was entirely irregular showing no periodicity at all. In such cases a diagnosis may be difficult and is often delayed unless the possibility of malaria is borne in mind and efforts made to find the parasites. In about 70 per cent of the cases the diagnosis was made within 48 hours of the onset of fever, but in a few instances it was not made until the tenth day of fever. The routine method of diagnosis was to use thin smears. Examination by the thick smear method would undoubtedly render the diagnosis easier.

The intervention of an attack of malaria in patients who were already ill was not entirely devoid of detrimental effects. Among the 51 patients there were fourteen deaths, seven of which seem to have been hastened by the malaria. Besides there were nine other patients, whose general condition was made worse and whose convalescence was unduly protracted.

In regard to the donors concerned in the thirteen cases presented in Table 1, data are available only in seven. One of the donors gave blood on as many as 42 occasions and each of them participated in giving blood to more than one patient who developed malaria after transfusion.

If it is assumed that such donors did actually transmit malaria to the recipients, it is of interest to study how close together these accidental transmissions occurred. In general they were within a period of a year or so. Donor 3808, however, gave blood for transfusions during 1925 and 1926 to ten patients, two of whom developed malaria; he was then not again used until 1933 after which, before this investigation was started, he took part in ten transfusions, three of which were followed by malaria in the recipients. He admitted having had malaria-like fever 20 years previously but never since.

In 18 donors a search was made for malarial parasites following the development of malaria in the recipients. In only one of them were parasites found. He was free of all symptoms of malaria at the time. Search for malarial parasites was made as a routine in thin smears, supplemented in a few cases by thick smears and cultures.

RELAPSING FEVER

In the past ten years, six patients have developed relapsing fever after transfusion. In only one of these did it occur after a single transfusion, while in the rest a series of transfusions were given. The source of infection was actually traced to the donors in two cases in which the intervals between the transfusion and the onset of clinical symptoms were four and five days respectively. Spirochetes were usually demonstrated in the blood wihtin 24 hours of onset of fever, but in one case they were accidentally found 24 hours before the rise of temperature. In another they were not found until the fourth day of fever. Except in one patient who, in spite of specific treatment, relapsed twice during her stay in hospital, the patients were easily cured with neoarsphenamine. In two patients it was noticed that the general condition of the patient

TABLE 1. *Cases in which malaria developed after a single transfusion*

Patient						Donor						
Case	Sex	Age *yrs*	History of malaria	Incubation period *days*	Relapse	Donor number	No. of transfusions	No. of malaria cases	Date of each malaria case	Palpable spleen	Search for malarial parasites	History of malaria
1	M	12	None known	5	Pt. died	(a)	—	—	—	—	Not searched	Not mentioned
2	M	15	,, ,,	60	None known	(a)	—	—	—	—	,, ,,	,,
3	M	6	Negative	16	One	(a)	—	—	—	—	,, ,,	,,
4	M	3½ mos.	None known	3	Pt. died	(a)	—	—	—	—	,, ,,	,,
5	F	1 mos.	Negative	20	None known	(a)	—	—	—	—	,, ,,	,,
6	F	48	,,	15	,, ,,	(a)	—	—	—	—	,, ,,	,,
7	M	61	,,	13	,, ,,	2320	42	6	Jan., April, June, July, Oct., 1933; May, 1934	No	,, ,,	,,
8	F	29	None known	12	,, ,,	3743	4	2	April, Dec., 1933	,,	Neg. in thin smears	,,
9	M	43	,, ,,	11	,, ,,	3767	10	4	June, Oct., 1933; Jan., July, 1934	,,	Neg. in thin and thick smears	15 yrs ago
10	F	43	Negative	10	,, ,,	3172	20	2	July, 1932; Feb., 1934	,,	Not searched	Not mentioned
11	M	60	None known	10	,, ,,	3767	10	4	June, Oct., 1933; Jan., July, 1934	,,	,, ,,	,,
12	F	30	Negative	8	,, ,,	3898	20	5	Sept., Oct., 1926, Oct., Nov., 1934; Feb., 1935	,,	,, ,,	,,
13	F	2	None known	18	Pt. died	3898	20	5	Sept., Oct., 1926; Oct., Nov., 1934; Feb., 1935	,,	Neg. in thin smears	Denied

(a) Unfortunately these records have been lost.

became worse after an attack of relapsing fever, and the convalescence from the primary disease was unduly long.

One pregnant woman, who received a transfusion from a donor in whose blood spirochetes were later demonstrated, developed in due course an attack of relapsing fever during which she had miscarriage. The premature infant also developed the disease and died of it. Scott (3) has reported a somewhat similar case. The following are the details.

Mother: A Chinese woman of 40, admitted April 16, 1935, seven months pregnant, and at the same time suffering from general anasarca and orthopnea of three weeks' duration. Blood examinations showed anemia with 2.9 gm hemoglobin per 100 cc of blood and 1.5 million red cells per cubic millimeter. The symptoms were thought to be due to the severe anemia and a transfusion of 470 cc blood was given the day after admission. Five days later patient developed a fever which gradually rose to 40°C. On the third day of the fever she gave birth to a premature baby. Three days later spirochetes were found in her blood and patient was given 0.6 gm neosarsphenamine, which terminated the fever. The placenta was reported to be normal. No special method was used to demonstrate the presence of spirochetes.

Infant: Immediately after delivery the infant was placed in the premature room. He weighed at birth only 1920 gm but otherwise appeared normal. He was fed on mother's milk by bottle, occasionally supplemented by evaporated milk, appropriately diluted. There was irregular fever between 38°C. and 39°C. on the second and third day after birth. The temperature was normal, however, by the fourth day but again rose on the seventh. Spirochetes were found in the blood on the tenth day when the temperature was 39.3°C. The infant appeared very ill and slightly cyanotic. Later the temperature dropped to 36.4°C. and the infant showed signs of collapse. Adrenalin, followed by 0.04 gm of sulpharsphenamine, was given. In spite of treatment the infant died an hour and a half later.

Donor: Two days after giving blood to the mother on April 17, the donor became suddenly ill with chill and generalized aching. After April 21 he had high fever. On April 25 he was admitted to hospital, when spirochetes were at once easily found in the blood. Spontaneous crisis occurred the next day and patient left the hospital. No further information could be obtained.

DISCUSSION

When a patient develops malaria following a blood transfusion serveral possibilities exist as to the source of infection. It may be a spontaneous relapse of pre-existing chronic malaria bearing no relation to the transfusion or perhaps merely precipitated by it. It is even possible that the patient happened to be naturally infected shortly before or after the transfusion. The patients' denial of malaria in the past and the development of symptoms shortly after the transfusion are points in favour of the direct transmission of the infection from the donor to the recipient. Further, the facts that several patients develop malaria following transfusions of blood from the same donor and that the infection is easily cured with a short course of quinine also speak in favour of this view.

In the particular case here reported in which malarial parasites were demonstrated in the donor's blood there can be no doubt on this point. If blood transfusions tend to provoke a relapse of chronic malaria, then we should expect similar relapses following subsequent transfusions. As a matter of fact malaria never occurred more than once in patients receiving a series of transfusions from different donors. The possibility of malaria among these patients being due to natural infection is also unlikely because the patients were living under the protection of a modern well-screened hospital when malaria occurred. It is, therefore, safe to assume that in most of the 54 patients under discussion malaria was the result of direct transmission from donors.

The same arguments as those advanced for the direct transmission of malaria may be used in favor of the view that cases of relapsing fever following blood transfusion are also the result of direct transmission. The number of patients in this hospital who have developed relapsing fever after transfusion has been much fewer than in the case of malaria. This is probably to be explained by the natural rarity of human carriers of *Treponema recurrentis*. The question of the congenital transmission of relapsing fever is an interesting one. In the present case the infant was probably infected through the placenta, though the possibility of infection through skin abrasion, during its passage through the birth canal, or through the mother's milk can not be entirely excluded.

It goes without saying that the transmission of disease by blood transfusion is to be sedulously avoided. Our own experience suggests that the accidental transmission of benign tertian malaria or relapsing fever to an individual whose health is already undermined by some per-existing disease is an undesirable risk. In regions where subtertian malaria is endemic the effect may even be disastrous. The loss of the infant is a further and special warning.

The detection of malaria and relapsing fever in blood donors may be a very difficult problem. The cases of transmission here reported occurred in spite of realization of the danger and careful examination of donors. Great care must be used, both at the time of enlistment and before each transfusion, in questioning the donor in regard to past and present malaria and relapsing fever and in examining him for evidence of either of these infections. Probably all candidates with a recent or severe history of malaria, or with splenomegaly, should be rejected. There are circumstances, however, in which the use of such a donor may seem almost unavoidable. In such instances, the blood must be most carefully searched for parasites, including the use of thick smears and dark field. Even though such examinations give negative results, the possibility of infection remains, and the donor should be used with this in mind, if at all. If a donor's blood appears to have transmitted malaria or relapsing fever to a patient, it is wisest to eliminate him entirely from use, at least pending the lapse of a proper time after he can be regarded with certainty as cured. Such a donor should be examined promptly and treated as the case may indicate. In emergencies and in regions where blood transfusion has not yet won general recognition as a therapeutic measure and where donors are scarce, the difficulties of administering an efficient and safe transfusion service are great. Where malaria and relapsing fever are endemic, it is only by the strictest vigilance that one can hope to keep to a minimum the incidence of accidental transmission of these diseases through blood transfusion.

SUMMARY

Fifty-four cases of benign tertian malaria and six cases of relapsing fever have occurred following blood transfusions in the Peiping Union Medical College Hospital during the ten-year period 1925-1935, in which 3,700 transfusions were performed. These include one interesting instance in which a pregnant mother having been infected with relapsing fever through a blood transfusion, apparently passed it on to her premature infant who died of it.

Without special effort it is difficult to demonstrate the infecting organism in the donor's blood. In only one case of malaria and two cases of relapsing fever was the disease actually traced to the donors concerned. For this reason it is not easy to eliminate entirely the transmission of these infections to the recipients. Only by constant vigilance can the incidence of such accidents be held low and undue suffering or even unnecessary shortening of life prevented.

In the presence of an unexplained fever in a patient who had received a recent blood transfusion, malaria and relapsing fever should always be borne in mind so that an early diagnosis may be made and an unhappy outcome avoided, particularly in endemic areas of malignant tertian malaria

LITERATURE

1. *Chue, C. Y., and Wang, S. H.* A system for obtaining Chinese blood donors. Chinese Med. J., **46**: 31-42, 1932.

2. *Stein, H. B.* Transmission of malaria by transfusion. Am. J. Dis. Child., **44**: 1048-1054, 1932.

3. *Scott, A. V.* Relapsing fever: A case in an infant aged eight days. Nat. Med. J. China, **17**: 782-783, 1931.

24. Canine Leishmaniasis in Peiping

Lee, C.U. *Chinese Medical Journal*, 51:951, 1937.

李宗恩《北平的犬黑热病》，载于《中华医学杂志》，1937 年，51:951-953 页。

翻译概要 作者首次报告了在北平确诊的两条感染黑热病犬及被其中一条感染的一个 5 岁 8 个月的患儿。病犬的脾脏可经注射致仓鼠感染黑热病。此前有报道称，在张家口发现过一例黑热病犬。

Chinese Medical Journal, **51**: *951-952, June, 1937.*

CANINE LEISHMANIASIS IN PEIPING

A PRELIMINARY COMMUNICATION

C. U. Lee

Department of Medicine, Peiping Union Medical College, Peiping, China.

This is merely to record the finding of two dogs in Peiping infected with a protozoal organism morphologically indistinguishable from *Leishmania donovani.* It may be recalled that in 1935 Dr. Mary Andrews reported a case of leishmaniasis in a Boston bull terrier originating from Mukden.*

The first was a stray dog caught in the streets of Peiping by the Municipal dog-catcher on the night of December 13th, 1936, was delivered to the Peiping Union Medical College animal house the next day and thence to the Department of Physiology for experimental purposes. Since November 9, 1936 the Department of Physiology at the request of the Department of Medicine sends as a routine, specimens of the spleen, liver and skin of every dog experimentally sacrificed. On receipt of the specimens, smears of the liver, spleen and skin are made and searched for the presence of leishmania infection. The dog in question, the 90th dog thus examined, was a bitch weighing 11 kilograms and was killed on December 19th, 1936 after an acute experiment on the brain. The person who opened the abdomen to secure specimens of the liver and spleen did not notice any appreciable enlargement of the organs. The specimens were received three days after sacrifice during which period they were kept in the ice-chest. Smears from each of the specimens showed numerous leishmania organisms. Sections demonstrated the presence of these organisms in the macrophages in the liver, spleen, and under the epidermis. Emulsion of the spleen was injected into 20 hamsters the majority of which were later found by liver puncture to be infected with the same organism.

*Trans. IX Congress F.E.A.T.M. Vol. 1. 679, 1935.

The second dog, an impure breed of German police dog, was from a Chinese house in association with a case of proven kala-azar in a child 5 years and 8 months old. The father of the child is a physician and director of a well known research institute in Peiping. He and his family have been residing in their present house since August 1933. The family consists of father, mother, and six children ranging in age from 12 to 5 $\frac{8}{12}$ years, the two youngest children being twins. The children except for going to school are not allowed out of the house very much, the outer gate of the house being always kept closed. Being of pre-school age the twins seldom had occasion to leave the house; only once in a long while they accompanied their mother on a visit to a friend's house in the afternoon. During summer months they have occasionally been taken to the hills outside Peiping for the day but never to stay overnight.

The house in which they reside is a typical well appointed Chinese house with many rooms built about paved courtyards in which there are a number of trees and flowering bushes. All the living rooms have plaster ceiling and wooden or cement floor. The house was built about 50 years ago.

Our little patient took ill in the early part of February, 1937, with tired feeling and fever. He was admitted to the Peiping Union Medical College Hospital on February 25, 1937 and kala-azar was diagnosed the next day by finding typical *Leishmania donovani* in marrow smear from a sternal puncture. He presented a picture of moderately advanced kala-azar.

A visit was then made to the house and all the members of household, including the servants, were examined for enlarged spleen, but none found. Two dogs and three cats (household animals) were subjected to liver puncture. The older of the two dogs which had been with the family for 5 years was negative. The younger was 10 months old and was a two months puppy when first introduced into the house. Leishmania organisms were easily found in smear from the liver. These two dogs were not allowed out of the confines of the house and therefore were never in contact with street dogs. The three cats were negative.

25. Neostibosan and Experimental Kala-Azar in Chinese Hamsters. I. Normal Hamsters

Wang, C.W. and Lee, C.U. Normal hamsters. *Proceedings of the Society for Experimental Biology and Medicine*, 38:670, 1938.

王季午、李宗恩《中国仓鼠作为黑热病的动物模型：I Neostibosan 对正常仓鼠的药理作用》，载于《实验生物医学学会会议记录》，1938 年, 38:670-674 页。

翻译概要 在治疗黑热病的药物中，Neostibosan 对黑热病人有较高疗效，且可皮下注射。对正常仓鼠，Neostibosan ［1］最高非致死剂量（容忍剂量）为 1 克/每公斤体重；［2］最高非致死剂量为 11-40 克/每公斤体重，与仓鼠的性别和体重无关，；［3］反复用药证明 Neostibosan 有累积效应，推荐治疗剂量为 0.4 克 / 公斤体重；［4］如动物已经接受中毒剂量，继续用药将在两个月内导致死亡。

9978

Neostibosan and Experimental Kala-Azar in Chinese Hamsters. I. Normal Hamsters.

C. W. WANG AND C. U. LEE. (Introduced by F. R. Dieuaide.)

From the Department of Medicine, Peiping Union Medical College, Peiping.

The problem of chemotherapy of experimental kala-azar was investigated by Smyly,[1] who used 4 drugs, to treat infected Chinese hamsters, *Cricetulus griseus*. None of Smyly's infected animals was cured of the infection, although sodium antimonyl tartrate was given in large doses for a period sufficient to effect a cure in man. Hindle, working with Johnson,[2] obtained similar negative results with neostam, novostiburea, antimosan, and antimonyl tartrate, all of which have been successfully used in the treatment of kala-azar in man. Roehl[3] studied the action of tartar emetic, antimosan, stibosan, and neostibosan, in infected European hamsters, *Cricetulus frumentarius*, and was able to keep his treated animals free of parasites for months. Recently, Kikuth and Schmidt[4] obtained similar positive results with solustibosan. The contradictory results of Smyly and Hindle on one hand and Roehl and Kikuth and Schmidt on the other, in the opinion of the last two workers, are due to the different species of animals used. Whether Chinese hamsters, infected with *Leishmania donovani* can be cured of the infection, and whether the difference in species explains the difference in results, are the problems under investigation. Neostibosan was used because it possesses high curative value in human kala-azar and can be given subcutaneously.

Experiment 1. Determination of the *maximum non-lethal dose, maximum tolerated dose,* and *universal lethal dose* of neostibosan for hamsters. By *maximum non-lethal dose* we mean the amount given as a single injection, without killing any of the animals; *maximum tolerated dose* is the amount given as a single injection, which kills most of the animals; *universal lethal dose* is the amount given as a single injection, which kills all the animals. One hundred normal hamsters were used. Seventy-two percent of these animals weighed 30 g each; the rest varied from 25 to 36 g. The animals were divided into 5 groups, each con-

1 Smyly, H. J., *Trans. Roy. Soc. Trop. Med. and Hyg.*, 1926, **20**, 104.

2 Quoted from 4.

3 Roehl, W., *Ind. Med. Gaz.*, 1929, **64**, 563.

4 Kikuth, W., and Schmidt, H., *Chinese Med. J.*, 1937, **52**, 425.

sisting of 10 males and 10 females. Each group received a single injection of one test dose. Five test doses, 0.8 g, 1.0 g, 2.0 g, 3.0 g, and 4.0 g per kg were used. Neostibosan was freshly prepared each time in a 5% sterile aqueous solution, and given subcutaneously in abdominal wall of the animal by means of a tuberculin syringe. Any death within 48 hours after injection was considered as due to the drug. This arbitrary time limit was chosen because the excretion of pentavalent compounds of antimony is approximately 50% in the first 24 hours.[5, 6, 7] Any death occurring later than 2 days after injection is not likely to be due to the direct effect of antimony. The results of the 5 test doses are given in Table I.

TABLE I.
Mortality Rate of Hamsters to Test Doses of Neostibosan.

Group	Dose, g per kilo	No. of animals	No. of deaths	Mortality %
A	0.8	20	0	0
B	1.0	20	0	0
C	2.0	20	5	25
D	3.0	20	13	65
E	4.0	20	20	100

Among the 5 animals in Group C which died there were 2 males and 3 females, each weighing 30 g. Among the 13 deaths in Group D there were 6 males and 7 females (11 weighing 30 g each, and 2 weighing 29 g each). It seems that males are just as susceptible to the drug as females. From the table it is evident that among the doses tried, 1.0 g per kilo is the maximum non-lethal dose, 3.0 g per kilo, the *maximum tolerated dose,* and 4.0 g per kilo, the *universal lethal dose* of neostibosan for Chinese hamsters.

Experiment 2. Relation of body weight to the *maximum non-lethal dose.* Thirty hamsters were used. The results are shown in Table II.

TABLE II.
Relation of Body Weight of Hamsters to Maximum Non-lethal Dose of Neostibosan.

Body wt. (g)	11	12	14	15	16	17	20	24	29	30	32	34	37	40
No. of animals	1	4	2	2	2	5	3	2	1	2	2	2	1	1
No. of deaths	0	0	0	0	0	0	1	0	0	0	0	0	0	0

Except for one death among the 3 animals which weighed 20 g each, the *maximum non-lethal dose* is universal to animals weighing

[5] Weese, H., *Chinese Med. J.*, 1937, **52**, 421.

[6] Boyd, T. C., and Roy, A. C., *Ind. J. Med. Res.*, 1929, **17**, 94.

[7] Brahmachari, U. N., Chondbury, S. C., Das, J., and Sen, P., *Ind. J. Med. Res.*, 1924, **11**, 829.

TABLE III.
Cumulative Effect of Repeated Doses of Neostibosan.

Dose (mg/kilo)	200	300	400	500	600	700	800	900	1000	1200	1400	1600	1800	2000
No. of animals	20	20	20	19	19	19	19	17	17	17	15	10	5	2
No. of deaths	0	0	1	0	0	0	2	0	0	2	5	5	3	2
Mortality %	0	0	5	0	0	0	10.5	0	0	11.7	33.3	50	60	100
Cumulative mortality	0	0	5	5	5	5	15	15	15	25	50	75	90	100

TABLE IV.
Effect of a Second Injection of Maximum Non-lethal or Toxic Dose of Neostibosan.

Dose (g per kilo)	First injection			Second injection			Interval between injections in days
	No. of animals	No. of deaths	Mortality %	No. of animals	No. of deaths	Mortality %	
1	20	0	0	20	5	25	34·50
2	20	5	25	9	4	44.5	34·51
3	20	13	65	5*	5	100	34·65

*Two animals only received 2.0 g per kilo in the first injection.

from 11 g to 40 g. The single death out of 30 hamsters may be considered as an accident. There seems to be no difference, therefore, in the susceptibility of hamsters of different body weights to the *maximum non-lethal dose* as previously determined.

Experiment 3. Cumulative effect of repeated injections and the determination of the *probable therapeutic dose*. Since repeated injections of neostibosan are required to effect a cure of kala-azar, one must know whether there is increased tolerance or cumulative effect, and find out a dose suitable for repeated injection at certain intervals with least toxic effect, to the animal.

Ten males and 10 females, each weighing 20 to 27 g were used. Injections of 1% solution of neostibosan were given subcutaneously, twice a week. The doses began at 200 mg per kilo, and were increased by 100 mg steps up to 1 g per kilo, and then by 200 mg steps up to 2 g per kilo. The results are given in Table III. The mortality rate following a single injection of 2.0 g neostibosan per kilo body weight was 25%, but after injections of increasing doses given twice weekly of doses increasing up to a final dose of 2.0 g per kilo, the mortality rate increased to 100%. This strongly speaks for a cumulative effect, and against increased tolerance. One hamster out of 20 was killed when the dose reached 700 mg per kilo. For therapeutic use in infected hamsters, it would seem, therefore, that a constant dose of 400 to 500 mg per kilo body weight, given twice a week, might be regarded as the *probable therapeutic dose* of neostibosan, but various possible influences of the infected state of hamsters with kala-azar require investigation.

Experiment 4. Effect of a second injection of *maximum non-lethal dose,* and *toxic dose.* Any dose greater than the *maximum non-lethal dose* must be regarded as a *toxic dose.* The following experiment is to observe the effects of a second injection of the same *maximum non-lethal dose* and of *toxic doses* in animals which have survived a previous injection. The interval between the injections varied from 34 to 65 days. The number of animals used for the second injection was necessarily smaller than that for the first as many died of the first dose and some were otherwise lost. The results are shown in Table IV. There was a higher mortality following the second injection, even after one or 2 months, during which the animals were expected to have recovered from the previous dose. This decreased tolerance may mean that the first dose though not fatal, damaged the organism in some way so as to lower its tolerance to the subsequent injection.

Summary and Conclusions. 1. In normal Chinese hamsters it was found that the *maximum non-lethal dose* of neostibosan is 1.0 g per kilo body weight; the *maximum tolerated dose,* 3.0 g per kilo body weight; and the *universal lethal dose,* 4.0 g per kilo body weight. 2. The sex and body weight of hamsters played no significant rôle. The *maximum non-lethal dose* was found universal to animals weighing from 11 to 40 g. 3. There was no increase of tolerance after repeated injections of gradually increasing doses of neostibosan. A cumulative effect was clearly shown. A *probable therapeutic dose* was found to be about 0.4 g per kilo body weight. 4. After an animal had been poisoned by a large dose of neostibosan, the repetition of the same or greater amount even after an interval as long as 2 months usually resulted in death.

26. Neostibosan and Experimental Kala-Azar in Chinese Hamsters. II. Infected Hamsters

Wang, C.W. and Lee, C.U. *Proceedings of the Society for Experimental Biology and Medicine*, 38:674, 1938.

王季午、李宗恩《中国仓鼠作为黑热病的动物模型：II Neostibosan 对被感染仓鼠的药理作用》，载于《实验生物医学学会会议记录》，1938 年，38:674-678 页。

翻译概要 被感染的仓鼠对 Neostibosa 的耐受性减低，有效剂量为 0.2–0.5 克 / 公斤体重，死亡率 31.6%。虽然所有存活的仓鼠都被治愈，但只有一半为彻底治愈，所以停药后仍需注射疫苗已确保永久治愈。

9979

Neostibosan and Experimental Kala-Azar in Chinese Hamsters. II. Infected Hamsters.

C. W. Wang and C. U. Lee. (Introduced by F. R. Dieuaide.)

From the Department of Medicine, Peiping Union Medical College, Peiping, China.

This report deals with observations on the effects of neostibosan on kala-azar in Chinese hamsters. As this work was started before Part I was completed, the *probable therapeutic dose* of neostibosan suggested in that communication was not used.

Twenty-six normal and 26 infected hamsters were equally divided into 4 groups, each consisting of 13 hamsters. Groups A and C were given repeated injections of neostibosan, while Groups B and D were kept as controls. Treatment was started 47 days after the infection with kala-azar. One percent sterile aqueous solution of neostibosan was given twice a week by means of a tuberculin syringe, subcutaneously in 7 hamsters and intramuscularly in 6 hamsters of each group. Hamsters were weighed weekly or fortnightly and the amount of neostibosan was given according to the latest weight. The first dose was 8 mg per kilo, which was continued for 6 weeks; this amount was chosen because it is effective in human kala-azar. As soon as this dose was found to be ineffective and the *maximum non-lethal* dose was found to be 1 g per kilo, the amount was raised to 200 mg per kilo and gradually to 800 mg. Altogether 32 injections, a total of 7 g per kilo, were given to each hamster in a period of 114 days.

Difference in tolerance of normal and kala-azar hamsters. The results are shown in Table I. The mortality rate is higher in Group A than in Group C which seems to indicate that tolerance for neostibosan is less in infected than in normal hamsters, but the difference is not statistically significant. No difference in mortality rate was seen between subcutaneous and intramuscular routes of administration.

TABLE I.
Tolerance of Normal and Kala-azar Hamsters for Neostibosan.

Group of animals	No. of animals	No. of deaths	Mortality %
A. Infected hamsters receiving drug	13	7	53.8
B. ″ ″ ″ no drug	13	3	23.0
C. Normal ″ ″ drug	13	4	30.7
D. ″ ″ ″ no drug	13	2	15.4

Curative value of neostibosan in hamsters infected with kala-azar. The 32 injections of neostibosan given to Group A constituted a course of treatment. Group B served as controls. During the treatment several infected hamsters died. At autopsy the size of spleen and number of parasites were found to be decreasing with the increasing intensity of treatment. When a total dose of 2.3 g per kilo was reached, parasites were absent in almost all cases in smears made from the liver pulp obtained by puncture, while numerous parasites were found in smears of splenic pulp obtained by puncture. When a total of 7 g per kilo was reached, none of the 6 surviving hamsters showed parasites in smears of splenic pulp. A further splenic puncture was done 3 weeks after completion of the treatment in 3 of the animals and none of the smears showed parasites. Without further study one would consider these 6 hamsters apparently cured.

On completion of the treatment of kala-azar hamsters in Group A, 3 out of 13 controls in Group B had died. At autopsy all were found to have big spleens and leishmania were seen in smears. Liver puncture was done on each of the 10 survivors, and all but one were found to be heavily infected. In the negative case, the animal was later sacrificed. Its spleen and liver were found to be normal in size and no leishmania could be found in smears from these organs. It appears that this animal spontaneously recovered within about 5 months after infection, although infected hamsters usually show no such tendency.[1, 2]

[1] Smyly, H. J., and Young, C. W., PROC. SOC. EXP. BIOL. AND MED., 1924, **21**, 354.

[2] Young, C. W., Smyly, H. J., and Brown, C., *Am. J. Hyg.*, 1926, **6**, 254.

TABLE II.
Amount of Neostibosan Received by Apparently Cured Hamsters.

Hamster No.	1029	1032	1035	1036	1041	1044
Avg wt of animal, g	26	24	20	25	24	23
Total dose, mg	192.8	174.8	149.8	185.3	181.9	156.7
" " g per kilo	7.4	7.3	7.4	7.4	7.6	7.0

Further study was made of these apparently cured hamsters (Table II), except for one (1036) which was too decomposed for use. Hamsters 1029, 1032, and 1041 were sacrificed 10 days, 3 weeks, and 3 months respectively, after completion of treatment. The spleen of each of these hamsters was ground in 3 cc normal saline solution and 0.5 cc of this emulsion intraperitoneally inoculated into 6 normal hamsters. The spleens were all small and smears made from the emulsions were all negative. Two to 4 months later the normal hamsters which had been inoculated with the emulsions from hamsters 1032 and 1041 came down with kala-azar, proving that these 2 apparently cured hamsters were not actually cured. The normal hamsters which had been inoculated with the spleen emulsion of hamster 1029 never contracted kala-azar, proving that this apparently cured hamster was actually cured.

The other 2 apparently cured hamsters, 1035 and 1044, were re-inoculated 2 to 4 months after completion of treatment with 0.2 cc splenic emulsion containing numerous *Leishmania donovani*. Two months later they were killed. Hamster 1035 was found to have enlarged spleen, with parasites in spleen and liver, while hamster 1044 was found to have normal spleen and liver, with no parasites in these organs. This showed that one was not reinfectable, while the other had either been reinfected or possibly suffered a relapse. It is noteworthy that only one (1029) of the 5 apparently cured hamsters was proved to be actually cured; while a second (1044) may have been cured. No difference was seen in the curative effect of neostibosan between subcutaneous and intramuscular routes.

Further observations on the curative value of neostibosan in hamsters infected with kala-azar. A new lot of 25 hamsters which had been infected with *Leishmania donovani* for 43 days were given bi-weekly subcutaneous injections of 1% solution of neostibosan. Nine injections were given, beginning with a dose of 200 mg per kilo, and gradually increasing to 900 mg per kilo. Four hamsters died during the course of treatment, while 21 survived the treatment, each receiving a total of about 5.0 g per kilo. All of these were apparently cured (negative liver and spleen punctures). Three of the apparently cured hamsters were sacrificed 10 days, 18 days, and 3 months respectively after completion of treatment. All the smears made directly from the liver and spleen were negative for parasites. The spleen of each of these hamsters was used for hamster inoculation. The inoculated test hamsters were sacrificed 2 to 5 months later and the results showed that 2 of the 3 apparently cured hamsters were actually cured, but not the third whose splenic emulsion, though showing no parasites on direct study, was still capable of causing kala-azar. Twelve of the apparently cured hamsters were subjected to reinoculation 3 months after completion of treatment. About 2½ months after reinoculation one of the 7 hamsters which had received 0.1 cc of the infective material, showed evidence of kala-azar, but the 6 others were free from the infection. On the other hand, 3 out of the 5 hamsters which had received 0.2 cc of the infective material, showed evidence of kala-azar which, however, failed to develop in the others. In all, 4 or 33.3% of the 12 apparently cured hamsters were reinfected, or possibly had a relapse, while 8 or 66.7% were refractory to reinfection. The reinfectability of the apparently cured hamsters varied with the reinfective dose. Among 20 normal hamsters which had been inoculated with the same infective material as that given to the 2 apparently cured hamsters in the preceding experiment and 12 in this experiment, all except one developed kala-azar at end of 2½ months. Six of the apparently cured hamsters were kept under observation for 5 months after completion of treatment and then sacrificed. Four of the 6 were found to have enlarged spleens and livers, all harboring *Leishmania donovani*, a relapse rate of 66.7%. The 2 others had normal-sized spleens and livers with no parasites in these organs, and were apparently cured (Table III).

TABLE III.
Curative Effect of Neostibosan in 26 Apparently Cured Hamsters.

Nature of test	Result	No. of animals
Hamster inoculation test	Cured	3
	Not cured	3
Reinoculation test	Reinfectable	5
	Not reinfectable	9
Observation for relapse	Relapse	4
	No relapse	2

Discussion. There were altogether 26 apparently cured hamsters among the 38 which were systematically treated. Of these apparently cured hamsters 6 were tested by hamster inoculation and 3 were found to be actually cured, giving a cure-rate of 50% among the hamsters which survived the treatment. It is obvious that for experimental purposes the most reliable criterion of cure is inoculation of a splenic emulsion into normal hamsters. The 12 hamsters which died during the course of treatment indicate a high mortality, 31.6%. As the natural death-rate of hamsters, either non-infected or infected (Table I) is considerable, it is difficult to say how far this mortality was directly attributable to neostibosan.

The range of the effective dose of neostibosan for hamsters seems to vary from 200 to 500 mg per kilo. This dose agrees well with the *probable therapeutic dose* of 400 mg per kilo proposed in Part I. The total amount of neostibosan per kilo body weight used to effect cure in a hamster is about 100 times the human dose. In view of this, the failure of Smyly and Hindle to obtain cures in their experiments was probably due to inadequate dosage and insufficient treatment, rather than to the difference in species of hamster. Even with this enormous dose the cure rate was only 50% among the hamsters which survived the treatment and were tested by hamster inoculation, much lower than the cure-rate in man. Whether or not a 100% cure rate can be achieved in experimental kala-azar is a problem for further investigation.

That 9 of the 14 hamsters apparently cured of kala-azar by neostibosan (Table III) were refractory to a second inoculation with *Leishmania donovani* is suggestive of immunity, but one can not be sure that a focus of infection was not present. The relapse rate of 66.7% is considerable, and further suggests that the treatment given was insufficient. The occurrence of spontaneous recovery is interesting, but rather infrequent. On the whole it seems that kala-azar is more difficult to treat in hamsters than in man.

Summary. Chinese hamsters infected with kala-azar seemed to have a lower tolerance for neostibosan than normal hamsters, but the difference was not statistically significant. Five to 7 g of neostibosan per kilo body-weight constituted a course of treatment. The range of the effective dose was from 200 to 500 mg per kilo. The mortality rate during treatment was 31.6%. The apparent cure-rate in hamsters surviving the treatment was 100%, but the actual cure-rate was only 50%. An inoculation test is necessary to prove actual cure. Nine out of 14 apparently cured hamsters were refractory to a second inoculation with *Leishmania donovani*. Spontaneous recovery from and relapse of kala-azar were seen in Chinese hamsters.

27. The Seasonal Incidence of Kala-Azar and Its Significance in Relation to the Transmission Problem of The Disease

Yuan, I.C., Chu, F.T. and Lee, C.U. *Chinese Medical Journal*, 56: 241, 1939.

袁贻瑾、诸福棠、李宗恩《黑热病的季节性发病与其对传播的意义》，载于《中华医学杂志》，1939 年，56:241-264 页。

翻译概要 作者统计了在协和住院的、未满一周岁的黑热病患儿的发病时间（因为他们只有一个被感染的季节），结果都在 5–9 月白蛉的繁殖季节，而且黑热病小体可于该季节在白蛉的体内成熟并繁殖。此结果支持白蛉是黑热病的传染媒介的假设。

Chinese Medical Journal, 56: 241-264, *September*, 1939.

THE SEASONAL INCIDENCE OF KALA-AZAR IN INFANTS AND ITS SIGNIFICANCE IN RELATION TO THE TRANSMISSION PROBLEM OF THE DISEASE*

I. C. Yuan, F. T. Chu and C. U. Lee

Departments of Public Health and Medicine, Peiping Union Medical College, Peiping

The occurrence of kala-azar in children in the first year of life presents certain unusual advantages for the study of the epidemiology of the disease. In the first place, the simple life of an infant with respect to diet, contact and whereabouts renders many of the possible channels of infection in an adult relatively unimportant in a young child, thus greatly reducing the epidemiological factors to be considered. Secondly, information concerning an infant, generally speaking, can be obtained more accurately than in the case of an older child, partly because his personal history is brief and partly because he is usually under the close attention and care of his mother. These are no small advantages in a disease the onset of which is, in most cases, insidious and the incubation period of which is little known except for its being rather long and variable. Finally, infancy affords a unique opportunity to ascertain whether the transmission of the infection is limited to a certain season, or whether there is, in the year, a period of greatest infectivity. Such a finding, if established, would rule out possibilities of little significance, and throw new light, on the transmission problem of the disease.

Important as these considerations may be, and in spite of the fact that kala-azar has been known in some countries to be especially prevalent among young children, epidemiological studies based on a sufficient number of such cases supported by adequate data are lacking. In a paper

* Presented before the P.U.M.C. Faculty Medical Society on January 18, 1939.

on the epidemiology of kala-azar in China, Young and Hertig (1) discussed the importance of the study of the seasonal incidence of the disease in young children. They stated that in view of the sharply marked seasons in the endemic area of China and the sandfly season for all species known in this country to be limited to the period from the end of May to the end of September, the presence of any considerable number of infants born in or after November and shown to have kala-azar before the following May would render the sandfly hypothesis difficult to maintain. However, their cases were few and, with the exception of two, were not supported by adequate data. Two of the eight patients whom they cited were admitted to the P.U.M.C. Hospital and both had experienced an entire summer, which fact we have been able to confirm by establishing their exact dates of birth. Of the remaining six cases, diagnosis of one was made by finding the parasite, of another by globulin precipitation test and clinical symptoms but not by demonstrating the parasite, and of the other four probably on clinical basis alone. The dates of birth of these patients were based on unverified ages in months as given on admission. The authors did not draw any conclusion on the basis of these cases.

Hindle (2) reported a case of kala-azar in a Chinese infant based upon the information obtained from a physician of the London Mission Hospital at Tientsin. This is one of the above cases cited by Young and Hertig. The patient was brought to the hospital on March 19, 1926, at the age of four months, presumably born in November, 1925. Diagnosis was made by finding the parasite. Hindle concluded that the child could not possibly have been exposed to the bites of sandflies, as their season ended approximately two months before the child was born, and that it was difficult of explanation except on the hypothesis of congenital transmission, although the mother showed no obvious sign of the disease. Apparently, no attempt was made to verify the age of the patient.

Outside of China, we have the well-known case recorded by Low and Cooke (3) of a young child, born in England, on September 12, 1925, and shown to have the disease on September 20, 1926. The authors stated that the source of the child's infection, occurring as it did in England, was undoubtedly the mother, as she was known to have the disease and to have suffered a relapse at that time. The mode of transmission was thought to be either intra-uterine or by direct contamination.

Napier and Das Gupta (4) reported a case in India, at the eighth month of life, seen on November 15, 1927. The child was born in April and remained well for three months. He developed fever in July. The mother showed no sign of the disease. The authors concluded that the period of incubation was almost certainly less than three months, and the infection was transmitted during April, the latter half, May, June or July.

There is, in the literature, a number of other reports on kala-azar in infants chiefly dealing with the clinical aspects of the disease but none of the authors has attempted to correlate the seasonal incidence of kala-azar in infants with the question of the time of infection. In a paper on the age incidence of 1,346 patients, Paradiso (5) recorded 189 cases of children in the first year of life, 21 under 6 months and 168 between 6 and 12 months. However, no data were given as to the time of birth of the patients.

THIRTY-SIX CASES OF KALA-AZAR IN INFANTS

In the present study we have analysed 36 cases of kala-azar in children in the first year of life diagnosed in this hospital from 1923 to 1938. The selection of cases was based upon the following criteria: (a) The diagnosis was made by finding Leishmania donovani; (b) the duration of illness between the onset of symptoms and first medical examination was not longer than six months; (c) the date of birth of the patient was known; and (d) the onset of the disease occurred during the first year of life. Abstracts of case records with special reference to the diagnosis, time of onset and date of birth are appended. The important points of each case are tabulated in Table 1. Five possible cases were excluded. Three of them had a history of more than six months, and the dates of birth of the remaining two could not be ascertained. We shall have more to say about these cases later.

TABLE 1. *Kala-azar patients in the first year of life*

Case No.	Sex	Residence	Birth date	Onset	Age in months		
					At onset	At Ist. exam.	Diagnosis made
H- 47156	M	Peiping	11-19-34	Nov. '35	12	14	14
H- 60904	M	,,	11-22-37	E. Oct. '38	10.5	10.5	12.5
H- 61858	M	,,	11-25-36	L. Nov. '37	12	14	14
H- 53180	F	,,	12-25-34	E. Dec. 35	11.5	11.5	14
H- 61592	M	,,	12-26-36	Dec. '37	11.5	12.5	12.5
H- 4002	M	,,	1-3 -23	L. Oct. '23	10	11.5	12
H- 57270	F	,,	1-3 -37	L. Oct. '37	10	16	16
H- 35524	F	,,	1-13-31	E. Dec. '31	10.5	14.5	14.5
H- 61582	M	,,	1-14-37	E. Nov. '37	9.5	12	12
H- 48939	F	,,	1-16-34	E. Dec. '34	10.5	14.5	14.5
O-393584	M	,,	1-17-37	Dec. '37	11	16	16.5
H- 38708	F	Tsinghua Yuan	1-18-32	Dec. '32	11	11.5	11.5
H- 62268	M	Peiping	1-22-37	Jan. '38	12	13	13
H- 65582	F	Haitien	1-29-38	L. Sept. '38	8	11	11
O-392654	M	Peiping	2-12-37	Feb. '38	12	14.5	14.5
H- 43708	M	,,	2-16-34	Oct. '34	8	13	13
H- 5092	M	,,	2-16-22	Feb. '23	12	15	15.5
H- 47814	M	Shihchiachwang	3-20-34	Nov. '34	8	10	10
H- 48918	M	Peiping	3-31-34	Jan. '35	9.5	9.5	12
H- 58377	F	,,	4-2 -37	E. Jan. '38	9	13	13
H- 29553	M	,,	4-10-30	E. Sept. '30	5	5.5	5.5
HFT-83-3	F	Huai-fang	4-17-36	Jan '37	9	9	12
H- 9403	F	Peiping	4-18-24	E. Oct. '24	5.5	6	6.5
H- 57277	M	,,	4-20-36	E. Oct. '36	5.5	5.5	8.5
H- 35137	M	,,	4-28-31	L. Dec. '31	8	10	10.5
H- 64925	F	,,	5-8 -38	E. Aug. '38	3	3	5.5
H- 65547	F	,,	5-8 -38	L. Aug. '38	3.5	7.5	7.5
H- 36583	M	,,	5-12-31	Dec. '31	7	10.5	14
H- 28282	F	,,	5-14-30	Feb. '31	9	9.5	9.5
H- 33980	F	,,	5-25-31	E. Nov. '31	5.5	5.5	6
H- 45070	M	,,	5-28-33	Nov. '33	5.5	8.5	12.5
H- 35684	M	Tsinghua Yuan	5-29-31	Jan. '32	7.5	10.5	10.5
H- 36286	M	Peiping	6-13-32	Nov. '32	5	6	6.5
H- 61665	M	,,	6-17-37	E. Dec. '37	5.5	7	7
O-394686	M	Wuchinghsien	6-19-37	E. Jan. '38	6.5	11.5	13
H- 46576	M	Peiping	9-23-34	E. Mar. '35	5.5	5.5	6

E. = Early; L. = Late

Of the 36 cases, 23 were examined by one of us (F.T.C.) at the time of illness. For establishing the diagnosis the demonstration of the presence of the parasite was required in addition to clinical symptoms and findings and in most cases confirmed by another person or by a different technique. In difficult cases judgment of an expert was always sought. The exclusion of cases with histories longer than six months was to avoid possible errors of information likely to occur in cases of long duration.

The ascertaining of the dates of birth of the 36 patients was not as simple as the matter might appear to be, because official registration of birth and keeping of birth records are novel institutions in China and have not yet been satisfactorily carried out even in large cities. In this hospital, the age of an infant patient was usually stated in months and the date of birth was not recorded until three years ago after a simple solar-lunar calendar chart was made available, by means of which a Chinese lunar date can be readily transcribed into its solar corresponding date. The recording of the date of birth was instituted in this hospital for in-patients in 1936 and for out-patients in 1938. Every effort was made by one of us (I.C.Y.) to ascertain the date of birth of each patient. Fortunately, 30 of the 36 patients were born in Peiping and many were still local residents at the time of inquiry. Eight patients were born in this hospital. For another ten patients the original records of birth written at the time of birth were found in the local police, health or midwifery institutions. The dates of birth of four more patients are almost as certain as those obtained from birth records, since they were confirmed by either dated events or records of another source. For the remaining 14 patients the date of birth was ascertained or confirmed from death records in two cases, by correspondence with the patients' parents in two cases, and by personal interviews with the parents, mainly the mothers, in ten cases. While information in the latter cases is not based on documental evidences, its reliability is probably of a high order because unusual importance is attached to one's hour, date, month and year of birth due to certain social traditions in this country. It is therefore extremely rare for a Chinese mother not to remember the date of birth of her children.

Information on the time of onset of illness in any patient cannot be for obvious reasons as accurate as the date of his birth. In kala-azar the onset of which is in most cases insidious, it is as a rule very difficult to fix the date of onset. Other factors which further complicate the matter are the variety of initial symptoms in different cases* and the frequent occurrence of remissions and relapses in the early course of the disease. Lastly, the information obtained from mothers concerning events which had occurred many weeks or several months previously may not be entirely reliable. Special effort was made to check the histories taken at different times and by different persons and to accept only those taken carefully and thoroughly. In ascertaining the time of onset, we took into account not only the above points, but also the physical and laboratory findings and the clinical course of the disease in each patient. In view of the gradual development of the clinical onset usually seen in kala-azar, an attempt was made to determine the earliest possible time of onset in every case. While we arrived at a conclusion on the approximate time of onset only after a careful scrutiny of all the available information bearing on the question, some degree of inaccuracy was unavoidable for reasons just mentioned. However, it may be pointed out here that, as the main object in ascertaining the time of onset is to find out whether the occurrence of kala-azar in infants exhibits any seasonal prevalence, such random error which may cause an increased variation in the distribution of the seasonal incidence will not in all probability alter the general picture of seasonal prevalence.

There are 23 males and 13 females. The majority of cases are of recent years, 16 within the last two years and only three before 1930. Of the 36 patients, 12 were born in Peiping and definitely known to

*One of us (C.U.L.) and Chung, in an article on the early manifestations of Chinese kala-azar, made the following statement regarding the clinical onset of the disease in children (Chinese Med. J. 49: 1281, 1935): "In children it may be night cries, fretfulness and general irritability, that first engage the attention of the parents. In some cases gastro-intestinal complaints are the presenting symptoms, a mild diarrhea with or without mucus in the stools or constipation. In children complaints of abdominal pain are rather frequent in the early days of their illness. Anorexia is not a prominent symptom among adults but in infants refusal or regurgitation of feedings may be the first sign that led the parents to suspect something amiss. In a few cases children were brought in by parents merely on account of an undue pallor and upon examination were found to have a moderate degree of anemia which later turned out to be due to kala-azar." It may be added that in young children an attack of coryza or mild cough with or without fever is very common at the onset of the disease, probably only next in frequency to fever which is undoubtedly the most frequent symptom at any stage of the disease.

have remained in the city, and 18 were born and resided locally, but without information as to whether the patients had ever been taken out of the city, except one who, at the age of two months, was taken to an endemic area of kala-azar in Shantung during a summer and stayed there for one month. Of the remaining six patients, four came from places a short distance from the city, one was brought here from Shihchiachwang, and another from a village 40 miles south of Peiping. It may be noted that 30 out of 36 patients were born and resided in Peiping, and probably contracted the disease within the city.

The cases according to the age at onset are distributed as follows: 1 at 3 months, 9 between 3.5 and 5.5 months, 10 between 6.5 and 9 months, and 16 between 9.5 and 12 months. On the whole, these cases sought medical examination comparatively early: a few days after onset, 8; 0.5-1 month, 6; 1.5-3 months, 13; and 3.5-6 months, 9. In other words, 75 per cent of the cases came to medical attention within three months following the onset. Diagnosis was made in the majority of cases soon after the first medical examination: a few days, 19; 0.5-1 month, 8; 1.5-3 months, 5; and 3.5-4 months, 2.

ANALYSIS AND FINDINGS

The incidence of the disease by month of birth of the patients shown in Table 2 is most interesting. We have two or more patients born in each month from November to June and one patient born in September, but none born in July, August and October. Grouped by intervals of four months, 17 patients were born between November and February, 18 patients were born between March and June and only one was born between July and October, namely in September. In order to ascertain whether this finding is really peculiar to kala-azar patients in the first year of life, we also record in Table 2 the distribution by month of birth of 35 patients whose onset of the disease occurred in the second year of life. The other criteria are the same as used in the selection of cases of the first year group. There are two or more patients born in each month throughout the year. Grouped by intervals of four months, the distribution appears to be remarkably even: 13 patients born between November and February, 10 patients born between March and June, and 12 patients born between July and October. This is a distinct contrast to the rarity of patients born between July and October as found in the first year group.

TABLE 2. *Distribution of patients of the first and second years of life according to month of birth*

Month of birth	Number of patients			
	First year		Second year	
November	3	17	5	13
December	2		4	
January	9		2	
February	3		2	
March	2	18	2	10
April	6		3	
May	7		3	
June	3		2	
July	0	1	2	12
August	0		3	
September	1		3	
October	0		4	
Total	36		35	

The frequency of cases according to the month of onset is given in Table 3 showing that there is a definite seasonal prevalence, the highest incidence occurring in the period of November-December. Napier (6) reported that the highest seasonal incidence of Indian kala-azar occurs between November and February. Adler and Theodor (7) stated that the disease in the Mediterranean countries is prevalent throughout the year but in Catania is commonest in March and April. The seasonal occurrence of kala-azar by onset in Chinese patients was studied by Patton and Hindle (8), and also by Young and Hertig (1). Based on 301 and 850 patients of all ages respectively, they failed to discover any seasonal prevalence. The advantage of studying the seasonal incidence of the disease by using records of patients in the first year of life is worth noting. Those cases whose incubation period of infection was long and tended to obscure the picture of seasonal prevalence would have been most likely excluded, as the maximum period by definition could not be longer than one year. It is also our experience that the disease runs a more acute and severe course in young children. (In the present series 50 per cent of the patients died during the treatment or soon after the treatment was completed). Consequently, the incubation period is likely to be shorter and less variable. Hence, the seasonal prevalence becomes more apparent among young patients.

TABLE 3. *Seasonal occurrence of kala-azar according to month of onset*

Month of onset	Number of cases	
July	0	2
August	2	
September	2	8
October	6	
November	7	16
December	9	
January	6	9
February	3	
March	1	1
April	0	
May	0	0
June	0	
Total	36	

In connection with the time of onset two more points deserve mentioning: First, none of the patients born in and after November was shown to have the disease before the following summer. Second, 35 of the 36 patients had lived through the latter part of June and the whole month of July before they developed the disease.

An examination of the age at onset in relation to the month of birth will show that patients born in winter months were on the whole older than those born in the spring or the early summer months, and patients born in the spring months were on the whole older than those born in the early summer months. Table 4 shows that the average age at onset was 11.5 months for patients born during November and December, 10.4 months for patients born during January and February; 7.4 months for patients born during March and April and 5.8 months for patients born during May and June. The differences of these averages are statistically significant. The youngest patients for the four bi-monthly groups were 10.5, 8.0, 5.0 and 3.0 months old respectively. Of the ten patients whose age at the onset was under six months, three were born in April; four were born in May; two were born in June; and one was born in September. All except the last patient were born within a short time before or during the early part of the summer. None of these patients was born in the winter months. Owing to the approximate nature of the time of, and age at, onset, one must not over-estimate the significance of the individual averages and figures. What is really important is the indisputable uniform trend exhibited by these averages and figures.

Table 4. *Average ages at onset of patients and ages of the youngest born in various periods of the year*

Month of birth	Average age in months	Age of youngest in months
Nov.—Dec.	11.50±.16	10.5
Jan.—Feb.	10.38±.26	8.0
Mar.—Apr.	7.44±.43	5.0
May—June	5.80±.38	3.0
July—Aug.	—	—
Sept.—Oct.	5.5*	—

* One case only

PERIOD OF GREATEST INFECTIVITY AND ITS BEARING ON THE TRANSMISSION PROBLEM

What conclusion or conclusions can we draw from these findings? In the first place, the rarity of patients born between July and October, the absence of patients born in and after November and shown to have the disease before the following summer and the fact that none of the ten patients whose age at onset was under six months was born during the winter months must indicate that the fall and winter months are of little importance in the transmission of the disease. Secondly, the existence of a definite seasonal prevalence, especially in a disease the incubation period of which is highly variable, suggests that there is, in the year, a period of greatest infectivity, probably of narrow limits. This period must be some time before August, because the youngest cases appeared in the latter month and the peak of the seasonal incidence occurred in November-December. Thirdly, the nearer to the early part of the summer the patients were born, the less their average age at onset, a fact indicating that the period of greatest infectivity must be later than April. It seems, therefore, logical to conclude that the period of greatest infectivity must be some time between April and August. Can we delimit this period more sharply than just stated? Although it is no easy matter, with the small number of cases available at present, to fix the limits, we may place that interval, with reasonable certainty, between the middle of May and the middle of July. The latter part of July probably is of no great importance, because if it were we would have some patient or patients born between the latter part of June and early part of July. Actually, the birth date of the last patient born in June was on the nineteenth and none was born in July or August. The placing of the middle of May as the other limit is not unreasonable, in the light of the finding that patients born in May and June were on the average younger than those born in March and April and also in view of the indication that the period of greatest infectivity probably is of short duration. At present, it is difficult to state whether the latter part of May is important in the transmission of the disease. When we have accumulated a larger number of cases, we will be in a position to answer this question by ascertaining whether patients born in June are on the average younger than those born in May.

What is the significance of the patient born in September and shown to have the disease in the following March? The existence of a period of greatest infectivity need not exclude the possibility of occasional infection during other months of the year. This patient obviously must have acquired the infection after birth and before the time of onset, as the mother of the child showed no sign of the disease upon examination. But the rarity of such patients suggests strongly that periods other than the early summer months are of little importance in the usual transmission of the disease. It is conceivable that the infection of occasional cases can occur outside the designated interval and the mode of transmission of such cases may be entirely different, but it cannot play an important rôle in the transmission of the majority of cases.

As stated previously, five possible cases which failed to satisfy the criteria of selection were not included in this study. It may be interesting to point out that even these cases fit in well with the general epidemiological picture which has already been brought forth. The approximate dates of birth of these patients fall between February and June, and their approximate months of onset, between November and February.

The relationship between the period of greatest infectivity and the time of birth and of onset of the individual patients can be best shown by means of a chart. A horizontal bar is drawn according to a daily-monthly scale, representing the age of each patient at onset. One end of the bar corresponds to the date of birth and the other end, the approximate time of onset. The period of greatest infectivity is indicated by fine vertical lines. An examination of the graphic representation of the seasonal case incidence with reference to the period of greatest infectivity as designated between the middle of May and the middle of July will enable one to rationalize completely all the facts which have been brought forth and may be summarized as follows.

1. All patients, except one already shown to have little importance on the problem of the usual mode of transmission of the disease, lived through the whole or a good part of the summer prior to the onset of their illness.

2. There is a definite seasonal prevalence of the disease, the highest incidence occurring during November-December.

3. The average age at onset of patients born during the winter months is greater than that of patients born during the spring or the early summer months, and so is the average age of patients born during the spring months as compared with that of patients born during the early summer months. The ages of the youngest patients born in the respective periods show the same trend.

4. There is only one patient born between July and October, namely, in September, in contrast with 17 patients born between November and February and 18 patients born between March and June.

5. None of the patients born in and after November was shown to have the disease before the following summer.

6. Of the ten patients whose age at onset was under six months, nine were born just before or during the early summer months and one was born in September. None of them was born in the winter.

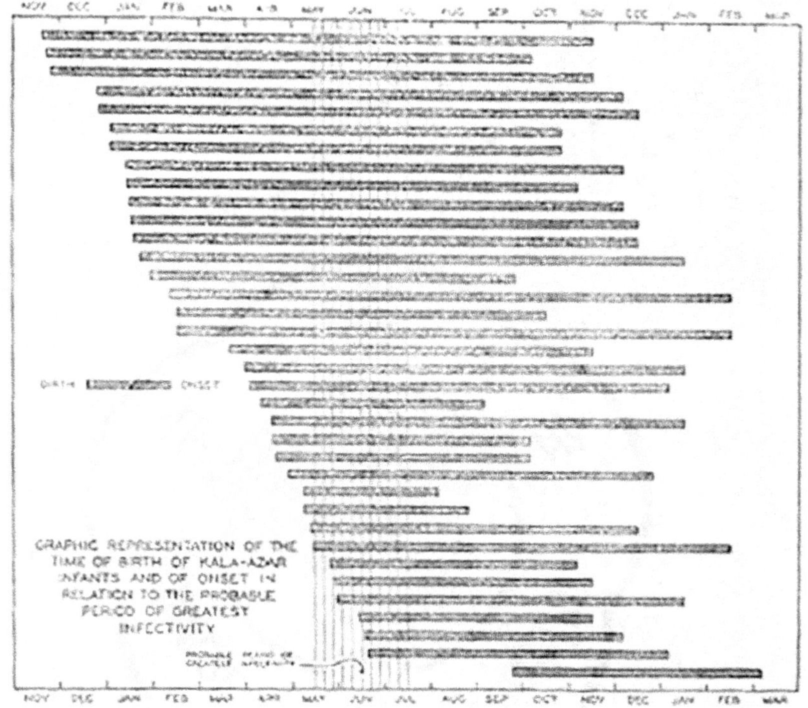

What is the significance of the existence of a period of greatest infectivity corresponding to the early part of the summer in connection with the transmission problem of the disease? Inasmuch as the present study is based upon cases of very young children, the question of congenital transmission must be first considered. If the latter mode of transmission were of any importance, we should have discovered a number of the mothers of our patients suffering from the disease. But this is not true. Not a single mother was known to have the infection. Furthermore, it would be extremely difficult to explain why congenital transmission should occur almost exclusively in the early part of the summer. The latter argument may be used with equal effectiveness against the contamination theory of transmission, not to mention already well-known epidemiological evidences contrary to such a theory. On the other hand, our present inference of the early part of the summer as the period of greatest infectivity speaks strongly in favor of the theory of the sandfly as the transmitter of the disease, especially in light of recent findings made in this country on this blood-sucking insect.

It is generally known that there are two important species of sandflies in the endemic area of China, *Phlebotomus chinensis* and *Phlebotomus sergenti*. Young and Hertig (9) found them in Hsuchow and Peiping. Patton and Hindle (10) found them in Shantung. Recently, Sun, Yao, Chu and Wu (11) found them in Tsingkiangpu in northern Kiangsu. In the paper just cited, Patton and Hindle gave a summary of the studies on the bionomics of Chinese sandflies. The species of *P. chinensis* first appears at the end of May, after which the numbers gradually increase until the middle of June. Toward the end of June, the numbers begin to fall, and after the middle of July, only occasional specimens can be seen. Its duration in various developmental stages is between seven and eight weeks, and there is probably only one brood in a year, which explains the fact that *P. chinensis* is rare in the latter part of the summer. The species of *P. sergenti* begins to appear simultaneously with *P. chinensis* at the end of May and continues without much diminution in numbers until well on into August; and throughout September occasional specimens can be obtained. Its duration in various developmental stages is about the same as that of the other species. It has probably two or more broods in a year. It is interesting to note that the seasonal prevalence of *P. chinensis* coincides with the period of greatest infectivity of kala-azar suggested by our study, namely, the early summer months.

According to Young and Hertig (9), the female of *P. chinensis* can be readily infected with *Leishmania donovani* by feeding on infected hamsters. The infection has been shown as high as 85 per cent. In it the parasites flagellate and multiply. The same is true in the case of the female of *P. sergenti*, but the rate of infection is considerably lower. These findings were confirmed by Patton and Hindle and others.

More recently, Sun and his co-workers discovered in Tsingkiangpu natural infection of *P. chinensis* caught in kala-azar houses with flagellates morphologically indistinguishable from those of *Leishmania donovani*. From June 6 to July 16, 1935, they (11) caught 769 sandflies of which 684 were females, and the large majority were *P. chinensis*. Of the 421 female *P. chinensis* caught and dissected, seven were found naturally infected with flagellates. These infected sandflies were caught from houses of kala-azar patients between June 18 and July 16; 1 on June 18, 3 on June 22, 1 on June 25, 1 on July 4 and 1 on July 16. In 1935, they (12) collected sandflies from the early part of June until September 15, covering practically the entire sandfly season. Among the 855 females caught, there were 731 *P. chinensis*, 2 *P. sergenti* and 53 of an unknown species. Of these, 483, 2 and 33 of the respective species were dissected and ten *P. chinensis* were found naturally infected. Again, the infected sandflies were caught from kala-azar houses between the middle of June and the middle of July; 1 each on June 16, 25, 28 and 29; 2 on July 2; and 1 each on July 3, 4, 9 and 13. It should be noted that very few *P. sergenti* were caught and dissected.

CONCLUSIONS

The existence of a period of greatest infectivity probably corresponding to early summer months, together with the recent discovery of natural infection in *P. chinensis* during June and July in kala-azar houses, the readiness with which this species can be artificially infected and its seasonal prevalence in the early part of the summer, strongly suggests this species as the most important transmitter of human kala-azar in North China. This theory also can adequately account for the patient of 5.5 months of life born in September, which is nearly the end of the sandfly season, by assuming that the infection took place soon after birth.

The proof of this theory must be sought through experiments. But the conclusion that natural infection in man in North China chiefly occurs in the early part of the summer remains significant. This conclusion renders unimportant those theories of transmission which cannot adequately account for the period of greatest infectivity.

At the same time it sets forth a principle that whatever the most important mode of transmission may be in this part of the world, it must be intimately associated with the early summer months, probably between the middle of May and the middle of July which our study strongly suggests to be the period of greatest infectivity.

In closing, it may be noted that our present position as summarized above with respect to the transmission problem of kala-azar in man in North China is based on epidemiological evidences brought forth for the first time from a study of human cases.

REFERENCES

1. *Young, C. W., and Hertig, M.:* The kala-azar transmission problem: Field and laboratory Studies in China. I. Epidemiology. Am. J. Hyg., **9**: 227, 1929.
2. *Hindle, E.:* Further observations on Chinese kala-azar. Proc. Roy. Soc., Ser. B., **103**: 599 1928.
3. *Low, G. C., and Cooke, W. E.:* A congenital case of kala-azar. Lancet, **2**: 1209, 1926.
4. *Napier, L. E., and Das Gupta, C. R.:* Indian kala-azar in a newly born child. Ind. Med. Gaz., **63**: 199, 1928
5. *Paradiso, F.:* The distribution in altitude of infantile kala-azar in Catania and the age of the children affected. Pediatria, **34**: 654, 1926; as reviewed in Tropical Diseases Bulletin: **24**: 131, 1927.
6. *Napier, L. E.:* An epidemiological consideration of the transmission of kala-azar in India Indian Med. Res. Mem., Supp. Indian J. Med. Res., Report of kala-azar commission, India. No. I., p. 219, 1924-25.
7. *Adler, S., and Theodor, O.:* Investigations on Mediterranean kala-azar. I. Introduction and epidemiology. Proc. Roy. Soc., Ser. B., **108**: 447, 1931.
8. *Patton, W. S., and Hindle, E.:* Notes on kala-azar in Shantung. Proc. Roy. Soc. Ser. B., **100**: 379, 1926.
9. *Young, C. W., and Hertig, M.:* The development of flagellates in Chinese sandflies (Phlebotomus) fed on hamsters infected with *Leishmania donovani.* Proc. Soc. Exp. Biol. and Med., **23**: 611, 1926.
10. *Patton, W. S., and Hindle, E.:* The North China species of the genus phlebotomus: Notes on the bionomics of Chinese species of phlebotomus. Proc. Roy. Soc., Ser. B., **102**: 546, 1927.
11. *Sun, C. J., Yao, Y. T., Chu, H. J., and Wu, C. C.:* Natural infection of *Phlebotomus chinensis* with flagellates morphologically indistinguishable from those of *Leishmania donovani.* Chinese Med. J., **50**: 911, 1936.
12. *Sun, C. J., and Wu, C. C.:* Notes on the study of kala-azar transmission. II. Further observations on the natural infection of *Phlebotomus chinensis* with *Leptomonas donovani.* Chinese Med. J., **52**: 665, 1937.

28. A Report on the Examination of 587 Normal Dogs in Peiping for Leishmania Infection. With Observation on the Experimental Production of Cutaneous Lesions on A Normal Dog Inoculated with A Canine Strain of Leishmania

Chung, H.L., Wang, C.W., Lee, C.U. and Liu, W.T. *Chinese Medical Journal*, 56: 354, 1939.

钟惠澜、王季午、李宗恩，刘纬通《对北平地区 587 条正常狗被利氏曼小体感染的筛查》，载于《中华医学杂志》，1939 年，56:354-359 页。

翻译概要 作者从 1936 年 11 月至 1937 年 11 月检查了北平的 587 条正常狗的肝、脾及皮肤，确认有 8 条狗感染了利氏曼小体（犬黑热病，1.4%）。作者将从病犬分离的利氏曼小体注射给正常狗的腹膜后，正常狗的皮肤呈典型的犬黑热病体征，从而确立狗亦为黑热病的中间储存宿主。

Chinese Medical Journal, **56:** *354-359, October, 1939.*

A REPORT ON THE EXAMINATION OF 587 NORMAL DOGS IN PEIPING FOR LEISHMANIA INFECTION

WITH OBSERVATIONS ON THE EXPERIMENTAL PRODUCTION OF CUTANEOUS LESIONS ON A NORMAL DOG INOCULATED WITH A CANINE STRAIN OF LEISHMANIA

KUEI-LAN CHUNG, C. W. WANG, C. U. LEE AND W. T. LIU

Department of Medicine, Peiping Union Medical College, Peiping, China

Canine leishmaniasis has been previously recorded in China by Andrews (1), Lee (2), Feng, Chung and Hoeppli (3), Chung and Feng (4), and Feng and Chang (5). The present communication merely records (*a*) the incidence of the disease based on microscopic examination of the liver, spleen and skin of 587 normal dogs and (*b*) the experimental production of gross cutaneous lesions on a normal dog inoculated with a canine strain of leishmania.

MATERIAL AND METHOD

Through the co-operation of the Department of Physiology of this College which has always employed a large number of normal dogs for physiological experiments, we have had an unusually good opportunity of procuring the necessary materials for the study of the incidence of natural leishmania infection of normal dogs in Peiping. Since November 9, 1936 the Department of Medicine has received, as a routine, specimens of the spleen, liver and skin of every dog experimentally sacrificed. On receipt of the specimens, smears of the said organs were made. These were stained with Leishman's stain and examined under the microscope with a high power oil immersion lens. In no instance was a specimen declared negative until a prolonged careful search for half an hour had been made. Grossly all the specimens received appeared normal, there being no evidence of perisplenitis, liver cirrhosis or ulcerations of the skin. The specimens of the skin were taken from the ear and the relatively less hairy part of the abdomen.

RESULTS

Altogether 587 specimens of the liver, spleen, and skin from 587 normal dogs have been examined during a period of a little over a year from November 9, 1936 to November 30, 1937. Out of these, 8 dogs (or 1.4 per cent) were found to be positive for kala-azar as shown in Table 1. In 5 of the 8 positives, organisms morphologically identical with Leishman-Donovan bodies were found in the smears made from the liver, spleen, and skin. The infection in these instances was moderately heavy. In the remaining 3 cases, however, the infection was so light that it was not recognized until the smears of the spleen were re-examined, the smears of the liver and skin in these instances having unfortunately been discarded before the re-examination.

TABLE 1. *Showing the number of dogs examined and the number of dogs positive in different months*

Time of examination	Number of dogs examined	Number of dogs positive
1936		
November	28	0
December	78	1
1937		
January	53	2
February	63	0
March	93	2
April	53	0
May	41	0
June	45	2
July	34	1
August	—	—
September	24	0
October	35	0
November	40	0
Total	587	8 or 1.4%

Since November 1937 many more dogs have been examined for leishmania infection. The incidence of canine leishmaniasis appears to be increasing, and this increase seems to be accompanied by suggestive parallel increase of cases of human kala-azar in Peiping as will be dealt with in a later communication. In most countries, where the incidence of canine leishmaniasis has been investigated, the percentage of naturally infected dogs was found to vary from 1.6 to 8.97 per cent except in Malta, Greece, and Turkistan where an infection rate of from 11 to 40.8 per cent has been encountered (7). The time of examination, and the number of dogs examined, however, varied with different investigations. Furthermore, the material subjected to examination also was not uniform. In general the frequency of the disease appears to have a definite seasonal variation, being more prevalent in the warmer than in the colder months of the year. The incidence of infection in our series is only 1.4 per cent. This figure was obtained, however, from a highly selected group of animals which were apparently healthy. Had the cases with definite skin lesions been included, the figure would have been raised many folds. Another fact is that in the material we examined, the age of the dogs was not ascertainable. It is obvious that if many young dogs of less than or barely one year old were included, the incidence of natural infection could have been considerably reduced.

EXPERIMENTAL REPRODUCTION OF CANINE LEISHMANIASIS

The first of the eight positive dogs, referred to above, has already been reported by one of us (2) in 1937. The strain of leishmania isolated from this dog has been maintained in hamsters and has produced in a normal dog gross skin lesions typical of canine leishmaniasis. Inasmuch as experimental reproduction of these gross skin lesions has not been reported on dogs inoculated with the parasites of either canine or human visceral leishmaniasis, it seems of considerable interest to record our observations on this dog.

The animal in question was a normal Chinese puppy of about 1½ months old when it was obtained in February 1937. To ensure against the very remote possibility of its being congenitally infected, it was subjected to several liver punctures which yielded negative results for L.D. bodies. As a precaution against insect bites, the puppy was kept in a specially constructed sandfly-proof kennel. On June 2, 1937, it was inoculated intraperitoneally with a saline emulsion of one-tenth of the spleen of a hamster, which had been infected intraperitoneally on December 23, 1936, with a saline emulsion of a piece of the spleen of a naturally-infected dog in whose internal organs and skin we demonstrated for the first time in North China the presence of numerous L.D. bodies as already reported by one of us (Lee). In spite of the extensive visceral leishmaniasis the dog was apparently normal.

On August 18, 1937, 2½ months after the inoculation, a liver puncture of the puppy was done. The smears showed no L.D. bodies. However, the latter were found in large number, when the liver puncture was repeated 3 months later on December 31, 1937. In the meantime the conjunctivae of the dog were found to be somewhat red, but there were no skin lesions. On June 24, 1938, another liver puncture was performed, which revealed many L.D. bodies as before. On January 13, 1939, about a dozen small depilated areas were observed on the chin near the muco-cutaneous junction. A few of these were somewhat red and slightly elevated. The conjunctivae were definitely red. The cervical lymph nodes were enlarged on both sides of the neck and the smears made from the fluid aspirated from one of them showed numerous L.D. bodies. The rectal temperature was 39.8°C. Examination of the blood on the same day showed 10,400 leucocytes, 13.7 gm hemoglobin, and a negative globulin precipitation test. On February 8, 1939 a smear made from the scraping of the skin of the left external ear revealed the presence of many L.D. bodies. The globulin precipitation test was weakly positive. However, apart from the depilated areas on the chin, there were no obvious skin lesions. By the end of March 1939, the hair over the ears began to fall off rapidly and, by the middle of April, most of the hair over the ears, around the eye-lids and on the face, was gone. The alopecia was patchy in appearance. The skin of the ears was somewhat thickened, slightly red, and felt warmer than normal, especially at their margins. There were also multiple minute ulcers over both ears covered with scabs and sero-sanguinous crusts. Some of these ulcers not infrequently bled, when the dog flapped its ears vigorously. The globulin precipitation test had become strongly positive. In the meantime it was noticed that the dog did not bark half as often as it used to. As a whole, it appeared less playful and was often definitely fretful. Figs. 1 and 2, show the skin lesions as well as the rachitic attitude as a result of the bow-legs due to rickets. Obviously prolonged captivity of the dog in the dark kennel and inadequate diet contributed a great deal to the development of this bone pathology.

From the 5th to the 30th of June 1939, a series of feeding experiments with *P. chinensis* and *P. sergenti* were performed on this dog as already reported by Feng and Chung (5). It was found that both species of sandflies became readily infected, and in the case of *P. chinensis* the flagellates were frequently found in the pharynx, buccal cavity and proboscis. By the middle of June most of the hairs over the neck, the body and the tail have fallen off. Scaling of the skin was also present in patches over the trunk. On July 6, 1939, a big ulcer measuring about 3 cm wide and 6 cm long was observed on the dorsum of the posterior third of the trunk. Multiple small superficial ulcerations were also seen over the left anterior thigh and leg. These were painted with a 1 per cent gentian violet solution which brought about rapid healing within five days. The dog is now used for sandfly feeding experiments.

In a separate communication we have shown that naturally-infected dogs with and without gross skin lesions show essentially the same histopathologic changes in the various internal organs. Obviously the presence of gross cutaneous lesions merely represents an advanced stage, rather than a different, form of canine leishmaniasis. The absence of gross cutaneous lesions may be regarded as characteristic of a relatively early infection, although a heavy infection may not be accompanied by any striking gross skin lesions. The fact that the gross skin lesions in our inoculated dog did not occur until many months after the establishment of a generalized leishmania infection also lends support to the above view.

SUMMARY

1. The spleen, liver and skin of 587 apparently normal dogs have been examined for evidence of leishmaniasis which was found to be present in 8, or 1.4 per cent, of the animals investigated.

2. Gross skin lesions typical of canine visceral leishmaniasis of natural occurrence have been produced experimentally on a normal dog 22 months after intraperitoneal inoculation with a strain of leishmania isolated from a naturally-infected dog of normal appearance.

Chinese Medical Journal, 56: October, 1939.

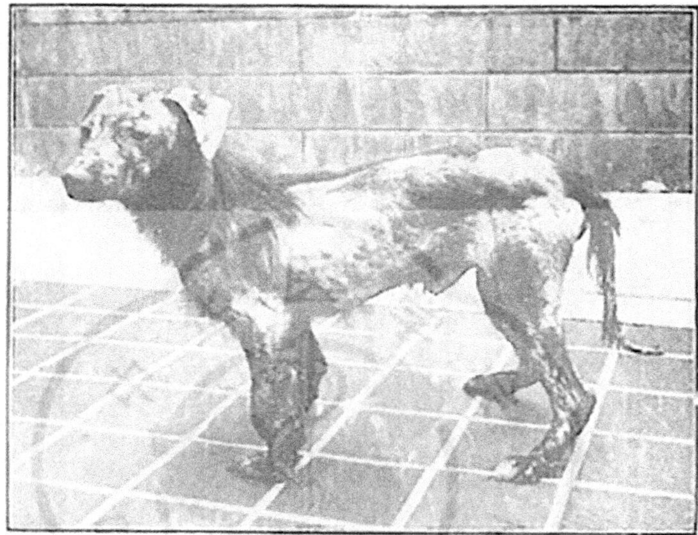

Fig. 1. Showing the skin lesions involving the head, body and limbs. Note the peculiar appearance of the tail due to loss of hair.

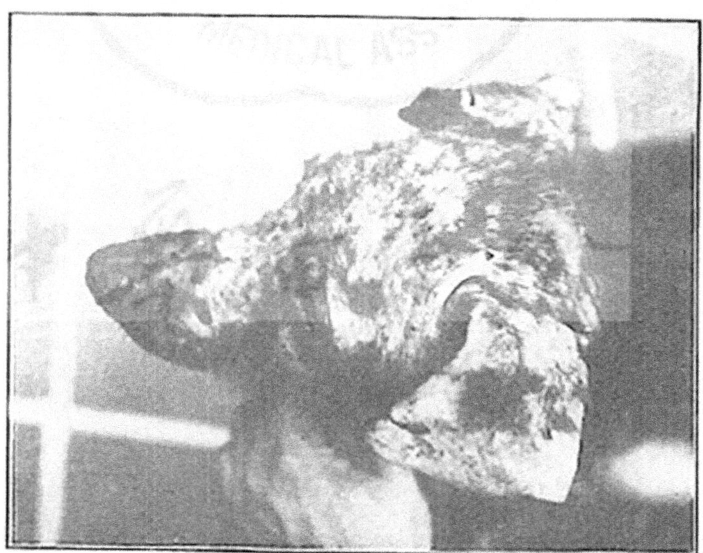

Fig. 2. Showing a close-up view of the lesions over the face and the ears.

H. L. CHUNG, C. W. WANG,
C. U. LEE AND W. T. LIU

REFERENCES

1 *Andrews, M. N.:* A case of canine kala-azar occurring in China. Trans. 9th Congress F. E. A. T. M., **2**: 679, 1935.

2. *Lee, C. U.:* Canine Leshmaniasis in Peiping. Chinese Med. J., **51**: 951, 1937.

3. *Feng, L. C., Chung, H. L., and Hoeppli, R.:* Canine leishmaniasis with skin lesions observed in Peiping. Chinese Med. J., **55**: 317, 1939.

4. *Chung, H. L. and Feng, L. C.:* Natural infection of *Phlebotomus chinensis* in Peiping with leishmania flagellates. Chinese Med. J., **56**: 47. 1939.

5. *Feng, L. C. and Chung, H. L.:* The development of leishmania in sandflies fed on dogs with canine leishmaniasis. Chinese Med. J., **56**: 35, 1939.

6 *Brumpt, E.:* Précis de Parasitologie. Paris, Masson et Cie, **1**: 282, 1936.

29. Solustibosan in Treatment of Kala-Azar

Chung, H.L., Wang, C.W. and Lee, C.U. *Chinese Medical Journal*, 61(2):77-82, 1942.

钟惠澜、王季午、李宗恩《Solustibosan 治疗黑热病之功效》，载于《中华医学杂志》，1942 年，61(2)：77-82 页。

原文概要　报告用 Solustibosan 治疗黑热病 24 例的结果，称适量之 Solustibosan 功效与 Ureastibamine 或 Neostibosan 相等，但因其所含锑量关系，用量远过于 Ureastibamine 或 Neostibosan。此剂有几种优点，为其它两种剂所不及，即其在水中始终坚定，毒性轻微，并可作肌肉注射等是。

Chinese Medical Journal **61**, 77-82, March-April, 1942

SOLUSTIBOSAN IN THE TREATMENT OF KALA-AZAR

HUEI-LAN CHUNG, C. W. WANG AND C. U. LEE
Department of Medicine, Peiping Union Medical College, Peking.

As a new remedy against kala-azar, Solustibosan,* a pentavalent antimony compound of hexonic acid has been tried clinically by several workers. Napier (1) reported a probable cure of 10 cases observed in India of which nine received 10 injections each and one 8 injections. The largest total dose was 87 cc and the smallest, 48 cc, the average being 73.6 cc. The drug was administered intramuscularly on alternate days in 6 cases and daily in 4. Struthers and Lin (2) reported 29 cases of which 22 were discharged as cured, 1 failed to respond, 3 did not complete the treatment and 3 died of serious complications having no relationship to the treatment, and 1 died within 6 months of some other disease. Yates (3) reported that in a series of 82 cases treated with the same drug 95.1 per cent. of them were discharged improved, but obviously no attempts were made to ascertain the rate of cure. The average total dose employed by the last mentioned 3 authors was 3.0 gm (60 cc solution) per patient given by the intramuscular route daily in a period of 11 days (Yates) or on alternate days in a period of 20 days (Struthers and Lin). Kikuth and Schmidt (4) who first introduced the drug for treatment of kala-azar believe that solustibosan is superior to neostibosan and that an average total dose of 60 cc or 3.0 gm is sufficient to bring about a cure in over 95 per cent. of the cases. Since 1937 we have treated 24 proven cases of kala-azar with solustibosan. Although in general our experience confirms the usefulness of this remedy, our observations as regards its potency and consequently its total curative dose are somewhat at variance with those of previous workers. As these observations may serve as a useful reference to clinicians interested in the chemotherapy of kala-azar in this country, they are here recorded.

MATERIAL AND METHOD

Altogether 24 cases of kala-azar admitted to the medical wards have been treated with solustibosan. In every instance the diagnosis was established before the commencement of treatment by the finding of *Leishmania donovani* in the material aspirated from the sternal marrow or from the spleen. Six of our patients were female and 18 male. They were between 12 and 62 years old, 20 of them being below 25 years. The duration of illness was between 3 weeks and 7 months in 16 cases and between 1 and 2 years in 8 cases. The drug was given intramuscularly (in 2 cases, it was given intravenously) every day in 2 cases, on alternate days in 13 cases and daily during the first 3 or 4 days but subsequently on alternate days in 9 cases. In the last mentioned group, the first 3 or 4 doses of the drug given in each case were 2, 4, 6 and 8 cc respectively followed by doses varying from 6 cc to 12 cc each on alternate days. In the rest of the cases, doses of from 6 cc to 12 cc each were maintained throughout the entire course of treatment. The total amount of solustibosan employed for the individual cases was 60 cc in 4 cases, 70 cc in 3 cases, 84 cc in 1 case, 100 cc in 8 cases, 100.2 cc in 1 case, 102 cc in 2 cases, 120 cc in 1 case, 144 cc in 1 case, 150 cc in 1 case and 162 cc in 2 cases.

RESULTS

The effect of treatment on fever. As shown in Table 1, the fever disappeared in 10 cases within 3 to 7 days after from 6 to 48 cc of solustibosan had been given and in 11 cases within 8 to 14 days after from 30 to 72 cc had been given. In the remaining 3 cases the temperature became normal

*Solustibosan is a colorless stable solution which contains 20 mg of metallic antimony per cc.

within 3 weeks after treatment with from 40 to 80 cc of the drug. Thus, as far as our experience goes, the effect of solustibosan on fever can be compared very favorably with that of either neostibosan or ureastibamine. Temporary spontaneous remission of fever occurs not infrequently in kala-azar and sometimes this renders the interpretation of the subsidence of fever during treatment difficult. In 4 cases in our series, a relapse actually occurred after the temperature had been normal for many days or weeks following a course of treatment. However, it appears safe to say that permanent disappearance of fever, as was the case with most of our patients, must be regarded as the beneficial result of treatment.

TABLE 1.—*The dosage and duration of treatment required to abolish fever in different cases.*

Case No.	1	2	3	4	5	6	7	8	9	10	11	12
Solustibosan cc.	30	40	6	40	30	60	30	80	20	60	18	8
Days	12	17	4	8	7	21	9	18	5	14	4	4
Case No.	**13**	**14**	**15**	**16**	**17**	**18**	**19**	**20**	**21**	**22**	**23**	**24**
Solustibosan cc.	24	30	42	36	60	42	48	32	30	72	18	54
Days	5	9	12	6	9	8	7	8	7	11	3	10

The effect of treatment on blood picture, plasma proteins, body weight and size of the spleen. As seen in Table 2, in all but 5 cases the treatment was followed by a definite increase of the hemoglobin values as well as the white and red blood cell counts. In 6 cases (Cases 2, 5, 12, 18, 20, 23) the blood picture became entirely normal or practically normal at the conclusion of treatment. It is interesting to note that in 5 out of these 6 cases the infection was relatively recent, being from 3 to 6 months old. In the 6th case, the duration of illness was 1 year. The amount and duration of treatment required to bring about a normal blood picture in these cases varied from 60 cc solustibosan in 12 days to 162 cc in 29 days. In the rest of the cured cases the blood picture did not return to normal until several or many weeks after cessation of the treatment.

In 9 cases of the present series the plasma albumin and globulin were studied before and after treatment. In 3 cases there was a rise of the albumin level with a simultaneous fall of the globulin content towards normal. In the remaining 6 cases no definite improvement of the plasma proteins was observed and no follow-up observations were made.

The spleen responded to the treatment with a reduction of its size in 18 out of 24 cases. The reduction of the size of the spleen was slight (1-3 cm) in 6 cases, moderate (4-6 cm) in 8 cases and marked (7-10 cm) in 4 cases. In the remaining 6 cases the spleen showed no appreciable decrease in size.

Under treatment the body weight showed an increase of from one-half of a kilogram to over 8 kilograms in 21 cases. In 1 case it was stationary and in the remaining 2 cases there was a decrease of 5 kilograms and 9.4 kilograms respectively. It is noteworthy, however, that all the last mentioned 3 cases were cured, whereas 4 out of the 21 cases which gained in weight during treatment required a second course to effect a cure.

Toxic reactions. The drug was well tolerated by all cases. Apart from the fact that its administration was followed by pain in the epigastrium and legs in one instance and generalized urticaria in another, no untoward symptoms attributable to it were noticed. Several patients had slight epistaxis and one had transient albuminuria which appeared during treatment. But these are common symptoms of kala-azar, hence they can hardly be regarded as toxic reactions to the drug. The low toxicity of solustibosan together with its suitability for intramuscular injections makes it a very useful drug, especially in infantile cases where the intravenous administration of other pentavalent antimony compound proves difficult. In cases complicated with Bright's disease or sensitive to neostibosan, ureastibamine or the like, solustibosan may prove to be a life-saving agent.

The effect of treatment on L.D. bodies, the total curative dose and the criteria of cure. The effect of solustibosan on L.D. bodies appears to be both direct and indirect. While its direct effect is not easy to demonstrate in vivo, its indirect effect seems obvious inasmuch as *Cases 1, 16, and 17* treated with a total dose of 70 cc, 102 cc and 144 cc respectively a permanent cure was obtained despite the fact that at the conclusion of the specific treatment L.D. bodies were still present in the lymph glands and in the sternal marrow. At least, it may be said that in these instances the body of the host having received a certain amount of solustibosan was able to carry on the fight against the L.D. bodies until the latter were completely eradicated without further treatment.

As seen in Table 3, of the 24 cases treated with a course of solustibosan from 60 to 162 cc, 4 (Cases 6, 8, 13 and 19) showed a persistence of kala-azar infection. In at least two of these cases (Cases 8 and 19) the failure was due to insufficient treatment, for a permanent cure was readily brought about by further therapy with 102 cc and 125 cc respectively of the same drug 4½ months and 2½ months later. *Case 6* might well belong to this category but nothing definite can be said about it as the patient failed to return for further

TABLE 2.—*Particulars of cases treated and the effect on blood picture, body weight, and size of spleen.*

Case No.	Age	Sex	Duration illness	Treatment Days	Treatment Amount	Spleen BT	Spleen AT	R.B.C. BT	R.B.C. AT	Hgb. BT	Hgb. AT	W.B.C. BT	W.B.C. AT	Body Weight BT	Body Weight AT
			Months		cc.	cm.		mil./cmm.		gm. %		No. per cmm.		kg	
1	12	M	12	16	70	20	20	2.7	3.0	8.5	8.4	3500	3100	27.2	27.7
2	32	M	6	20	70	12	8	2.8	4.1	9.0	12.9	2200	6300	47.6	50.3
3	24	M	24	14	70	18	18	1.2	1.4	5.4	4.9	2100	1920	50.2	52.8
4	29	M	3	14	100	7	3	2.9	3.1	9.3	10.4	2300	3280	46.3	53
5	14	M	3	21	100	10	5	3.7	4.5	9.5	13.1	2850	7750	42.0	42.5
6	17	M	5	30	102	8	8	3.0	3.9	8.5	12	2000	2600	43.2	49
7	62	M	3	20	100	11	8	3.20	3.7	9.8	11.2	1200	4100	50	48
8	37	M	13	20	100	12	10	0.90	1.8	3.8	7.1	1250	1900	46.6	51.3
8			2	16	102	15	12	2.3	3.1	6.7	8.9	400	2300	45.7	48.3
9	15	F	1½	15	60	10	6	2.6	3.6	5.9	10.5	1900	4250	38.5	38.7
10	19	M	2	24	100	8	1	3.4	3.5	10.1	10.2	2900	4950	43.1	48.5
11	17	M	3	16	60	8	4	3.7	3.8	9.5	11	1950	2800	50	52.8
12	12	M	4	12	60	10	6.5	3.2	5.1	10	15.5	2100	7200	29.3	33
13	18	F	4	24	190	10	9	1.9	3.9	6.1	12.1	1050	3900	45.9	46.4
			2	17	131	10	10	2.8	3.6	8.0	10	1800	2900	47.2	50
14	12	M	3	18	60	12.5	11	2.2	3.4	6.4	11.0	700	4400	27.9	29.7
15	16	M	12	22	84	12	12	3.1	3.3	7.8	9.8	1300	4450	39.9	34.9
16	12	M	5	22	102	6.5	5	2.1	3.0	9.4	11.5	2750	2700	30.4	31
17	27	M	24	22	144	16.5	16	1.5	2.1	5.1	7.5	900	2050	53	60.1
18	12	M	6	22	102	14	4.5	2.8	4.1	8.5	13	1600	5200	28.7	31.4
19	14	F	7	20	120	13	12.5	2.6	3.5	8.4	10.1	4900	5750	38.3	43
			2	23	125	10	6	3.2	4.0	11.5	14.5	4500	7500	46.5	49.8
20	13	F	3	22	100	14	9	2.1	3.9	5.5	11.2	3800	9100	21	22.9
21	20	F	24	22	100	14	7	3.1	3.5	9.0	10.5	2500	3650	39.3	30.4
22	27	M	6	23	150	12	9	3.4	4.4	9.0	11.1	2200	2450	49.1	57.3
23	19	M	12	26	162	10	3	2.9	5.9	8.6	16.4	2400	6900	50.1	57.2
24	21	M	12	29	162	20	15	2.4	3.0	5.6	7.8	2650	3450	45.5	50.2

BT = Before treatment. AT = After treatment.

treatment. On the other hand, in *Case 13* the kala-azar infection persisted despite a second course of treatment with 131 cc of solustibosan 2 months afterwards. The disease was finally cured with a course (2.0 gram) of ureastibamine. This case may be regarded as failure of solustibosan to effect a cure. But even here, the possibility of a third or fourth course of solustibosan being capable of finally bringing about a complete cure seems open. As may be seen in Table 3 the curative dose may be as low as 60 cc as in Cases 9, 11, 12 and

TABLE 3.—*Showing effect of treatment on L. D. bodies and end results.*

Case No.	L.D. bodies positive or negative	Follow up and end results
1	Positive in SG and EG 3 days after 70 cc	2½ years; cured
2	Negative in SG 3 days after 70 cc	26 days; probably cured
3	Neg. in Lv., Spl., BM & Gs at autopsy	Died of pneumonia and bacteremia 8 days after 70 cc. cured.
4	Pos. in SP 10 days after 70 cc (no puncture after 100 cc)	4 years; cured
5	Pos. in SP 6 days after 98 cc	3 years; cured
6	Pos. in Spl. 2 days after 102 cc	Worse 9 weeks after discharge; not cured
7	Neg. in BM 7 days after 100 cc	4½ months; cured
8	Pos. in SP 34 days after 100 cc	Relapse 4½ mos. later; SP positive
	Neg. in SP same day after 78 CC	1 year; cured
9	Neg. in SP 6 days after 60 cc	5 months; cured
10	Neg. in SP 2 days after 80 cc	17 months; cured
11	Neg. in SP 3 days after 60 cc	16½ months; cured
12	Pos. in SP 8 days after 60 cc	
	Neg. in Spl. 15 days after 60 cc.	
	Neg. in Spl. 4½ months after 60 cc	30 months; cured
13	Pos. in SP 7 days after 60 cc	
	Pos. in SP 7 days after 100 cc	2 months; not cured
	Pos. in Spl. 2 days after 131 cc	
	2.0 gm ureastibamine; neg. in SP 6 days after 2.0 gm	28 months; cured
14	Negative in SP 3 days after 60 cc	15 months; cured
15	Pos. in SP 1 day after 60 cc	
	Neg. in SP 7 days after 84 cc	15 months; cured
16	Pos. in SP same day after 102 cc	14 months; cured
17	Pos. in SP 1 day after 108 cc	
	Pos. in SP 1 day after 132 cc	
	Pos. in SP 21 days after 144 cc	13 months; cured
18	Pos. in SP 11 days after 60 cc	
	Neg. in SP 2 days after 102 cc	3 weeks; probably cured
19	Pos. in SP 5 days after 120 cc	
	Pos. in SP 2½ months after 120 cc	Relapsed 2½ months later
	Neg. in Spl. 8 days after 125 cc	16 days; probably cured
20	Pos. in G 7 days after 60 cc	
	Neg. in SP 6 days after 100 cc	15½ months; cured
21	Pos. in SP same day after 90 cc	
	Neg. in SP 6 days after 100 cc	6 weeks; "no relapse"
22	Pos. in SP 1 day after 60 cc	
	Pos. in SP 1 day after 102 cc	
	Pos. in SP 1 day after 120 cc	2 weeks; probably cured
	Neg. in SP 3 days after 150 cc	
	Neg. in SP 11 days after 150 cc	
23	Neg. in SP 2 days after 126 cc	
	Neg. in Spl. 3 days after 138 cc	33 months; cured
24	Pos. in SP 3 days after 126 cc	
	Neg. in SP 20 days after 162 cc	2½ months; cured

SG—submaxillary lymph gland; Lv.—liver; EG—epitrochlear lymph gland; Spl.—spleen BM—bone marrow; SP—sternal puncture; Gs—lymph glands

14, or as high as 150 cc as in Case 22. When the first course of treatment is insufficient and the therapy is not continued but resumed after an interruption of from 2 to 4 months the combined total curative dose appears to be very much higher, being 202 cc and 245 cc respectively for Cases 8 and 19. In Case 13, the infection persisted despite a combined total dose of 231 cc. It is therefore obvious that pending further clinical observations, it is neither advisable nor practical to recommend a fixed universal total curative dose. In our experience, as shown in Table 3, no relapse has occurred in any of the cases showing no L.D. bodies at conclusion of treatment. Should a patient show evidence of intolerance of the drug which we have never seen, when the clinical symptoms and signs of the disease have disappeared or very much subsided but the parasites have not entirely disappeared, one may let the patient go without further treatment. But such a patient should be followed up weekly for at least 3 months as a potential candidate of non-cure or relapse. We would regard any case still showing L.D. bodies 4 weeks after cessation of treatment as one of a non-cure due to insufficient therapy and such a case should without delay receive further treatment with the same drug or with neostibosan or ureastibamine. To safeguard against possible relapses every case of treated kala-azar should be followed up closely during a period of 6 months. Unless this is done, it is not absolutely safe to pronounce a cure. However, for patients showing completely normal physical and laboratory findings at conclusion of treatment, even a relatively short follow-up during a period of 2 or 3 months seems sufficient to permit a conclusion as regards cure or non-cure.

DISCUSSION

There seems little doubt that solustibosan is an effective remedy against Chinese kala-azar. The fact that out of 24 patients (see Table 3) treated with this drug, there were 17 permanent cures (without relapse in 1-3 years) and 5 immediate cures (diagnostic punctures negative for L.D. bodies at conclusion of treatment; no sign of relapse 2-6 weeks later) indicates its therapeutic value. Of the remaining 2 cases, one (Case 13) may be regarded as a failure since 231 cc of solustibosan (containing 231 x 20 mg or 4.62 gm stibium equivalent to that contained in 11.54 gm of neostibosan) did not effect a cure, and the other (Case 6), as a case of insufficient treatment (102 cc solustibosan containing 2.04 gm of Sb equivalent to that contained in 5.1 gm of neostibosan) rather than failure of therapy. Disregarding Case 6 which was insufficiently treated, and adding the cases of immediate cure and those of permanent cure together, we have only 1 failure in 23 treated cases, that is to say, a cure rate of 95.6 per cent. This figure compares very favourably with the cure rate obtained in either neostibosan or ureastibamine therapy.

But if we compare solustibosan with neostibosan and ureastibamine (containing 40% Sb respectively) in terms of their antimony contents, then it will be seen that, gram for gram, antimony in the form of solustibosan seems to be definitely less effective than antimony in the form of either neostibosan or ureastibamine. For only 2.5-3.0 gm of ureastibamine containing 1.025-1.35 gm Sb or 3.0-4.0 gm of neostibosan containing 1.2-1.6 gm Sb are required to cure an average adult case of kala-azar, whereas, as shown in Table 3, a total dose of over 140 cc of solustibosan containing 2.8 gm Sb was frequently required to produce a cure. In Case 13, even a total dose of 231 cc of solustibosan containing 4.62 gm metallic Sb failed to cure the infection. In this particular case there was an interruption of 2 months between the 2 courses of therapy. Whether this had anything to do with the failure of treatment and whether further treatment with solustibosan would have eradicated the infection, it is difficult to say. In Case 19 a total of 245 cc of the drug containing 4.9 gm Sb was required to render the patient parasite-free. Here again it should be pointed out that 125 cc of the drug were given 2½ months after 120 cc of same had been administered.

In clinical therapy we are more interested in good therapeutic results than the economy or the absolute amount of the drug used. It seems clear that in adequate doses solustibosan is an effective remedy against kala-azar. Besides, the drug has several advantages. In the first place, it is stable and can be kept over long periods. Drugs like ureastibamine or neostibosan have to be prepared fresh before each intravenous injection which cannot be delayed longer than 10 minutes after dissolving the powder in sterile distilled water. In the second place, not like ureastibamine and neostibosan, the drug is not irritating to the tissues and hence can be administered intramuscularly without any local reactions making it suitable for certain infantile cases where intravenous injections are difficult. Finally solustibosan has a low toxicity and is very well tolerated by patients in large doses. This fact makes it a drug of choice for cases of kala-azar with renal complications.

In our series, 22 patients received their injections on alternate days, and 2 had them once daily. It seems that 2 or 3 injections daily may yet shorten the course of treatment considerably. This problem is now being investigated.

SUMMARY AND CONCLUSION

The results of treatment of 24 cases of kala-azar with solustibosan are reported. In adequate doses the drug is as effective as ureastibamine or neostibosan, but in terms of its antimony content, the amount required to produce a cure is much larger than that of ureastibamine or neostibosan. The drug has several distinct advantages over the last mentioned 2 preparations in that it is stable in aqueous solution, low in toxicity and can be administered intramuscularly.

REFERENCES

1. *Napier, L. C., Chaudhuri, R. N. and Chaudhuri, M.N.R.* A stable solution of antimony for the treatment of kala-azar. Indian Med. Gaz. **72**:462, 1937.
2. *Struthers, E. B. and Liu, L. C.* The treatment of kala-azar with solutibosan, a new antimony compound. Chinese Med. J. **52**:335, 1937.
3. *Yates, T. M.* "SDT 561" in treatment of kala-azar. Chinese Med. J. **52**:339, 1937.
4. *Kikuth, W. and Schmidt, H.* Contribution to progress of antimony therapy of kala-azar. Chinese Med. J. **52**:425, 1937.

節　略

Solustibosan 治療黑熱病之功效

鍾惠瀾　王季午　李宗恩

報告用 Solustibosan 治療黑熱病廿四例的結果，稱適量之 Solustibosan 功效與 Ureastibamine 或 Neostibosan 相等，但因其所含銻數量關係，用量須遠過於 Ureastibamine 或 Neostibosan。此劑有幾種優點，為其他二種劑所不及，即其在水中始終堅定，毒性輕微，並可作肌肉注射等是。

30. Epidemiological Studies on Kala-Azar

Yuan, I.C., Chung, H.L. and Lee, C.U. Unpublished.

袁贻瑾、钟惠澜、李宗恩《黑热病的流行病学研究》（未发表）

杂稿

以下为李宗恩从1938年初至1962年3月去世前留下的讲演稿、报告、报刊文章、信件和日记（1958年2月1日至1962年2月28日）。所有文稿按时间顺序排列，个别原文中没有注明日期的，则根据与其他相关档案材料的年代排序。所有英文内容的中译文附于原文之后，以供读者参考。

筹备国立贵阳医学院之经过[1]

1938 年 3 月 6 日在贵州省政府纪念周讲演稿

主席！诸位先生！

刚才听见主席报告，说要请兄弟演讲，这演讲两个字，是兄弟不敢当的。兄弟刚由汉口来，来到这有许多革命光荣历史而且为中华民族复兴策源地的贵州，尤其是更有机会和诸位先进见面谈话，这在兄弟是觉得十分光荣。今天所报告的，是筹备国立贵阳医学院的经过，报告以后，还要请各位指正。

国立贵阳医学院虽然表面上是本年一月十一日由行政院会议通过，可是研究它的因素——也可说是根苗，却是比较的早。在二十六年六月兄弟在汉口时，即已奉得教育部的命令，着手筹备国立武昌医学院，当时各事均弄得颇有头绪。不幸沪战发作，兄弟因为职责——医师——的关系连忙赶到上海去办理救护事业，一直拖挨到十月左右。在这时期，还接到教育部的电报，说经费仍是固定，催促赴汉。可是因为兄弟原是北平协和医学院的供职，有许多教务事务，须待本人前去处理，于是赴平一趟，等到处理好了，上海已是陷落，只好绕道香港，来到武汉，此时是十二月半光景，南京、芜湖均已失守，武汉已经变成了国防上之第一前线，在这样局面之下，武汉已失去了开办医学院的意义，于是有在贵阳成立医学院的提议，挪用原来的经费，开办现在的贵阳医学院，所以直接了当的说，贵阳医学院和武昌医学院，在历史上是有关系的。

为什么要筹备贵阳医学院呢？这包含两种使命，第一是临时使命。这自然不用说了。自卢沟桥事变以来，平津京沪均已陷落，这许多地方，本是我国文化中心区域，以我国医事人才之少，这许多医科失学青年，自然应该予以收容，尤其是在这非常时期，无论前方作战，和后方防疫，都正需要大批医事人才应用。贵阳医学院正是应这种临时需要而产生的。第二是永久使命，这也是很明了的。西南各省对于医学人才之欠缺，这是毋庸赘言。在过去，贵州虽曾办过贵州大学医科，但后来因为经费师资不足的关系，不久停办，直到民国二十六年，贵州省政府当局，因感到卫生事业未来之需要，遂一面开办卫生行政

[1] 贵州省档案馆，全宗号 99，目录 1（下略），卷号 510。

人员养成所，招收高中或旧制中学毕业生，训练十个月；一面拟行筹备医学院，以谋根本的解决。这种感觉，不仅是在贵州，即四川、云南诸省，亦莫不如此，每因医事人才之缺乏，而致卫生事业之设施，无法措手，这种实际困难，在民政厅所编的“贵州省卫生行政概况”一书中，已经是充分的流露了。所以要发展西南诸省的卫生设施，第一先要解决人才培养问题，这才是本学院之最高使命，也可说是本学院的特殊使命。不过，中国的医事现势，已渐向“公医制度”途径上迈进，医学人才之造就，在其服务社会，为大众谋利益，并非“开医院”“发财”为个人利益打算，而致提高社会之负担。尤其是中国精华在于农村。农村繁荣，中国才有出路，所谓都市不过是外国资本家的销货场所而已。所以，本学院以后毕业学生，完全是要深入农村，为农民解除痛苦，谋真正的福利，这种精神的培养，是本院所特别留意，而应该补充报告的。

关于本学院组织方面，可分为本科、医事职业两种，其中医事职业科，更包括护士、助产士两部分。本来医师、助产士、护士是有密切关系，过去分别办理，训练医师的是医学校，训练助产士的是助产学校，训练护士的是护士学校，不特糜耗经费、师资，而且道不为谋，被此牢挚，以致卫生设施上发生了不少的纠纷和障碍。本学院打破此种篱障，使医学教育系统融汇一体，这是中国医学教育上一大改进，以后对于西南卫生建设上，尤有不少的便利。

在过去，贵州全省卫生人才本来极其缺乏，此次本院创立于贵阳，拥有多数特殊专门人才，如果利用此种机会，与社会发生联系，则一方面可以便利教学，同时他方面对于社会卫生事业，亦能有相当的协助，此种改进社会事业，也要说是大学的真正使命。

第一，为保健事业之进行：自然“治病不如防病”，这好比一个警察，他本是有缉盗的责任的，但是如果能于事前防止窃案之发生，这自然要比事后“追捕抄赃”为好。本院刻正拟与地方药局联络，准备筹设城市卫生实验区，乡村卫生实验区，以为各种卫生事业之改进，使现代化医学之福利，能直接达到每个民家，不致成为少数资产阶级所专利，他方面兼为本学院学生实习之场所，予以精神上之发扬训练而树立“公医制度”之基础。

第二，为医疗事业之协助：自然在现在医学状况下，有若干疾病，简直无法预防，而且纵使科学如何发展，一部分疾病仍然可以发生。本院如利用各项临床专家，进与省立医院合作，一方面固可训练学生临床知识，它方面若干困难病症，亦可代为诊疗，这对于省会民众方面，也是不无小补的。

以上所述，只为个人脑海一时所想起，非常没有头绪。本院使命重大，以后有赖于在座先进之协助者甚多。希望常赐指教。

国立贵阳医学院筹备委员会工作报告[1]

1938 年 4 月

案奉教育部二十六年十二月三十一日令，聘宗恩为国立贵阳医学院筹备委员，并派朱章赓、杨崇瑞为委员，又指定宗恩为筹备主任，旋又聘任为国立贵阳医学院院长。宗恩遂于本年一月一日在汉口成立筹备委员会，即编具筹备委员会临时费、预算书，并奉教育部六日令饬国立武昌医学院筹备费移拨应用，又于二日拟具本学院组织规程及经常费、临时费、概算书呈送在案。又奉教部加聘杭立武、张志韩为筹备委员，嗣以各项筹备事宜大致就绪。为适应工作环境上之便利计，宗恩遂于二月中旬由汉口经重庆转道来筑，设立本学院临时办事处于贵阳禹门路一三三号，继续筹备未了事项。迄二月底止将筹备工作告一结束。谨将所有筹备工作之经过情形择要分述如下

一， 接收国立武昌医学院筹备委员会。本会奉部令略开以国立贵阳医学院筹备等费，暂由武昌医学院筹备委员会经费移用。经该会先后将结存现款三万六千九百四十一元零七分拨交本会查收。

二， 接收国立北平第一助产学校武昌办事处。本会奉命接收国立北平第一助产学校武昌办事处，旋经该处于一月十日将印章、文卷、款项、文具、家具、及图书、药品、医疗器械等件移交本会接收，业经会衔呈奉，令准备案。

三， 办理招收学生。此次所招学生仍以战区内失学医学生及护士助产士为原则。招收地点分汉口、长沙、重庆、西安、贵阳等五处。汉口长沙系一月二十四日至二十六日报名，二十七日至二十九日办理入学手续；重庆、西安、贵阳系二月五日至十日报名，十一日至十三日办理入学手续。现在学生合格者共计二百五十余人之谱，惟为便利远道学生求学起见，尚留贵阳一处在未正式开学之前仍通融报名。

四， 送学生来筑。本学院自经招生办理入学手续后，即预备运送学生来筑。乃因湘黔公路车辆缺少，而学生人数过多，无法供应。乃决定集中汉口乘轮至重庆再行陆续分批来筑。

---

[1] 贵州省档案馆，卷号 282。

五， 租定校舍。自宗恩抵筑后，即请贵州省政府当局协助觅定贵阳两广会馆及三圣宫两处为临时校舍。因原屋破漏不堪均须修理，业已招商估价动工装修并令限期修竣，以资应用。

六， 商借教学设备。本学院各科系、图书、仪器等需要甚多。限于经费未能购买，乃向各地卫生医事教育机关商借应用，现已接洽者有中央卫生实验处、卫生署、公共卫生人员训练所、贵阳联合试验室及军医学校之生理学系。图书仪器现正设法装运来筑。

七， 与贵州省卫生医事机关合作。本学院为便利发展贵州省卫生事业起见，与贵州当局共同拟具合作办法，一俟计划确定另行专案呈报。

以上各项筹备期内工作情形，除已呈报教育部备案外，敬祈公察。

筹备主任李宗恩

欢迎词[1]

1938 年 6 月 1 日

诸位同学，

诸位为了求学，能不辞辛苦，很远地从各地到这里来；今天我能和诸位同学同聚一堂，觉得非常愉快。今天趁着我们头一天聚在一起的时候，我愿意有几句话和诸位谈谈。一方面，可以说是我代表学院向诸位致的欢迎词，一方面也可以说是我们初次见面时候我送给诸位的见面礼。

我知道诸位能不辞辛苦地到医学院来求学，当然对于医学院所负的使命，是非常关切的。所以我愿意先拿出这点来和诸位谈一谈。

国立贵阳医学院的成立，总括起来是抱了两大使命。一个是永久的，一个是临时的。所谓永久的使命，简括地说一句话，就是开发内地。我们知道，西南各省的文化水准，由于所处地域的关系，因而比较落后，是无可讳言的事实。关于医疗卫生事业，则其落后的程度，更为厉害。我只要拿一件事情来证明，就可以明白它落后的情形。根据最近的调查，贵州全省 1000 万人口中，经过中央卫生署立案的医师，仅仅 12 人；以这样推算起来，在贵州一省，平均每 80 多万人口，只有一个医师。人才的极度缺乏，是显而易见的。在这种情况之下，即使我们有充分的经济能力可以用来发展本省的卫生事业，也是不容易成功的。所以我们医学院的第一个使命，就是替西南各省造就一批医事人才，普遍地分布到西南各省，尤其是西南各省的农村中去，为建设新的西南，尽我们最大的能力。

所谓临时的使命，那是更容易明了的。自从抗战开始以来，日本用他新时代的战争利器，来和我们作战，以致在不到一年的时间中，相继攻破了我们沿海一带文化水准区域；并且专以卑劣的手段，肆意破坏文化机关，使成千成万的青年学子，因而失学。其中医学生失学的也很多。所以我们第二个使命就是要来设法救济这部分失学的医学生，使他们能够继续求学，不至中辍。况且，在抗战期内，前方后方对于医事人才的需要，并不下于火线上作战的士兵。所

[1] 贵州省档案馆，卷号 534。

以从积极方面，也可以说是使这部分失学的医学生，在一定的期间内，成为有用的人才，参加到前方后方去，以他们所学的，来替国家尽一部分国民的天职。

根据上面这两个使命，我愿意向诸位提出几个简单的要求。希望诸位不但能在在校时遵守，并且希望诸位能在他年服务社会时，也常常记着这个原则。

第一点要求就是合作精神，这一点可以说是人类共同生活所必须的条件。很不幸的，在我们中国，由于个人主义的极度发展，这一点是非常之缺乏的。我们往往忽略了别人，忽略了社会，忽略了我们对社会应尽的责任；任自己一个人的好恶，随便做事，这是很不对的。我们应该学习怎样一方面不失去自己的个性，而他面又能顾到别人，顾到社会。拿一部机器来说，他的各部门是有各部分的用处的，可是合在一起又是互有关系的，若是一部门走快或是走慢，或是根本不走，全部机器必至出毛病或因而停顿。在社会上也是如此，一切事业的各部分是各有关联的，一个人做一件事，决不能和全体脱离关系。若是他不能顾到全体，随便地做，必致影响整个事业。尤其是现在的医学事业，已由“私人行医制度”，逐渐转变成“公医制度”；由“做医生发财”这个观点，逐渐转变成“在集体行动之下替社会上一般贫民服务”的观点，更应该有合作的精神，才能成功。在这里，我愿意提一提关于纪律的问题，我觉得所谓纪律，就是学习合作精神所必应有的步骤。因为在纪律训练之下，我们最容易学习共同生活和共同工作的习惯，学习如何彼此协助，然后合作，这也是希望大家注意的。

第二个要求是要有肯耐劳、肯吃苦的精神。时才我已经说过，现在做医师的观点是替社会上一般民众服务，那么，在现在中国社会极度贫穷之下，我们自己能希望优裕的生活吗？诸位不要误解我的意思，以为我是站在人道主义的立场上，认为大家吃苦，我也得吃苦。其实我是要诸位明了，若是我们不肯吃苦，我们就不能为一般平民服务。这是简单而容易了解的，若是我们替一个穷人做事，我们当然不能希望好的报酬；推广起来，我们若是要为一个贫穷的社会服务，当然也不能希望好的报酬。同时，在现在中国的医事人才是非常之少的，而需要却非常之大，我们孜孜终日还恐怕做不过来，当然更不应该贪懒图舒服了。所以我希望诸位自今日起就来练习吃苦，练习耐劳。

第三个要求是本地化。刚才已经说过，我们第一个使命开发内地是替西南各省服务，当然我们就应该先在生活上和内地人民打成一片，除了他们的坏习惯之外，我们应该学习他们的生活习惯。这样子我们才可能和他们接近，和他们生活在一起，逐渐了解他们，知道他们的痛苦和需要，才可以为他们服务。否则，我们和他们站在两个阶层上，我们不明了他们，他们不明了我们，完全是隔膜。这样子，我们为他们服务，他们不但不容易接受，而且甚至于反对我们。同时，即使就我们自己方面着想，若是我们不能习惯本地人的生活，而要居处在本地人中来服务，也会感到痛苦与不便的。所以我提出的第三个要求就是本地化。

这三个要求：纪律化、勤俭化和本地化，我提出的不过是原则，如何能达到这样的要求，还是需要我们大家将来在日常生活随时体会的。

最后，我愿意向诸位报告一下医学院成立的种种困难，以及学院所需要大家互助的地方。

第一点可以说到的是时间的仓促。我们知道国立贵阳医学院是今年一月十一日才经行政院通过的，在短短的几个月中就要成立开学，当然是有许多地方不能周到的。况且，我们来贵阳的时候较晚，许多好一点的地方早被其他来此地的机关占去，以致我们不容易找到一个合适的地方。

第二个困难是，贵阳是一个比较偏僻的地方，对外的交通是非常不便的。所以一切的向外购置物件，以及通信等，都很费时日。从贵阳寄一封信到重庆或是香港，要用十天左右，旅行及运输当然更其不便。这也给我们的事业许多困难。

第三个困难是经济的拮据。我们要知道，在现时长期抗战之中，各方需钱的时候，政府还要拿出一部分金钱来办学，已是很不容易的事情，所以钱虽然少，我们会因而感到困难，但是我们仍旧应该谅解政府的苦衷。只要我们努力，肯用这少数财力，产生最大的效果，就是我们对得起自己，对得起国家的地方。

以上所述的，不过是许多困难中的较大的三个，希望诸位能够明了。从今天起，我们应该知道我们是要从无中创造出有，要在荒地上开发出新园地。在这创造时间中，我们每个人都是主要的一份子，我们绝对不容许在我们之间有院方和学生的明显划线——认为学院是院方的。要知道，学院是我们大家的，我们大家是属于这一个有机体的。只有全体的努力，才能使学院蒸蒸日上。以后学院的扩大发展和成功，就是我们每一个人的胜利，我们每一个人的光荣。

国立贵阳医学院报告书[1]

1938 年

沿革

民国二十七年一月十一日，经国民政府行政院院务会议决议于贵州省会之贵阳创设一国立医学院，树立内地医药发展之基础，其最大之使命及夫急切之目的有二。第一，尽量使战区退出之医学学生，及护士助产学生，得以继续学业，俾就国难期中及未来医事人材来源不至间断。第二，尽量集合各停办医科学校受良好训练及有经验之师资人员，继续努力医学教育工作，教育部乃聘定李宗恩（北平协和医学院内科副教授）杨崇瑞（国立北平第一助产学校校长）朱章赓（教育部医学教育委员会秘书）杭立武（管理中英庚款董事会总干事）张志韩（贵州省教育厅厅长）等五人，组织筹备委员会，并指定李宗恩为筹备主任，共襄进行。

在学校之组织中，医科学生及中级医事人员（如护士及助产士）之课程讲授，不分为独立科别，希望能以此种教育制度上之合并，消除各种医事人材逐渐分为独立职业之趋向，同时促进医事职业整个之更和谐合作，至于学校课程，悉遵照教育部所颁布之课程标准，并依实际情形，略为改变。

一月中旬，筹备委员会开始登记战区失学学生，分在汉口、西安、重庆、长沙及贵阳等五处，设立招生处，总计共收医科学生及护士助产学生三百人，几全数系自停办之学校而来，因学生毫无经济来源，顾设法自汉口经重庆来黔，舟车运送费用，均由学校担负，四月初全部如数到达贵阳。

贵州省面积为七万六千四百一十六方哩，人口约一千万，其中十二万人汇居省会贵阳。全省中资格符合之医生，寥寥无几。虽无疾病之统计，然天花、疟疾、斑疹、伤寒等流行病，时有所闻，故本省急需完善之医事设施，至为急迫。此间省府当局洞鉴此种情势，现正采取一贯政策，提高医事职业之标准。本学院当曾向省政府商洽，允准利用现有之省立医院为本学院实习医院，该医院初仅有病床二十四张，现已计划增至八十张，然新病房亟需另行扩充建筑，

---

[1] 贵州省档案馆，卷号 282。

为时需六七个月之时间，始可完成。

值此国家抗战期间，因政府财政之资源受以限制，本学院预算中，开办费截止二十七年六月底止，已减低为十三万元，内中包括中英庚款补助费七万元，尚有中华文化基金会二十七年度补助费五万元在外。

临时校舍，业经此间省政府指定租借两广会馆三圣宫等处，俟修缮完毕俾可早日开始工作。

预算

二十六年八月，中央建设事业专款审核委员会通过二十六年度补助教育部十六万元，用以在武昌设立一医科学校，嗣因抗战以来，该校之筹备工作，无法进行，后因贵阳设立国立医学院事通过后，经呈准教育部将武昌医学院之补助费七折（十一万二千元）移归贵阳医学院，该款分配方法列后：

筹备委员会经费（二十七年一月至二月）	四,OOO,OO 元
学校开办费	三八,OOO,OO 元
经常费（二十七年三月至六月，每月一七五 OO 元）	七 O,OOO,OO 元
总计	一一二,OOO,OO 元

开办费预算

校舍修缮费	一九,OOO,OO 元
设备费	三,三 OO,OO 元
电线装设	四,OOO,OO 元
运输	一一,七 OO,OO 元
总计	三八, OOO,OO 元

经常费预算

薪俸	一一,七九 O,OO 元
教员	九,七二 O,OO 元
职员	一,五九 O,OO 元
工资	四八 O,OO 元
办公费	一,七三 O,OO 元
购置费	一,七 OO,OO 元
特别费	二,二八 O,OO 元

总计	一七,五 OO,OO 元

中华文化教育基金会补助费预算

图书	一 O,OOO,OO 元
科学设备	三五,七 OO,OO 元
仪器	二九,七 OO,OO 元
药品	六,OOO,OO 元
运输费	四,三 OO,OO 元
总计	五 O,OOO,OO 元

中英庚款补助费预算

图书	一 O,OOO,OO 元
修缮费之一部	三,一一 O,O 八元
家具及电线装设	一五,OOO,OO 元
显微镜四十座	一四,OOO,OO 元
科学设备	四一,O 七 O,OO 元
运输费	六,七 OO,OO 元
总计	八九,八八 O,O 八元

职员

院长	李宗恩
教务主任	贾魁
教务副主任	管葆真
注册主任	何战白
会计主任	徐曾渊
秘书	丁书翰
事务主任	常仁
出纳主任	刘晴皋
图书馆管理员	李宗瀛

教员名册

薪俸表

	原定薪额	实支薪额依照百分之五十之标准
教授	三九〇——四七〇元	二二〇——二六〇元
副教授	二五〇——三五〇元	一五〇——二〇〇元
讲师	一五〇——二三〇元	一〇〇——一四〇元
助教	五〇——一三〇元	五〇——九〇元

此处应堪注意者，本学院教职员支给对折薪俸，实为全国中仅有之学校，国家在抗战期中，人人愿得一献力国家之机会。然以后其他学校之薪俸仍继续高出于本学院时，如经相当时期后，欲维持原有标准将感困难，故拟自二十八年一月起，薪俸之折扣不得不稍加以更改，以便与他校同为一律。

课程

本学院课程拟遵照医学教育委员会二十四年规定之课程标准，依目下情形稍加改变，现另创设一"人文科"，尚为一种实验性质，该科所教授者为与基本科学及医学有关，但不包括其中之科目，如哲学、社会学、语言、心理学、医学史、医学伦理学等，该科聘请洪士希博士主持，洪先生为哲学研究家，对于自然科学有基本之造诣。

为应战时需要，本学院决加紧授课，连续牺牲二暑假，自二十七年六月一日至二十八年九月三十日，以便在十六个月中，完成四学期课程，此纯为一种紧急中之措置，不能认为完善之实验教育。

校舍

贵州省政府指定两广会馆之一部为本学院校址。经加修缮后，现有教室十及实验室九，另又租赁房屋两处为学生宿舍，一住男生一百六十四人，一住女生约一百六十人。

本学院现向省政府请求拨定永久校址一处，在东门外五里处之高地约计四百二十五亩，旁有小河一，除八十五亩稻田需出资购买外，尚有荒冢若干均须迁移，此地三分之一留为省立医院新院址。省当局已允拨六万元，本学院方面现正进行绘制二层楼房图样，此项楼房之特征，自以"简单"、"坚固"、"庄严"，并适宜医学教育之用为准则。该项建筑当尽量采用本地材料及人工，钢骨水泥之使用，须尽量减少，（盖水门汀之价格为普通之六倍，而钢筋所值亦为常价之五倍故也。）惟此项建筑费为数甚巨，须设法筹划，除向教育部呈请拨发一部份外，另须设法其他之补助。

医院

因经费限制，欲建设一附属医院，殊非不能，省政府已接受与本学院合作计划，允将省立医院做本学院实习医院，医院院长及各科主任亦由本学院聘任，已订五年合同，期满得延长。

此间省立医院由本学院接收时，至为简陋，设备不完，全院仅病床二十四，现省政府已拨六万元，拟扩充为一百四十床，其较昂贵之科学设备，本学院当予以协助购置，以期提高使合于实习医院标准，但吾人深感一原有之普通医院，自不能适合于临床实习之需要，将来须建一附属医院，以符现代医学教育之要求。

设备

健全之科学人才问题解决后，继须取得适当之教学及实验设备。目前运输费用之高昂，外汇之管理，均使设备购置事发生影响，一时未易解决。本学院现尽量设法在本地制作科学仪器，现聘有经验丰富之玻璃技士一人，制造各种烧瓶、试管及气体分析器等，如将来能设一小工厂，对于设备问题之解决，将有可观之进展。

学生

尽量收容战区失学之医学及护士助产学生，以便使战时及未来之医事人材源源不断，俾完成本学院成立最初之使命，现有学生总共医科学生二百二十七人，护士助产学生七十六人（见下表），来自四十九个医科及护士助产学校，吾人希望能加以基本医学之训练，使彼等成就为正轨之医事职业。

<table>
<tr><td rowspan="16">学生人数表</td><td rowspan="6">医科</td><td>年级</td><td>男</td><td>女</td><td>合计</td></tr>
<tr><td>1</td><td>30</td><td>14</td><td>44</td></tr>
<tr><td>2</td><td>53</td><td>16</td><td>69</td></tr>
<tr><td>3</td><td>32</td><td>22</td><td>54</td></tr>
<tr><td>4</td><td>22</td><td>8</td><td>30</td></tr>
<tr><td>5</td><td>23</td><td>7</td><td>30</td></tr>
<tr><td></td><td>总计</td><td>160</td><td>67</td><td>227</td></tr>
<tr><td rowspan="4">护士</td><td>1</td><td>1</td><td>1</td><td>2</td></tr>
<tr><td>2</td><td></td><td>15</td><td>15</td></tr>
<tr><td>3</td><td>4</td><td>16</td><td>20</td></tr>
<tr><td>总计</td><td>5</td><td>32</td><td>37</td></tr>
<tr><td rowspan="4">助产</td><td>1</td><td></td><td>12</td><td>12</td></tr>
<tr><td>2</td><td></td><td>14</td><td>14</td></tr>
<tr><td>3</td><td></td><td>13</td><td>13</td></tr>
<tr><td>总计</td><td></td><td>39</td><td>39</td></tr>
<tr><td colspan="5">总计：男生 165 人，女生 138 人，共计 303 人</td></tr>
</table>

未来之希望

本学院未来之希望，尚须有赖于三项问题之改进。

（一）政治之稳固：贵州省已整个在中央政府之治下，现任省主席吴鼎昌先生，曾一度为实业部长，洵为不可多得之能才，其在行政计划之下，各方面社会均有迅速之进展，吾人希望此种步伐，得以继续推进，以期达到最完善之政治区域。

（二）交通之进步：贵州省地交通工具之缺乏，公路制度难以应付大量之运输，如欲发展贵州省使成一教育中心，必须先将交通问题解决，自贵阳通长沙之铁路线尤为需要，湘黔铁路如能完成通车，贵阳无疑将为西南之交通中心。

（三）国立大学之设立：依据上述之情形，设立一医学院本属可能，然欲使其充分发展，必需有大学文化空气所造出不断之刺激，俾就事实上之趋向，为本学院吸收人才之导引，新设立之大学须包括理、工、医、农及教育等五学院之设备。

1938 年国庆日讲演[1]

1938 年 10 月 10 日

今天是国庆日，是抗战建国以来第二个国庆日，又是我们学校第二学期开始的第一个纪念周。在这样一个机会，我们不必要什么庆祝的话，也不必须回溯什么以往的光荣，这些都是我们早已知道，不用我再来重复。今天我愿意借这个机会来和你们谈一谈团体生活的基本观念。我们知道，抗战建国的最迫切的需要是举国上下团结起来，向一个目标往前迈进。所以团体生活的养成，是非常重要的。二十七年四月，中国国民党临时全国代表大会通过的战时各级教育实施方案纲要以及七月间政府向国民参政会提出的各级教育实施方案，都热切的提到训练学生团体生活的必要。今天我讲这个题目也是这个意思。

我们要讲团体生活，就必需先知道团体生活中个人应有的几个基本态度。我们知道，人类是非常复杂的，各个人之间显然有许多相同的地方，但是却有更多不同的地方。古人所谓"人心不同，有如其面"，就是这个意思。现在我们要把这些各有个性的人，放在一起，叫他们在一起生活，若是没有这点共同的态度，那完全是不可能的事。所以在团体生活之前，我们每个人必须有几个基本的态度。

团体生活内，个人的基本态度，我认为大要可分为三点，即是不在团体内，也是处世处人应有的态度。

第一点是"诚"，也就是我们校训的第一个字。而民国二十七年七月间政府向国民参政会提出的各级教育实施方案，也说"应遵从先哲遗训，以'诚'字为训练人生之中心目标"。这个"诚"字，换句话说，就是"不自欺，不欺人"。在团体中，我们若是能做到这一点，彼此能以诚相见，那么不管我们的意见是怎样的分歧，我们的主义是怎样的不同，我们不妨把自己的意见，自己真正所想的，公开提出，彼此讨论，彼此批判，在自己发现自己错误的时候，勇敢地承认。如果能做到这一个地步，我们就不难获得彼此的谅解。根据这个彼此谅解的条件为出发点，我们也就不难产生和谐的团体生活。反之，我们若是不能够以诚

---

[1] 贵州省档案馆，卷号 534。

相见，尽希望用歪曲的手段来达到自己的目的，口是心非的对付别人，那么你能这样对付人家，人家又何尝不可以同样的手段对付你，以致弄成彼此猜忌，彼此提防。试问这样子还有什么团体生活之可言？所以，简单地说一句，彼此谅解是团体生活之基础，而“诚”又是彼此谅解的基础。“诚”字的重要，就可以明显地看出来了。

第二点，就是彼此尊重。要知道，一个和平理想的团体，是这个团体内的各个份子，都是处在平等的地位，而不是分阶级的。既然彼此都是处在平等地位之上，我们若是自己尊重自己的意见，同时又希望别人尊重自己的意见，当然自己也必须尊重别人的意见。反过来说，就是孔子说的“己所不欲勿施于人”。然而，什么叫作尊重别人的意见呢？尊重别人的意见，并不是服从别人的意见，这是我们必须清楚区别开来的。所谓尊重别人的意见，乃是说我们应该尊重每个人发表他自己意见的权利，并且应当予以充分的考虑，不应该因为他的意见不合我的，就不考虑他的意见，甚至侮蔑他的意见。刚才我们已经说过，人与人之间，意见是不能完全相同的，在别人意见和我的不同的时候，我们彼此尽可善意地批评，公开地讨论，但绝不横加侮蔑；因为你能侮蔑人家的意见，人家就能侮蔑你的意见，这样彼此侮蔑，试问还有什么团体的和谐可言！

第三点，我们必须承认一个最大的团体，为我们最高的准则。显然的，人类所组成的团体非常之多，有政治的，有社会的，有教育的，若是我们不能认定一个比较普遍的团体为我们最高的归依，则各个小团体之间必至常常冲突，而没有一个平衡的标准。要提起人类的团体，最普遍的当然应以全人类为一个最高最大的团体，但是这样的想法，在现在只可以是一种理想，很难立即实现，所以我们只好不得已而求其次，暂时以民族为我们的最高最大的团体，一切行动，都要以民族的利益为依归，也就是说，要拿民族的利益为一切的大前提。我们这样的说法，并不是否认了世界大同的可能性，而流为偏狭的民族主义。要知道，若我们全人类为一个大团体，我们必须先以各民族间的平等为基础，但是事实告诉我们，各民族之间，现在是无平等可言的，所以我们只有以民族利益为最大前提，争取民族的自由平等，来达到全人类的共存共荣。我们若是希望越过这一步去，恐怕我们永远不会达到世界大同的目的的。

以上就是我个人认为团体生活应有的三个态度，让我来重复一遍：（一）

我们要有诚意；（二）我们要尊重自己尊重别人；（三）我们要以民族利益为一切团体利益的最后归依。

上面三点，已经说过，是一个人，不但是在团体内，并且在团体外也应遵守的态度。现在让我们把这三点记住，再来谈各人在团体内应有的行为，也就是说，团体对团体内各份子的要求。

第一点，每个团体，都是有它存在的目的的。团体的成立，不是为了实现某一个理想，就是为了谋求团体内各份子的共同利益。一个民族国家的结合，是为了谋求民族国家内各份子共同的保障；一个宗教团体，是为了谋求某种理想天国的实现；一个政治团体，是为了谋求某种政治主张或社会制度的实现。无论它的方式手段怎样不同，目的是不可少的。所以，我们在一个团体之内，我们最高的责任就是要谋求这些理想或利益的实现；换句话说，我们在一个团体之内，我们就有责任，向着这个团体的目的努力；否则，我们就等于背弃了这个团体，我们不配再在这个团体内存在。不过，我们必须注意一点，我们刚才已经说过，我们必须承认国家民族是我们最高的团体，我们的一切行动，必须以国家民族的利益为准则。所以，若是我们在一个较小的团体内，这个团体有些利益与国家民族的利益有冲突，我们应该怎么办呢？我觉得在这种地方，我们就应该为了更多人的利益而牺牲，我们应该使这个团体，为了更高的利益而放弃它自身的这一部分主张或利益。

第二点，人与人之间，是决不能完全相同的。各人有各人的个性；人类的个性，可以说是一切进步的根源。失去了这些，人类的生活就变成干燥单调，而很难产生进步。所以团体生活之下，个性也是不应该完全牺牲的。在许多地方，个性和团体没有冲突，当然不成问题；可是许多地方，个性常常发生冲突。这时候，我们怎么办呢？这是很难解答的一个问题。我在没有回答这个问题之前，愿意先举一个例子。在欧战的时候，有些反战的人，觉得没有人有权利要求他们不忠于他的思想，所以宁可接受团体的任何处置，以致自己牺牲了生命，而不愿意放弃他反战的思想去打仗。这一件事情，至少告诉我们一点，就是团体也必须尊重个人的意见。团体尽可制裁个人单独相反的行动，但绝不能强制个人改变他自己认为对的思想。这一点是非常重要的。历史告诉我们，没有一种思想是永久的真理，有些思想在一百年前是认为离经叛道的，百年后却成为家喻户晓了；有些思想，百年前是人人奉行的，而百年后却没人相信了。所以，今天我有个思想，纵使人人反对，这也不见得就是于人没有利益的。这种思想，若是我相信，而因为大多数人的反对，不敢坚持，那么渐渐的，这种思想被人忘却，甚至永远没有重视的机会。万一这思想确是一种进步的思想，那岂不是文化演进的损失。所以我认为，为了人类的进步，团体尽可制裁个人反于团体的行动，却不能强制他变更自己的思想。而个人方面呢，自己有一种思想，也应该勇敢地发表，这不但是你的权利，也是你对人类文化的义务。这一点，你们要仔细地去思想，不要误会我的意思。

第三点，每一个团体，都有它经常的规则，要求团体内各份子的遵守。这我们当然要遵守，是不成问题的。不过，我们在奉行这些规则的时候，我们最应该记着，我们遵守这些规则，不是受了别人的压迫，而是自动地愿意去遵守。因此，我们要养成习惯，不论在人前人后，我们要把这些规矩引为我们在无论什么地方做事的信条。我们并不是怕处罚，或是怕别人的批评，而是觉得这是我们的责任，我们的团体的责任。

上面这些意思，可以说是我在双十节向同学的赠言，我希望你们能在日常生活中，切实地实行；在遇到困难或问题的时候，大家讨论。我们从今天起，决心做一个我们团体中有用的份子，做我们国家的一个良善的公民。国家需要我们这样作，在抗战建国中的国家，尤其需要我们这样作。

第一次开学典礼讲话[1]

1938 年 12 月

今天是本学院第一次的开学典礼。上半年六月初开学时，因为一切都是刚开始，不能就绪。所以不得不把这次开学典礼推迟到现在才举行。今天承各位来宾在百忙之中，抽出功夫来参与这次聚会，我们觉得非常荣幸，非常之感谢。不过，本校从六月初开学到现在，不过半年，这短短的半年中，在成绩上是没有什么可报告的。今天，我愿意就本学院成立的动机，及现在的教育方针两方面，做一个简短的报告。

我们一谈到本学院成立的动机，马上就会引出两个问题来。

第一个问题，为什么要在抗战期间成立一个新的医学院？第二个问题：为什么要在贵州设立这个新的医学院？

现在让我先回答第一个问题，为什么要在抗战期间成立一个新的医学院。我们知道，在中国，专门技术人员是非常缺少的，在医事方面，也是如此。在抗战开始之后，这种缺乏表现得更加明显。所以我们可以说，在抗战期内，努力培植专门技术人员是非常重要的事情。不但如此，就是将来战争完毕以后的建设，也是要靠大量的专门技术人员来完成的。若是我们现在不事先预备，到将来也是要感到困难的。所以，在抗战期内，为了目前的战争，为了将来的建设，专门教育都是应该继续的。但是，由于战事的关系，许多地方沦为战区，许多学校因此不得不解散或者停顿。因此有许多失学的学生，那时所存留的医学院很少，绝对难容纳这么多的失学学生。因此，我们必须在短期迅速地预备之下，成立一个新的医学院来容纳这许多失学的医学生，使他们能够完成学业，不至于半途荒废。

但是我们为什么要在贵州成立这个医学院呢？这点也是需要答复的。我们知道，教育部的大学方针，是把全国割分为若干大学区，每区设国立大学或独立学院，以应这区的需要。贵州也是一个大学区，医学院之成立在贵阳，可以说是教育部大学教育方针的部分实现。但是我们不应忽略许多旧有的文化区现

[1] 贵州省档案馆，卷号 534。

在都已沦为战区，为了使教育能够继续，我们不得不在比较安全的后方，开展新的文化区，贵阳在这方便是比较合适的。医学院之设在贵阳，这也是原因之一。事实上，自从医学院在这里设立之后，卫生署也在这里设联合实验室，中央医院、湘雅医学院也先后搬到这边来，贵阳事实上已是一个后方的医事中心了。

上面两个问题的回答，就可以代表本学院成立的动机。现在让我再就本学院的教育方针及其实施方面，做一个简单的报告。

教育的原则。在这方面，我们已经作到的以及最还要作的，可以分三项来说。

第一项是加紧工作，缩短训练期间。刚才已经说过，本校的成立是为了救济战区失学医学生，所以大部分的学生，都因战事影响，耽误的时间很多。我们在六月开学的时候，就决定各年级的上下学期同时开班，并且取消今年和明年的暑假。这样子，由于同仁以及同学的合作和牺牲，我们可以从今年的六月到明年九月的十六个月中，完成四个学期的功课，这点是值得提出的。

第二项，对于平时医学教育缺点的补救。这点在今年四月中国国民党临时全国代表大会通过的战时各级教育实施方案纲要中也说到。在这纲要的序言中，曾经说到："教育为立国之本，整个国家之构成，有赖于教育，在平时然，在战时亦然。国家教育在平时要健全充实，在战时即立著以功能；其有缺点，则一至战时，此等缺点即全部显露，而有待于急速补急与改正，所贵于战时教育之设施者，即针对教育上之缺点，以谋根本之挽救而已。战时教育之必大有异于平时也。"这句话明显地告诉我们，战时教育之最大目的，就是在于改正平时教育在战时所暴露的缺点。这种改正，不但在战时，即在战事完毕之后，也是应该继续实行的。在这方面，我们值得提出的是人文科的设立。中国的大学教育，一向就是偏重技术知识的灌输，而对于学生整个人格的建立、治学治世治人的良好态度的养成，常常忽略。尤其医学教育更是如此。所以本院在一成立的时候，就决定设立人文科，除了语文之外，还添上哲学、心理学、科学方法论、社会学、文化史等等的科目。这种设施，就是希望学生能在一方面对文化有相当的认识；另一方面，能够养成一个健全的人生观，以为他们将来研究学业、服务社会的基础。这点若是我们能做得好，一定是对于国家有很大的贡献的。

第三项，就是给学生战时应有的知识。在这方面，我们在未开学的时候，就组织救护训练班，一方面加强军事训练，一方面给学生一些战场急救、担架、伤兵运输、战地医院等等的普通军医知识。但在这方面，我们觉得还不够，希望最近在课程中增加一些军医知识和军医训练。

其外，学校为了救济战区出来经济困难的学生，我们设立了不少免费及贷金的名额。现在领贷金的学生有XX人，领免费的学生有XX人，总计XX人。差不多等于全校学生人数的百分之X。这也是值得附带报告的。

以上所说的，是本学院教育方针的第一点。但更重要而永久的，还是我们的第二点，就是，我们要使我们的教育，切合贵州省实际的需要。刚才我们已经说过，贵州是教育部所划的大学区之一，本学院的设立，是要应贵州这一区的需要，替贵州培养医事上的工作人员。所以我们在教育及训练方面，处处都顾到这一点。我们一方面领导学生参加贵州的各项社会工作，希望他们能切实明了这里的实际的需要。另一方面，我们还用种种方法来鼓励本学院的毕业人员在这里服务。这都是为要达到这一个目的。因为我们在这里是永久性的，所以我们必须找一个永久的校址，在这方面，省政府帮了我们不少的忙，替我们在城外找到了离城不远的校址。现在我们正在设计校舍的建筑，一等我们在经济上有办法的时候，就可以开始建筑。

当然，由于战时交通的不便，国家经济的困难，我们在推行这些工作的时候，免不了要遇到许多困难的。在过去，有许多困难，我们已经克服。我对各界对本校的关心和合作，表示敬意，同时，对今天的各界来宾，敬致谢忱。

青年会成立讲演稿[1]

1938 年 12 月

今天是青年会成立，XX 要叫我来说几句话。我平时对于宗教和青年会的事业很少研究，不能有什么很好的意见贡献给你们。不过我喜欢和你们随便谈谈，多多的交换我们的意见。所以我愿意把我平常感觉到的提出来给你们讨论。

信仰是一种力量，这是大家都承认的，在历史里面也可以找到很多的例子。我们可以看到一种信仰对于个人，对于人类社会所尽的推动力量。在人类社会的进化史里，几乎没有一个英雄事业不是靠着一种信仰所造成的集团意志。打一个比方说，信仰就好比是航海家的罗盘。当一个航海家驾驶一条船在风狂雨骤的大洋里面走，四面看不见边，若是他没有一个罗盘，他就不知道向哪一方面走，结果他一定弄得手足无所措，失去了一切希望，也就失去了一切力量。反过来，如果他有力量，因为他有了罗盘，他相信可以靠着这罗盘把船驾驶到目的地去，于是他无形之中就对于工作有了热忱，也就有了力量。信仰也是这样，他帮忙人在这个浩浩不可测的宇宙中得到一个坚定不移的人生态度，使他可以努力为人类服务。

我这里所说的信仰虽然不见得一定是宗教，但是我们不得否认宗教是信仰的一种，也就是说宗教对于个人对于社会具有其他一切信仰同样的力量。有些人认为宗教是一种麻醉剂，它叫人满意于现在的一切．不求改进，这句话固然有一部分真理，但是它们只看到了宗教的消极方面而没有看到宗教的积极方面。当我们听 Back（巴赫），Handel（汉德尔），Beethoven（贝多芬）的音乐的时候，或是读 Jolotoi（托尔斯泰）的小说的时候，我们不能不承认这些伟大的作品是由于宗教的信仰所启发。当我们看到回族团结力的强大，我们更不能不承认宗教在集团中所发生的积极的作用。

青年会是一个社会组织。这个组织的最大目的，不是要来传教，而是要使

[1] 贵州省档案馆，卷号 511。

青年在里面彼此帮助，培养自己的人格，得到一个正确而坚定的人生态度来服务人群，来服务国家。尤其要注重的是这是一个青年组织，所以它的积极性比其他任何宗教要大。它不是要给青年们空泛的安慰，而是要教青年们学习如何从服务人群的工作中去求得安慰。青年会在中国已经有相当的历史。固然在它发展中也有一些毛病，但是它对中国社会所尽的责任是不能泯灭的。在中国虽然有许多学校，但是由于学校的教育要注重知识的灌输，青年在学校中很少学习和衷共济及服务同辈的精神，反过来青年会在这方面却有相当的努力，因为它给了中国青年学习服务人群的机会，它替中国造成了一些社会上各部门的领导人才。

今天是本学院青年会成立的第一天，我愿意大家能够努力把这一个组织发展成我们活动的核心，同时把我们的精神发扬出去，来服务学习，服务人类。

致王世杰函[1]

1939 年 3 月 22 日

雪艇先生道席:

久未奉问，时殷念念。辰维公私迪吉，为慰为颂。敬启者，宗恩奉命主持本学院院务以来，栗六如恒，乏善可陈，此间工作进行上因筹备期限之匆促，及内地环境之种种拘束，始于六月一日开学来，学院院址已先租定，临时院舍等处暂可应付，其永久院址亦经与省府交涉，觅得城郊空地一方，约有四百亩，其中数十亩或须收买，且将若干坟墓迁移尚需的款。至建筑一项亦已进行设计，务求建筑物以朴实耐久适用为原则。学院师资及教学设备，目前所聘教员连各卫生医事机关协助者共计七十二人。惟各项教学设备向各机关商允借用外，必需购置者充分利用本国出品，但尚有一部分仍须向外阜择购，且因外汇兑换之手续颇需费时日，再此次所收战区失学学生计达三百零五人(其中医本科二二九人医事职业科【护士助产】七六人）学校来源计有四十九单位，其中大部分学生均系失学已久，顾本学院如谋补习缺课，及推进抗战时期后方教育工作之力量，爰有改订学程之计划。自本学年六月一日起至二十八年九月三十日止共计十六个月，分为两个学年，並两次暑期均不放假，籍以统筹办理。顾此计划之实施教学工作，殊觉繁重，宗恩自惭才浅，勉力为之，所幸各教职同仁深体战时国民应尽之天职，而全部学生亦能洞悉学校创办与夫培育人才之使命，师生均能同心合作共济时艰，私用欣慰。再此间战区失学生大部分均为家在战区，经济无力接济者，除学杂费免收外，其受贷金学生几占三分之二，并为顾及此辈学生毕业后出路及协助推进贵州全省卫生事业计，已与省卫生当局订定毕业生在黔服务办法，期为二年，按贵州省卫生事业始于本年春间，经吴达铨主席之倡导成立省卫生委员会（为全省最高卫生行政机构），又在省会设卫生事务所，及定番等七县次第成立卫生院，推进卫生工作不遗余力。如春季扩大种痘运动，霍乱预防宣传周及卫生展览会等，本学院依照部令兼办社会教

---

[1] 贵州省档案馆，卷号 242。

育之规定，随时参与协助该项卫生保健工作。年来黔省政治自主任莅任以来，锐意刷新，渐入轨道。近因各方民众迁徙入黔者多大部分集中省会，因而贵阳已成为一新兴都市之雏形，又中央文化机关不少移黔，故社会文化目前颇有畸形之开展。顾此种现象终难持续。战争平定后虽不致一反故步，即目前之地位已难持久，如将来西南交通开展，有望贵州地处西南之中心，社会文化事业将有发展之可能。但医学教育之展望，仍有赖于其他社会文化事业之发达，互相扶助，以资集中人才物力，故黔省需一设备完善之最高学府以谋文化建设之基础。

先生关切西南教育文化之发展，及爱护本学院尤具热忱，感佩同深，用特摅陈琐琐，烦渎清听，定所乐闻也。尚祈不弃远方，时锡教益，俾利进展之处，尤深企祷。为此匆匆奉候。籍颂

勋绥

李宗恩 敬启

疟疾的预防问题[1]

1939 年 4 月 30 日

当此全面抗战的时候，疟疾确实是一个很严重的问题，因为我们目前一方面固然是在抗战，而一方面却又在建国。既要建国，则在这后方西南，便应加紧建设；要建设，我们认为有两件事是应该注意的：一是鸦片，一是疟疾，这两种东西，都是建国期间的障碍，我们不得轻易忽视。

抗战以来，疟疾在军队中蔓延之广，实属骇人听闻。前方部队里，差不多有百分之七八十是患疟疾的。我们常常看到许多士兵因为患了疟疾，以致不能作战，甚至不能动作，于是只好退到后方来，在医院里休息。因此在后方医院里，就我们所知道的，第一期抗战时，所收容的伤兵，多半是属于外科方面的；可是迄到现在所收容的伤兵，则多半是属于内科方面的了。说是属于内科，而实际上就是指疟疾占最大多数。此种现象，确是非常危险的。如不谋补救，对于抗战的实力，实有相当大摧损，尤其在这抗战建国的过渡时期，我们更应该予以注意。

疟疾既然属害，治疗当然是不可缓的。谈到疟疾治疗，看来尚觉得简单，不外金钱同组织两个问题。如这两方面都有办法，倒还是一件比较有把握的工作。

预防方面来讲，是不应该十分困难的。然而经验告诉我们，我们虽有许多关于疟疾的科学知识，而事实上，一直到今天，对于预防疟疾，还没有万全的办法。我们现在将预防问题，分作两种不同的对象，一是指某种团体（如军队工程队），富有时间及移动性者，一是指疟疾流行区域的居民，我们对此不得不考虑及之。

以上系说明预防疟疾时应注意的地方。还有几点关于预防工作的基本常识，我们也可以在此提出。

（一） 关于虐蚊。我们知道，蚊子的种类很多，不凡是蚊子都能传染疟疾。并且雌性蚊子咬人传染疟疾的蚊子不过几种“安拿非利”的蚊

[1] 贵州省档案馆，卷号 282。

子罢了。而且各种虐蚊的传染能力亦各有不同，有时限于环境，在某地可以传染疟疾，若另换一个地方，也许它又不会传染疟疾了。再还有几种虐蚊，其能力亦稍有差异，比如传染某一种疟疾，它是可能的，若传另一种，也许它又不可能了。此其二。最后还有一种虐蚊，其雌性的传染能力，亦各有不同，此其三。总之，虐蚊的情形复杂，预防实不甚容易。

（二） 关于虐蚊的习性方面，亦是一个复杂的问题。有时在白天咬人，有时在晚上咬人。而且咬了人后，或呆在屋子里，或飞到外面去。呆在屋里的，它如已受传染，他就能将疟疾传递给同住的别人。因为虐蚊习性不同，灭蚊的方法也是很困难的。

至于蚊子的幼虫，讲起它们的习性来，更是各有不同。比方说，虐蚊的幼虫，在比较清洁的水中生长，有时候它必需择那又清又活的水，才能够繁殖。但是，有几种疟蚊在积水中，在某种情形之下，还是能繁殖的。

疟疾原虫的生命史是相当复杂的。它寄生在人的红血球里。繁殖的方式有两种，一种是“无性繁殖”，最初为一个小细胞，慢慢长大，以至变为分裂体，在这时期，将红血球撕破，便有许多“分生子”散开，每个分生子或几个分生子再钻进另一个红血球里，如此循环繁殖，破坏了不知多少的红血球，因此使患此病的人容易发生贫血的症候。这些形体是致病的形体。

第二种是有性生殖。在成千成万的分生子之中，有一部分的分生子，还另外负有一种特别的使命。当它钻进一个红血球以后，它不像其它的“胞虫”那样活动，亦不会分裂，只渐渐长大起来，成为一种所谓“配偶体”。如果仔细检查一番，可以分别出它是雌性还是雄性来。不过这些配偶体，在人体内并无多大作用，它的作用，是为散播疟疾原虫给疟蚊，再由疟蚊传染给无病的人。

以上是我们对疟蚊应有的基本常识，若果稍加认识，对于将来用药品治疗和预防方面，都有很大的帮助。

现在来讲预防。讲预防，我们可以暂分几方面来着想。一就是将疟蚊扑灭到相当的程度，使其在量上减少；一是用可能的掩蔽物，如蚊帐，使疟蚊不能与人接近。前者倘使用蚊烟熏蒸，或是用类似扑杀的方法，一定可以获得相当效果。至于后者，是要具有普通经济条件方办得到。

不过，有一点应该注意到，便是乡人所居的处所多系茅屋，矮小黑暗。若要采用扑灭的方法颇不易办。同时又为一般经济情况所限，蚊帐等设备是不易办到的。

至于消灭幼虫，那就更发不易了。需要大量的财力，而且还要有“卫生工程”的设施，才能希望有成绩。

在目前中国这种社会情形之下，扑灭疟蚊，非常不易。而扑灭幼虫，尤应多加考虑。不得已而求其次，用药物治疗及预防，在预防工作上是不是有功效呢？

消灭疟虫还是奎宁最为有用。一来价钱便宜，二来没有毒性，所以现在一般人都很普遍的采用。虽然现在有他种新发明的药品，奎宁可以说是一种主要的药品。我们现在将三种药品的口服量列表于下：

	缩写	日服	治疗	预防
奎宁	Q	每日	1.0-1.30 克，7-10 日	0.4 克，每日
阿涤平	A	每日	0.3 克，7-10 日	0.2 克，每星期二次
普虐母星	P	每日	0.02 克，7-10 日	0.02 克，每星期二次

这三种药品服用时应当注意。若单服前两种，一时好了，日久又可复发，比方在一百人中，大概有五十人会有此种现象。故除一方面给奎宁丸外，同时再酌给少许 P，则复发的趋势便可减少。

奎宁与 P 可以同时服用，但 A 同 P 则不可同时并服，不过服过 A 后，再服 P，那倒很好，没什么关系。

以上所说的，是有疟疾者的治疗法。至于军队方面，若有任务而要跑到某疟疾流行区域工作时，为维持他们的工作力量，可用药品预防方法使他们至少在工作期间不要发生疟疾的病症。如每日服奎宁丸，那么只要 0.4 克兰姆即可，服阿涤平每周两次，每周 0.2 克兰姆。普虐母星的作用，在治疗方面，有相当的效能，上面已经提及，但它的特别用处，在于能消灭血脉中配偶体，尤其恶性疟疾的配偶体，故患疟疾者，如先服奎宁或阿涤平，然后再服少许普虐母星，则所有原虫，均可杀死。

在此有一点，在有组织及纪律的团体中，每日在一定时期应集队在负责长官亲自看他咽下去。

因为这是几种药品，可以治疗疟疾，若是有大批药品的话，便可散给各处有医学知识而可靠的人，如学校教员，让他们发给病人服用，这样可以减少死亡率，也可以减少疾病率，并且在工厂方面能增加生产力量，对于抗战，也可以增加战斗力量。

在军队里或各种团体组织之中，如果经济可能，一方面酌量制发蚊帐，减少与蚊子接触的机会，少受疟疾的传染。一方面可发给药品，以资预防。

假如现在我们已有防疫队的组织，要到疟疾流行区域去，我们觉得非从详细调查疟疾流行的情形入手不可，但是怎么样才能知道呢？第一，应注意各该地学校的儿童，因为曾犯疟疾的儿童，血内带有“配偶体”者最多，因之传播能力最大，所以凡要做这种工作的人，必须检查儿童的脾脏是否肿大，是否有其它变态，同时如有相当的设备，可取血片检查，看看究竟是属于哪一种的疟疾，配偶体的多少。这种材料经过分析之后便可知道疟疾的流行情况。当地疟疾流行的节令，普通说善性疟疾的发生，不善性疟疾在温带地方哪一季都可以有的，恶性疟疾，则以秋季为最流行。这是什么原因呢？第一因为传染恶性疟的疟蚊在秋天特别繁殖得快，还有一个原因，就是恶性虐的原虫，要有比较高的温度，才能活跃起来。所以我们每当这个季节来到时，应该事先有妥善的防范。

最后，还有一件事我们不可忘的，便是采集疟蚊。采来后，一方面加以检查或解剖，到底百个蚊子之中有多少是带有疟疾原虫可以传播疟疾的。（一方面）幼虫生殖的习惯亦应有详细的调查，宣传工作亦是不可少的，以获得民众的信仰。

有此种调查工作后，才能拟定预防的办法。开始设计，经过相当时期，然后再来一次检查等类的工作，便可知道预防的工作有否实际的功效了。

为什么提倡健全生活[1]

1939 年 7 月 1 日

要讲“为甚么要提倡健全的生活”，先得说明甚么是“健全的生活”。对于“健全生活”的解释，一般人往往只说到身体一方面，把“健全”这个字解作身体的强健，把“生活”两个字的意义缩小到生理的范围以内，这也许是因为受了“健”字的习惯的解释的影响。我认为“健全生活”的意义，就字面来说，应该多注意在“全”这一个字上面，单是某一方面的健，不能说是健全，要各方面都顾到的健全，才是真正的健全。而且，我有一种这样的想法，就是“不全的健”是不值得我们提倡的，我们要提倡“全”的“健”，要提倡“健”而且“全”的生活，不是单单提倡健的生活。

怎样才是“健”而且“全”的生活呢？我们的整个生活究竟可以分开哪几方面呢？据我想来，身体的强健当然是一个方面，这可以说是生理的方面，与生理方面并行的，应该还有心理的方面。至少要身心都健全的生活才配说得上健全的生活。不过生理的健全，大家很容易明白，耳朵听得清，眼睛看得明，吃得下，做得动，这是谁都懂得的生理健全的现象，心理的健全是怎样说法呢？因为心理这个词儿不很通俗，所以比较难讲。心理就是一个人受了外面的刺激，引起的冷、热、痛、痒等感觉，跟喜、怒、哀、乐等情感；从零星的感觉同他的反应积聚起来，就是我们处事的经验，为一面的情感可以陶养成功有规则的情绪等等。健全的心理的表现，就是一个人的行动，受了经验的指示，能够适应环境，以及能够运用以往的经验来改造环境。同时心理健全的人，他的情绪一定很稳定的。在应该喜的场合欢喜，在应该怒的场合愤怒，而且他的喜怒哀乐都有一定的分寸，一点不会过分。反过来说，一个喜怒无常的人，就因为他的心理不健全，他的生活就不能算是健全的生活。所以我说“健全的生活”，除了他的身体很强健以外，还要他的心理反应能够保持着正常的状态，就是他们的行动很得当，情绪很稳定。

单是生理的健全同心理的健全这两个方面，还包括“不尽健全的生活”。应

---

1 《国立贵阳医学院院刊》第 12 期，1939 年 7 月 1。

该还需要一种力量去推动，使强健的身体跟正常的心理相配合，来表现人生的意义，达到健全生活的标准。这种力量，我现在用“精神”这个词儿来代表。让我们来一个比喻：一个兵拿着一支很好的步枪，这枝步枪就代表健全的身体，他把这只步枪的使用法操练得很精熟，能够百发百中，这好比强健的身体与正常的心理得了适当的配合。他用了这只步枪去和敌人拼命或者用来欺负老百姓，这就要看他使用这只步枪的动机了。这里所说的用枪的动机，就是上面所说的推动生活上生理方面同心理方面的一种力量。这种力量如果没有正当的动机来支配，就要闹出乱子来。所以，我认为健全的生活应该分为“健全的”生理，“健全的”心理与“健全的”精神三方面，要有健全的身体，正常的心理，良好的精神才可以说得上健全的生活。说到这里，应当来一个说明：我的意思并不是提倡健的生活，无需注意生理的健全，是说单注意身体的强健是不够的，还有心理与精神两方面应该同样的加以注意。

或者有人要说，身体强健诚然只是健全生活的一方面，不能概括健全生活的全体，但是正常的心理应以健全的生理为基础，健全的精神寄托在健全的身体上，所以身体的强健应该是健全生活的主要方面。我以为不尽然，强健的身体未必是健全生活的重要方面，如果要在这三方面中指出哪一种比较重要的话，我的想法应该是“精神”。单是生理健全的人可以是一个愚笨的人，可以是一个怪癖疯狂的人，身体强健心理正常的人有时候受环境的支配也可能成为一个有害社会的坏人，或者没有志气没有出息的人，这些人的生活都算不得健全的生活。反过来说，有志气有良好的精神的人就是身体上或者生理上有些缺陷，他还有机会可能做出一番有益社会的事业，进一步来说，我们要锻炼强健的身体，修养正常的心理，就要发挥我们良好的精神，所以健全的精神才是健全的生活主要的部分。

健全的精神是哪里来的呢？这固然跟健全的生理健全的心理有密切的关系。但是，有健全生理、健全生理的人，未必都有健全的精神。健全的精神另有它的来源。我想，人的健全精神的来源，或许是“宗教”或许是“主义”。在我们中华民族的健全分子，我想应该是孙中山先生在他三民主义里特别指出的，以忠孝为本的，我国固有的道德。从此次英勇抗战发扬起来的，给全世界敬仰的民族精神，就是这种以忠孝为本的，我们固有道德所开的花。所以，贤明的最高领袖蒋委员长要提倡精神“总动员”，指导我们全国同胞，来养成适应抗战建国需要的健全生活。

上面把解说健全生活的话说的太多了！这是因为，健全的生活这个名词一般的解释，不免把范围看得太窄小了，把内容看得太简单了，要下一番辩证的功夫，自然不免要说些话。好在这些话已经把为什么要提倡健全生活的意思连带的说了一些。现在为着时间的关系，只好用极概括的话，来说明为什么要提倡健全的生活。

第一，生活应该是有意义的。我们不能够醉生梦死的空活一辈子。我们活一天要有一天的成绩。我们要从自己的志愿由实现的当中取得满足。我们要让自己到了老年没有什么懊悔，临死都一点不觉得遗憾，这就是每个人必须有一个职业，或者干一番事业，或者研究一种学问。做事情跟研究必须能耐劳耐苦，有胆量有决心，能彻底，有乐观的态度，能够继续不断地求进步。要这样就必须有健全的生活，健全的心理，以及健全的精神，一方面也不可以缺少。

第二，生活应该是有声有色的，是内容丰富、色彩浓厚的。我们除了使自己的生活有意义而工作以外，还要能为人服务，要有热烈的情绪，要有广泛的同情，能够在空闲的时候有正当的娱乐。要这样，试问健全的生理，健全的心理，以及健全的精神有哪一方面可以缺少?

第三，我们生在这样的大时代中，我们要能够担负起抗战建国的使命来。无论当兵也好，做生产建设工作也好，担任后方政治工作也好，以至于防空、救灾、照料伤兵、帮助难民等等，这些繁亘的工作如果没有健全的身体，健全的心理以及健全的精神，很不容易贯彻始终的。关于这一层，尤其可以见得健全精神的重要。如果没有健全的精神，就不能达到“国至上，民族至上，军事第一，胜利第一，意志集中，力量集中的目标”。甘心做汉奸顺民的人家，就是他们的精神不健全，多一个汉奸顺民，抗战建国前途就多一重障碍。少一个汉奸顺民，就能够早一天达到胜利的目的。所以在今天提倡健全生活，必须特别指出精神健全的重要来。

以上的话不是我故意要提出一点特别的意见来，因为关于生理方面物质方面的健全生活的条件，别人说的太详细了，不必我再来重复。所以把什么是真正的健全生活，为什么提倡健全的生活这两点提出来讲一讲。我们要提倡的是生理健全，心理健全和精神健全的健全生活。我们为着使生活得有意义很丰富很浓厚而且能够担负当前抗战建国的使命，所以提倡这种生理心理精神三方面的健全生活。

《学艺》发刊词[1]

1940年2月3日

有几位同学在课外组织了一个学艺社，他们为着选辑材料、发表心得，练习写作技能，要出版一种刊物，取名《学艺》。这刊物就要发刊了，要我给他们写几句话在头上。他们这样的勤恳，并且肯虚心的向人请教，使我非常高兴，因此乐于写几句话给他们。

第一点，我们出刊物写东西，必须认定目的，切实地朝着目的走去。这刊物的宗旨，既是要把科学研究所得的用通俗化的文字发表出来，我们就得认清，工作的首要目的是科学研究，用通俗化的文字发表乃是一个副目的，也可以说是配合着这首要目的的一种手段。必须这样，这个刊物所发表的文字，才总是"言之有物"的，这个刊物才是一个有根底的东西。刊物应该是"花"，要花好，根本枝叶须要茂盛。如果要我们的《学艺》像个样儿，必须"学艺社"是一个生气蓬勃的团体。否则，光以办刊物为目的，结果不免落到"办刊物到头给刊物办了"的末路里去的。

第二点，因为学术工作最要紧的是求真，所以关于学术的文字，最要紧的是把学问上的真理切实表达出来。学术文能够诚诚恳恳的求"真切"。如果斤斤于文字的美，结果不免是求美失真，反为不美。即以"通俗化"这种功夫来说，也不可以忽略了"真"。我们要使真理普及给一般人，决不可以为着"通俗"而混淆了，甚至于歪曲了真理。学术文字的通俗化是很不容易的技术，非对于真理有透澈的了解，是办不到的。我们千万不好放松了求"真"的功夫，千万不好小看了"通俗化"的技术。小有才的要笔杆的朋友，是不容易写出"美"的学术文、"通俗化"的学术文的。

我提出这两点意思出来，希望学艺社要好好的注意这个刊物，为这刊物写文字的要从科学研讨好好的去锻炼他的写作技术，使这刊物成为科学研讨会所开的美好的花。从小规模做起，从浅近的做起，"好大喜功"，"舞文弄墨"在科学研讨方面、在学术文"通俗化"方面是不会有什么成就的。

---

1 《贵州日报》1940年2月3日。

院长对首届毕业生临别赠书[1]

1940 年 2 月 7 日

二十九年甲级诸同学：

诸位在此艰难困苦的非常时期，修毕大学医科的学程，得到医学士学位，我热诚的向诸位道贺。但是从我的职务上，以及对于诸位的私谊上，都感觉彼此相处的日子太短了。我对于诸位有无限的希望，在诸位毕业离校的时候，愿意从自己的生活经验中提出一些重要的心得来贡献给诸位。

我们无论求学、办事，都必须有科学的态度。我对于科学态度的解释，认为应该是避免主观，注重客观。主观太强，理智容易给感情蒙蔽，会不知不觉的走入错路。注重客观就必须有冷静的头脑，才可以充量运用他的智慧来求学来办事，才会有良好的成就，才会有不断的进步。就是处世方面，也要有科学的态度，才能够检讨自己，体谅他人。这种心平气和认真做事生活的风格，实在是受过高等教育者应有的修养。

求学办事仅有科学的态度还是不够，如果没有一种动力，所谓成就与进步还是没有把握的。这种动力必须有健全而有意义的精神生活的人才有。在西洋社会宗教信仰是人们健全精神的基础。有人说，主义信仰也可以成为人们健全精神的基础。我以为一个人能够有一种固定的事业欲，也可以使他的精神生活达到健全而有意义的境地，因为有固定的事业欲的人必然是意志坚定的，必然能够不惜牺牲为他的事业向前作艰苦的奋斗，像有宗教信仰或者主义信仰的人一样。这样的人，他一定能够从他的事业中得到满足，得到他特有的乐趣，他活一天觉得有一天的意义，他的心境永远是乐观而且积极的。

我有千言万语要对诸位讲，可惜我缺乏演说的天才，又没有充分的时间。以上两点，就是其中扼要的部分，我特地写出来给诸位。如果诸位能够接受了，应用到实际生活里去，那么我所没有说出来的千言万语，诸位也不难体会到了。再会，祝诸位前程无量！

---

[1] 《国立贵阳医学院院刊》第 16 期，1940 年 2 月 7 日。

中学生进修科学应有的条件[1]

1940 年

中国的教育，差不多是分成三个阶段：小学教育，中学教育，大学教育。这三个阶段之中，小学教育和中学教育是占着很重要的地位，大学教育倒是居在比较次要的地位。这是很显然的，一个人格的养成，一个人才的造就，主要的还是中小学教育的使命，到了大学，差不多一切都有了定型，很少能改变的了。诸位都是从事中学教育的工作人员，对于中学教育，一定都有充分的学识和经验，不必我来说什么。我是从事专门高等教育的人，对于中学教育并没有经验，而且也不是一个专门研究教育的人，所以我今天只能就我这个立场，根据个人的以往经验，提出一点意见来供诸位参考。我所要提出的题目，就是中学生进修科学应有的条件。在这个题目上，我只能提出几个条件加以说明，至于这些条件应如何在中学生之中培植起来，那还要靠诸位的努力了。

（一）**要诚实**：我这里所指的诚实，是指在求学问上的诚实而言。我们学科学的人，最大的使命就是探求事物之“真理”，我们要求真，就是不要自欺欺人来蒙骗自己，蒙骗真理；反之，我们必须要诚实，我们要“知之为知之，不知为不知”，我们要勇于认错。唯有具备这种态度，我们才有接近事物之真理的希望。

（二）**要有浓厚的兴趣**：现在许多学习科学的，他们之所以选择某种科学来作他们研究的范围，大部分是以这种科学的出路为先决条件，而忽略了个人的兴趣。这是不对的。虽然出路的问题有时不得不考虑到，但我们必须知道，我们对于一种学问，如果是没有兴趣，就很难有热忱，也就不会有成就。

（三）**要有热切的求知心**：所谓热切的求知心，就是对于一切疑问具有一种解决的要求，不让任何一点不了解的事情马马虎虎的忽略过去。牛顿若是对于苹果为什么往下掉这个问题，没有发生怀疑，没有要求解答，那么，发现万有引力的恐怕就是另外一个人了。

[1] 贵州省档案馆，卷号 510。

（四）**要有坚决的意志**：仅有热切的求知心，还是不够的，我们必须有不怕失败的百折不挠的精神。在一个科学家作一个实验的时候，他不知道要经过多少次失败，才能成功。若是我们没有坚强的意志，一遇失败，立即灰心，那是永远不会成功的。

（五）**要有创造的天才**：每一个学问上的进展，都要靠着一些独立卓越的创造思想来完成，这是很明显的事实。若是每个人都模仿前人，墨守成规，不知进取，一切都是不会有改良和进步的。

（六）**要有虚心容纳的态度**：要知道学问是没有边境的，不但在书本上，即使在我们四周围的环境里，所闻、所见、所遇，也没有一件不是学问；只有肤浅的人才会相信他自己的学问是足够了；反之，渊博的人却总是钻研，会觉得自己的学问之不足，因而更加不断的努力。我们知道孔夫子在他那时代这样一个大学问的人，尚且说"三人行，必有吾师焉"，于此我们就可以想见学问之道了。

（七）**要有判断的能力**：现在的科学，说一句老实话，离"完全"还差得远，所以许多地方，由于材料的不足，研究的不够，结果所得的仅是一些学说或假设的问题。因此一人有一人的学说，一人有一人的的假设。一人既不是全能，当然也就不能完全都对。所以学科学的应该有冷静的判断能力，来采取或寻求自己认为对的学理，不应该死板的去迷信某个"权威者"或是先生的学理。

（八）**要有精确的观察能力**：科学的使命是在于观察自然界的事实，就观察所得，加以分析；再把这些分析，归纳起来成为原则；再用这些原则来解释各个的事实。所以，整个的出发点在于观察事实。所得结论的对或是错，先要看观察的对或是错，由此可见观察力的精确是十分重要的。

（九）**要有合作的精神**：研究科学决不是研究单独的一个个的问题，而是研究许多相互有关系的问题中之一个，所以我们应时常交换所得知识，彼此讨论。若是我们把自己的一点结果，秘而不宣，那么，你这一个问题研究，恐怕就很难再有新的发展。有许多研究问题，范围很广，非一人的学识精力所能到达，那么，更需要有合作的精神，大家来共同努力。

（十）**要有强健的体格**：无论我们做什么事，强健的体格总是一个先决的条件，学科学的尤其重要。因为以研究科学为战志的人，必需要有不会疲乏的体力和精神来努力的工作。否则，这短短的人之一生，是很难有所成就的。

以上十点，可以说是我个人就经验中所得的结果，希望诸位能拿来作一个参考。

中学生升学选择医科前应有之认识[1]

为中学导师及中学生之参考

1941 年 10 月 16 日

一，绪言

在中国医事人才之缺乏，是大家都公认的事实。由于医事人才的缺乏，一方在民族健康没有保障的社会，新的建树无从开始，一方因求过于供而减低从业者的固定性。这实在是现在一个重要的社会问题，需要我们尽力解决的。

解决这问题的唯一方法，就是增加医事人才的培植，这个责任当然大部要落到我们从事医学教育者的肩上，但更要各关系方面的联系，才能完成这个使命。充实医学教育的内容，加强其训练，尽量多招收学生是我们可以尽力的，但一讲到尽量多招收学生，则学生的质的方面就难顾到了，学生的志趣好尚能力以及既往的训练是否合适，我们都无法顾到。为了达到量的增多，牺牲了质的要求，势必粗制滥造，以人命为儿戏，贻害社会无穷的危险。

这个问题，初看起来，似乎无法两全其美的得到根本解决；其实却不然。要知道我们今日之所以质量不能兼顾，并不是因为全国中学毕业生中近乎学医或够得上学医的人少，而却是因为他们缺乏自我的意识，许多近乎学医够得上学医的学生不知学医，而有些不近乎学医够不上学医的人却偏要学医。换一句话说，中学毕业生在选择学科的时候不曾对自己以及自己所想选的学科仔细检讨一番，可以学医的人，有些却走向别的道路，有些不宜于学医的人，初则盲目从事，继则中途而废，但个人及国家所蒙受损失却已不小了。这种现象恐怕是普遍的，但在医学教育方面为尤甚。我们只要分析一下中学生选择医科的动机，就可以瞭然了。

根据个人观察，医学生选择医科的动机，约有下列数点：

（一）家庭传统之支配：这可以从两方面讲：积极的鼓励和强迫是少数，消极的受环境暗示而选修的很多，医生家庭物质较高的享受及职业地位的优越，却是很大的诱力。

[1] 《国立贵阳医学院院刊》34 期，1941 年 10 月 16 日。

（二）中学教员之影响：大部分中学生的兴趣是不稳定的，多方面的，对各课无显殊之偏爱，一位良好的教员可以使所授的课目变得有特别诱惑性，往往使学生因此认定了自己个性的趋向。

（三）不负责任的医师造成的反作用：病者或病者的亲属因关切及痛苦常是特别敏感，对一些医师不负责任的处理反感必深，这种反感经升华作用，就成为一种豪侠精神，毅然从事医业，欲使别人能免去自己曾身受的痛苦。

（四）习尚或社会的重视：医师为病者的精神寄托所在，以其工作能救人济世，为社会所崇尚，由于这种影响而从事医学的为数不少。

（五）青年人的热诚：青年常以公义、仁爱、助人为己任，医师的职业颇有牺牲为公的精神。

（六）少受环境的支配：青年人爱好自由、独立的生活，医师职业在固定性的工作中可算最自由的，尤其是不受政治变迁的影响，颇能投合一部分青年的脾胃。

（七）兴趣和特殊才能：这是一个最理想的动机，但自己的兴趣才能，能很早确定的为数很少。

（八）经济问题：在校时可受公医学生的待遇，毕业后职业得有保障。

以上各种动机，也各有可取的地方，但大致说来，多为盲目的，被动的；不是决定于感情作用，就是受了一些偶发的事实的影响，很少周密的考虑。因之中途而废的，不知凡几，以国家社会今日的经济力言，实是非常重大的损失。因此我们觉得如果事前把医学教育及医师职务的内容概况，其过程中之困难便利的情形，学医者各人应具备之条件，提供出来，实在是必要的。如果因此而使中学毕业生在选择学科前多一番考虑，不近于学医的，尽早改学他科；近于学医的，多多选择医科，那我们的目的就可算是达到了。在这方面，我们需求中学导师以及中学生自身的合作。

二、医学界的概况

（甲）医学教育的概况：医学的对象为最复杂的人体，在医学校课程之完毕，并不就是医学教育之完成，以我个人的估计，一个良好的医生，须经过十年的训练，这十年中学习的方式不同，可分作两个阶级。

一、六年大学：这较普通大学长，而所受的训练也较严格，六年内学课的分配如下：

普通基本学课　一年
医学基本学课　二年
临床　　　　　二年
实习　　　　　一年

二、四年的经验：人体是复杂的多变动的，因之病状因人而异，所以经验为一良好的医师所必需，四年经验是起码的条件。

（乙）医师职业概况

一、职业问题：医学生毕业之后，从业的范围是很广的，可供职于卫生机关、教育机关、做研究工作或私人开业，不论是哪一项，只要以社会的福利为前提，则自有其价值存在，社会之地位亦必高。就以私人开业来说，现在也趋于社会化了。自然目前医学界中，还有许多败类存在，在抗战期间，大发其国难财。

同时，医师绝无失业的可能，我国国民约有四万万五千万，以一万人需一医师计，最少要有四万五千个医师，而现在的医师仅一万人。医师当然是不会无事可做的，这些便利也许可以算是艰苦的长期训练的补偿。

二、工作的性质：在前面关于医师的地位、对象、及医师业务的社会性已约略提过，这里要提出的是这种职业的两个特点：

1. 工作份量：一个医师工作的时间是不能机械的规定的，疾病的变化常使医师在廿四小时内无间断的工作，不同其他职业有固定的工作时间，时间一过就可以自由了。因之，医师职业从份量上看，是较其他职业为重。
2. 工作环境：医师的工作是在病榻之间，疾病的传染可能很大，同时精神上不时为病人的痛苦所侵蚀，这种工作的环境，非体力及精神上的绝对的健康，不足以应付之。

（丙）公医制度：所谓公医的意义是很广的，不以医来牟利的都可以称为公医，最近中央卫生机关已订立公医制度办法，教育部为了奖励公医，推行公医制度起见，规定了公医学生待遇暂行办法和服务暂行办法。

三、医学生应具的条件

对于医学生及医师的情形，上面已大略说明，进一步我们希望中学生考虑个人学业所近，同时顾虑国家需要缓急，我们更希望中学导师，指导学生明确的道路，俾所率从，关于鉴别宜否学医的条件，有下列几个原则：

（甲）兴趣是否近于理科：医学是多方面的科学，除超现实的艺术较少与他发生联系外，理科方面的知识都有应用之处，无论对某一种科学有特长，在医学上都有充分发展的可能。

（乙）意志是否坚定：从事任何事业都必须有坚定的意志，六年学习中课程的繁重，毕业后工作环境的特殊，都足以减少从业的勇气，若没有坚定的意志很难继续下去。

（丙）身体是否健康：医学生在学习期间及毕业后做医师的工作均甚繁重，其他如传染疾病之接近，医院空气的刺激，都非有绝对的健康不能应付。因之健康为考核是否合格之重要原则。就是精神上也需要充足的健康。思想沉着、富理解力，性情乖僻、举动浮躁的绝不适于学医。

最后，希望普遍的瞭解，增加一般人对医学的兴趣，从吸收与鼓励的努力，收较高的成效，使医药卫生事业，迅速开展，成为抗战建国的原动力。

国立贵阳医学院院史[1]

1941 年 10 月 16 日

民国廿六年抗战军兴，中央政府有鉴于医药人才之缺乏，为谋战时急切之需，并树立西南之医学基础，救济沦陷区医学生之学业，乃有设立贵阳医学院之议，至十二月卅一日教育部聘任李宗恩、朱章赓、杨崇瑞三人为国立贵阳医学院筹备委员，并指定李宗恩为主任委员。廿七年元月一日筹备委员会即在汉口成立，并由教育部加聘张志韩、杭立武二人为筹备委员，延聘师资，举办招生，关于院舍及教学设备等重大问题，均得顺利进行。初由教育部令饬移用国立武昌医学院筹备费十六万元，按七折计十一万二千元，为本学院筹备费。又令饬接收北平第一助产学校武昌办事处。于一月中旬至二月初旬，分别在汉口、重庆、西安、长沙、贵阳五处设招生处，招收战区退出之医学生及护士助产学生，共计登记者约三百人，除贵阳区外，均由各招生处负责输送入黔。三月一日本学院正式成立于贵阳，院长一职，即由李宗恩充任，六月一日在阳明路两广会馆正式开课，编定医科一年级第一学期至五年级第一学期共九班，盖因招收学生程度不一，不得不采此因时制宜之办法。同年十月，敷设医事职业科，内分护士班及助产班各自一年级至三年级，共六班。廿八年十月奉令特设卫生工程专修科。廿九年九月解除前与贵州省卫生委员会借用省立医院为本学院学生实习场所之合作办法，在两广会馆本院自设临时门诊部，復于本年特将门诊部扩充为附属医院。兹分人事、行政、设备、院舍四项概述于次。

（一）人事

本学院自廿七年元旦，在汉口成立筹备委员会，经诸位筹委悉力擘划，于三月一日正式成立，暂假禹门路王公馆为办事处，六月一日在阳明路两广会馆正式开课，聘贾魁为教务主任，徐曾渊为秘书主任，并聘洪士希、汤佩松、林绍文、严镜清、柳安昌、侯宝璋、贾魁、杨静波、杨崇瑞等分任人文科、化学科、生物形态科、公共卫生科、物理生理科、病理科、内科、外科、妇产科主任。同年十月聘管葆真为医事职业科主任。廿八年奉令改组秘书处为总务处，

1 《国立贵阳医学院院刊》 34 期，1941 年 10 月 16 日。

聘杨济时为总务主任。同年三月改组生物形态科为生物科解剖科，分聘林绍文、尹觉民为主任。十月，奉令特设卫生工程专修科，聘杨铭鼎兼任主任职务。卅年八月设数理科，聘王成椿为主任，并改组物理生理科为生理药理科，由祝维章医师代理主任职务。

（二）行政

本院自廿七年秋正式开课后，行政机构初具规模。分设教务处、训导处、秘书处。属于教务处者，为注册组、图书馆，后于廿八年增设出版组及图形制作组；属于训导处者，为军事管理组，又于廿八年增设生活指导组及体育卫生组；属于秘书处者，为事务组、出纳组、文书组。此外设会计室，直隶于教育部会计处。廿八年二月奉令改组秘书处为总务处，并于院长室加聘秘书一人。廿九年九月，成立临时门诊部，设主任一人，由各科医师处理诊务。卅年秋将门诊部扩充为附属医院。

（三）设备

关于教学设备，因本学院成立在战时，由于经费有限，运输不便，购置颇感困难，惟经多方设法，向内地及当地医药卫生机关转购或商借，并自制各种实验仪器，得以免敷应用。廿七年十月间曾向广州孙逸仙博士医学院订购生理学仪器，又向安亚公司订购化学药品仪器，长沙永盛隆玻璃公司订购玻璃仪器，后因广州失陷，长沙大火，均遭遗失。此后在香港订购解剖课器械，化学科药品仪器，并向德商仕德洋行订购之显微镜廿五架，又因欧战爆发，均被阻于途中，去年始另运到美国出品之显微镜廿架，及其他教学设备一小部分，此项购置，连同已到及未到者合计，共值国币六万元，美金五千元，港币六千元，此外尚有已购得之图书，计值一万元。

（四）院舍

本学院成立之初，租定阳明路两广会馆及三圣宫两处为临时院舍，在修缮期间，暂租禹门路王姓公馆一所为办事处，并供络续抵筑之教职员及大部分学生住宿之用，另有一部分男生及女生则分住于省立医院及新世界旅社。五月二十日阳明路院舍落成，并于两广会馆左侧隙地自建办公楼一栋，上下共十二间。在两广会馆正院，分佈礼堂、教室、图书馆、实验室、办公室等，其后院花厅为女生宿舍，三圣宫全部为男生宿舍。廿八年“二四”本市被轰炸后，本院为谋疏散计，商得贵州盐务办事处同意，借用其六广门外空地建筑茅舍十九栋，作为前期学生临时院舍，并另建住宅，在打儿洞者三栋，在大垇者五栋，供本院教职员租用。至廿九年三月，六广门外临时院舍告成，即将医科一、二、三年级及卫工科一年级，并有关各科，及教务处训导处同时迁至城外。本年八月，两广会馆之门诊部扩充为附属医院，复将门前城墙拆穿，佈成石级，以利空袭疏散。院本部已于九月二十日，迁设三圣宫内办公。

以上所述，仅其大略，至于"人事"一项，更动颇多，见下载教职员名录，兹不复详，三年以来，本学院于人力物力维艰之际，得由中央之督导，地方政府及各界之掖助，本学院同仁之通力协作，辛苦经营，已完成初步基础，迄今医科毕业者五十三人，卫生工程专修科毕业者五人，护士科毕业者五十一人，助产科毕业二十一人，均受政府征调服务于前方及各省卫生机关或医院工作。胜利在望，益用淬励，愿以"敬往思来"共勉之。

医学生的质与量的问题[1]

1942年8月1日

在中国，医事人才的缺乏，是大家都承认的；但这也是必然的。新医的输入中国，不过是近百年来的事；医学教育开始至今也不过五十年上下；在这短短的时间中，要产生充分足用的人才，当然是不可能的。再加上医事行政上的缺点，人才不能适当分配，充分利用，这种缺乏乃更行显著。补救这种缺乏，医学教育者当然要负大部分的责任。近九年来，政府之增设医学院校，公医学生待遇办法颁布，以及最近命令各医学院校多收学生，这都足以表现政府在这方面的苦心和努力。

但中国医事人才的缺乏，并不单纯是一个量的问题，仅求数量的增加，并不能解决这种缺乏。有些人虽是医师，而没有病人敢请教，其结果等于零；有些医师非但不能为病人减病，反而替病人增病，则更引起相反的作用了。因此，从事医学教育者所应注意的，不但是要造成多量的医师，而且要造成够得到一定标准的医师，换句话说，就是医师的量与质，应有一个适当的平衡。是要以最低限度的质为标准，来造成最大可能量的医事人才。

下面，我们愿意先从一个医学院的立场来申述，这质与量的平衡。

我们先讲量。根据各国以往办理医学教育的经验，我们知道一个医学院每班人数以六十人为最合适。至少最好有四十人，最多可至一百人，若班次太小则太不经济，这是不言而喻的；若班次太大，则教员的精神不能遍注，不能对每个学生加一番考察，而给以适当的指导。

但这个数量的规定，并不是单方面的。我们若是忽略了这些学生的本实，以前所受的教育；大部分课程的实验课可以不成问题，但医院的设备就不同了。根据我们以往的经验，医院病床数与每班人数至少应为三与一之比；否则学生之实习即不足。以此为例，一个每班六十人之医学院，其附属医院至少需有病床一百八十张，方能足用。

一个医科毕业生，他的本质和前后训练能如上述，则在质方面可以说已及

[1] 《国立贵阳医学院院刊》第43期，1942年8月1日。

最低标准。这样一个毕业生，在临床诊断方面，至少可以有相当把握，不至犯重大错误，不至不识病症，乱投药石。其实一个医师最重要之点，也就在他的诊断，看出患者的病症；至于治疗，那是比较简单的问题，只要知道是什么病，怎样治是比较容易解决的。至于特别有天才或领袖能力的学生，则校中教员自愿多予注意和指导，使他可以完全发展，有较大的成就。

反过来说，如果质素太低，不及这个标准，则所造就的医师，必定不能胜任；他们在诊断治疗方面必定要出种种错误，不但不能替病人减病，反而替病人增病，成为社会上的祸害。不但如此，现在新医的位置，在一般人的心理上还没有完全建立起来，必使新医失去人们的信仰，而在发展上受到无穷的困难，并且这一班粗制滥造的医师到了社会上去，必然要占住一部份地位，将来比较优良的医师，如果能够训练出来，也必要受他们的排挤，这更将成为新医发展前途的不幸。

因此，我们认为一个医学院虽应以每班六十人为标准，但如果在师资设备方面不足，千万不能拘泥于人数，而造一些低劣的医师，遗害社会，遗害学术本身。自然一个医院如果师资或设备方面不足，仍应该发展下去，力谋各方面的充实，再逐渐增加学生人数，以期达到饱和。

再就中国整个医学教育政策而言，也是一样。我们一定应该注重量与质的平衡。如果想增加医学人才，我们应先从充实现有的医学院的内容起，使每个医学院均有充实的师资和设备，再增大班次至饱和；不应不顾内容，而徒求数量上的增加。

增加医学人才的另一个办法，当然是增设医学院，但这一点我们认为暂时不应该鼓励，这有两个理由；第一、现有医学院的内容还不充实：如果经济上许可的话，应该先充实现有的医学院，使其能多招生。这不但成效易见，而且比较经济。

第二、中国新医教育的开始到现在不过五十年左右，造成的师资自然不多，即就现在几个医学院说，已感到师资不够，这一点现在办医学教育的都感到，若是再增设医学院，师资必更嫌不足，结果造成中国无一完整的医学院的现象，必使医学教育日见退步。

最后，我们愿意附带的提出，中国现在医事人才的感到缺乏，不定全是一个量的问题，我们在本文开端时，已经提出，人才不能适当的分配利用，也是一个大原因。我们若是能够仅现有的人才作适当的分配，乡村方面，固然应该鼓励人去，但不应该强迫，减少医师工作的热忱，而城市方面，也不应该完全取放任态度，应尽量促进城市医师的组织，和适当的分配。这样，人数虽不必增加，而其成效可以提高，所得结果还是一样的，这一方面，自然需要医事行政者的思考和努力。

在中国西南建立一个新医学中心的呼吁[1]

1943年5月10日

National Kweiyang Medical College.
Kweiyang, Kweichow, China.
May 10, 1943

An Appeal for a New Medical Centre in South West China.

Modern medicine in China has received in war time both a setback and an impetus. Its Mecca, the Peiping Union Medical College, founded by the Rockefeller Foundation, has ceased to function, but several national schools have been strengthened and one new school has been created to keep up the training of medical personnel to meet the national emergency.

The National Kweiyang Medical College came into existence in 1938 at a time when a large number of medical teachers and students were thrown out of their respective schools as a result of the Sino-Japanese war. The Government made the timely decision to create a new medical centre in an interior province with two definite objectives: first to accommodate refugee medical, nursing and midwifery students so that they might continue their studies, thus ensuring the supply of medical personnel during the war and in future, and secondly to establish permanently a modern medical training centre in China's South West. Thus when the college began its first teaching session in June 1938 it had an enrolment of 227 medical, 37 nursing and 39 midwifery students rallying from 49 different medical and vocational schools. In February 1939 the first class of nurses and midwives and a year later the first class of doctors were graduated. By July 1942 altogether 90 doctors, 59 nurses and 20 midwives from this new school were serving the country.

Kweiyang is the capital of the province of Kweichow with a population of 180,000, while the province itself, with an area of 69,000 square miles, almost half the size of Japan, supports a population of about 11,000,000. Kweichow has been one of the backward provinces of China both economically and culturally. Prior to 1938 modern medicine had hardly gained a footing. There were less than a dozen qualified doctors in the whole province. The war has, however, turned the little known city of Kweiyang almost over night into an important medical centre in free China, since besides the National Kweiyang Medical College five other medical institutions have temporarily established themselves in the city, but the Kweiyang Medical College is the only institution that will remain in Kweiyang after the war as a modern centre of training for medical personnel in China's South West. Looking ahead, China's South West will, even before the present war is over, possess a significance never before anticipated. It is also certain that Kweiyang will become a city of some importance when the railway comes through Kweilin and Canton and as a centre of medical education will have an assured position. The urgent demand for well trained personnel

---

[1] From the application of National Kweiyang Medical School. RAC, CMB, Inc. Box 96, folder 685.

to staff the eighty-three district health centres in the Province of Kweichow itself must somehow be met.

The National Kweiyang Medical College has, however, not yet attained any degree of permanency in the way of a campus. At present its preclinical departments are housed in a series of bamboo and straw structures on a rented site outside the north gate of the city, while its clinical departments, with its teaching hospital and the attached vocational school, are located in an old guild house within the south gate of the city and the administrative offices in a nearby temple. Such scattered premises are highly unsatisfactory in administration and co-ordination. After much prospecting and unavoidable delay and a great deal of red tape, a permanent site of 28 acres has been recently acquired. It is situated a short distance to the south west of the city. From the points of view of accessibility, salubrity and availability of water supply it is in every respect an ideal site for the realisation of our building program.

The first part of the program includes an erection of a series of simple permanent buildings on the new site to replace the existing temporary bamboo and straw structures which have served during the past three years as lecture rooms and laboratories for the preclinical division and dormitories and residences for a part of the student body and teaching staff. They are now toterring on their last legs. For the new buildings good local materials will be chiefly depended upon, but provision will be made for future improvements when modern building equipment becomes available. The motives of the building will be simplicity, durability and dignity.

A large building fund will have to be raised. A part of it will be granted by the Government but a substantial proportion will have to come from other sources.

（译文）

国立贵阳医学院

贵州，贵阳，中国

1943 年 5 月 10 日

在中国西南建立一个新医学中心的呼吁

在战争时期，中国的现代医学受到了很大的冲击．如医学圣地——由洛克菲勒基金会成立的北平协和医学院就被迫关闭了。不过也有进步的地方，比如有几所国立学校变得比先前更强大了，而且为了满足国家的紧急需求，还成立了一所新的医学院。

中日战争的爆发，使许多医学院校的学生和老师被迫离开了校园。为了收容这些医学、护士学和助产学的学生，让他们能够继续学业，从而确保战时和未来医务人员的供应，同时在中国西南地区建立一个永久的现代化医疗培训中心，政府及时决定在内陆省建立一个新的医疗中心——国立贵阳医学院于 1938

年应运而生。1938 年 6 月，贵医的第一学年正式开学，227 名医学生、37 名护士和 39 名助产士学生报到上课，他们来自 49 所不同的医学院校和职业学校。1939 年 2 月，第一批护士和助产士毕业；一年后，第一批医学生毕业。到 1942 年 7 月，一共有 90 名医学生、59 名护士和 20 名助产士学生从这里毕业，走向社会，为国家服务。

贵州省占地 6 万 9 千平方英里，几乎是日本的一半，人口约 1100 万；贵阳是贵州的省会，人口 18 万。无论经济还是文化，贵州都是比较落后的地区。在 1938 年之前，现代医学在这里几乎无迹可寻，全省合格的医生连 12 个都不到。战争使贵阳这个名不见经传、尚未受战争干扰的小镇一下子成为了中国重要的医疗中心，除贵阳医学院，另外还有 5 所医疗机构在这里搭建临时据点。不过在战后只有贵阳医学院仍将留在这里，为中国的西南地区培养现代医学人才。展望未来，甚至在战争结束之前，中国的西南地区将扮演之前从未有过的重要角色。此外，待通过贵阳的贯通桂林和广东的铁路建成，贵阳将会变得越来越重要，贵阳作为医学教育中心的地位就更毋庸置疑了。眼下的当务之急是，必须采取相应的方式，对贵州省 83 个地区的卫生中心的工作人员进行严格的培训。

但糟糕的是，贵医现在连确定的校址都没有，其临床前期还租住在城北门外的几间茅草棚里；临床部门及其教学医院，还有附属职业学校，安置在南城门内的一个很旧的公馆内；行政办公室则设在附近的一间寺庙里。各院系四处分散，这对行政和各部门的协调合作都是极为不利的。经过大量的实地考察，办理繁杂的文件手续及其他耗时的琐事，最近我们终于在离城西南很近的一个地方收购了一块 28 英亩的土地，用作永久校址。从方便性、供水及其他各方面考虑，这块地对于我们实现修建校舍的计划，都是非常理想的地方。

我们计划第一步先在新址上修建一些简单的永久性建筑，以取代过去临床前期的教室和实验室及一些老师和学生用作宿舍的竹蓬屋。现在这个计划已进入最后准备阶段。建筑材料将主要采用本地一些比较好的材料，不过等有了现代的建材和设备后，我们会做一些改进。修建这些建筑的宗旨是：简单、实用且大气。

因此我们现在需要募集大量的建筑基金。政府会拨一些款项，不过相当一部分资金，我们还得从其他途径募集。

医师业务的探讨[1]

1943 年 7 月 23 日

中国今后需要的医师据估计须在十年内造就二十三万余人。但目前已登记的合格医师却不过一万余人，如何从这样小的数字来达到那样大的理想的数字，实在是一个非常重大的问题。第六届中华医学会在重庆开会时，大家细心研讨的结果，认为最大的可能，恐亦不过能造就十万人左右。因为数量的增加，需要许多客观条件如经费、师资等等，如果客观条件不具备，数量问题决不能得到正常的解决。况且医师业务关系人命，训练决不能苟且。一个合格的医师，至少在学识经验与技术上都要能符合起码的要求，但这个起码的要求，决不能在短期内做到。如果匆匆了事，训练马虎，结果所造就出来的医师，大多学识短浅，经验缺乏，技术低下，则其可能给予社会的危险，那真不堪想像。这是我们造就大量医师的时候，所不能不特别注意的。

我国幅员广大，人口众多，就现有医师和全人口比例来说，数量上的缺乏，当然显而易见；但如果仅就各大都市的情形来说，实际上的问题却不完全在乎数量的不够。即就贵阳市而论，除公立医院的医生之外，开业医师亦不下四十人。假定贵阳市人口约为二十万人，则平均每五千人有医师一人照顾，以观医药事业最发达的美国，平均一位医师亦须照顾三四千人，相差不过一二千人。但关于人民医疗卫生问题，却不能像他们那样得到比较合理的解决。可见除了数量不足之外，还有其他因素，值得我们注意。

我觉得这里面的主要因素有四：1、是医师业务没有合理的分配，人人各自为政，互不相谋。以致有许多力量互相抵消，不能尽量发挥他们的效能。2、是医师与患者之间，没有建立一种良好的关系，患者对医师不能完全信任，医师对患者不能诚意负责，结果医师与患者之间，仅是金钱的交易。3、是医师不能在社会上取得合法的地位，中国古时每以医巫并列，至今尚以医师与道士同流，即上层社会的人民，亦很少认识医师的责任与地位，因此医师不能彻底执行他的职务。4、是社会对于公立医院不能尽力予以支持，因此公立

[1] 《贵州日报》1943 年 7 月 23 日。

医院，也不能不藉收入来维持生命，也不能不受许多社会因素的障碍，结果，公立医院也不能做到它本身应尽的责任。

我国医师，数量上既如此缺乏，再加上这些人为的因素，使仅有的一些医师尚不能充分发挥他们的效能，无怪乎我国的医疗问题，不能逐渐地得到合理的解决，所以要尽量努力以达到理想的数字之外，一定要在下述几点，同时谋彻底的改进。

第一、便是要医师能分工合作，分工是使他们都能贡献他们的特长，合作是各人所贡献的能力不致互相抵消，且集中起来对社会发生更大的效果。换句话说，就是要把医师的业务，作合理的分配与严密的组织。一个医师并不是样样都懂，也不是样样都精，如果他要做他所不懂的，或是勉强做他所不精的，那是一种浪费，同时也是一种危险。所以欧美各先进国家，非常注意到这一点。就我所知道英国情形来说，他们把医师分为普通与专门两种，普通医师的知识比较广博，关于医疗的各种常识都很具体。他们是直接和人民发生关系的，是人民家庭中的卫生顾问。一般轻微的疾病，固然由他们照顾，就是平日的饮食起居，也负有相当责任。如果遇有疑难的疾病，他们便介绍给专门医师然后由专门医师指示他去诊治。这种普通医师，大多是在学校毕业后不久，在医院实习了一二年，为经济及兴趣等等关系，不能继续深造，于是便开始执行业务。也有的是毕业后便跑到有名望的普通医师那里学习了一二年，取得了相当经验之后再单独执行业务的。专门医师又可分为临床各科、基础医学各科及公共卫生的专门医师三种，后两种因与本问题没有多大关系，故此忽略而不谈。临床各科的专门医师，是对于内科外科及妇科等有专门的学识与经验者，即普通所谓的专门医师。他们平日不随便诊病，只是接收那些由普通医师介绍来的比较疑难的疾病，经过他们诊断之后，再指给普通医师去治疗，所以他们不直接和病者发生关系，而是对普通医师负责。他们是从医院里经过了长期的实习与锻炼，由很低的地位慢慢升上来的，现在他们在社会上已经负有相当的名望，每月医疗的机会虽不多，但已经可以解决生活问题，所以还有空暇的时间义务担任医学院的功课，及公立医院的诊疗工作，以便增进自己的学识经验，以便在社会上树立更普遍的信誉。

普通医师与专门医师这样的分工合作，有几个很显著的优点：第一、因为普通医师的来源容易，人数较多，所以社会上的卫生问题可以得到更多的人去照顾；第二、有些疑难的疾病可以得到专家的指导；第三，可以节省专门医师的精力，让他有进一步的造就；第四，普通医师可以从专门医师那里不断地学习以增长自己的知识和经验。

在英国，不但医师的工作有这样合理的分配，就是医疗机构，也有严密的组织。他们的医院，大概分为公立医院，实习医院，私立医院，或团体合组的诊疗所，及个人诊疗所四种。公立医院完全由社会的力量维持，亦完全以服务为目的，普通的医药费几乎完全不收，所以他们的对象大多为平民阶级，反之，私立医院及个人诊疗所却收费较高，所以大多是以中上层阶级的人民为对象。在这种情形之下无论哪一种阶级的民众，医疗问题都可以得到相当的解决。

然而反观我国目前医师工作的状况，却与此相差很远，开业医师，不分普通与专门，彼此之间，以竞争代合作。为了扩充业务，吸收病人，处处迎合病人的心理，往往滥用许多治疗用方与手续。例如一些用不着特殊医治的病也要"无的放矢"！一些其他医师治不了的病，也得敷衍。结果，在病人方面，浪费了金钱，延误了疾病！在医师方面，浪费了精神，毁坏了道德！真可说是两败俱伤。至于公立医院的专门医师，也因为缺乏分工制度，以致许多极普通的病，犯不着专家医治的，也常是集一身，影响他的工作技能。这种情形实宜及早挽救。

其次，便是要建立医师与患者间的正常关系，医师的医疗工作，能否收到最大的效果？便完全视此种关系如何为转移。在患者方面，要紧的是信任医师，做终身的健康顾问。不但有病时要找他医治，就是平日的起居饮食，也要时常向他请教，换句话说，个人整个的健康就完全交付与他。在医师方面就应有服务诚意，负责的热忱，不但做患者的健康顾问，而且能做患者的忠实朋友，处处以患者的幸福为服务的目的，在平日医师要随时供给患者各种预防疾病的知识及各种养成卫生习惯的方法。一旦有了疾病，便要诚心诊断，遇有疑难的疾病，便要介绍给专门医师。并且有许多疾病，病人有自然恢复的可能，医师便要多方面加以指导和协助，使这种可能性能及早实现。这样，才算是尽了医师应尽的责任。总之，医师的工作完全建筑在与患者的关系之上，如果患者不信任医师，朝秦暮楚，或医师言之谆谆，而患者听之藐藐，又如果医师以营利为目的，虚伪欺骗患者，那不但会失医疗的意义，而且要引起不幸的结果。

第二、是要严格规定医师的业务范围，同时在法律上要予以合法的保障，使医师能在其所规定的范围内，充分行使其职权。本来医师资格的取得，政府已有严格的规定，如果依照规定审查合格的，就应该予以充分的信任，因为医疗工作是一种专门的学术，局外人决不能妄参末议肆意批评！否则，一定要引起严重的问题，对于医师与患者都不利。举一个很显浅的例子来说，病人在手术后不幸死亡，这里的情形很复杂，病人所患的病若是不治之症，不用手术便全无生望，用手术也许有一线生机，如果不幸手术后死亡，这在医师便没有什么责任；但若是因医师在诊断上或手术上偶尔错误，无意中发生不幸的事件，这在医师当然有相当的责任，但在法律上却不便加罪，因为偶尔的错误，任何职业界的人，都难避免；但若医师为贪一时之利，用了某项不必用的手术，或用手术时不合条件，如医师自己心神不安，或消毒不够等，结果致病人死亡，那么医师便要负法律上的完全责任；由此可见，虽同是在手术后死亡，但医师的责任却因情况的不同而大有差别。如果法律上对于这种情形不严加区分，或是社会上对于此种情形不充分认识，淆乱是非，妄加批评，其结果有些医师为省却麻烦起见，凡遇有疑难与危险的疾病，便只好敬谢不敏，使病人只好求之于一知半解的庸医，以致疾病愈弄愈糟，所以归根结底，受损害的还是社会。

最后便是要以社会的力量来充分支持公立的医院，使公立医院能真正地成为社会上大多数人民的诊疗所。目前各公立医院为了经费不够，常常要籍收入来维持生命，结果有钱的人才有看病的资格，没钱的人只有病以待毙。这在私立医院和私人诊所，未可厚非，如果号称社会服务的公立医院，也因为经济条件不够，不得不将大多数贫苦的病人驱逐门墙之外，就不免失掉本意了。所以如何使公立医院不直接和病人发生经济上的关系实在是目前一个非常迫切的问题。这个问题的解决，所依赖的条件很多，如前述医师分工以后使一班专门医师有余力义务在公立医院担任治疗，就为公立医院解除一部分经济负担。除此之外，最基本的是要社会全体人士能充分认识公立医院对于社会整个福利的关系，平日能尽量在经济上舆论上充分维持它并爱护它。同时，还要提倡一种健康保险制度，以便平时有了准备，一旦有病临身，也不致如大祸临头。其实平时所花的一点钱，也许不及疾病时耗费的十分之一。现在一般病人，每每感觉到医药费太贵，有一病万金之叹！其实反躬自问，造成这种结果的，自己难道没有责任吗？况且有许多人，平日情愿花不少钱用在无用的迷信上，更是情不可原。谈到这处，问题又要牵涉到整个社会的教育程度，一般人民对于医院的认识不够，自然与其教育程度有关，所以要解决这个问题，还要同时从教育方面入手。

以上数点，本来卑浅无甚高论，唯就目前中国医疗工作现状言之，似为切要之图。我国的科学医学，历史尚短，根基不厚，倘若开始时即误入歧途，则差之毫厘，谬以千里，将来的结果，殊未可乐观！况当抗战建国期间，人力物力，都要力求经济，总裁谆谆有言，一人应做十人所应做的事，意即人力的浪费，在所不许。今政府于物资极端困难之中竭力谋医师数量的补充，我医界同仁，尤当健全本身，分工合作，诚意服务，发挥最大的工作效能，以弥补数量上之不足。同时希望社会人士，应尊重医师的地位，认识医师业务的范围，尽量设法支持公立医院的设施，使医师能充分行使其职权，公立医院能真正担负其使命，则我国医药业务的前途必可日新又新，社会人民的健康，从此亦有充分的保障了。

医学院附属医院的任务[1]

1944 年 5 月 1 日

本学院自成立附属医院迄今，转眼已经二年了。这二年以来，赖地方人士的爱护与协助，暨医院工作人员的埋头苦干，始能具有现在这样的一点规模，并且能相当地尽到了它所应尽的责任。兹者欣逢它二周年纪念，本人特地代表本学院表示其无限的谢意。

无论是普通的医院抑是一个医学院的附属医院，它就是一个社会的机构。所以要使一个医院办得有成绩，一方面固然要有专门人才和合理的组织与管理，但另一方面还是要社会人士的真诚合作，这里所谓合作，就是它的计划和设施，社会人士尤其是患者能够照着去实行；同时它的需要，也能给予种种的帮助。

凡是一个比较理想的医院，为了要指挥它的工作效能起见，便不能不有很精密的分工合作。就拿医师的任务来说，不仅在横的方面依照病的性质的不同，有内科外科及妇产科等分别，就是在纵的方面，同在一科之中，各人所负的责任也不一样。在名义上，依照他的学识经验分为主任、主治医师、住院医师、助理住院医师及实习医师。在任务上，主任和主治医师都是处于指导的地位（大概要诊断上发生了困难才请教他们），住院医师同助理住院医师才直接和病人有密切的关系，举凡关于病人身体的初步检查与普通疾病的诊断及治疗，都由他们负责。实习医师是一种学习性质，他们除了纪录病历及化验等工作之外，也负有协助处理的任务。经过这样分工之后一般病人的初步诊治可以有人负责，不必一定都要主任和主治医师去处理，但一旦遇有困难的时候，则主任和主治医师便可以展其所长，加以诊断，然后指示给住院医师等去处理。这样，一方面可以节省专门医师的精力，好让他们继续研究，另一方面住院医师等又可从他们那里得到许多新的知识。

但是社会上许多人士不明了这种情形，无论他患了什么病，甚至一点伤风

[1] 《国立贵阳医学院院刊》59&60 合刊，附属医院二周年纪念专刊。1944 年 5 月 1 日。

或皮肤上生了一个小疮，总希望都定主治医师来诊视才好，有时不惜花许多精力，辗转托人介绍。专门医师为了应付起见，也只得什么都自己来。结果因为病人太多，不得不草草了事。这不但浪费了专门医师的光阴，而且难免有延误病人的危险。这种情形，实在是两头吃亏。所以在医院方面，我们虽然有了合理的组织，但要是社会人士不予合作，则此种组织便不能表现他的效能，在工作的推进上便发生了许多困难。

其次一个医学院的附属医院，除了像普通医院一样，以服务社会为宗旨之外，还负有教学的任务。也可以说，在我们附属医院里面，对于一些较为疑难的疾病，都是用一种研究的态度，目的在避免诊断上有不周到的地方，并求得比较更确实的原因与解释。也就是所谓“精益求精”的意思。所以我们常有一大群医师围着一个患者讨论研究的情形，这虽然增加患者一点麻烦，可是对于患者总是有益无损的。倘若因为他所患的病而得到一种新发现或新启示，那么他对于人类还是一种很大的贡献哩！这一点，也是要请社会人士加以明了的。

末了，一个比较理想的医院应该要有相当的设备。虽然在此物力艰难之际，不能如何求其完备，但最低限度的标准，总不能不做到。如果要做到，在目前百物昂贵的状况下，经费是相当可观的。可是一个医学院的附属医院，并没有单独的经费预算，只能自给自足。为了平衡收支起见，只好在病人身上多收一点费。我们一方面深感不能使医药事业普及一般平民，一方面，又觉得不能使学生得到较多的病例来见习，也引为遗憾。不过国家财政的困难情形，人所共知确是心有余而力不足。所以唯一切实可行的办法还是希望社会热心人士的赞助。前次本院为添置病床，承蒙社会人士慷慨乐捐，不久便达到预定的数目，可见这种社会事业，只要大家群策群力，并没有不成功的道理。所以关于本院今后的发展，还希望社会人士多多协助。

关于中华医学基金会和协和医学院的备忘录[1]

September 2, 1944

MEMORANDUM ON THE C.M.B. AND THE P.U.M.C.

In reply to the many queries put to him by Dr. Forkner just before he left China in March 1944, the writer ventures to express his personal views on the C.M.B. and the P.U.M.C. under the following headings:

1. The contribution of the P.U. M. C. through the activities of its graduates.
2. Criticism of the educational policy of the P.U.M.C.
3. Concerning the CMB.
4. Suggestions for the future.

THE CONTRIBUTION OF THE P.U.M.C. THROUGH THE ACTIVITIES OF ITS GRADUATES

The real contribution of an educational institution can best be measured by the activities of its graduates. In order to estimate the influence of the P.U.M.C. graduates on medical education, health promotion and the standard of professional practice, it is necessary to have some understanding of the Chinese personality.

For thousands of years the social unit in China has been the family. The preservation and continuance of the family clan play a dominant part in the moulding of the individual character. It tends at least to restrict his horizon and personal ambition. The traditional attitude towards education is another factor of importance. Since China has always been ruled by men of literary attainments, orthodox education became the only path by which a person could advance himself and his family. This gave rise to the attitude of looking upon education as a means rather than as an end, and generations of literary training resulted unfortunately in divorcing the individual's mental activities from the factual world. With this background in mind, one finds the average educated Chinese as compared with his equals in the West, mentally less mature. He lacks in neither intelligence nor diligence, but is less integrated in the sense that he is less capable of acting in relation to his experience as a whole, and more easily distracted by passing impulses. His sense of social responsibility stops short of his family clan, outside of which he tends to be a rank individualist. In temperament, he is more intuitive than ratiocinative more cautious and conservative of his vital resources and less venturesome and spendthrift. He is more interested in peaceful contentedness on earth rather than ultimate truth. He has never had to fight for his intellectual freedom, nor has he been subjected to the discipline that comes from the co-operative life in an industrial community. The complicated system of "face" also tends to create all sorts of unnecessary difficulties in his social relationships. He is apt

[1] RAC, CMB, Inc. records (FA065) Box 118, Folder 856.

to be unreasonably intolerant of any situation that hurts his self regard. Probably because of this, he is incapable of any genuine sentiment of hero-worship in the best sense of the term. Under such circumstances, it is often difficult for native leadership to be effective.

In her efforts at industrialization and social reconstruction, China needs at the present day, not only leadership in every technical field, but also leadership in all public and social services. The discovery and training of such leadership must therefore be the primary object of every branch of higher education.

The first class of medical and nursing students of the re-organized P.U.M.C. graduated in 1924. During the period of 1924 to 1942, altogether 295 doctors and 171 nurses have been qualified. If from these we deduct the number of graduates who completing their course after 1938 have not yet had the time or opportunity to show their ability and leadership, we are left with 212 doctors and 114 nurses whose activities and achievements might be reviewed as a measure of the contribution of the P.U.M.C. to the development of modern medicine in China. The writer through his fourteen years of connection with the P.U.M.C. and subsequent service in the field of medical education, had the privilege of being personally acquainted with about seventy percent of them, and would be aware of any notable contribution made by them. Yet without detailed investigation into every case, he is only justified in setting down below some of his impressions in regard to the achievements of the group as a whole.

In the field of medical education, it can without qualification be stated that the P.U.M.C. graduates and its associates have played a very important part in raising the standard of technical training in every medical school with which they happen to be associated. They introduced modern methods in undergraduate teaching and a degree of efficiency in performance. Under favorable conditions many are productive investigators in the laboratories. Indeed, they are responsible for whatever progress was achieved in medical education in China within recent years.

In Public Health, many P.U.M.C. graduates are occupying important posts. Undoubtedly, they have strengthened the health services in a technical sense. With a few outstanding exceptions, however, none have made any noteworthy contribution to the movement as a whole. This is probably due in large part to social backwardness, but one somehow misses qualities of statesmanship among members of the P.U.M.C. group taking leading parts in the movement. In Red Cross and war work, a number of them have shown up most creditably under able leadership. Their loyalty to a worthy cause and spirit of self sacrifice are certainly commendable, but such are not many.

Some graduates have taken up private practice but there is no evidence that they have contributed in any way to the ethical standard of professional practice.

From the above, one reluctantly comes to the conclusion that as a whole, the P.U.M.C. graduates have among them many technical leaders but their social and intellectual contributions have not come up to expectation.

CRITICISM OF THE EDUCATIONAL POLICY OF THE P.U.M.C.

In order to find some possible explanation of the above impression, an examination of the educational policy adopted by the P.U.M.C. may not be unprofitable.

Before proceeding it might be appropriate to make a few observations on university education in China in general. In China, American influence has always predominated in the development of modern education. There are several types of universities. First of all, there is the missionary type of private universities such as St. John's University in Shanghai, West China Union University in Chengdu, Cheeloo University in China etc. Among their graduates, there are many notable social and intellectual leaders, but as a group their lack in social and cultural background often hinders their full development as active leaders in China's efforts at social reconstruction. On the other hand, there are the government and Chinese private universities staffed mostly by returned students from different western countries. Their graduates wield considerable influence in the educational and political spheres, but as a group show some deficiency in modern view points and methods of approach. Besides these two types of universities, there is an intermediate type notably represented by the Yenching University in Peiping, under the enlighted leadership of President Leighton Stuart. This university combines the merits of both the above-mentioned types of institutions and should serve as a model for future educational projects of foreign support.

Though supported by non-missionary interest, the P.U.M.C. in many respects still reminds one of the missionary types of institution in its social and intellectual isolation. It somehow suggests a mere transplantation on China's soil of a first-class medical college from America which did not become an integral part of the national programme of medical education. Many of its students come from missionary colleges. Even those from Yanching University, being separately prepared from the medical course, do not possess the broad liberal background the other Yenching students seem to enjoy. The religious and social department of the P.U.M.C. was a sort of after-thought and its activities seem to have had very little influence on the students. This state of isolation is further enhanced by the adoption of the English language as the official medium of instruction. True, a medical student in China must have a thorough command of at least one modern European language and English is probably the most useful, but it should not be at the expense of his own tongue. The inability to handle with ease the Chinese language among so many of the P.U.M.C. graduates, may account partly for the slow rate at which modern medicine takes root in China. The net result has been that the students, after spending the most impressionable years of their life in a closed circle of comparative ease, acquire a highly technical training at the price of losing touch with the social problems that bristle around them.

CONCERNING THE C.M.B.

Since the establishment of the P.U.M.C., one understands the C.M.B. had devoted all the income from its capital fund in support of the P.U.M.C. The writer had not the exact figures at hand, but if he remembers correctly, the annual sum was round about $1,500,000.00 Chinese currency which at two and a half to one rate of exchange, would be equivalent to US$600,000.00. This sum was supplemented annually by a special grant from the Division of Medical Science of the Rockefeller Foundation which amounted to US.$420,000.00 in 1937-1938.

Since the seizure of the College by the Japanese, its available funds have been used to maintain and strengthen existing medical colleges in Free China. Selected National Colleges have been materially aided. This means that the Board instead of maintaining one special institution has spread out its resources to embrace the whole field of medical education in China and thereby broadened its influence. In the field of nursing education, it resuscitates the P.U.M.C. Nursing School in Chengdu in collaboration with the West China Union University Hospital.

SUGGESTIONS FOR THE FUTURE.

In creating the China Medical Board, in 1916, it was the aim of the Rockefeller Foundation to promote the gradual and orderly development of a comprehensive and efficient system of medicine in China (Second Annual Report of the China Medical Board, 1917). At that time, all the medical colleges of any standing in China were supported by foreign missions. Under the stimulus of the P.U.M.C. a national programme of medical education has since been gradually evolved. Now, several national medical schools, such as the National Central University Medical College, the National Shanghai Medical College, the recent nationalized Hsiang-ya Medical College (formerly Hunan-Yale) and the newly established National Kweiyang Medical College, may all be considered to be developing along modern lines. During the war, the C.M.B. will naturally involve two main problems: First, the re-opening of the P.U.M.C. and secondly, the desirability of continuing its war time policy of direct assistance to medical education in general.

Since the re-opening of the P.U.M.C. is of greater consequence it might be considered first. It is hoped that its buildings in Peiping will be intact, but complete re-equipment may be inevitable. But, a much more important question must first be considered, that is, whether Peiping will continue to be the strategic centre from the standpoint of future development of medical education in China. This depends, of course, on the outcome of the war and subsequent political development in China. Where the future site of the political capital will be is still uncertain. It will largely depend on the nature of the final settlement of Manchuria between China and Japan. If it is unconditionally returned to China, the capital will certainly be in Peiping. If otherwise, the decision will probably be in favor of Sian in the North West. In the former case, Peiping may still be considered a strategic site for the future P.U.M.C. in spite of the distractions of a political centre. In the latter case, the wisdom of re-establishing the P.U.M.C. in Peiping, needs some consideration. With the national capital in Sian, Peiping will no longer be China's educational centre of gravity and it might again develop into a focus of international bickering. Taking a long view of the situation, Hankow or its vicinity might be worth considering. In any case, the ultimate decision should be made only after a careful survey of the post-war political situation.

As to the future educational policy of the P.U.M.C., it should be consonant with the aim of the Rockefeller Foundation explicitly stated in the Second Annual Report of the China Medical Board, referred to above. Instead of setting a standard of training without reference to what prevails in the other medical schools, its main effort should be to improve the quality of other schools by direct relationship. The P.U.M.C. did of course in the past, assist in the development of other medical schools by giving appointments or making small grants to individuals to work at the college either in a junior capacity or for short periods of time. But, with an under-graduate school of its own its primary attention must be on its own graduates. The tendency has been to confine its facilities to a small group of students and to maintain a high average standard among them. But mere attention to average standard of technical training does not necessarily favor the discovery of native leaders. Dr. Houghton, after surveying the educational systems in Europe, said that while the American system makes Fords, the British system tends to produce Rolls-Royces. What he meant was that the British system is more selective and pays less attention to the average standard than the American system. Time will probably be ripe after the war for the P.U.M.C. to widen its field of selection and to relieve itself of the responsibility of conducting an under-graduate school of its own. Its emphasis should be placed on post-graduate training and scientific research. Selection of candidates among graduates of other schools should be by competitive examination including practical and oral texts. Successful candidates are to be admitted as interns in the clinical, and externs in the pre-clinical, departments for at least two or three years training. It may be difficult at first to get students with sufficiently sound basic training, but in a short time the other medical schools will surely catch up, the same as in pre-clinical sciences, the colleges had caught up with the required basic science training and made it unnecessary for the P.U.M.C. to continue its pre-medical school. It does seem that time has now arrived for another forward step to be taken. In this post-graduate school, particular attention should be paid to the discovery of native talents and special opportunities provided for them. Formal short term courses may also, of course, be given in special fields to applicants from other medical schools. Fellowships abroad should be rather liberal so as to attract the best talent into the fields of medical education and public health. The whole plan should be to permeate medical education in China as effectively as possible, with modern medical ideology and methods of training. Incidentally, academic freedom is much more easily secured from the government for post-graduate school.

The second post-war problem the C.M.B. will have to face is the continuance of its war time policy of direct assistance to medical schools other than the P.U.M.C. and the wherewithal to do it. After six and a half years of experience, the writer feels that the pre-war budget of the P.U.M.C. was unnecessarily large. It was about three million dollars Chinese currency per annum (C.M.B. $1,500,000.00 + Hospital receipts $400,000.00 + Rockefeller Foundation special subsidy $1,000,000.00). For comparison, we might take the National Kweiyang Medical College. The latter with its small 75 beds hospital has at the moment of writing an estimated annual expenditure of about NC.$12,000.00. If we convert it to its pre-war value assuming an average increase in costs of 600* times, the budget dwindles to NC.$20,000.00 pre-war currency per annum. This means the Kweiyang Medical College spends 150 times less than the P.U.M.C. Assuming our standard is a hundred times below that of the P.U.M.C., we believe in normal times an annual budget of NC.$2,000,000.00 should be ample to run a first class post-graduate medical college in China. If the Rockefeller Foundation continues its annual grants, they can be used as grants in aid to other Medical schools.

*This figure represents the average rise in costs of all items, i.e. daily necessities as well as scientific supplies.

（译文）

备忘录：中华医学基金会和北平协和医学院

本文是作者对福克纳医生（按：时任中华医学基金会驻华主任）1944 年 3 月离华前所提出的一些问题的答复。在文中，作者冒昧地从以下几方面表述了他对中华医学基金会和协和医学院的一些看法：

（一）以毕业生的业绩来评估协和医学院的贡献

（二）对协和医学院教育方针的批评

（三）关于中华医学基金会

（四）对今后的建议

以毕业生的业绩来评估协和医学院的贡献

评估一个教育机构的真正贡献，最好的方法是考量其毕业生的业绩。而要评估协和医学院毕业生对中国医学教育、卫生事业和医疗专业水准所作出的贡献，我们就要先对中国人的性格有一定的了解。

数千年来，家庭是中国社会的基本单位。家族的延续和传承在个人性格的形成中起着决定性的作用，至少，它限制了个人的知识面和抱负。另一个影响个性的重要因素是中国人对教育的传统态度。由于中国的当权者历来由科举考试产生，接受传统教育就成为读书人扬名显亲的唯一仕途，因此形成了把教育作为手段而不是目标的态度。不幸的是，古来读书人重文轻理，思维活动脱离现实世界。鉴于此，有一般教育背景的中国人与受同等教育的西方人相比，心智显得不够成熟。他缺少的并不是智慧或勤勉，而是不善于从过去的经验中获取智慧，容易感情用事；他也缺少社会责任感，除了为自己的家族牟取利益之外，以自我为中心的倾向十分明显；在性情上，他依赖于直觉而少用推理；在生活资源上，他小心谨慎，不喜欢冒险和浪费，对生活的安稳比对探求终极真理更感兴趣。他不曾为思想的自由奋斗过，也没有遵守过工业社会中分工合作的集体规则。错综复杂的“面子”，又为他的社会关系设置了各种障碍，使他无法冷静对待任何有伤自尊的事情。正因如此，他不会真心实意地崇拜任何英雄。而这也是本土领袖难以发挥作用的原因。

在致力于工业化和社会重建的进程中，中国目前需要的，不仅仅是各个技术领域的精英，也需要公众事业和社会服务方面的领袖。因此，发现和培养这种领导人才，应该成为每个高等教育机构的主要目的。

协和医学院改组以后，第一届医学生和护士生于 1924 年毕业。从 1924 到 1942 年间，一共有 295 位医生和 171 位护士从协和医学院毕业。我们还应该从这两个数字中减去 1938 年以后毕业的人数（因为他们还没有足够的时间去表现他们的能力和领导才干），以剩下的毕业生（212 位医生和 114 位护士）的业绩，来衡量协和医学院对发展中国现代医学的贡献。作者曾在协和工作了十四年，此后继续在医学教育界服务，有幸和这些毕业生中的百分之七十相识，对他们的成就有所了解。但因为没有详查每个人的情况，我只能对这些毕业生作一个整体的评价。现将我的印象分述于下：

协和对于医学教育事业的贡献，是通过到其他医学院校工作的协和毕业生和教职员们显现出来的。他们卓有成效地把现代教学方法使用到医学本科的教学中，大大地提高了这些学校的教学质量。如条件许可，他们中的很多人也在各自的研究领域作出了出色的成绩。的确，近年来中国医学教育中所取得的进展，归功于他们的努力。

在公共卫生领域，很多协和毕业生都在重要的岗位上工作。无疑，他们在技术方面提高了公共卫生的水平。但除了几个极为突出的例子外，协和毕业生对中国的公共卫生运动还没有起到有力的推动作用。社会的落后自然是一个很重要因素，但另一个原因是，在公共卫生领域官居要职的协和人似乎缺少政治家的智慧。在红十字会和抗战中，他们之中很多人在卓越的领导下恪遵职守，这种对事业的忠诚和自我牺牲的精神确实令人敬佩，但这样的人毕竟太少了。

有些协和毕业生选择了私人开业，他们对医疗职业的道德标准作出的贡献，似乎微乎其微。

综上所述，我们不难得出结论：协和的毕业生中有很多技术精英，但他们对社会和思想领域的贡献还没有达到预期的程度。

对协和医学院教育政策的批评

为了对上述结论提供一些诠释，我们有必要审查一下协和采用的教学方针。

首先，我们应该了解一下中国大学教育的状况。在中国近代教育的发展进程中，美国的影响尤为重要。中国的大学可分为几类：第一类是私立教会大学，如上海的圣约翰大学、成都的华西大学、济南的齐鲁大学等等。这些学校的毕业生中，有很多社会活动家和知识精英。作为一个整体，他们在社会和文化背景方面的不足，不利于他们成为社会建设中的领袖。另一类是国立和私立大学，其大多数教员是从欧美回来的留学生。这些学校毕业生对教育界及政界有相当大的影响，但作为一个整体，他们缺乏现代的观念及思维方式。除了这两类，还有另一类大学，其代表是在司徒雷登校长卓越领导下的北平燕京大学。这所大学融合了上述两类大学的优点，应为将来投资教育的外国人所效仿。

虽然与教会没有关联，协和医学院在很多方面，很像一所没有融入中国社会和知识界的教会学校。它给人的印象似乎是，一所移植到中国来的美国一流医学院，而不是中国医学教育规划的一部分。其原因为：许多协和的学生来自教会大学，即使那些来自燕京大学医预科的学生，也没有像其他燕京大学的学生那样，有广博的人文基础知识。协和的宗教和社会系比较薄弱，对学生的影响力有限。另外，协和使用英文教学，也是造成其孤立的一个重要原因。诚然，一个中国医学生必须精通至少一种西方语言，而英文可能是最有用的，但这不能以失去母语作为代价。很多协和毕业生不能自如地使用中文，这可能是近代医学在中国生根如此缓慢的一个原因。其结果是，这些学生在一个象牙塔中，渡过了他们最宝贵的年华，接受高度专业的训练，但他们却失去了接触周围社会的机会。

关于中华医学基金会

自协和成立以来，中华医学基金会一直将投资基金的全部收益用来支持协和。作者没有确切的数据，若他没有记错的话，这笔钱每年约为 150 万元中国货币，按 2.5 汇兑折算则为美金 60 万元。洛氏基金会的医学科学部每年为协和提供特别补助金，如在 1937-38 财政年度中，这笔补助金为 42 万美元。

自日本占领协和以来，中华医学基金会将其资金用于维持和巩固在自由中国的各医学院校，并给予某些国立医学院物质援助。这就意味着，基金会将原来给一个医学院的资金，分配到全中国的医学教育事业，从而扩大了它的影响。而且，基金会还与华西联合大学附属医院合作，在成都恢复了协和护校，支持了中国的医护事业。

对今后的建议

中华医学基金会在 1916 年成立时，洛氏基金会为其制定的目标是，在中国渐进有序地发展一个综合而有效的医疗系统（见 1917 年中华医学基金会第二年度报告）。当时，所有中国比较好的医学院都是由外国教会支持的。之后，协和医学院促进了中国医学教育规划的发展。现在的几所国立医学院校，都在这一规划之中，如国立中央大学医学院、国立上海医学院、最近收归国有的湘雅医学院（前湖南雅礼）、以及新近成立的国立贵阳医学院。在战争时期，这些医学院都得到了中华医学基金会的资助。和平以后，有两个问题基金会应该考虑：一是协和的复校，二是继续其战时的政策，直接援助所有医学教育机构。

因为协和复校事关重大，应首先讨论。但愿协和在北平的校舍完整无损，不过完全重新装备在所难免。复校首先要选择校址，这将取决于北平是否继续是战略的中心，和由此带来的对中国医学教育的影响。北平的前景将受制于战争的结果，和由此而发生的政局演变。将来中国的政治首都在何处，主要取决于中日之间如何解决满洲问题。如果日本无条件地把满洲交还中国，首都肯定会在北平；否则，首都可能会在位于西北地区的西安。如为前者，尽管政治中心将会很混乱，北平仍可为协和复校的校址。如为后者，协和是否要在北平复校就值得考虑了。如果首都设在西安，北平将不再是中国教育的重心，而可能变成国际争端的焦点。从长计议，汉口或其邻近地方也许值得考虑。不管怎样，协和在何处复校，需在谨慎研究战后的政治局势之后，才能作出最后的决定。

至于协和未来的教育政策，应该恪守上述洛氏基金会在中华医学基金会第二个年度报告中所明确的宗旨。协和应为提高其他医学校的教学质量，提供直接的帮助；切不可订出一套自己的教学标准，不考虑其他医学院校的具体情况。过去，协和为了帮助其他医学院的发展，也曾聘任有关人员，给予少量奖学金，让他们来协和做助教或短期工作。不过，协和有医学本科，培养自己的毕业生是首要的。比如，协和的设备历来优先让自己不多的学生使用，从而保持高标准教学。但仅提高平均技术水平，不一定有助于发现中国的领导人才。

胡恒德博士在考察欧洲的教育制度后曾说，美国生产福特（Fords，按：一般汽车，产量大），英国生产劳斯莱斯（Rolls-Royce，按：质量高的汽车，产量小）。他的意思是，与美国的制度相比，英国的制度不追求平庸的产品，更具有选择性。战后，协和扩大其选择范围，放弃自办医本科的时机将会成熟，而后应把重点放在研究生的培养和科学研究工作上。研究生可从其他院校的毕业生中，通过实际操作和口试等方法择优录取。录取的学生可进入临床各科作实习医师，或入前期各科作进修生，学习过程至少需要两至三年。开始时，也许没有足够学生具备扎实的基础知识，但其它医学院校的水平必将在短期内相应提高。而过去协和停办医预科，也是因为其他大学基础科学水平提高了。在研究生院中，应特别关注有才干的本土学生，着重培养。我们还可以为来自其他医学校的进修生，设立特别短期课程。为了把最优秀的人才吸引到医学教育和公共卫生事业中来，应该提供到外国学习的充足的奖学金。全盘计划应当是，把近代医学理念和教学方法贯穿到中国医学教育之中。而且，中国政府更可能给予研究生院多一些学术自由的空间。现在，协和向前迈进一步的时机似乎已经来临。

中华医学基金会在战后面对的第二个问题是，是否继续资助除协和以外的医学校及资金的来源。根据作者六年半的经验，战前协和的花费每年约为三百万法币（基金会一百五十万，医院收入四十万，洛氏基金会特别津贴一百万），这是一个不必要的庞大数字。相比之下，国立贵阳医学院拥有一个75张病床的小型医院，在写此报告时估计每年支出约一千二百万法币。如果折合为战前的价值，假定物价上涨六百倍（此数字代表所有项目的平均涨价，包括日用必需品和科学器材），就相当战前每年法币二万元。这说明贵阳医学院的费用只是协和的一百五十分之一。假使我们的标准比协和低一百倍，我们相信，在正常时期，每年二百万法币足够在中国维持一所一流医学院。如果洛氏基金会每年继续提供资助，其剩余部分就可用以赞助其它医学校了。

致中华医学基金会驻华主任福克纳医生信[1]

1945年2月3日

National Kweiyang Medical College
Chungking
Feb. 3, 1945

Dr Claude E. Forkner,
Director,
China Medical Board, Inc.,
c/o West China Union University
Chengtu

Dear Claude:

Thank you ever so much for your letter in care of Dr. Loucks which I deeply appreciate. I am very much disappointed, however, that we cannot meet in Chungking and talk things over. I have so many problems on hand that I wish to have your advice on. I received none of your letters which you referred to. The postal service is certainly undependable these days. I am returning to Kweiyang in a few days' time but will be back in Chungking in early March when I do hope to see you before you leave for the States. I shall appreciate if you will let me know your movements during the next two months.

The recent crisis in Kweiyang played havoc with our school. Acting on the order of the military authorities, our school evacuated on December 7th, 370 strong, of whom 160 tracked north on foot. With the retreat of the enemy order was gradually restored in Kweiyang but the presence of large numbers of troops and refugees made the immediate return of the college impossible. The cost of living has soared to a level three times that of Chungking and there is the possibility of acute food shortage in the affected area in the coming spring. The college premises and staff residences have all been occupied and some destroyed by troops and need extensive repairs before they can be used again. The teaching hospital is now being used for sick refugees.

Under these circumstances the decision is therefore forced upon us to seek refuge in Chungking. With the generous cooperation of Dr. H. P. Chu of the Shanghai Medical College the preclinical classes as well as those for the nursing and midwifery students have already been resumed at Koloshan on Jan. 22nd. As to the senior classes it is planned to send them back to Kweiyang at the earliest possible date. On my return to Kweiyang in about ten days I shall try to resuscitate, in part at least, our teaching hospital and to cooperate with the Kweiyang Central Hospital, which is now very short of staff following the withdrawal of the Hsianya personnel, so that some of our clinical teaching could be taken care of there. I have persuaded all of our clinical staff to return to Kweiyang, some at the end of February and others at the end of March, with the exception of a few junior members who I think will be much benefitted by remaining

[1] Letter Lee to Forkner, Feb. 3, 1945, RAC, CMB, Inc. Box 96, folder 685.

a period at Koloshan with Drs Loucks and Gordon King. The whole school will return to Kweiyang at the end of August when arrangements could be completed for their reception.

Apart from expenses of evacuation the loss sustained by the school consists of damages to the buildings and furnitures and some hospital equipments. These must needs be repaired and replaced at some cost.

The China Medical Committee of the AMPAC at its meeting on Jan. 27th agreed to an emergency grant of NC$2,660,000 for additional buildings and furnishings at Koloshan which will tide us over the period of exile. I stipulated that this should be regarded as an emergency grant and that the grant of NS$2,400 for residences and that of NC$200,000 for the farm project both in Kweiyang already passed by the ABMAC but being held over on account of the military crisis should be on call in June when we shall need them to enable us to return to Kweiyang.

Disastrous as the episode has been it is not without some compensations. The present cooperation with the Shanghai Medical College will be a great stimulus to our teachers and students and will, I feel, surely lead to future plans of collaboration in frequent exchange of teaching personnel between the two schools. A school in the interior such as ours will certainly need such connections with a more favorably situated school as the Shanghai Medical.

So far I have not yet replied to your questions but the above statement of what had happened and of our plans for the future will make my answers more intelligible.

(1) When the crisis was on in Kweiyang we sent away all our laboratory and hospital equipment by pack horses to an out of the way village some thirty miles from Kweiyang. After the crisis we had them brought back again by the same means. Now they are safely in Kweiyang. Since the preclinical section of our school is to be temporarily located in Chungking we shall transfer such equipment as microscopes and microtones to Chungking for use but it does not seem wise or necessary to ship any fragile equipment or chemicals up here. The Shanghai Medical will share their supplies with us. We shall, of course pay for extras used. The Shanghai Medical is short of cadavers of which we shall prepare a few to send up as they seem to be easier to procure in Kweiyang. Our department of physiology and pharmacology has only four sets of kymograph and these were borrowed from the Army Medical College. We very much wish to obtain at least five new sets with all accessories from Chengtu. In Chungking we also would like to purchase some locally made apparatus for our Physics department to improve its practical teaching.

So if the CMB could make a special grant to take care of the items listed below it would release just so much from our ABMAC receipts to allow some readjustment in living subsidies for staff members now returning to Kweiyang where prices have risen to a very high level.

Five sets of kymograph with accessories	NC$500,000
Apparatus for Physics department	NC$200,000
Glass wares and chemicals needed in Chungking	NC$200,000

The figure for kymograph is an estimate. The exact sum required could be ascertained from Prof. Chai of the National Central.

(2) The recent happenings have wrought great hardship to some of our staff members especially those senior members with families. Children's education has become quite a problem with many of us. The UCR, as you know, appropriated a sum

for subsidising key personnel under the administration of the China Foundation. I understand three of our senior members have already been approved including myself. Each will receive monthly NC$10,000. This will be of some help but will not touch the problem of children's education. I would like to recommend a special subsidy for some of our staff's children going through middle schools or colleges according to their individual needs. I, myself, am in debt to the extent of $100,000 for my children's education. A personal problem of my own has to do with the payment of my insurance premium which comes to G$234.90 annually. It is a policy I took out while I was in Peiping with the Manufacturers Life Insurance Company. Up to last January I was able to meet the annual premium from a gold deposit with the company representing my only savings during my years of service with the PUMC which is now exhausted.

(3) As to fellowships abroad I have several names I could confidently recommend. Three of them are teachers who have been with us several years and I feel well deserve such opportunity. Their records are enclosed herewith. Besides there are two younger men, our own graduates, who while showing promise have not yet had sufficient investigative opportunities but should be next in line. Records of their experiences are also here appended.

With kindest personal regards,

Yours sincerely,

C. U. Lee

（译文）

国立贵阳医学院（重庆）

1945 年 2 月 3 日

成都西部联合大学转

中华医学基金会驻华主任克劳德• 伊•福克纳医生

亲爱的克劳德，

非常感谢您请娄克斯医生带来的信。不过，我为失去了在重庆谈话的机会深感失望。我现在有好多棘手的问题，都想听听您的意见，可是这次却无法在重庆跟您碰面，这真是太遗憾了。您说给我寄过信，可是我一封都没有收到。现在的邮递系统实在太不可靠了。我过几天就要返回贵阳，然后三月初再回重庆，希望那时能赶在您回美前跟您见一面。如果您能告诉我您下两个月的行踪，那就再好不过了。

近来贵阳的战争给我们学校造成了极大的破坏。按照军方的命令，我们全校 370 人于 12 月 7 日撤离贵阳，其中 160 人徒步北上。敌军撤退后，贵阳逐渐恢复秩序，但路上兵慌马乱，所以我们没有办法立即返校。现在贵阳物价暴涨，生活费用是重庆的三倍，而且开春后极有可能面临食物短缺的危机。学校的教室和职工宿舍被军队占去后遭受了很大的破坏，如果不彻底维修，完全无法使用。教学医院现在也被用作难民医院了。

面对这种情况，我们不得不在重庆寻求避难。在上海医学院的朱恒璧医生的大力帮助下，临床前期医学生以及护士和助产士学生已于1月22日在歌乐山安顿下来；高年级学生，我们则计划让他们尽早返回贵阳。我大约10天后返回贵阳，届时我将尽力先恢复附属医院；在湘雅撤退后贵阳中央医院的员工短缺，我会争取跟他们合作，这样的话，我们的一些临床教学就可以在那里进行了。我已经劝服所有的临床教师，让他们分别在2月底和3月底返回贵阳，只有少数年资低的教员，基于对他们更好的考虑，会让他们和娄克斯医生及金医生（Gordon King）暂留在歌乐山。到8月底时，贵阳那边的事情应该会安排妥当，届时滞留的学生将全部返校。

这次大撤退，学校遭受了很大的损失，除了转移的开销外，学校还必须花钱修建被严重损坏的建筑、家具和医院器材等。

美国医药援华会（ABMAC）的中国医学委员会1月27日召开了会议，同意紧急拨款NC$266万用于我们疏散到歌乐山后的安置费用，这将帮助我们度过这段流亡的时间，我们将把这笔钱作为紧急补助金。之前，医药援华会已经批准了我们申请的用于宿舍的NC$240万和用于农业项目的NC$20万资金，但因为最近的战争危机，这笔款项暂缓发放。他们将在6月份考虑放款，届时这笔款项可以资助我们返回贵阳的费用。

虽然形势一直很糟糕，我们还是有一些收获的。目前与上海医学院的合作对我们的学生和老师都有很大的激励，我确信以后我们还会有频繁的交流与合作。像我们这样在内陆的学校，确实需要与像上海医学院这样在发达地区的学校保持联系。

写到这儿，我还没有回答您在信上提出的几个问题，不过上面对现况的介绍和对未来的计划应该会帮助您更好地理解我下面的回答。

1. 贵阳爆发战争的时候，我们已经把实验室和医院的所有器材打包，用马车运到离贵阳约30英里的一个村庄。战争结束后，我们已经用同样的方法把它们运回来了。我们将把显微镜、切片机等运到重庆供临床前期教学使用，但把易损坏的仪器和化学品留在贵阳，同时付费给上海医学院，以共用他们的设备。现在这些设备在贵阳是完全安全的。上海医学院现在缺乏解剖用的尸体，我们会准备一些运给他们，因为在贵阳获取尸体标本似乎要容易些。我们的生理和药理学系有四套从陆军医学院借来的记纹鼓。我们希望能从成都弄到至少5 套配件齐全的新的记纹鼓。另外，我们还希望能在重庆为物理系购买一些本地制造的设备，提高学生的实习教学。

如果中华医学基金会能提供下列资助的话，那么我们从医药援华会申请到的款项就可以补贴一下重返贵阳的员工们，因为现在贵阳的物价涨得太高了。

5 套完备的记纹鼓：NC$ 50 万

物理系仪器：NC$ 20 万

重庆所需的玻璃器皿和化学品：NC$ 20 万

记纹鼓所需的经费目前只是一个预估值，具体的数目可以从国立中央大学蔡教授那儿得到。

2. 最近发生的事情给我们的员工尤其是那些年长的有家属的员工，带来了巨大的困难。我们中很多人都被孩子上学的事情困扰。你也知道，经中国文化教育基金会(China Foundation)授权，联合救援会（UCR，United China Relief）拨了一笔款资助核心人才。包括我在内，我们学校有三名高级员工都在被资助名单内。我们每人可以得到 NC$1 万的资助，但这笔钱对于解决我们孩子的教育问题来说，只是杯水车薪。我建议，对有孩子要上中学或大学的家庭，提供有针对性的特别资助。我自己为了孩子的教育问题，已经借债 NC$10 万了。我个人面临的另一个问题是，必须缴纳我的年保险费 G$234.90，这是我在北平的时候在人寿保险公司买的保险。截止到去年 1 月，我一直靠过去在协和工作时的积蓄支付这笔费用，但目前这笔钱已空无分文。

3. 关于出国深造的事情，我确实有几个人想推荐给你，我对他们很有信心。其中三人是在我们学校任教多年的老师，我觉得他们应该得到这样的机会。我把他们的履历附在信内。另外还有两位从我们学校毕业的年轻的男士，他们很有培养前途，但还没有机会做深入的研究，下次应该轮到他们。我把他们的履历也一并给您寄去。

致以个人最诚挚的问候！

真诚的，

李宗恩

致中华医学基金会驻华主任福克纳医生信[1]

1945 年 3 月 8 日

National Kweiyang Medical College

Kweiyang,
Kweichow, China

March 8, 1945

Dr Claude E. Forkner,
China Medical Board, Inc.
c/o American Embassy
Chungking

Dear Claude:

Your letter of Feb. 3 enclosing one from Miss Pearce, crossed with mine of the same date. I left Chungking on the morning of the 8th and your letter was relayed to me from Koloshan. Your remittance of CN$507,500 was received in Chungking but I don't know whether my representative Dr. Chia has issued an official receipt and if not please let me know and I will do so at this end.

The grant for department of chemistry will be used for teaching expenses at Koloshan while those for the departments of medicine and public health will be spent in Kweiyang as both of these departments are now reestablished here. T. S. continues to be in charge of our department of public health though much of his time will be occupied with his official duties of Commissioner of Health. He wishes to devote the CMB subsidy largely to improvement of the teaching facilities at the city and Huachi Health Stations.

The material loss sustained by the College during and after the crisis is staggering particularly on the campus outside the city. Only the outer shells of the buildings are left standing. One of the buildings lost all its windows. All the laboratory furniture have disappeared. Apparently, a period of anarchy prevailed after the crisis. Realizing that we are not in a position to restore the buildings to their original state I decided to concede to the U.S. Army request for the use of them as a go-down for medical supplies. The U.S. Army will undertake to repair them and put in electricity and water supply. Should our preclinical departments return in the fall they will pay us a sum of money sufficient for us to rent some temporary premises elsewhere. It is the best possible arrangement that I could make under the circumstances for the preservation of the existing buildings. Our hospital premises inside the city have been used as a refugee hospital but the administrative quarters have been much damaged by soldiers. Much repairing needs to be carried out. I am exerting every effort to take over the refugee hospital and run it as a teaching hospital after March 15th when some of our clinical staff will be back in Kweiyang.

---

[1] Letter Lee to Forkner, RAC, CMB, Inc. Box 96, folder 685.

Your letter of Feb. 22 came a few days ago for which very many thanks.

I am sorry I was late in sending in applications for fellowships abroad for some of our staff members. I hope they can be given a chance after July 1st of this year. The data you needed from them will be in your hand before you leave China. My order of choice would be first Mr Tso-kan Chang, second Mr Ta-hsiung Chin and third Mr Chih-chun Wang. Drs Ken-tien Li and Chen-hua Liu can wait for their turn next time. College regulations compels me to state in my letter guaranteeing each candidate a post on his return that it will be difficult to carry a person's full salary for longer than six months during his absence from the College.

In reference to assistance to key personnel I would like to tell you about a plan being adopted at Koloshan influenced by similar practices at the Shanghai Medical College. Any wife of any staff member with college or vocational education and capable of doing some teaching, clerical or administrative work is given a post in the college so that the combined income of the couple be sufficient to care for the family. Take as an illustrative case Dr Chia, himself, Mrs Chia having had some experience in accounting helps in the accounting office and gets a monthly income of NC$22,312.00. Thus, the total monthly receipts for the Chia family comes to NC$55,684.00 a sum sufficient to get by. But there are wives who are either not qualified for office work or prefer to take care of their family at home; in which case the family receipts must be supplemented from other sources. We must by hook or crook guarantee a married person a monthly income which would provide a minimum standard of living. Now I have a few key persons who suffer because their wives for various reasons are unable to contribute to the family earning.

Dr Y. T. Chou, our professor of surgery and a graduate of PUMC, has been with us for six years whose wife is non-earning and whose monthly family income is about 40,000 which in Kweiyang must be raised by at least NC$15,000 a month. Dr Tso-kan Chang our histologist is in the same position but living in Chungking requires less assistance. Dr Veh-the Lieu whose wife is a qualified nurse and sometimes does private nursing but during slack times needs some help. Those whose wives draw salaries from the college need for the time being no consideration. I don't like this system of husbands and wives drawing pay from the same institution but what can one do under the present state of inflation which makes one feel so impotent and helpless?

I just heard unofficially that the New York ABMAC Headquarters turned down the recommendation of its China Medical Committee to make the emergency grant of NC$2,600,000 to us which I reported in my last letter. Our finances this year will be further strained.

You mentioned the possibility of taking care of my insurance premium. I wrote to the company a few days ago requesting a loan on my policy to pay for this year's premium. I enclose hereby a copy of my letter and the company's notice of payment for premium due on Jan. 28th, 1945. If you could make a grant to cover it please pay direct to the company against my policy no. 550,998. This is the only protection I have for my family.

I hope to get to Chungking before the end of the month and to meet you before you leave for the States.

Yours,

C. U. Lee

（译文）

国立贵阳医学院

克劳德• 伊•福克纳医生

中华医学基金会

请重庆美国大使馆将信件转交

亲爱的克劳德:

您 2 月 3 日的信我已于 3 月 8 日在歌乐山收到，正巧我那时也在给您写信，而且在准备离开重庆。夹在您信中的皮尔斯小姐的信，我也一并收到了。我在重庆时还收到了您的汇款 507,500 元（国币），不知道我的代理人谢博士是否给您开具了正式收据；如果没有，请告诉我，我会来处理此事。

化学系的资助款将用于歌乐山的教学支出，内科和公共卫生系已回贵阳，所以该部分的资助款将在贵阳使用。尽管施正信花大量的时间做他的政府卫生专员的工作，但他仍继续负责我们的公共卫生系。他希望能把中华医学基金会的大部分补助用于改善花溪卫生站和贵阳的教学设施。

战乱给学校尤其是城外的校区造成了极为严重的损坏，教学楼几乎只剩下空墙；还有一栋楼连窗户都没了；所有实验设备也都不翼而飞。危机过后，无政府状态盛行。当我意识到我们无法将校舍恢复原状时，就决定接受美军的请求，让他们储存医疗物资。美军将负责维修这些建筑，并安装水电设备。秋天我们的临床前期返筑时，他们会支付租金，让我们在附近找临时房屋使用。这是我们当下保存现有校舍的最好方法了。我们市内的附属医院已用作难民医院，而且办公室被士兵们破坏得很厉害，需要彻底修缮。我正竭尽全力接管这个“难民医院”，希望在我们的医务人员 3 月 15 日后返回时，能将其恢复为教学医院。

你 2 月 22 日的信件我前几天就收到了，非常感谢。

关于迟交我院员工国外奖学金申请表的事情，我感到非常抱歉。我希望今年 7 月 1 日后，他们还能再有一次机会。我会把您需要的数据在您离开中国前交到您手上。下面是我推荐的顺序：1、张作干（Tso-kan Chang）；2、金大雄（Mr Ta-hsiung Chin）；3、王志均（Mr Chih-chun Wang）。李耕田（Ken-tien Li）和刘震华 Chen-hua Liu 医生可以等待下一次机会。根据校规，我得在信中保证给每位候选人在进修后仍保留原职位，但如离校超过 6 个月，继续全薪就很难了。

关于如何帮助核心人员的问题，我想给您讲讲我们在歌乐山采用的一个方法，这是借鉴了上海医学院的一些类似实践。任何员工的妻子，只要是有大学或专科学历并能做一些教学、文书或行政工作的，我们就让她们也来学院工作，这样夫妻的双份收入就能够照顾家庭了。例如，谢博士的夫人有财会经验，如果她能在财务室工作的话，每月就可以获得 22,312 元（国币）的收入。这样，谢家全家的月收入就变成了足够生活的 55,684 元（国币）。但有些员工的妻子不够到办公室工作的条件，或者她们自己想在家照顾家庭，这样情况的家庭，就得用其他的方式来补贴了。我们必须通过双职工的薪酬或其他曲线办法，保证已婚员工的月收入能满足他们家庭的最低生活开销。现在我们有几个资深员工，由于他们的妻子因各种理由不能赚钱，生活非常艰难。

毕业于协和医学院的周裕德医生是我院的外科教授，已跟着我们 6 年了。因为他的妻子没有收入，家庭的月收入只有 40,000 元左右，这样他们家每月至少要增加 15,000 元才能保证在贵阳的基本生活费用。组织学家张作干博士也面临同样的情况，不过他的家在重庆，需要的补助少些。刘维德医生的妻子是一位护士，她也做一些私人护理工作贴补家用。对那些妻子可以从学院领工资的员工，我们现在可以不用考虑。尽管我不喜欢这种夫妻两人在同一个单位领工资的方式，但现在通货膨胀严重，我们又能有什么办法呢?

我刚从小道消息得知，纽约美国医药援华会总部拒绝了他们中国医学委员会的给我院 260 万（我在上封信中提到的）紧急捐款的建议。我们今年的财务状况恐怕将会更加紧张了。

您信中提到帮我助支付保险费的事情，我几日前寄给保险公司一封信，请求用贷款的方式来支付今年的保险费。我把这封信以及保险公司的 1945 年 1 月 28 日保险费到期的通知单一并寄给您，如果您能赞助这笔钱的话，请直接交款给保险公司，我的保险账号是 550998。这是我给我家人的唯一保障了。

希望我能月底前赶到重庆，在您回美国前跟您见一面。

此致，

李宗恩

1945 年 3 月 8 日

国立贵阳医学院为谋发展所拟各项建议之呈文[1]

1946 年 3 月 11 日

谨呈者：本学院创办迄今已逾八载，前者因抗战关系，西南人才荟萃，故虽物质条件极感困难，而员生来源不虞匮乏，是以院务推进尚称顺利。今战事胜利结束，形势大为改变，其可能发生之情况太多，而其中影响最大者莫如员生之移动。以教员而论，本学院教员十之八九为外省籍，彼辈离乡别井，多年在外，一旦有机会返乡一省，亦为人情之常。且收复区范围广大，需才孔殷，将来交通畅达，人才流动性增大，亦为意料中事。其次，本学院所有学生籍本隶本省者为数寥寥，以现有学生而论，黔籍者仅有七人，此外各生皆属外省籍贯，彼辈前此就学此间，或系不堪敌伪压迫逃难来此，或系父兄徒居后方随同迁来。今者形势不同，义民纷纷返乡，择其距离较近之学校入学，亦在情理之中。故无论就教员抑就学生之来源而言，今后困难必然日益增加，苟欲使本院继续维持于不坠，对于上述二项困难，不可不预谋解决之道。窃以为在教员方面，首宜给予种种进修机会，鼓励其上进。盖不少教师，前者以战事关系，有志进修而不可得，多年服务于此，虽恪尽职守、力求进步，无如交通梗阻，文化交流缓慢，其固有之学识自不能与外界之新知识并驾齐驱，而有彼此脱节及落伍之感，今正宜乘此机会，给予国外国内进修机会，使彼辈能利用今后一二年之时间，充实其学问，扩大其经验，使成为督学上更有效之师资，此不仅有利于本学院之前途，则对于整个督学教育言，亦良有裨益也。但此举不但不能解决目前之师荒问题，亦且足以促使本问题益趋严重．是则不能不另谋补救方法。盖欧美各国复员以后，人才济济，一部分行将告老之教员，欲利用退休前一段时间，赴国外作种种实际工作者大有人在。苟国家能订出具体办法，延聘此辈人才前来讲学，绝非不可能之事。如果成功，不但师荒问题可以获得一部分解决，亦且对于教育水准可以相当提高。其次，则为如何谋教员生活之安定，以便罗致人才。假设生活安定，应包含食宿问题之合理解决，返乡旅费之津贴及教学设备之充实。故希望政府方面能迅予拨出巨宗款项，迅予建筑合理

[1] 贵州省档案馆，530-1 卷。

之教职员宿舍及住宅，并希将返乡旅费津贴办法作具体之决定。对于教学设备之充实，尤希尽可能速予进行。苟生活安定、工作环境适宜，则人才之罗致有所依据，进行自比容易。至于学生方面，本学院固可将标准略予降低，吸收较多学生，但标准之降低仍有一定限度，否则无法施教。故拟请钧部今后对于边疆各校之学生，其开班人数不予名额上之限制，即少至五六名亦须准予开班，相信此种情形系过渡期间必有之现象，苟学校基础稳固，学生人数必随之加多也。此外，边疆学校学生待遇亦希望能全部公费，一方面可予学生术学、物质上之鼓励，一方面亦可表示政府对于边疆教育之重视也。窃以西南为抗战时期之重要基础，相信在建国时期亦有其价值，而本学院之维持，亦为事实上所必需，同时钧部亦有维持之决心，则如何衡量客观情势作为今后之努力之准绳，实为目前刻不容缓之要图，用贡一得之愚，聊作决策之参考。如何之处，敬候钧裁。

国立贵阳医学院院长　李宗恩

民国三十五年三月十一日

教育部指令

令贵阳医学院：

卅五年三月十一日阳字 4825 号呈一件。为谋本院今后发展建议各点，祈鉴核由。呈悉。分别核示如次：

一、 聘请外籍教授，现正拟订办法，俟呈奉核定饬遵。

二、 后方各省国立专科以上学校教员服务奖励办法业经订定并呈院核示，俟奉准后饬知。

三、 教授休假、进修，本部已订有办法，应遵照该项办法办理。

四、 每班学生人数，应视将来实际情形再行决定。

五、 学生待遇，本部已予注意并正核议中。

以上各项仰即知照。此令。

部长　朱家骅

民国三十五年四月八日

本学院现状及今后计划[1]

1946 年 9 月 15 日

本学院自民国廿七年开办，迄今九载，其间适值抗战，艰难困苦缔造之情形，谅为社会人士所能想像，兹不赘述。自去岁抗战胜利，本学院奉部令于九月全部自渝迁返贵阳，实为学校复员之第一个，惟当时原有在太慈桥永久院舍为盟军供应站征用，本学院向贵阳市政府暂借前市立商业学校校址为前期学生上课及住宿之用，并租若干民房以为教职员宿舍。至十一月盟军供应站撤退，其所留存之医药设备全部移交国际善后救济总署，再由国际善后总署移交行政院善后救济总署，从事分配予临近数省医药卫生机关。而同时本学院前期学生全体迁入，分配工作赓续进行，院舍亦相继腾出，各科实验室随之设备。至三月份善后救济总署分配工作完毕，本学院新建之办公室亦告落成，爰将总办公室自城内迁入办公，各科实验室更加扩充，自是本学院之大本营奠定于永久院舍。仅附属医院为诊务便利，仍暂设于黔明路原址。设备方面：本学院蒙行政院善后救济总署捐赠一百六十张病床设备，医院设备，焕然一新；前期各科，亦承美国医药助华会捐赠药械二十余箱，较前更为充实，足敷学生实习及教员研究之用。人员方面：本学院旧有人员除少数出国进修外，余均未异动，现并尽量延揽各项专门人才，阵容当益整齐。本学院复员工作即告完成，今后计划，拟于永久院舍内修建疗养院一座，收容需长期修养之病人。因自中央医院迁移后，本院附属医院门诊及住院病人倍增，原有床位不敷分配。又本院教职员家眷大部尚住于租赁之二三宿舍内，今后拟修建教职员住宅若干幢，以期生活更为安定。至学生人数亦年有增加，去年增设药学专修科一班，本年度复奉令增收先修班学生一班，原有宿舍不敷应用，拟再建男女生宿舍各一幢。其余本学院永久院舍之建筑计划亦当次第完成。内容方面更力求充实，当本百年树人之旨，以建立西南医学教育之楷模。

1 《国立贵阳医学院院刊》复刊第一期，1946 年 9 月 15 日。

向贵医师生报告医学教育考察之行[1]

1947年4月15日

这次离开贵阳四个月，在旅行中的时间感觉，因为今天到这里，过几天又到那里，各处接洽的事情繁多，似乎日子过得很快；有时遇到等车候船，又牵挂学校和家庭，便觉得日子过太迟慢。这次走了许多地方，回来后觉得大家的生活仍尚安定，甚为安慰。院务也能与日俱进，表示慰问和感谢！

此行第一个使命，向教育部报告本学院复员后情形，第二个使命，顺便转赴沿海一带考察复员后的医教卫生，各方师资分配情形，及各地校友之工作表现，并参加武大浙大医学院筹备工作。自去年十一月十二日乘邮车赴渝转飞汉口，参加武汉大学医学院筹备，本人战前曾参与武昌医学院筹备工作，旋因战事，部令移拨该项筹备费创办贵阳医学院，故贵医与武大医学院颇有历史渊源。近来中央认为武汉地理关系的重要，仍须成立一个完善的医教机构，我们的计划，应做较长的准备，今秋开始招生，由理学院作基础学科训练，而在两年内训练成自己的师资，附属医院先行筹设，用武大城内原有校舍，由行总拨发设备，教育部确定修建费，现由杨济时大夫负责主持，也有校友在那里协助，很快的开展工作，已有很满意的成就。本人留汉一周余，于十一月二十七日飞往上海。

在沪所得的一般印象，第一是“大”，宽广的马路与天相接，其他叉路纵横，稍不经意，很易迷途。第二是“平”，四周全无山峦的影子，市内除苏州河上几处大桥以外，绝无坡道，所以从战时代替汽车的三轮车，才能成为很便利的交通工具。第三是“乱”，全市人口在四百五十万以上，贫富悬殊，房荒特甚，路上各种车辆首尾相接，每一叉路口有红绿灯管制交通，从外滩到跑马厅，汽车须行二十五分钟。行人摩肩接踵，在大马路上如欲穿过对面行人道，须等候十数分钟，才能过去。到处显得紧张混乱，尤其抢劫迭闻，火警频赴，物价跳涨，失业众多，生活极不安定，一般厂商均感不易维持，彼时正遇摊贩事件，实为混乱局面的大暴露。

[1] 《国立贵阳医学院院刊》复刊第8期，1947年4月15日，第1、2页。

上海医学院正在开始恢复，原有的皇宫式房屋尚未修复旧观。且于搬回时损失三船器材，颇受影响，学生甚多，现有实习医院二处，一为红十字医院，又为邻接的中山医院，院长沈克非氏，有病床三百余，规模较为完善。宝隆医院为同济的实习医院，接收美海军的中美医院设备，最为富丽堂皇。卫生局因受政局牵制，仅能勉强支持，不宜发展。

杭州为名胜地，西子的美丽不减当年，只是湖滨的几所庄子（别墅），多已破败失修，显得褴褛毕露。全市人口四十万，仅有一个市立医院，两个教会医院，共有病床一百四十张，因沪杭距离较近，有钱病人多赴沪就医，以致医院业务颇形落后。杭州医专有悠久历史，复员后正在恢复期中。浙大迁回后，学生增三倍，原校舍不敷应用，已得行总竭力援助，当可逐渐建立新舍。医学院去冬已招新生一班，理学院的教授们颇为帮忙，设备也可借用。竺校长尚在美未回，拟与武大医学院采取同样的准备计划。附属医院因无房屋，尚未成立。

十二月二十六日由杭抵京，晋谒朱部长，报告本学院复员以后情形，承示贵医决予继续维持。南京中央医院，大致已恢复战前规模。中央大学医学院，因房屋不敷，戚院长现在竭力于初步恢复中。在京参加第二次武大医学院筹备委员会会议后，于十二月三十一日折回上海，原定一月五日飞平，因故改作海行，四天抵秦皇岛，天气奇冷，在零下二十二度。乘火车一天，于一月二十四日到北平。

离开十年的北平，觉得景象依然，引为快慰。有几处的道路较前更宽，惟入晚萧条异常。清华校舍损失颇大，梅校长正在全力设法恢复中，燕大设备亦颇受损失。北大设备图书均甚充实，北大医学院亦很像样，可称上轨。协和原址，无大损害，近为军调部借用。北平原为文化中心，至今觉得人才过剩，生活甚苦，燕大学生吃的只是窝窝头和青菜，其他也可想而知。二月十日离平赴津。

天津中央医院，近由重庆迁往，院长陈崇寿氏，现有房屋百余栋，门诊已开始，医院尚仅病床四十张，最近可接收美军医院。在津留二天，搭美机仅三时半返沪。二月二十三日乘轮赴香港。

三月七日抵广州，参观中山大学医学院，岭南大学医学院（孙逸仙博士医院，院长李廷安氏），及中央医院等。广州市挂牌医师极多，实为中外稀有的现象。十二日乘粤汉火车抵衡阳，转搭邮车于三月二十一日返筑。

本学院适与沿海相反，僻处西南，环境较为安定，惟因交通不便，师资不易延揽，设备不易补充耳。

本学院在初创时招收各陷区流亡学生，毕业后仍散布各地，均能适应环境，受人欢迎，且均有求知的进取心，以冀在学术界站得住，这是最可宝贵的现象，也引为衷心的快慰！

最近协和董事会电邀本人回平服务，当利用国际机会，为协助我国医学教育而努力，至于本学院的前途，只要能将最近两年维持过去，将来交通畅通，师资得以充实，发展不应成甚问题。

致协和董事会主席胡适先生信[1]

1947 年 4 月 3 日

Dr. Hu Shih,
Chairman, Board of Trustees,
P.U.M.C., Peiping

Dear Dr. Hu:

A week of careful consideration convinces me that in view of my past happy connection with the institution and my interest in medical education it is my duty to place my service and whatever experience I may have had in the field of medical education in China at the disposal of the P.U.M.C. Board of Trustees. This therefore confirms the telegram I dispatched on March 31, 1947.

"ACCEPT TRUSTEES APPOINTMENT KEENLY CONSCIOUS HONOUR CONFERRED AND RESPONSIBILITES INVOLVED STOP UNABLE LEAVE KWEIYANG BEFORE EARLY MAY STOP PLEASE ADVISE GREGGS DECISION AND TIME ARRIVAL CULEE"

I gratefully acknowledge the honour the Trustees conferred upon me in offering me this opportunity of service but feel very keenly of the responsibilities of the office. In accepting it I derived much courage from your encouragement and the wisdom of the Trustees in inviting the cooperation of Dr. Allan Gregg. Under your direction and guidance, I will do my best.

At this end I feel I must do what I can to ensure the continuance of this college. I have already written to Dr. Y.T. Tsur to sound out at the Ministry as to who my successor is likely to be. I hope it will be somebody who from his previous connection with this college will command the wholehearted support of the faculty here. Otherwise it will fall to pieces. It will not be in the interest of medical education in this part of China for that to happen. As soon as I hear from Dr. Tsur I'll formally submit my resignation. The handing over will also take time. Hence I fear I shall not be able to make a move before the early part of May.

Your telegram of April 1 was received yesterday. I hope Dr. Gregg will revise his decision. His presence in Peiping will be so vital to the work of the initial period. Please keep me informed of further development.

As it is not possible for me to make a move until I hear from Nanking there is no immediate need for funds. In the meantime, I shall appreciate if Miss Mary Ferguson will mail me copies of whatever records or dockets that bear on the history, administration, organisation, curriculum, etc. of the college. They will help me to get my bearing.

In the local paper a few days ago there was a vague report which seems to point to the passing away of Mr. Roger Greene. If it is true and you are sending a message of condolence to Mrs. Greene please include my name.

---

[1] PUMC Achive.

With kindest regards,

Yours very sincerely,

C.U. Lee

（译文）

北平协和医院董事会主席胡适博士收

尊敬的胡博士：

经过一周的深思熟虑，鉴于过去我在协和的愉快经历以及我对中国医学教育的强烈兴趣，我认为有责任接受协和医学院董事会的任命，将我在中国医学教育领域的一些经验贡献给协和医学院。我1947年3月31日曾发出受命电报，此为确认函。

“接受董事会任命，深感其荣誉和责任。但 5 月初之前不能离开贵阳。请告知格雷格医生的决定和到达的时间。”

董事会授予我这样（为协和医学院）服务的机会，是我莫大的荣幸，同时也感到责任的重大。您的鼓励给了我很大的勇气，能邀请格雷格博士来协作也是董事会的明智之举。在您的指引下，我会全力以赴。

在离开（贵阳）之前，我必须竭尽全力确保这所大学（贵阳医学院）能够继续下去。我已经写信给周诒春博士，咨询谁可以来接替我的位置。我希望这个人此前就与贵医有关联，并能全力支持这里的老师。否则的话，这个学校很可能会毁于一旦，这将给中国的医学教育造成极大的损失。一旦收到周博士的回复，我会立即正式提交我的辞呈。不过交接工作也需要一些时间，所以恐怕我5月初之前是无法动身离开的。

您 4 月 1 日的电报昨天刚刚收到。我希望格雷格医生能改变他的决定。如果他能来北平，将对我们初期的工作起到至关重要的作用。若有新消息，请及时告诉我。

我在得到南京的消息之前不能离开，所以现在还不需要款项。同时，烦请福美玲女士寄给我一些（协和医学院）历史、行政、组织和课程方面的资料，这样我可以早做准备。

前几日在当地的一份报纸上，我看到一个消息好像说顾临先生去世了。如果消息属实，您给顾临太太发吊唁函的时候，请帮忙转达我的慰问。

致以最诚挚的问候！

您最真诚的，

李宗恩 敬上

1947 年 4 月 3 日

致胡正详教授信[1]

1947年4月4日

National Kweiyang Medical College
T'aitsechiao, Kweiyang, China
April 4, 1947

Dr. C.H. Hu
O.M.E.A.
P.U.M.C.
Peiping

My dear C.H. :

It's almost two months since we parted in Peiping. It took me some six weeks to work my way back to Kweiyang via Shanghai, Hong Kong, Canton and Hengyang. When in Canton I was told by somebody that you were in Nanking, attending some conference, I expect, in connection with the O.M.E.A. I intended to write to you as soon as I got back home but on my return I had so much to do that I could hardly find time for personal correspondence, hence the delay in getting into touch with you. I suppose you yourself have had a busy time in getting the executive headquarters out of Peiping and consequent retrenchment of your own organization.

The PUMC development took me by complete surprise. I rather suspect much of it was your doing. After very careful consideration, accompanied by severe searching of the soul I felt I have to accept the challenge and be prepared to do my best. In accepting the appointment, I derived much courage from the wisdom of the trustees in inviting Dr. Gregg's cooperation. I understand, however, it is not yet certain that he will consent to the trustees' proposal. His presence in Peiping seems to be so vital in starting the difficult work of reorganization, I still hope we can get his service at least for the initial period. His cooperation will be invaluable in the building up of a strong nucleus of teaching personnel.

At this end I feel it is my duty to do my utmost to ensure the healthy continuance of this college for the existence of which I am directly responsible. Much depends on who my successor is likely to be. Unless we can have a man who, from his qualification and personality, can command the respect and wholehearted cooperation of our faculty here, the thing will fall to pieces. Rather than for that to happen, I personally would prefer to close it down altogether and make better uses of its equipment and staff elsewhere.

This, however, the Ministry will never consent to. The next best thing will be to get somebody capable of holding together and gradually developing it into an up-to-date teaching institution. I am making every effort to sound out indirectly intentions of the Ministry. As soon as I can be sure of the right person being appointed to take up my place I shall formally submit my resignation. Then the handing over will also take

[1] PUMC Archive.

some time. I am therefore not yet in a position to say when I shall be ready to take up my new duties. Provisionally I plan to fly to Peiping sometime in May. My family may have to wait until the children finish their school term and then leave by land and sea for the North.

What are your plans? Though I am not in a position to make any commitments I would like to express the opinion that nobody is more qualified than you to take up the deanship of the college. Of all people your cooperation I shall value most. I do hope you will keep this in mind. In the meantime this, of course, is only between you and me and the doorpost.

After four months of hard travelling covering something like 8,000 miles of distance, I thought I could look forward to a period of comparative quiet and peace, but alas, there is never any rest for the wicked. However I continue to feel quite fit and forty. I hope you are also gradually recovering your former health and vigour.

With affectionate regard to you and yours,

Yours always,

C.U. Lee

（译文）

国立贵阳医学院

中国贵阳太慈桥

1947 年 4 月 4 日

胡正详博士收

O.M.E.A.

北平协和医学院

北平

亲爱的正详：

北平一别已快两月。我一路经由上海、香港、广州和衡阳到达贵阳，差不多花了 6 周的时间。途径广州的时候，听人说你在南京参加会议，希望是在讨论与 O.M.E.A.有关的事情。我本打算一到家就给你写信的，没想到回来后事务缠身，实在不得空处理私人信件，以致拖到现在。把军调处搬离北平，随之而来的裁员工作，恐怕也让你忙得不可开交吧。

协和医学院的进展完全出乎我的意料，我猜这也许有你的参与。经过深思熟虑，内心深处的声音告诉我，必须接受挑战并全力以赴。我明白，虽然格雷格医生不一定会接受董事会的提议，但董事会能邀请他来协助已是非常明智之举，这也给我接受任命增加了很多信心。格雷格医生如能来北平的话，对启动艰难的复校工作将起到至关重要的作用，尤其是在建立强大的核心教师团队方面，格雷格医生的价值更是不可估量，所以我仍非常期望至少在初期能得到他的帮助。

这里的情况是，我必须保证我一手创办的贵阳医学院能够健康持续地办下去，这是我的责任，不过这很大程度上取决于谁来做我的接班人。如果我们不能找一个德才兼备并取得我们教员的绝对信任的人来接任，贵医恐怕将毁于一旦。要是这样，我个人更情愿把它彻底关掉，这样所有的设备和员工还可以在其他的地方发挥其价值。

不过，教育部无论如何都不会同意这样做的。那么最好选一个得力的人，让全院团结一致，并逐步将本院发展成为一个与时俱进的教育机构。我也在竭尽全力向部里申明我的意愿。一旦合适的接班人确定下来，我会立即正式递交辞呈。工作交接恐怕要耽误些时间，所以我现在也不确定到底何时我会到新职位上任。我现在暂定 5 月飞去北平，家人估计得等到孩子们完成这一学年，再通过海陆交通北上。

你有什么打算呢？虽然我并不能承诺什么，但我个人认为，没有谁比你更能胜任教务长的职位。纵观所有能共事的人，我对你的评价最高。我希望你能明白这一点，不过此事仅你知、我知、天知、地知。

经过漫长的 4 个月、近八千英里的长途跋涉，我原本期待一段短暂而安静的休息，但生命哪有停歇！不过，我自己感觉还是像40岁时那样健康。我也希望你能早日恢复昔日的健康和活力。

向你及家人致以最诚挚的问候！

永远是你的，

李宗恩

致施正信教授信[1]

1947 年 4 月 16 日

National, Kweiyang Medical College
T'aitzechiao, Kweiyang, China
April 16, 1947

My dear T.S.

Many thanks for your letter of March 19th which came to hand on the 28th. Before its receipt I wrote to Dr. Y.T. Tsur asking him to see Minister Chu to find out in a circumspect way some indication as to my successor here. We would like to put in a man who has had previous support of our faculty members. You are our first choice. As it is a rather delicate point with the Ministry we don't want to appear to deprive it of the right of free choice. I therefore asked Dr. Tsur to use his kind office to get the reaction of Minister Chu. I postponed writing you until I could get a reply from Dr. Tsur which came yesterday. From it I read that Minister Chu is well disposed to our suggestion and asked Dr. Tsur to approach you. I therefore hasten to solicit your cooperation in the solution of our problem. I do hope you will give this preposition your favourable consideration. Without a qualified leader such as yourself at the helm there is the grave risk of the whole set up here falling to pieces. It would be a great pity to allow that to happen, not only from the point of view of the development of modern medicine in this part of China, but also of the effort that we put into it. In equipment we are second to none south of the Yangtze River and recently the Ministry has given us over $500,000,000 for buildings and equipment. At present we are short of teachers but with the return of these we sent abroad this year we shall be able in time to get over that difficulty. When the PUMC gets really properly established there shouldn't be any difficulty in working out some plan of cooperation. All in all I am quite optimistic of the future of this college. With patience and expert direction it should develop into a really worthwhile medical centre. It would be, of course, a personal sacrifice on your and Joan's part, but I am sure that would not constitute a too serious consideration with you. As far as basic living conditions are concerned there is a great deal to be said for Kweiyang. I am therefore waiting with considerable eagerness for an affirmative reply from you.

The PUMC development was indeed a surprise to me. I was quite in the dark until I got back to Kweiyang on the 21st of March. It was, of course, an honour as well as a challenge. In view of my past happy connection with the college and my life interest in medical education I have no choice but to accept it. I don't know what my contribution will amount to, but I am prepared to do my best. I am indeed grateful to you for your good wishes and also for your views and counsel on the future of PUMC.

In regard to your first point that the function of the PUMC is to train social doctors rather than aristocratic doctors, I suppose what you mean is that we should train doctors

---

[1] PUMC Archive.

willing and qualified to meet the present social needs of the country. This should, of course, be the object of any branch of higher education dealing in social sciences. It is important to train students not only in technical efficiency, but also in the development of a proper attitude towards problems they have actually to face. It is, however, much more difficult to develop character traits such as enthusiasm, perseverance, spirit of sacrifice, patience, devotion, loyalty, doggedness, etc. Rigid scientific discipline may contribute to some extent to their development. Mere social or human contact does not necessarily make leaders. I often wonder whether it is not true that the leaders are born not made. If you can devise a reliable test by which one can pick out leaders from a crowd, you will make the greatest contribution to the problem of higher education in China.

As for your second point on postgraduate training, I fully agree that it should be more emphasized than ever before. I would like you to be more specific in the methods of postgraduate teaching in Public Health. I should be very much interested in suggestions for new experiments. You say something about products must meet the demands and needs of the market. Is it not also true that we can create the right kind of demands and needs for the products we have to sell? I wonder how much the PUMC can contribute to the creation of such demands and needs. So much depends upon political, economic and social progress.

Do you detect any signs of a fresh breeze in the political atmosphere of Nanking? Is there going to be an all-round shake-up, or just reshuffling of political heads? Let's hope it will be a change for the better. Life here is fairly peaceful and living conditions are rather comfortable. My plans for the near future very much depend upon your decision. When the future of this college is in safe hands, I intend to make a move for the North, leaving my family behind until the children finish their school term when they can travel together to Shanghai. I look forward to getting good news from you and Joan.

With warmest regards,

Yours very sincerely,

C.U. Lee

（译文）

国立贵阳医学院

中国贵阳 太慈桥

1947 年 4 月 16 日

亲爱的正信：

3 月 28 日收到你 3 月 19 日的信，我感激备至。接到你的信之前，我已经写信给周诒春博士，请他设法从朱部长那里得到一些我的继任者的消息。我希望能有一个我们教职员信任的人来接任。你是我们的首选。不过部里的事情很微妙，我们不想干扰他们的选择权。所以我请周博士办公室探听一下朱部长的意向。周博士的消息昨天才到，这也是为什么我推迟到现在才给你回信。周博士的消息说，朱部长请他转告我，他很愿意考虑我们的建议。因此我赶紧来征询你的意见，是否能一起解决我们的问题。我真诚地希望你慎重地考虑一下这个邀请。如果没有一个像你这样合适的掌舵人，贵医已经建成的一切很有可能毁于一旦。从中国现代医学发展的角度，倘若这个学校垮掉，我们注入的大量心血也将付之东流，那将会令人非常痛心和惋惜。在长江以南，我们有最好的设备；近日部里又给我们拨款 5 亿元（$500,000,000）的建筑和设备费。虽然我们现在师资短缺，待我们今年出国深造的老师回来，这个问题就会迎刃而解。协和医学院复校后，两校之间寻求一些合作应该不成问题。总而言之，我对贵医的未来充满信心。在耐心的专业人士的带领下，贵医一定会成为一个有价值的医学中心。尽管你和琼（Joan[1]）要牺牲很多，但我相信这一定不会太影响你的决定。就基本生活条件而言，贵阳也有很多可圈可点之处。因此我殷切地期待能够得到你肯定的答复。

协和医学院的事情对我来说实在是太意外了。这事我一直蒙在鼓里，直到 3 月 21 日回到贵阳才知晓。这对我来说很荣幸，当然也是巨大的挑战。鉴于我过去在协和的愉快经历以及我对医学教育的强烈兴趣，我别无选择，只能接受这个任命。我也不确定我能为协和做多少贡献，但我已经做好了全力以赴的准备。谢谢你的祝贺，同时也非常感谢你对协和未来发展的意见和建议。

你第一点提到，协和的功能应该是培养有社会意识的医生而不是贵族医生，我想你的意思是，我们应该培训无论是能力还是意志都能满足中国当今社会需求的医生。这应当是高等教育中所有社会科学课程的目标。培养学生，不仅要培养他们熟练的技能，也要培养他们以后面对各种困难的态度。至于培养学生品格，如热情、毅力、耐心、忠诚、责任感以及牺牲奉献精神，就难上加难了。严格的科学训练可能会在一定程度上帮助他们的发展，不过更多的社会实践和人际交流并不一定能培养出领导者。我常想“领导能力是天生的而不是后天培养的”这句话是否有道理。如果你能发明一个科学的测试，从茫茫人海中挑出天生的领导者，那么你就为解决中国高等教育的问题作出了最杰出的贡

[1] 编者注：即王春箐，施正信夫人。

献。

你在第二点中提到研究生的培养，我完全赞同你的观点，这一点，现在比以往任何时候都更需要被重视。关于培养公共卫生领域研究生的方法，希望你能说得更具体点。你说产品需要满足市场的需求。难道我们不能为自己要销售的产品创造相应的需求？我不知道协和对创造这样的需求能做些什么。这在很大程度上取决于政治、经济和社会的进步。

在南京，你有没有闻到什么新的政治气息呢？是要全面改组，还是只重组重要领导？无论怎样，希望都是往好的方向变化吧。现在这里的生活很平静，物质生活也很惬意。我接下来的计划很大程度上取决于你的决定。如果贵医能迎来一个可靠的掌舵人，我准备自己先行北上，家人则等到孩子们完成这一学年后再一起去上海。期待从你和琼那儿得到好消息。

致以最亲切的问候！

你最真诚的，

李宗恩

致协和董事会主席胡适先生信[1]

1947 年 8 月 30 日

August 30, 1947

Dear Dr. Hu:

Herewith I send you a tentative Operating Budget for the PUMC for the year 1947-48. There will be ample opportunity for full discussion of this budget when the Executive Committee meets at your call for this purpose. It may perhaps be helpful to you, however, to have before you a statement of the underlying principles which have guided us in framing this budget.

When the Trustees did me the honor of offering me the directorship, the determining factor in my acceptance was my conviction that medical education in China, which the end of the war found at a low ebb needed a fresh start and that the PUMC which had been the model in the past should resume that place in the postwar period. My own entry into the field of educational administration at Kweiyang had been more or less accidental and due to the war, but I was interested in the opportunity of bringing the experience thus gained to the problems of medical education as I could not have done had I stayed on there. At the same time I believed that I could perhaps help the Kweiyang Medical College and other similar institutions from the outside even more effectively than as a part of the local administration. I had not seen a copy of the report of the Rockefeller Foundation Commission at that time nor did I have any detailed information about the financial status of the College. I did, however, have a deep concern for the future of medical education in China, a vision of the part the PUMC should play in it, a willingness to make a try at bringing this to realization, and a readiness to withdraw from the picture if I did not succeed.

Although I had been a member of the PUMC Faculty for some thirteen years before I went to the southwest, you will recall that I was an associate professor, primarily concerned with teaching and clinical duties, and the administrative aspects of the institution as I began to look them over on my arrival in Peiping were new to me. The first thing that impressed me was the fact the PUMC is housed in an expansive physical plant. Medical education could be carried on at a high level in less elaborate buildings though not with less scientific equipment. The fact of the matter, however, is that we do have this physical set-up; this has to be accepted and reckoned with. This does not mean, however, that every effort to reduce the cost of operation should not be made. Indeed, one of my chief concerns in the few months that I have been in Peiping has been to examine the whole administrative structure with a view to reducing to a minimum the proportion of the budget which goes into administration and into the physical services. The Executive Committee has already approved my recommendation to combine the offices of the Recorder and the Secretary into a single Secretariat. May I call to your attention the desirability of revising the By-Laws at this

[1] PUMC Archive.

time in accordance with the principle approved in 1936 and confirmed in the spring of 1941, to provide for a single financial officer instead of the two now specified? I believe that such a revision with a restatement of the duties and responsibilities of that officer would be a further step toward economy and efficiency of administration. With your permission, I plan shortly to present a draft of a suggested revision of this section of the By-Laws for your consideration.

With the conception of the PUMC's future role as the arbiter in medical education in China, emphasis must be placed on quality not quantity. Whatever we undertake, however limited in scope, must be done well – we cannot have anything slipshod. In the past when funds were sufficient, working conditions favorable and the PUMC was being built up to a position of international eminence; attention was centered on excellence rather than on economy. Now we have to strive for the maximum excellence with the maximum economy. This is a new point of view. If we are to adapt ourselves to it and get maximum results, we must build up an esprit de corps with everyone working toward a common end. This brings us to the setting up of the salary scale, something which unavoidably had to be done before we could get any idea of the total budget. In devising the formula two main considerations were in mind:

1) We must give our staff end employees an income sufficient to remove constant anxiety over daily necessities, so that they can devote themselves to their duties in order to secure the desired excellence of performance.

2) We must find some way of offsetting the rise in prices through inflation.

Since the Executive Committee on June 21st approved the formula I then proposed, we have in the interest of economy revised that formula downward as you know. Details of that revision will be reported at the next meeting of the Executive Committee. As our salaries now stand, our lowest paid workers are receiving about 40,000 times their pre-war wages; those in the middle brackets about 10,000 times; those in the top brackets about 5,000 times. With living costs at present more than 40,000 times pre-war, it is evident that our present salaries can truly be said to be maintenance salaries and not at pre-war levels except in the case of the lowest paid workers whose pre-war wage was only a maintenance wage. It is true that our salaries are about double those paid at Pei Ta and other local educational institutions, but I am certain that we can expect work of high quality from a full-time staff which does not have to seek outside remunerative employment to provide bare maintenance. Even so our salaries are not at the top level of the salaried classes in Peiping.

The actual working out of these two principles and applying them within our budget calculations, especially as to providing sufficient margin in the budget to offset inflationary increase in costs, emphasized three main problems:

1) Exchange – a factor outside our control. When we began to draw up the budget we soon realized that unless an exchange rate of not less than 40,000 to 1 should prevail, it would be impossible to cover more than existing commitments to the School of Nursing and Health Station. Fortunately, in the last week of budgeting the new exchange provisions were announced. It is our hope that if marked price increases during the coming year send the Index of the cost of living up, these will be offset by corresponding changes in the open market rate of exchange.

2) The present exorbitant cost of coal – which makes it the dominating factor in all our considerations.

3) The rigid demarcation by the China Medical Board as between funds for

operation and funds for rehabilitation. In the first year of resumed activity it is not always easy to make a hard and fast distinction between what is operation and what is rehabilitation, and a little elasticity between these two sections of the budget would have made our task somewhat less exacting. I appreciate, however, the great concern of the China Medical Board that in our enthusiasm for reopening we should not jeopardize the re-equipping which is so necessary if we are to maintain a program of high quality, and so we have accepted this limitation with good grace and perhaps in the end have profited by the hard necessity of framing our operating budget within the total of US$320,000 and rehabilitation within $200,000, instead of working out the two budgets ourselves within the total of US$520,000.

The budget as now presented provides for maintaining the School of Nursing and Health Station, the two units already functioning, together with the Library, Administration and Power Plant; and adds provision for the Medical School departments of Anatomy, Physiology and Biochemistry. We have arrived at the budget as presented only by the most careful scrutiny of every item, section by section, and strict economy in personnel and expenses. You will note that there is no provision for the Hospital in this Budget. This is not because we are not all agreed on the importance of reopening the hospital at the earliest possible date; the Nursing School needs it, the community is clamoring for it, and it should be well established before the first year class which we hope to admit this year is ready to begin clinical work two years from now. Under present circumstances, however, we can not squeeze out of the $320,000 which we hope for from the China Medical Board, enough to cover the cost of running the Hospital even for a three-month period. The thing which makes this impossible is the high cost of operating the power plant. We are continuing to explore every possibility for reducing that item. There is some reason to hope that we may be able to work out a plan which will effect sufficient savings on the power plant to enable us to open the Hospital by April 1, 1948. I can assure you that we will do everything within our power toward that end. Aside from its place in our educational program, the Hospital is important as a medium for creating and sustaining interest on the part of the local community from whom we hope eventually to secure some measure of financial support.

Although the budget here presented deals with the current year only, in working over it we have kept in mind the fact that this is not an isolated year's operation but rather the initial year in an expanding program. We have attempted therefore to view all commitments in that light. We have also kept before us the important long-term policies toward which we aim. The PUMC must play its part in the national development of medical education and has a unique opportunity through the younger medical schools which have our graduates at their head and on their faculties, and are following the PUMC pattern. This increases our responsibility. We must keep in close touch with them; in so doing we will not only help them to develop and maintain standards but will also profit by our contact with the main stream of Chinese medical education.

Sincerely yours,

C.U. Lee,
Director

（译文）

1947 年 8 月 30 日

胡适博士：

随信一并送上 1947-48 年度北平协和医学院(PUMC)的预算草案。在您为其召开的执委会上，它将得到充分且深入的讨论。以下是我们编制预算所依据的原则，或许对诸位会有帮助。

我接受董事会委任我为院长一职的思想主导是我对发展中国医学教育的信心。中国医学教育在战争后期走向低谷，亟待重振。过去曾是中国医学教育楷模的协和医学院，战后应重新取得这一领先的位置。我进入医学教育行政工作——去组建国立贵阳医学院并担任行政领导——多少有些偶然，要归因于抗日战争的爆发吧！工作中我积累了一定的经验，一心想把这些经验加以推广。这一点，如果留在贵阳医学院就很难做到了。从外部来帮助贵医和其他一些类似于贵医的医学院，比在其内部做行政工作或许更为有效。那时我还没有看到洛氏基金会的报告，对医学院的财务情况，也知之甚少。但基于我对未来中国医学教育的忧虑和对协和医学院应起的作用的了解，我愿为之一搏。如果失败，我准备随时引退。

在去西南之前，我在协和医学院工作了约 13 年。您是知道的，我的职位是襄教授，从事教学和临床。这次一回北平，就要直面行政工作的方方面面，这对于我是陌生的。给我印象最深的是协和医学院的庞大建筑。办好一个医学院可以没有非常堂皇的楼宇，但不能没有精密、优良的仪器设备。而我们已经有了这样的条件，这是要认真对待的现实。这并不是说，我们就不能设法缩减一些开支。事实上我们正在考虑怎样把行政开支缩减到最低限度，在全部开支中占最小的比例。例如：执委会已经批准的我的建议，把书记和秘书两个办事处合并成为一个秘书处。也请您允许我旧事重提：按 1936 年提出 1941 年进一步确定的原则修改的章程的细则，把原来规定的两个财务官员改为一个。这一修改，能加强财务工作者的权限和责任感，是在精简机构中迈出的有效的一步。得到您的同意后，我将尽快地提出一份可行的缩减行政开支的修改草案，供执委会讨论时参考。

为使协和医学院今后能在中国医学教育界成为执牛耳的角色，重点必须放在质上而不是量上。不管我们做什么，事无巨细，都必须认真对待，不得马虎。过去经费充足，工作条件好，协和医学院曾享有国际声誉，注重的是追求卓越的成绩，而不在于省钱。现在则必须在最节约的基础上，做出最卓越的成绩，这是我们新的着眼点。要适应它并获得最大的成果，就必须建立团队精神，迈向一个共同的目标。在总预算还没有确定前，我们就必须把各个级别的工资待遇定下来。在决定工资级别前，又必须先考虑以下两个问题：

（1）必须让我们的员工有不必再为温饱操心的工资收入。只有这样，他们才能勤于职守，全心全意地投入工作。

（2）必须让他们在物价上涨时所受到的损失得到补偿。

您也许已经得知，6 月 21 日执委会上通过我提出的方案，考虑到节约开支，已经做了些削减。修订的具体内容将提交下次执委会会议。目前，收入最低的员工的工资数额是战前的 40000 倍，中层员工的工资数额为战前的 10000 倍，高层员工是 6000 倍。在生活指数远高于战前 40000 倍的今天，显然他们的收入都只能维持最低的生活水平。除了在战前收入也只能维持最低生活需要的工人外，其他人员的生活水平都远远低于战前。不过，我们的待遇仍然是北大或其他地方教育机构的一倍。但我认为，只有不必为温饱去疲于奔命、去打工的人，才有可能提供优质的工作。再说，在北京地区，我们的待遇目前也不是最高的啊！

为了做到上述两点，并把他们列入预算，特别是在预算中留有余地，以抵消通货膨胀的影响，就必须强调以下三点：

（1）汇率：这是我们无法控制的。在制定预算时，我们就意识到只有保证汇率不低于 40000 的情况下，护士学校和医学院才能勉强维持下去。幸运的是，就在我们做预算的最后一周，新的汇率真的宣布了。希望以后物价上涨时，生活指数也能随之提高。这样，或能抵消市场汇率上涨给员工生活带来的损失。

（2）目前，燃煤价格高居不下，它已成为我们忧虑的中心问题了。

（3）中华医学基金会对年度经费和修复经费的规定十分严格。事实上，在复校的第一年度里，这两项经费是难以分开的，有些项目既可以是常用经费，也可以说是修复经费，所以需要一些灵活性。但我还是感谢中华医学基金会的关心，在我们努力复校时，也应该维修更新设备，这是保持一个高质量的长远计划所必需的。因此我们愿意按这个规定，把预算分成两个部分，年度经费 320,000 美元和修复费 200,000 美元两个预算，而不是 520,000 美元的总预算。

现在所呈上的这个预算，包括护士学校、卫生事务所这两个已经开始运行的机构，图书馆、行政部门和供电所，加上医学院解剖、生理和生化三个系科的设备。对这个预算我们做到了逐条逐款仔细认真的审核，并落实到每个人和每一笔费用上。您也许会注意到，在这个预算中没有列入附属医院的经费。这不是说，我们对尽早恢复附属医院的重要性认识不足。护士学校需要实习医院；社会呼吁医院能早日开放；今年入学的新生两年后要在医院里开始临床实习。但目前我们实在没有可能从中华医学基金会拨给的 320,000 美元中，挤出即使只是维持附属医院三个月的开支！最主要的限制是供电所运转所需开支太大。我们正在尽一切努力减少这笔开支，让附属医院能在 1948 年 4 月 1 日开业。我向您保证，为此我们将竭尽全力。附属医院不仅是我们教学计划中不可或缺的，它还为医学院和地方提供相互支持的机会。我们希望最终能从社会上取得一定数量的经济支持。

虽然这只是本年度的预算，但在其制订中我们始终明白，这不仅是一年的计划，也是一个长远规划的开端，因为我们必须承担此后的全部责任，而且我们必须遵守为达到使其成为长远规划这一目标所制定的各项有关政策。协和医学院要在中国医学教育的发展进程中发挥作用，这是我们的机遇，也是我们的责任。我们有的毕业生已经成为一些新建医学院的负责人，他们采用的是协和医学院的办学模式。我们要与这些毕业生保持紧密的联系，这不仅能帮助他们的发展，保持一定的学术水准，而且我们还能通过他们与中国医学教育的主流互动，并从中受益。

你真诚的，

李宗恩

院长

任协和校长时的讲演[1]

1947年10月9日

本人离开协和差不多有十年，最近回到本校服务，一方面觉得非常的荣幸，一方面能有机会同诸位老朋友老同事在一起工作，感觉到非常的愉快。

因为都是老朋友老同事，用不着什么正式的介绍．所以兄弟回来北平之后并没有举行任何仪式，同诸位见面谈话。

明天是双十节，总务处陈先生提议今晚举行一次同乐会，借此给本人一个机会同大家见见面，谈几句话，我就很高兴的答应了。

今晚是同乐会，我不愿意多用时间做一种演讲式的谈话，不过有一点意见，愿意提出来同大家互相勉励。

我们抗战是胜利了，但是经过这几年的破坏，政治、经济、社会以及教育各方面一时都不能上轨道。在这种不正常的环境之下推动一件工作，确是有很大困难的。本人回到协和，首先就感觉到协和虽然经过一个长时期的停顿，她的一种特殊精神依然存在，这种精神就是"不论任何一件事、一件工作，要么不做，要做的话就要达到一种标准。"绝不马虎，绝不苟且。这种精神目前在任何其他机关是很少见到的，这种精神我们必须保持。

但是这种精神是经过许多年培养成功的——在抗战以前，我们的经济力量比较充裕，所以我们在工作方面能集中我们的注意力，造成一种最高的理想的可以给别人做榜样的标准，有时候是不计代价的。

现在环境不同了，拿我们现在的经济力量同过去比，只有八分之一。换句话说，从前有八块钱，现在只有一块钱，假设因此我们就降低我们的标准，这是万万不应该的。

最近董事会决议，先恢复协和医学院，医院暂缓开办。这项决议亦就是因为要保持我们协和的标准，设备不齐，经费不够，我们不愿意轻举妄动。

我是最不赞成贴标语的。假设一定要提出口号，那么就是"在最经济的条件之下来维持我们协和的特殊精神。"我不愿多费诸位的时间，现在我请主席

[1] 协和医学院档案室。

开始今晚上的节目。

致协和医学院和护校全体毕业生信[1]

1948 年 1 月 1 日

To all graduates of the Medical College and School of Nursing:

The New Year is traditionally a time for settling accounts, reviewing the accomplishments and disappointments of the year that is ended, and planning for the year that is beginning. This newsletter is such an accounting to all of you who are an integral part of the PUMC's past and who have so keen an interest in the future of your Alma Mater.

To each one I send my heartiest good wishes for a New Year full of the satisfactions of accomplishment and service, wherever you may be.

From each one I bespeak in return a New Year pledge of understanding interest and support for the PUMC, which will bring us through this year and the years to come in ever-growing usefulness.

As a motto for the year 1948 I give you a quotation from a statement made by the late Dr. George E. Vincent, president of the Rockefeller Foundation, in one of the early reports which resulted in the establishment of the PUMC:

"The greatest need of China is not, after all, for highly trained scientists, although they are essential; it is not, after all, for the greatest technical skill, although that is absolutely necessary if the great end is to be attained. But the great need of China is scientific knowledge and technical skill dominated by idealistic loyalty to the highest and best influences in human life."

This statement is as full of wisdom and insight today as it was when it was made more than thirty years ago. Let us together face the coming year in that spirit, and in it find the NEW HAPPINESS with which we greet each other on New Year's Day.

C. U. Lee

（译文）

致协和医学院和护校全体毕业生：

新年是辞旧迎新之际，人们总是习惯在这时总结过去一年的得与失，并为新的一年开始新的计划和打算。今天的这个简报，算是我给你们的一个新年献词吧，在过去你们是协和的一员，在未来你们也是最关心母校的人。

无论你们在何方，我都衷心地祝愿每一位同学在新的一年里，能够悬壶济世、志得意满。

可以预见，未来你们对母校的关注和支持，会让协和的影响力与日俱增。

---

[1] 《协和校刊》, Peiping Union Medical College, 复校后出版两期英文版，1948 年 1 月 1 日。

作为 1948 年的赠言，我想把已故洛克菲勒基金会主席乔治 · 文森特 (George E. Vincent，1864-1941)[1]博士在一份报告中的一段话送给你们，也正是因为这份报告，协和医学院才得以成立。

"为了实现伟大的目标，训练有素的科学家和精湛绝伦的科学技术缺一不可，但对于目前的中国来说，真正最需要的其实是'一切科学知识和技术技能都以为人类创造福音为宗旨'这一坚定的信念。"

文森特博士的话虽然说于 30 多年以前，但现在看来，这句话仍然充满智慧和洞察力。让我们带着这种信念，迎接新一年的到来，也在这种信念中，寻找到新的幸福。

李宗恩

[1] George E. Vincent，洛克菲勒基金会主席 (1917-1929)，中华医学基金会主席（1917-1928，1934-1936）。

在中华医学基金会年会上的讲话[1]

February 2, 1948

Address to China Medical Board

To save time, I would ask permission to present a brief statement on the progress that is being made in the reopening of the PUMC. Before doing so, I would like to express my deep appreciation of your kind invitation to visit this country, thereby conferring upon me the honor and privilege of meeting the members of the Board.

Though my appointment was made at the meeting of the Trustees on March 12, 1947, it took me some time to liquidate my obligations to the National Kweiyang Medical College, of which I was then in charge. I arrived in Peiping at the end of May 1947. After an absence of nine and a half tragic years, it was indeed gratifying to find that all the buildings and a considerable part of the College's scientific equipment were more or less intact. A rapid survey of the situation convinced me that immediate effort must be made to put them into good use or else we would run the risk of losing an opportunity of providing a timely stimulus to medical education and of rendering humanitarian service at a time when it was most needed. Also, a group of well-constructed, desirable buildings standing idle obviously would invite occupation by others. The time available for preparation was short, but we went ahead.

Before producing a budget for the current year, we had to devise a scale of enumeration for staff and employees, compatible with our resources. We had to adopt a formula which, in terms of income to individual members of the staff, especially of the upper strata, became subsistence allowances rather than salaries. While the scale is somewhat above that of government educational institutions, it is still below that of banks or some government industrial organizations or even certain private educational institutions.

We deeply appreciated the prompt action the Board took in approving the budget for 1947-1948, which allowed us to proceed with the enrollment of the first-year medical students and the lining up of teaching personnel. Registration of twenty-two medical students was completed by October 22nd, and teaching began the following day. Though we were late in the season in making appointments to the faculty, we succeeded in inviting visiting or part time teachers from other schools, who now are taking care of the teaching schedule satisfactorily for the current academic year. This arrangement has the advantage of allowing the College more time to canvas the field for a permanent staff. Full programs are being carried in the nursing school, in cooperation with other hospitals, with an enrollment of fifteen in the freshman class, and the health station, which has been kept going against great odds throughout the war period.

It has been repeatedly pointed out that in the budget for 1947-1948 no provision was included for the operation of the hospital. It is an omission that must be remedied at the earliest opportunity, not only for the service that we can render but because of

---

[1] Report made by Dr. C.U. Lee, February 2, 1948, RAC, CMB Inc. Box 47, Folder 334.

the urgent need for providing a practice field for the nursing school. In this respect, we are getting much encouragement from the CNRRA, the Chinese counterpart of UNRRA, in a special allocation of equipment equivalent to that of a two hundred and fifty bed unit, which is in the process of being shipped to Peiping. We have also been promised material help from the United States Post-UNRRA program, to be spent in the rehabilitation work of the hospital. An appreciable item of funds can thus be released from our rehabilitation grant for this year. If these savings can be applied to the operation of the hospital, we believe that we can make a start with our clinical services sometime in April, so as to justify our acceptance of such help. Our being a going concern is important from the point of view of getting such assistance.

The exchange situation continues to give us concern. The gap between the present official open market rate and the Peiping black market rate has continued to widen, so that at the time I left Peiping in the middle of December, the difference was about fifty per cent. In other words, we were getting only half of the actual purchasing value of that portion of U.S. currency that has to be exchanged for local expenditures. An arrangement has just been reached in Shanghai with the Central Bank by which a preferential rate for PUMC funds gives us twenty-five per cent better than we could get on the official open market.

As to future outlook, it must be frankly admitted that a categorical statement is not possible in the face of so much uncertainty in the political, economic and social situation that exist in North China. Assuming continuation of the present political regime, it should be possible to build up by slow stages a center for the development of teachers for the other medical schools of China – compared with which we are still better housed and equipped, and, being privately endowed, have more freedom for educational experiments. It is true that in view of the appreciable devaluation of the American dollar and of the out-of-bound inflation of the Chinese currency, with consequent marked reduction in the purchasing value of our income and coupled with it the greatly increased overhead expenses, largely due to the price of coal, it may not be possible to attain our former standard. It is, nevertheless, my belief that we can do a worthwhile job, retain a leading position among the schools, and be an essential cog in the wheel of medical education. To do so, it may be even necessary to curtail some of our existing commitments and concentrate on the absolute essentials.

At this point, I would like to stress one of the fundamental conditions in the building up of strong teaching personnel: namely, a fellowship program, for which we have made no provision this year on account of the limitation of funds. But serious consideration must be given to it in the future.

This is assuming that the present situation holds out. The possibility of a major political change in North China involving Peiping cannot be ignored. In that eventuality, it is still reasonable to hope that educational activities will continue to enjoy a large measure of freedom from political interference, though some shift in emphasis is possible. Emphasis may perhaps veer more toward the social aspects of medicine, at the expense of scientific education and standard.

In closing this brief statement, I would like to take this opportunity to express the deep appreciation to the Board of the College administration in making possible Dr. Loucks's presence in Peiping during the period of intensive planning last summer. Without Dr. Loucks' cooperation and constant encouragement, our task would have been even more difficult.

（译文）

致中华医学基金会

为了节约时间，请允许我简要地介绍一下协和医学院复校以来的工作进展。不过，我得先向基金会的邀请表示深深的谢意，让我有幸与董事们会面。

1947 年 3 月 12 日的董事会年会上，我被任命为协和医学院院长。彼时，我正担任国立贵阳医学院校长，在交接完贵阳医学院事务后，我于 1947 年 5 月底抵达北京。阔别九年半之后，我欣慰地发现，虽然经过了这一段悲惨的岁月，学校所有的建筑和相当一部分科研设备基本保存完好。经过初步考察，我认为应该尽快复校，否则将错过促进医学教育发展和提供人道主义服务的最佳时机。如果任其空置不管，这些美观而坚固的建筑很可能被挪作它用。时不我待，我们火速投入到复校工作中。

在制定本年度预算之前，我们按照现有的资金制定了一个支付教职员工的方案。我们没有采用简单的薪酬等级制，而是考虑每个员工的具体情况，尤其是高级员工，以满足他们的生活所需。尽管我们的标准稍高于政府教育机构，但仍低于银行、一些国营企业及某些私立教育机构。

我们非常感谢董事会及时批准了 1947-1948 学年的财政预算，使我们能够招收第一批医学生，让教学人员准备就绪。截至 10 月 22 日，22 名新生注册；第二天正式开课。尽管我们错过了本季度教职员工的聘用期，但还是成功地从其他学校邀请到了客座老师或兼职老师，他们正在为本学年提供高质量的教学。这也给了学校更充足的时间选聘永久教职人员。另外，战时坚持办学的护校和卫生事务所都恢复了正常，开始与其他医院合作，护校已有 15 名新生正式注册上课。

我曾经提过，1947-1948 学年的预算并不包括附属医院的开支。我们必须尽早纠正这个遗漏，这不仅因为医院可以服务社会，更重要的是它可满足护校实习的急需。在这方面，我们得到了中国善后救济总署（下属于联合国善后救济总署）的大力支持，为我们分配了相当于 250 个床位的器材，现在这些器材正在运往北京。之后，美国政府也承诺为修复医院提供物资援助。因此，今年我们可以从复校的经费中省下一笔可观的资金。如果把节省下来的资金用于修复医院，我们应该在 4 月左右就可以诊治病人了。这些物资援助对我们确实起到了雪中送炭的作用，而我们也物尽其用，且好钢用在刀刃上。

兑换率也是我们担心的一个问题。目前官方市场兑换率和北京黑市兑换率的差价不断扩大，我 12 月中旬离开北京时，差价大约为 50%。换句话说，在经过官价兑换后，我们只得到了可从黑市兑换的美元价值的一半。不过，我们已经和上海的中央银行达成了一项协议，他们将为协和医学院提供高于官方市场 25%的优惠兑换率。

展望未来，必须坦率地承认，在中国北方政治、经济和社会形势如此动荡的局势下，我们很难做一个笼统的保证。假如目前的政治局势不变，那么协和医学院是有可能逐步地为其他医学院培养一批教师的，因为我们仍有较好的建筑、设备、私人捐助和相对的学术自由。但是，美元贬值和中国失控性的货币膨胀，造成我们收入的购买力明显降低，与此同时燃煤价格的上涨，又使我们的开销迅速增高，这些都可能使我们达不到先前的标准。尽管如此，我仍然坚信，事在人为，我们将继续领先于其他医学院，并成为医学教育事业的中坚。为了实现这个目标，我们也许应该减少次要的开支，而集中精力专攻当务之急。

讲到这里，我想向大家强调一下建立强大的教师队伍的一个重要环节：奖学金。由于资金短缺，我们今年没有这一款项，但在未来我们一定要认真考虑这件事情。

以上所述，是以目前政局不变为前提的。不容忽视的是，包括北京在内的中国北方，很有可能发生重大的政治变革。如果这种情况发生，医学的重点可能会从科学教育转移到社会方面，我们仍然希望，教育活动能够不受政治的干预，继续享有相当大的自由。

最后，由衷感谢校董事会能够让娄克斯医生在去年夏天——我们的重要规划时期——亲临北京。如果没有娄克斯医生的合作和不断鼓励，我们的工作会更加困难。

致中华医学基金会主席帕克先生信[1]

1948 年 12 月 28 日

Mr. Philo W. Parker
Standard-Vacuum company
Shanghai

Dear Mr. Parker:

It is a keen disappointment to all of us that existing circumstances prevent the visit from you in Peiping which we have long anticipated. We had looked forward to showing you the institution in its present state of activity, disussing with you our plans for the gradual resumption of full activity over the next year or two, and getting from you the ideas of the China Medical Board as to the future. Instead, we have to be content with sending you as full information as possible by letter, with the hope that you may find it possible to let us hear from you by letter or telegram with such advice as you may feel like giving to us at the present time.

A number of enclosures accordingly accompany this letter. The first is a copy of a circular letter I sent to the Trustees of November 22nd covering the situation up to that time. Attached to this is a copy of the Home-Coming Day News Bulletin and the Staff List brought up to date. The return to the Index of the Cost of Living as the basis for adjusting salaries and the subsequent improvement in rates of exchange were real life-savers, ——the former for the staff and employees who for more than a month previous had of necessity been paid at a sub-maintenance level, and the latter for the College whose resources thereby became adequate once again to cover the budget with salaries adjusted to the Index.

The second enclosure is the Second Revision of the Operating Budget for 1948-49 with the Controller's memorandum dated December 7th, and the third is the Revised Rehabilitation and Re-equipment Program, both of which were approved and adopted by the Executive Committee under date of December 8th. The Controller's memorandum calls attention to the important features of the revision of the Operating Budget and needs no further comment from me, except to emphasize our satisfaction at the improved budgetary position in comparison with that at the beginning of the fiscal year.

The statement of the Rehabilitation and Re-equipment Program is of special interest in that it summarizes all the appropriations and grants which we have received for this purpose, giving the impressive total of US$389,267.46 of which $247,833.33 has come from funds specially appropriated for that purpose by the CMB, US$47,830.54 has been allocated from CMB-provided operating funds (1948-49 budget), and US$93,603.59 from other sources, chiefly from the China Relief Mission (CRM) and the Economic Cooperation Administration (ECA). Since that statement was prepared, we have received from the ECA two further grants of Gold Yuan 300,000 and Gold Yuan 375,000 for rehabilitation of the Hospital. With these grants

[1] Letter Lee to Parker, December 28, 1948, RAC, CMB Inc., box 125, folder 910.

and the other funds available in the Rehabilitation Budget, it is believed that our hope of completing the major rehabilitation of the whole institution before the end of the year 1948-49 will be realized. When we remember that about a year ago we thought it would take four or five years to accomplish this program, we feel that we have reason to be gratified at what it has been possible to do thanks to the continued support of the CMB and the substantial help from the CRM and ECA.

As I said at the beginning of this letter, I wish you could see for yourself just what these figures represent. Perhaps a few figures of a different sort may help to give a picture of what we are doing. During the months of October and November our 95 hospital beds were nearly 95% occupied, a very high percentage of occupancy by usual standards; in October there were 3,288 visits registered in our outpatient clinics, and in November the clinic visits numbered 3,312. December figures are not yet available. On January 3rd we plan to open one more ward in the hospital which will increase our bed capacity to 125 which is about 35% of our prewar number. Other wards are rehabilitated and ready for opening whenever our situation as to budget and personnel permits.

In the Medical School and School of Nursing classes have continued without interruption and our student bodies have stayed calm and undisturbed in spite of the uncertain and troublous times. The morale of the staff is excellent, and everyone concentrates on his daily work and responsibilities, so that academically we are not suffering by reason of the present situation. We have even found it possible this past week to present diplomas to ten members of the Class of 1943 in the Medical School whose course was interrupted by the closing of the College in 1942, and who completed their work elsewhere but because of regulations of the Ministry of Education had never been able to get a valid diploma or degree from any other institution. These ten have recently completed all the PUMC requirements for the degree and were then awarded our diploma.

Our coal stocks amount to some 5,000 tons which is enough to see us through most of the next half year. We have stocks of staple food stuffs in the hospital for about three months. The city is without light and water which makes us realize how fortunate we are to have our own power plant and wells so that there is no interruption in our work from the lack of these essential utilities. The residence compounds are supplied with PUMC water but were cut off from our electricity by the Japanese, and so those of us who live in the compounds share with the rest of the city the necessity of using kerosene lamps for lighting while enjoying unlimited water supply.

You will see from all this that we are operating as usual without any plan or intention to do otherwise. Of course, we cannot say with assurance that any new regime that may take over this region will not interfere with us, but it is my conviction that the thing for us to do is to go ahead until circumstances outside our control force us to stop. What we have heard of initial contacts in Mukden, Tsinan and at Yanching University seem to indicate that it may be possible to carry on, and it is our earnest hope that this will prove to be so. The only alternative would be to close the institution and abandon the plant, the results of which none of us would care to contemplate. To do so might leave a chasm which we could never bridge in the future. As the Executive Committee stated on November 11th "it is the desire and intention of the Trustees to carry on work as usual in Peiping, without any thought of moving away from this city". That is the desire and intention of us all.

We will do everything we can to keep in touch with the Trustees and with the CMB. I give you my personal assurance of loyalty to the principles and purposes of the founders and supporters, and that I will do everything in my power to bring the institution through the present vicissitudes intact and playing its part in the development of modern medical education and practice in China.

I cannot close without telling you what a satisfaction it is to us all and in particular to me to have Dr. Loucks here as representative of the CMB. He is a tower of strength and his presence here is an important factor in the stability of the institution. At the same time it must mean everything to you to feel that you have on the spot representing your board so wise and sound an observer and adviser.

With kindest personal regards and regrets that there will be no chance to see you in Peiping,

Sincerely yours

C. U. Lee

（译文）

亲爱的帕克先生:

我们对您因为局势不能来访北平的消息深感失望。我们一直盼着您能亲眼看看学校现在的一切情况，盼着和您讨论我们在今后 1-2 年内把学校全部恢复的计划，听取您告诉我们中华医学基金会对未来的展望。但是，我们只好把所有这些写在这封信及附件里，希望您通过信件和电报告知我们您的意见。

随信附上以下文件。第一份附件是 11 月 22 日寄给所有董事的信，汇报学校之前的情况；返校节的校刊和教员名单；调整薪酬依据的兑换率，教职员在之前的一个多月仅能维持生活；及改善后的兑换率，使学校的资金得以支付根据生活指数调整的薪酬而正常运转。

第二份附件是 1948-49 年预算的第二修改稿，还有总务处 12 月 7 日的说明。第三份附件是 12 月 8 日执行委员会批准并开始执行的修缮及设备预算的修改稿。总务处的说明中列出了修改要点，我就不多说了。比起本财政年开始，我们对于改进后的财政情况比较满意。

特别提出的是，修复和装备项目的报告总结了我们为此花费了 389,267.46 美金，其中 247,833.33 美金来自中华医学基金会的指定款项，47,830.54 美金来自基金会 1948-49 年的运行款项，93,603.59 美金来自其他地方，主要是中国救援会（CRM）和经济合作委员会（ECA）。那以后，我又从 ECA 收到两笔为修复医院提供的资金，300,000 金圆卷和 375,000 金圆卷。这些资金，加上其它预算中的复校用款，我们相信，全面复校工作可以在 1948-49 学年完成。就在 1

年前，我们还觉得需要 4-5 年才能完成复校，现在我们有理由感谢基金会、CRM 和 ECA，帮助我们完成这一计划。

如上所述，我希望您有机会看看这些数字说明了什么。也许告诉您如下的景象，可能更说明学校的现状。10 月和 11 月，医院的 95 张病床的利用率达 95%，按一般标准，这是一个很高的利用率；10 月的门诊病人为 3288 位，11 月为 3312 位，12 月的数字还没有统计出来。我们计划在 1 月 3 日再开放一个病房，那时全部病床将为 125 张，为战前的 35%。其他病房将在资金和人力允许的情况下随时开放。

医学院和护校的课程始终没有停止，学生们没有受时局混乱和前途未卜的干扰。员工的士气高涨，每人都专注于自己的日常工作和责任，所以我们的学术工作没有被打乱。而且，我们本周会将毕业证书授予给 10 位 1943 年的毕业生，他们的学业因为医学院在 1942 年被关闭而中断，后来在其他学校完成了学业，但因为教育部的规定，没有得到那些学校的毕业证书。这 10 位学生最近完成了所有协和医学院的规定课程，所以获得我们的毕业证书。

我们的燃煤储藏够用半年，医院的食物储藏可用三个月。北平城已经没有电和水，这让我们庆幸有自己的发电厂和水井，让我们可以继续工作。宿舍原来由协和供水，但供电被日本人切断了，这让我们这些住宿舍的人和北平人一样点起煤油灯，不过我们还有用之不竭的自来水。

您从以上可以看出，我们一切运行正常，没有改变任何计划和意图。当然，我们不知道取代现政府的新政权是否会阻碍我们的工作，我认为我们应该照常工作，直到不能控制的因素迫使我们停止。从张家口、济南和燕京大学的消息表明，我们也许可以继续，我们也衷心希望继续下去。否则，唯一的选择是关闭学校，弃置发电厂，其结果对我们是难以设想的。就像执行委员会 11 月 11 日所说"董事会将照常工作，没有搬离此城市的意图，并将尽力帮助教师和学生克服任何困难。"这也是我们所有人的希望和决心。

我们将尽一切可能与董事会和中华医学基金会保持联系。我向您保证，忠实执行创始人和支持者的原则和目标，竭尽全力领导学校渡过这一动荡时期而完整无损，为中国医学教育和医疗工作作出贡献。

最后，我想告诉您，娄克斯医生在这里作为中华医学基金会的代表，对我们至关重要。他的存在给了我们强有力的支持，是学校保持稳定的重要因素。

同时，您应该为基金会有这样一个有智慧和主见的代表而高兴。

你真诚的，

李宗恩
院长

致协和董事会信[1]

1949 年 2 月 18 日

To the Board of Trustees:

It is a great satisfaction to be able to report to you that the College and Hospital have come through the past six weeks unharmed and without interruption of our academic and service program. Staff and students have gone about their regular work as usual. The Men's Medical Ward of 30 beds was opened on January 3rd, bringing the total number of beds in the Hospital to 125. During the month of January these beds were occupied for a total of 2863 patient-days, an increase of 250 patient-days over the month of December; clinic visits in January totaled 2688 of which 2299 were in the public outpatient department, an increase of 190 visits in the public clinic as compared with December.

On February 8th, the School of Nursing granted diplomas as the Class of 1948 to three women who started their course in Chengtu in 1945, returned with the school to Peiping in 1946, and had just completed the requirements for graduation. Four other members of this class unfortunately had left Peiping for personal reasons a few weeks earlier.

Payrolls have been covered as usual from our own resources, and there is no indication of any early change in this situation. The rehabilitation of the hospital wards and clinics has proceeded according to plan, and we expect it to be completed by the end of February with the exception of some interior painting which must be deferred until stocks of paint become available.

The Vice Chairman of the Board visited the College on February 11th on the occasion of his first trip into the city from Yanching University since early December, and it was a pleasure to have so favorable a report of the situation of the institution to give him. The officers are now beginning the preparation of the budget for the fiscal year 1949-50. With the resumption of rail communication with Tientsin, we hope to get a quorum of the Executive Committee together to consider the budget when it is ready. Postal service to points outside North China is not open, but telegraphic communications have not been interrupted and it has therefore been possible to keep the China Medical Board, Inc. informed as to the situation of the College.

No official pronouncements have been made in recent weeks on educational policies in general, or with respect to institutions like the PUMC. Such unofficial contacts as have occurred indicate an encouraging interest in the continuance of the College's special function of training medical teachers and leaders, and a friendly concern that the buildings and equipment should be protected from harm. What future developments may bring we have no basis as yet to forecast. We can only assure you of our keen sense of the weight of responsibility which rests on us to preserve and to further the fundamental purposes of the Founders and Trustees.

---

[1] Memorandum to the Board of Trustees, February 18, 1949, RAC, CMB, Inc, box 125, folder 910.

Sincerely your,

C. U. Lee
Director

（译文）

致董事会：

我非常满意地向你们汇报，学校和医院在过去的六个星期里一切如常，即没有受到损害，也没有中断正常的教学活动。有 30 张床的男病房于 1 月 3 日开放，现在医院共有病床 125 张。1 月份实际占用的总床日数为 2,863 ，比 12 月增加了 250；1 月的门诊病人总共 2,688，其中 2,299 是对外门诊病人，比 12 月增加 190 人。

2 月 8 日，护校给 1948 级的 3 位护士颁发了毕业证书，她们 1945 年在成都入学，1946 年和学校一起返回北平，刚完成所有学业。这个班级的其他 4 位学生不幸在几周前因个人原因离开了北平。

我们用自己的储蓄支付了工资，这一情况没有任何改变的迹象。医院和门诊的修复按计划进行，除了一些室内油漆因为买不到而没有完成之外，我们希望所有工作能在 2 月底结束。

2 月 11 日，副董事长自 12 月初后第一次从燕京大学到学校参观，我们很高兴向他汇报了学校的工作。管理人员现在开始准备 1949-1950 年的预算。如平津铁路按期通车，我们希望能在预算完成时执行委员会有法定人数开会讨论。与中国北方之外的邮政服务还没有恢复，但电报业务一直畅通，所以学校一直和中华医学基金会保持联系。

最近几周，官方一直没有对教育政策或对协和这样的学校发出任何通知。非官方的消息表明，官方对协和在培养医学教师和领导的工作很感兴趣，还善意地提请我们保护设备和建筑。对于未来的发展我们无从而知。我们向你们保证，我们清醒地意识到肩负着执行创始人和董事会制定的目标的责任。

你们真诚的，

李宗恩

院长

非正式医学教授会议总结[1]

1949年5月

Recapitulation of Informal Medical Faculty Conferences

January – May 1949

By Dr. C. U. Lee

During the past 5 months, a series of 12 conferences have been held, at which various aspects of medical education were taken up and discussed. It is my pleasure, today, to give a resume of our discussions and attempt some general conclusions.

In reviving the College two years ago we were fortunate in having before us a shining pattern evolved through years of experience and experimentation. Of course, from the very beginning we realized that the PUMC pattern was eminently a child of evolution which grows with time and is never static. So as soon as we got a nucleus of our faculty together, we set about arranging opportunities for reviewing our aims and objectives as well as techniques and procedures. I think we have all enjoyed the series of informal conferences we have had, and our discussions have resulted in a number of agreements on general principles tending towards the achievement of a unity of purpose which is of considerable importance at a time like this.

At these conferences topics have been introduced by one or two speakers who have not only reviewed the historical aspect of the subject on hand, which has given us a sense of continuity with the past, but at the same time have summarized for us its modern development bringing the group up-to-date on the subject.

The discussions following such introductions were always free and informal, being the kind of group thinking which is indispensable in developing our educational policy for the future.

Personal – Basic Doctor

Since problems of medical education are our primary concern, we attempted to estimate at the outset the kind of personnel most urgently needed in the development of a national medical service. In view of the size and complexity of the problem, it is, of course, difficult to reach any definite conclusion but we seem to be agreed on the urgent need of at least one category of personnel, the basic doctor, which will be the backbone of the profession. We indicated the essential qualities and qualifications of such a doctor: (1) He must himself enjoy both physical and mental health. By mental health we mean social adjustment, implying a sympathetic understanding of other people and a responsiveness to their needs as well as personal adjustment involving the individual's understanding of himself, his poise, and adequacy in coping with real situations. (2) He must have a background of reasonably sound general education. (3) He must possess a professional education which is well balanced and integrated giving adequate, if not equal, emphasis on the preventive, curative and social aspects of medicine. (4) Above all, he must have a sense of responsibility as a citizen and a

[1] PUMC Archive.

physician. I think we were agreed that the proper training for this type of personnel requires at least a period of 6 years with internship following senior middle school. We also felt that there is room for considerable improvement in the educational standard of the existing middle schools.

Aim of PUMC

As to the aims of special schools like the PUMC we are of one opinion that our future mission still lies in the preparation of teachers, specialists and investigators. We can best perform our specific function by maintaining an undergraduate school of high standing and at the same time undertaking graduate training in all the academic departments. Further we are not unaware of our social responsibilities as a medical school towards the continuous improvement of the quality and type of medicine practiced in the community.

Selection of Entrants:

In view of our interest in developing leaders among our graduates, we took pains to review our methods of selecting entrants. We rely not only on the applicants' college records but also on the observations and recommendations of premedical deans and teachers. All of us are also watching with interest the use of personal interviews as a selection device. This method is still in the experimental stage with us and it will be sometime before reliable results can be obtained to establish its worth in evaluating personality traits. The development of some appropriate aptitude test has also been recommended.

In the past, our field of selection has been almost exclusively confined to a small group of private colleges but efforts have been and are being made to widen our contacts so as to include some national collages with strong science departments.

I am sure the Committee on Admissions will soon be taking up the task of reviewing our present entrance requirements and method of selection, which has not been done for almost 30 years.

Undergraduate Teaching

The PUMC undergraduate teaching has been considered at three sittings on preclinical and clinical fields and public health and preventive medicine.

In these discussions, a number of important principles met with unanimous approval.

(1) Repeated stress is laid on the conception of the unity of medicine and that the students must be taught to view it in its entirety and not as a series of independent disciplines. Even the division of the study of medicine into preclinical and clinical fields is a matter of expediency.

(2) The acceptance of this viewpoint led to a great deal of emphasis on the question of integration and correlation of preclinical and clinical teaching. A number of experiments are under way from which we expect some interesting results. Dr. H. C. Chang of Physiology, for example, has been taking his students into hospital wards to be shown some abnormal physical findings, not to teach them diseases but to impress upon them the significance of normal findings by contrast. Dr. Chang Chun of Anatomy advocates that the teaching of special sense organs and female pelvis should be closely correlated with clinical teaching. The teaching of public health and

preventive medicine should be spread over the whole period of four undergraduate years. The clinical and public health department have recently been experimenting on joint conferences in presenting to the students certain pathological conditions.

(3) The importance of the social aspects of medicine seems to be accepted without question. It is also agreed that the teaching of the preventive, social, and environmental aspects of medicine in individual patients can best be done in the clinical clerkship years and by clinicians. Dr. H. C. Chang of Medicine also says that the humanistic element of medicine should be inculcated in the students along with the scientific, so that one will not be unduly emphasized to the neglect of the other. Treating of medical problems from the standpoint of the community is the function of the department of public health.

(4) Dissatisfaction is, however, expressed in the present shortage of teaching personnel which places such a heavy burden of routine on everyone that it retards the development of any investigative activities. Financial considerations also put a serious limitation on the number of free beds required for proper teaching. Remedies must be sought to improve the situation or else the educational standard of the College will deteriorate. Voluntary contributions from the community and government subsidy have been suggested but without adequate discussion as to their implications.

Examinations and Grading

Consideration and discussion of the present system of examinations and tests in grading medical undergraduates elicited a number of problems. The merits and demerits of the orthodox essay type and the more objective methods of examination were discussed as well as certain essentially subjective methods. The opinion of the group indicates that no single method answers all requirements and a combination of methods will always be necessary. With some of the methods more extended experience is required in estimating their degree of reliability. Dr. Zia emphasizes the importance of making teachers and students realize that examination is for the benefit of both and should therefore be a friendly exercise. The records of the PUMC students up to 1942 were studied and a comparison of their premedical, PUMC entrance and final grades show some rough correlation but also obvious discrepancies. An attempt to correlate their academic grades with their subsequent activities indicates that as of the present date only 1/5 of the 300 odd graduates turn out to be teachers and investigators, amongst whom the proportion of the best and mediocre students are about equal. A much higher proportion of the best and good students are in private practice, while the smallest proportion of the best students are in government and hospital services. Many outside factors, of course, have contributed to this present distribution so that no safe conclusion can be drawn from this analysis. In 1941, for example, only 8 out of 272 graduates were in private practices. The important thing for us to keep in mind is to ensure that our students are equipped to give creative service in whatever field they may be enlisted.

Curriculum Reform

On curriculum reform Dr. C.H. Hu rightly emphasizes that the success of a medical school depends largely if not entirely on the quality of the teachers and students and the nature of their relationship. Curriculum is a mere teaching program.

The development of the present curriculum is in line with the modern trend away from didactic teaching to practice in the laboratory and hospital wards, from textbook assignments to the use of library, from factual knowledge to fundamental principles and from spoon feeding to independent learning. There has been a reduction of total required hours from 4785 in 1922 to the present 3937 with weekly blocks of free hours for the students to pursue special individual interests. Here I would like to pay a tribute to Dr. Dieuaide for his lasting contribution to the building up of our model curriculum which embodies all the best principles in modern teaching. Curriculum must however be subject to constant review. There are subjects deserving more emphasis than they have received in the past such as psychsomatic medicine, social aspects of medicine, and medical jurisprudence but Dr. Hu has stressed the fact that such additions must be accompanied by corresponding reductions elsewhere in the curriculum and not by increasing the total number of hours. Dr. Hu also suggests that students should be encouraged to make more frequent use of the Chinese language in the expression of scientific ideas. The suggestion of conducting conferences on the CPC pattern in the teaching of psychosomatic or social medicine seems to meet with universal favor. Requiring student-clerks to recommend preventive measures in their history writing was also an interesting thought. The rest of the discussion on this subject was a reiteration of the principles already referred to.

Graduate Preclinical

Two sittings were given to graduate teaching in the preclinical and clinical fields. Dr. Adolph reminds us that our purpose in graduate instruction is to educate educators. Who are these educators that the preclinical departments undertake to train? They are either prospective teachers or investigators in any of the preclinical fields, or clinicians requiring a shorter or longer period of basic training in preparation for specialization in the clinical fields. It seems that the system of graduate teaching is much better organized in the clinical than in the preclinical fields. The demonstrator system parallel to the hospital resident system should be strengthened. This has, of course, certain financial implications but if by so doing we may encourage medical graduates to specialize in preclinical subjects it should be seriously considered. Aside from this, a greater degree of planning is needed for graduate training in the preclinical departments. The tutorial system should prove more flexible in meeting specific individual needs than formal courses. Arrangement for graduate students in one department to spend some time in other allied departments would broaden their training. The training of clinicians in preclinical fields is a special problem. We might consider the desirability of making a period of study in one of the preclinical subjects a prerequisite to taking up any clinical specialty, in line with the requirements of the U.S. Specialty Boards.

The limited opportunities for advancement in preclinical fields in comparison with those in clinical fields was cited as an important reason for the failure of medical graduates to be attracted to these fields. The possibility of padding preclinical salaries at a somewhat higher level than clinical salaries was suggested as one way of offsetting this situation. Some sort of certificate or degree at the conclusion of a program of preclinical studies might serve as an inducement. Medical graduates should be especially encouraged to take up such fields as pathology, pharmacology and immunology.

On the question of educational methods there was general agreement that to develop teacher's actual participation in teaching while under training, is essential. This is one of the reasons for maintaining an undergraduate school to ensure successful graduate teaching. Although the majority of the group felt that teachers are born rather that taught, seminars on educational methods are not without their value but the approach to teaching methods should always be experimental.

The development of graduate training in biophysics received some attention. The best way of developing the use of biophysical methods at the present time will be through inter-departmental cooperation.

Graduate Teaching Clinical

For graduate training in the clinical fields the residency system in vogue is eminently satisfactory and has been most productive. The value of straight internship is stressed and if 3 beds for each student in the two undergraduate clinical years is considered minimum for effective teaching than there should be 15-25 beds for each intern or assistant resident. As to non-resident graduate students these are usually fellows wishing to spend a period of time on some special study. Individual programs must be arranged for them. Intensive refresher courses used to be conducted regularly in obstetrics and gynecology and their revival in all the clinical departments may meet a special need at the present juncture when so much experimenting is going on elsewhere in mass production of medical personnel. We are not sure of the wisdom of such well-intentioned activities but if we could in some way influence the technical standard of those taking part in these experiments should we not plan some short courses for them provided such diversion of effort would not affect our own set program? The content of such courses will have to be carefully worked out.

（译文）

非正式医学教授会议总结

1949年1月-5月

作者：李宗恩医生

在过去的 5 个月里，（协和医学院的教授们）在 12 次会议中讨论了医学教育的很多方面。今天，我很荣幸能够对这些讨论进行一下归纳，并尝试得出一些结论。

两年前，我们开始复校。很幸运，我们有经过多年实践检验了的宝贵模式可以借鉴。从一开始，我们就清楚，协和模式就像一个正在成长的小孩子，必须与时俱进，而不能一成不变。因此，我们的核心教师队伍一组成，就立即安排重审协和的办学宗旨、目标、方法以及程序。我个人认为，大家在参与这些非正式的讨论中，心情都很愉快；而且对一些基本原则也达成共识。在这一特殊时刻，这些意见对于实现我们的共同目标至关重要。

每个在会议上讨论的题目，首先由一或两位发言人回顾这方面的有关历史，使我们明晰前人所作的努力；在此基础上，再总结这个题目的最新进展，从而让我们对此题目处于资讯最前沿。

在充分了解了每一题目之后，与会者畅所欲言，各抒己见。这样的群体意见，对我们未来教育方针的发展至关重要。

医生的基本素质

因为医学教育是我们关注的首要问题，我们首先就要考量什么样的人是国家医疗服务发展中最迫切需要的人材。鉴于此问题宽泛而复杂，我们很难得出一定的结论，但我们基本认同，至少有一类人是迫切需要的——基层医生——医疗事业的中坚力量。我们认为，从事医生工作，应具备如下基本素质和资格：（1）他应该身心健全。精神健康，我们是指社会适应能力，即对他人的同情和理解，对他人的需求给予回应，个人的悟性包括对自己的了解、自信和随机应变的能力；（2）他必须有足够的综合的知识积累；（3）他必须具备专业知识，具有平衡而综合地运用预防医学、治疗方法、社会学等各方面知识的能力；（4）最后，他必须具备作为一个公民和医生的责任感。我们一致认为，培训出这样的人材至少需要在高中毕业后再接受 6 年医学教育和临床实习。我们还认为，现在的中学教育水平有相当大的提高空间。

协和医学院的办学方针

我们一直认为，协和是一所特殊的学校，肩负的使命仍在于培养教师、专家和研究人员。这一特殊使命，我们可以通过保持我们高水平的（医学）本科教育来实现，同时在所有科系培养研究生。我们明白，我们的社会责任是不断提高医疗的质量和种类。

新生的选择

因为我们有意在毕业生中培养领军人物，所以在录取标准上应该格外用心。我们不仅要看申请人的大学成绩，而且还应该听取医学预科院长和教师的观察和建议。作为一种尝试，我们对把个人面试作为录取的手段之一也很感兴趣，这种方法对评估人格特质很有益处。还有人提议要开发出一些适当的资质测验。

过去，我们选择新生的范围基本局限于几所私立大学，但我们已经开始并将继续努力扩宽招生范围，包括一些拥有较强理科的国立高校。

我相信，招生委员会将会很快重审现在的入学要求和录取标准，这是一件30年来都没有完成的事。

医学本科教学

协和的本科教学侧重于基础医学、临床医学、公共卫生和预防医学三个专业。

在这些讨论中，一些重要的原则得到了大家的一致认可。

（1）要反复强调医学的整体性，即要教育学生把医学作为一个完整的体系来看，而不是一系列独立的学科。甚至基础医学和临床医学被分开来教，也只是一种权宜之计。

（2）就此而论，我们必须在教学中强调将基础医学和临床医学相互渗透和整合的重要性。我们正在进行一些实验，想必不久就会看到一些有意思的结果。例如，生理系的张锡钧教授带领学生去病房观察一些异常体征，目的不是为了教他们疾病知识，而是让他们通过对比异常情况来加深对正常体征的印象。解剖系的张鋆教授强调，特殊感觉器官与女性骨盆的教学必须结合临床进行。公共卫生和预防医学的教学应该贯穿于四年的医学课程中。最近，临床和公共卫生系开始用联合研讨会的方式，教授学生一些病理知识。

（3）社会医学的重要性得到了大家的一致认可。对于预防、社会和环境因素对医疗的影响，我们认为，由临床医生在学生实习时，针对个别病例进行教学是最好的方式。张孝骞教授认为，医疗中的人文元素应该随着科学知识一起讲授给学生，这样他们不会顾此失彼。从社区的角度解决医疗问题，是公共卫生系的职能所在。

（4）目前教学人员的短缺，使得每个人都肩负了沉重的负担，没有余力从事任何科学研究。开支问题也严重限制了正常教学所需的免费床位的数量。必须寻求补救措施来改善这种情况，否则学校的教学水平将会下降。有人建议寻求社会和政府的捐款，但这将产生什么影响，我们还没有充分地讨论。

考试与评分

对现行医学本科生考试和评分制度的考量，引起了热烈的讨论。我们讨论了传统的论文考试和比较客观的考试方法的优缺点，以及某些比较主观的测试方法。我们一致认为，没有一种方法可以满足所有要求，必须用多种考试方法才能达到目的。有一些方法需要更多的实践检验，才能确定其可靠性。谢少文教授强调，要让老师和学生们意识到，考试应该是一个友好的练习，对双方各有益处。我们研究了1942年以前协和医学院学生的记录，比较了他们的医学预科、医学院入学考试成绩和毕业成绩，发现它们之间有一些相关性，但也有明显的差异。我们试图比较他们的学习成绩和毕业后的业绩，截止目前的数据显示，在300多名毕业生中只有五分之一成为教师和科研人员，这与优秀生和普通生的比例是一致的。 最好和较好的学生在私人诊所的比例则要高得多，在政府和医院服务的最优秀学生的比例最低。当然，现在这种分布情况也受许多外部因素的影响，因此，无法从这些分析中得出绝对准确的结论。例如至1941年，272名毕业生中只有8名在私人诊所。但我们必须切记的是，无论他们在哪个领域工作，我们的学生都在提供创新式的服务。

教学改革

在教学改革方面，胡正详教授的发言被所有人认可：医学院的成功与否，如果不是百分之百，但至少很大一部分是取决于学生和老师的质量以及他们之间的关系，课程安排只是一个单纯的教学计划。

目前教学改革与现代教学的趋势是一致的，即远离说教式教学，采用在实验室和医院病房实习的模式；远离课本作业，利用图书馆；从书本知识到基本原理；从填鸭式教学到独立学习。我们已经把课时从 1922 年的 4785 小时所缩减到现在的 3937 小时，而且每周专门留出空余时间让学生们去做自己感兴趣的事。在这里，我要对狄维德医生在课程设置方面所作出的经历了时间检验的贡献表示敬意，狄维德（Francis R. Dieuaide，1892-1977[1]）医生所设置的课程体现了现代教学中的最佳原则。尽管如此，课程设置是需要不断进行审核的。根据过去的经验，我们认为，心理生理医学、社会医学和法医学等课程应该受到重视，但胡正详教授强调，如果增加这些课程，就必须相应地缩减其他课程的

[1] Francis R. Dieuaide，协和医学院内科主任（1927-1941）。

课时，以保证总课时不会增加。胡教授还建议，我们应该鼓励学生尽可能地使用中文表达科学概念。关于以临床病理研讨会（CPC）的方式来教授生理心理学或社会医学的建议，得到了一致赞同。另一个有意义的提议是，要求学生在书写病历时建议预防措施。关于这个话题的其他讨论，不过是对上面提到的一些原则的重复。

基础医学教学

我们为研究生设立了基础医学和临床医学两个专业的教学。窦威廉（Willian H. Adolph，1890-1958）[1]医生提醒我们，研究生教学的目的是培养教育者。那么谁将是这些将被培养成教育者的人选呢？他们具备成为教授、研究某种基础医学的潜质，他们也许是临床医生，希望通过时间或短或长的基础医学学习，准备进入某一临床专业领域。现在的研究生临床教学似乎比基础医学更规范化，因此，相应于实习医师的示范性教学，基础医学教学需要加强。这当然要把财务因素考虑在内，但如果实施，我们可以开始鼓励医学生专攻基础科目。此外，我们需要更大程度的规划基础医学毕业生的培养。与正规课程相比，导师制应该更灵活地满足个人的志趣。安排一个科室的研究生到另一个相关的科室工作一段时间，将会拓宽对他们的培训。对临床医生在基础医学方面的培训是一个特殊问题。我们可以参考美国的专业考试制度，把完成相关基础医学的必修课定位成进入临床专科学习的先决条件。

和临床领域的提升空间相比，基础领域的机会有限，这是医学毕业生对基础领域不感兴趣的重要原因。为改变这一现状，我们建议增加基础医学教员的工资，使其稍高于临床医生。另一个办法，是为基础医学培训结业时提供证书或学位。我们尤其要鼓励医学院的毕业生从事病理学、药理学和免疫学等领域的工作。

关于教学方法的问题，我们的共识为，对教师的培养，实际参与教学至关重要，保留医学本科的原因之一就是确保研究生教学的成功。尽管我们中的大

[1] Willian H. Adolph：1915 年获宾夕法尼亚大学博士学位，来华任教齐鲁大学。1926 年回国，1929 年来华任教燕京大学化学系，曾任系主任。太平洋战争爆发后，被日军拘禁，1943 年返美，任教耶鲁大学。战后返华，曾代理燕京大学校务长，1947-1950 年任协和医学院生化系教授，系主任。著有《近世无机化学》，由曹惠群编译，1922 年由博医会出版。

多数人认为教师是天生的，而不是教出来的，但教学方法的讲座仍然有它的价值。不过，每种教学方法都是一种尝试。

培养生物物理研究生的进展引起了我们的关注。大家认为，目前发展生物物理技术的最好的方式是通过跨部门的合作。

临床研究生教学

至于临床研究生培养，目前流行的住院实习医生制度非常令人满意，而且卓有成效。实习阶段的训练很有价值，为确保两年的本科临床教学有效地进行，每个学生至少要有 3 个床位，每个实习医生或住院医助理至少有 15-25 个床位。非住院医研究生一般希望花大量时间进行一些专业的学习，他们也会被安排学习一些特定的课程。精修课程过去只限于妇产科，现在所有的临床科室都可以恢复精修课程，这对很多地区因为急需大批医疗人员，开始进行速成医学教育，应该是有益的。虽然我们不确定速成医生教育是否是最好的解决办法，但我们能够在某一层面影响参与这些实验的教师的水准。基于这种考虑，我们应该在不影响我们自己工作的前提下，计划开设一些短期课程，为他们做一些努力。我们将对这些课程进行仔细地研究。

致施正信教授信[1]

March 22, 1949

Dr. T. S. Sze
Institute of Social Medicine
10 Parks Road
Oxford, England

Dear T. S.:

I was delighted to have your letter of February 5, which came a week ago after six weeks of postal interruption. It is good to know that you and your family are happily installed in peaceful Oxford. How fortunate you were in getting out of the country just in time before the storm broke!

We have been remarkably fortunate in coming through a period of siege lasting 40 days. You will be glad to know that we are all safe and sound. The work of the College was uninterrupted though the state of tension was quite acute while it lasted. About one hundred shells fell in various parts of the city; all the physical damage we suffered amounted to no more than a broken windowpane. The spirit and morale of the staff were excellent throughout. We were able to have a new ward opened in the early part of January as planned. The turnover was peaceful and orderly. If you were here now, you would not notice much difference, at least within the campus of this College. Indications are that we shall be allowed to carry on without much interference and naturally we have to make adjustments from time to time, but it will be a very interesting experience. We still hope that some understanding for a general peace will be reached in the near future. One does not get very much news from the outside world, but one has the uncomfortable feeling that the development in the international situation is not as constructive as could be desired. I hope, however, nothing catastrophic will really happen for with all the modern scientific weapons, the human race is quite capable of destroying itself; then where will be your humanism and all the rest of it?

I was very much interested in your remarks on the trend of medical education in Great Britain. I would like to hear more from you about the way the integrated course is run in Birmingham. Our faculty members here have fortnight conferences during which we study problems connected with medical education in China. Opinions tend to favor more coordination and integration of the various aspects of medicine in place of the old departmentalized method of teaching. Everybody seems to accept the principle but putting it into practice is another matter. Years ago, PUMC experimented on integrated courses but failed from the technical point of view. We are, however, getting ready to make another attempt at it. I have a feeling that whatever success one may attain in medical education depends ultimately on the quality of the staff and students rather than on curriculum itself. We have reasons to be well satisfied with our

[1] Letter Lee to T. S. Sze, March 22, 1949, PUMC Archive.

present second-year class composed of members who show exceptional intellectual maturity and independence. It is one of the best classes we have ever had.

One of our chief difficulties at present or in the near future is the securing of young blood to our teaching personnel. If you know of any of our compatriots studying in Great Britain, especially in the fields of Biochemistry and Pharmacology, I shall appreciate having from you any details about such people. Please keep it in mind in your travels and contacts.

It has been a long time since your father-in-law, Mr. Wang, called on us, but I believe he is still in Peking. Somebody has seen him recently on the street. Joan's letter in care of me was delivered to him. Please keep me informed of your plans and movements.

With kindest regards to you and yours, in which Jean joins me,

Yours sincerely,

C. U. Lee

（译文）

施正信医生

社会医学院

帕克路 10 号

牛津，英国

亲爱的正信:

在 6 个星期邮路中断之后，我很高兴在上周收到你 2 月 5 日来信，特别是得知你们一家已经在和平的剑桥安居。你真运气，在暴风雨到来之前离开了中国。

我们十分幸运地度过了围城的 40 天。你会高兴地知道我们一切都好。在情况最紧急的那段时间，学校的工作也没有中断。大概有一百发炮弹落在城里不同的地方，但我们唯一的损失只是一个窗户的玻璃。职工们的情绪一直很高。我们还按计划在 1 月初开了一个新病房。交接和平有序，如果你在这里，不会看出有什么不同，至少在这个校园内。迹象表明，我们的正常活动不会受到任何阻碍，我们当然不时要做出调整，不过那也会是很有趣的经历。我们仍希望不久的将来会有某种和平解决的方式。我们很少听到外面的消息，但总感觉国际局势的发展令人担忧。不过，我希望这么多现代武器不会导致大灾难，人类完全有能力毁灭自己，那么我们的人道主义及其他呢?

我对你信中提到的英国在医学教育方面的发展趋势极感兴趣。请告诉我伯明翰的综合课程的内容。我们这里的教员开了14个会议，集体讨论中国医学教育的问题。大家倾向于增加协调和综合的课程，取代旧式的按科系的教学方法。每个人都在原则上接受了，但实际做起来就是另一回事了。多年前，协和试验过综合课程，但因技术原因没有成功。不过，我们现在正准备再试一次。我的感觉是，医学教育的进步最终还取决于教师和学生的质量，而不是课程安排。我们对现在的医学二年级就十分满意，他们之中有不少人非常成熟和独立。这是我们有史以来最好的一班学生。

我们现在的主要问题之一是，如何保证教师团队中有年轻的教员。如果你知道或在认识人里知道有正在英国学习的华人，尤其是在生化和药理方面的，我非常感谢你能把他们的信息告诉我。

自从你的丈人王先生来访之后，好久没有他的消息了。不过我认为他还在北京，有人最近在街上见到了他。我已经把琼让我转交的信给他了。请随时告诉我你们的计划和行踪。

我和晋[1]向你们致以最亲切的问候，

你真诚的，

李宗恩

[1] 编者注，即夫人何晋。

致娄克斯医生信[1]

1949 年 7 月 8 日

Dear Dr. Loucks:

The attached copy of Mr. Bowen's letter of July 1st to Dr. Wilson[2] is of course no surprise except for his decision to leave so soon. I had hoped that he would stay on at least until after your return, but he appears to have decided on an early departure largely as a result of the recent labor difficulties which have brought him to the conclusion that his inability to use the Chinese language and his particular temperament as well as his being a foreigner combine to minimize to a serious degree his usefulness to the institution under the external circumstances in which we are now working.

The first I knew of his decision was when I received a copy of his letter to Dr. Wilson, so I had no chance to influence him in advance as to the timing of his departure. Yesterday and today, however, I have had long and satisfactory talks with him from which I was glad to gain the definite impression that his is not leaving any spirit of bitterness or dissatisfaction, but that he has rationalized the situation in what seem to him reasonable terms. It is true that after the initial dismissal of the eleven men which he did through an interpreter the subsequent course of events has of necessity developed apart from him although he has of course participated in the Business Division meetings at which all policies applied in the negotiations have been determined. In my conversations with him, I asked if he would be willing to defer his departure for a time, but he said that he prefers, for the reasons already stated, to leave without delay other than that involved in getting passage.

From your own observations in the months following the liberation of Peiping, I am sure you will understand when I say that in the present period of transition there is inevitably confusion and indecision even in the higher official quarters. The Communists themselves realize their lack of experience in government administration, especially as applied to urban situations. They are therefore deliberately tardy in making decisions and adopting policies, hoping to gain time and experience before actually formulating rules and regulations. Hence their technique of numerous conferences and lengthy discussions which much of the time are simply a delaying tactic. In the meantime, institutional administration is necessarily very hit-or-miss.

An example of the existing confusion is the situation arising from the failure to state clearly the difference from the union point of view between colleges and universities on the one hand and industrial plants on the other, although the higher authorities recognize such a difference. In our own case this has meant that the Central Labor Union instructed our Workers' Union that it should reorganize to take in all categories of persons employed in the institution, while at the same time the educational authorities state that apart from the Workers Union there should first be a staff union comprising the faculty, other teaching members and the clerical staff, with

---

[1] Letter Lee to Loucks, July 8, 1949, RAC, CMB Inc. Records, Box 47, Folder 334.

[2] Stanley D. Wilson, 协和医学院董事会董事（1941-1949）。

the intention of ultimately amalgamating the two groups into a single "vertical" union which would become a member of the Central Labor Union.

In the course of time such situations will be straightened out as new administrative techniques can be developed. The establishment of a Central Government and of some sort of international relations, whenever this takes place, should clarify things to a considerable extent. At the moment, however, it may be fairly said that everything is in a state of flux, governmentally. The educational authorities, the health authorities, and even the labor authorities are not ready to give rulings of guidance on problems of administration of such institutions as ours. At the same time, former rules and regulations no longer are accepted as valid. The best course of action for us therefore seems to be to avoid "incidents" whenever possible, to apply such palliative measures as may be required from time to time in specific situations, and to play for time until we have a definite framework of government within which to operate.

You will appreciate the irksomeness of such a situation to us all, but especially to a man of Mr. Bowen's temperament. I had hoped he would stay on for some months yet, and in the light of your reports of Mr. Parker's reactions to his going and to that of Mr. Alston, I have done what I could to hold him. I am truly sorry to lose anyone from our administrative group at this moment when it is none too large or strong, but he cannot see that it would be useful to the College for him to continue under present external circumstances, and there seems no possibility of getting him to reverse his decision. Incidentally, I think it is important to note that in my opinion his nationality has no bearing on this particular situation.

Since it seems definite that he will leave whenever passage is available, and since as you know that may come on very short notice, I asked him about his ideas on covering his various responsibilities. His suggestions are as follows:

1. Signing of checks – to be assigned by the Trustees to some other officer.
2. Cashier – to be responsible to the Director; to settle exchange and attend to other banking matters with the specific approval each time of the Business Division.
3. Acting Engineer – to be responsible to the Director for the operation of the physical plant and shops; to hold regular conferences with the Director once or twice a week, for reporting and discussing matters affecting the physical plant; to be ready to ask for periodic consultations with consulting engineers.
4. Purchasing Division – for the time being, Mr. Emslie to spend an hour or two a day in the division, checking on requisitions and orders.

You will see that except for the Purchasing Division, his proposals are in effect the transfer to my shoulders of the responsibilities assigned to the Treasurer. To meet the present situation I am ready for a limited period to take on these added duties, but in the course of the next few months some more satisfactory and permanent solution must be found, especially with the greatly increased load of attendance at outside meeting of one sort or another which has come to me with the new regime. I asked Mr. Bowen if he had any suggestions for a successor and he had none except to voice his conviction that it should not be a foreigner. When I told him that Alfred Sun had once jokingly said that he was tired of banking and when Mr. Bowen left would be glad to take his place, he was greatly struck with the idea and said he could think of no better choice. The more he thought about it the more enthusiastic he became, and the mere mention of this as possibility seemed to give him a real lift in spirit.

Yesterday Dr. Wilson telephoned to say that he had a sailing freighter, the SS Polar Bear, from Tientein July 16th, and in order to have a meeting of the Executive Committee before he goes, Mr. Chu is coming up from Tientsin on Sunday, the 10th. At that meeting Mr. Bowen's resignation will be brought up along with the proposals for the interim handling of his responsibilities. I am not sure that the question of a successor should be discussed at that time, but I will talk to Mr. Chu before the meeting as well as to Dr. Wilson to get their reactions.

You will notice that Mr. Bowen's proposals do not contemplate asking the Controller to assume any additional responsibilities. It is his opinion, in which I concur and with which I think you will agree, that Mr. Chen is now carrying the maximum that we should ask of him, and that we should guard against any planned or unwitting broadening of the scope of his duties.

Mr. Bowen continues to express complete confidence in the capacity of Archie Chang to run the physical plant and shops satisfactorily, and in his probity, he believes that any attempt to put anyone over him, whether foreign or Chinese, would be disastrous since Archie would probably under these circumstances refuse to stay on and the group of senior foremen who under him make a cooperative team might give rise to serious difficulties. Lacking the blueprints which the Japanese took away or destroyed, we are often dependent on the personal knowledge of this group as to the lay-out of the installation. Without them we would frequently be completely in the dark. (this makes me wonder if perhaps in the New York office there are blueprints of the various installations – electrical, mechanical, water and steam lines, waste pipes etc? if so it would be useful to have copies sent out to Peiping.)

It seems possible that we may need to wait until the new power plant materializes before we get the kind of engineer that Mr. Parker has in mind, and in the meantime to keep a constant vigilance over our present set-up. In our discussions this morning I pointed out to Mr. Bowen the fact that with the physical plant taking up 40% of our budget, we cannot afford to have it in any but competent hands. He repeated his conviction that Archie is thoroughly competent.

I hope to add a postscript to this after our meeting on Sunday, and then to ask Mr. Chu to take it back to Tientsin with him and put it in the hands of someone who will be leaving on the B & S sailing on the 12th, so that it can be mailed in Korea and reach you before you leave. In my cable of the 6th I included the information that the B & S ships are coming to Tientsin as usual and that we have informed the steamship agents that your reentry has been assured, so that you could make your plans accordingly. We will be glad when the cable comes that gives the actual date on which you expect to fly from the USA.

July 10th – 2 pm

We had just finished the Executive Committee meeting, and I enclose an annotated docket. I have nothing to add beyond the notes of the actions as shown on the docket, which you will see make Mr. Bowen's retirement effective as at the end of the month in which he leaves. (He is now trying to get on a ship one week from today, but if he fails to get that sailing, it may be another month before he gets off.) I was glad to have the trustees agree with me that the proposals for handling the Treasurer's responsibilities must be considered a temporary expedient only. They feel strongly that other more permanent arrangements must be made as soon as possible. – I will be cabling you tomorrow about the travel provision for Y.K. Feng and H.T Chang. I think that at the present time this action is a wise one.

CU Lee

（译文）

亲爱的娄克斯医生：

附上鲍恩先生 7 月 1 日写给威尔逊医生的信，他的决定应在意料之中，我原来希望他至少能等到你回来再走，没想到他这么快就要离开。最近的劳资纠纷让他觉得在当今的外界环境下，不会讲中文、他的脾气、还有作为一个外国人等因素，他对学校的用处有限，所以决定提早离开。

我是从他给威尔逊医生的信中得知他的决定的，所以我没有机会在之前影响他做出离开的决定。不过，我昨天和今天跟他进行了比较满意的长谈，从中我欣慰地了解到他没有怨言和不快，他是在理智地考虑了所有情况之后才做出了这个决定的。确实，最初他通过翻译解聘了 11 个人，接下来发生的一系列事情他没有直接参与，虽然他列席了总务处决定调解政策的所有会议。在我们的谈话中，我问他是否可以晚些离开，但他说，根据以上所说的原因，他宁愿一办好手续就走。

根据你对北平解放后的观察，肯定理解在目前交接时期，各级管理甚至高层都不可避免地会有感到混淆杂沓和举棋不定的问题。共产党本身也意识到他们缺乏政府管理的经验，特别是大城市。所以他们有意识地推迟作出决定、制定政策，希望在真正建立落实政策和制度之前积累时间和经验。他们的做法是开很多会，在长长的讨论中耗费时间。此间，学校的管理就只能靠猜测了。

仅举一个混乱的例子，虽然当局已经承认学校工会和工厂工会不同，但具体有何区别却无从而知。就我们的情况而言，总工会指示我们的工会面向学校的所有人员，但同时教育当局说除了工人工会之外，还要有一个由教授、其他教员和职员组成的工会，最后把两组人合并成一个由中央工会领导的"垂直"的工会。

希望不久在新的管理体制建立起来后，这种情况得到改善。现在中央政府成立了，待国际关系得以发展后，这些事情早晚应该得到一定程度上的解决。不过此时，政府方面的所有事务都不稳定。教育当局、医疗当局、甚至劳工当局还不能对我们这样一个机构的管理做出明确的指示。同时，过去的规则和政策又不再有效。所以对我们来说，最好的办法就是尽可能避免出“事故”，在特殊情况下使用这一缓兵之计也许很有必要，直到我们有一个政府的条例可以遵循。

你会理解这一情况让我们所有人都感到不快，特别是像鲍恩先生那样脾气的人。我曾经请他能再工作几个月，特别从你那里得知帕克(Philo W. Parker)[1]先生对他和 Alston 先生离去的反应，我尽了一切努力挽留他。此刻我们的管理队伍并不强大，我真不愿意失去任何人，但他看不到在现在的外部环境中，他对学校还有什么用处，让他改变这一决定已无可能。不过，我不认为他的国籍在这一事件中有什么特别之处。

因为一安排好行程他就会离开，我向他征求谁来做他留下来的工作，下面是他的建议：

1. 签署支票：请董事会找其他管理人员
2. 出纳员：向院长汇报；负责兑换和跟银行有关的事务，每次需经业务部门特别批准
3. 代理工程师：向院长汇报设备和修理问题；和院长每周开一至两次会议，汇报所有设备问题，按期向工程师顾问咨询
4. 采购部门：Emslie 先生暂时每天花 1-2 小时，处理采购和订单事务

你会看出来，除了采购部门，他的建议实际上把财务的责任转到我的肩上了。为了解决眼下的问题，我准备暂时担负起这些多出来的责任，但希望在今后几个月内会找到永久的解决办法，特别是现在新政府总要求我去开这样那样的会议，又增加了我的额外的负担。我问鲍恩先生是否可以推荐一个接班人，他说没有，但坚信不能是外国人。当我告诉他孙锡三[2]曾开玩笑说，他厌倦了银行工作，要是鲍恩先生走了，他可以补缺。鲍恩非常赞同，说想不到更好的人选了。他越想越喜欢，好像这个想法让他在精神上得到了解脱。

昨天威尔逊（Stanley D. Wilson）[3]医生打电话告知，他计划乘 7 月 16 日从天津起航的 SS Polar Bear，为了在他离开之前召开执行委员会开会，朱先生将

[1] Philo W. Parker, 中华医学基金会主席（1945-1956）。

[2] 孙锡三，T. Alfred Sun，中孚商业银行总经理，协和医学院董事(1941-1944, 1947-1951)。

[3] Stanley D. Wilson, 协和医学院董事会董事（1941-1949）。

于 10 日从天津赶来。会议将讨论鲍恩先生的辞职及如何继续他留下的工作问题。我不确定是否那是讨论他的继任者的最好时机，但我会在会前和朱先生和威尔逊医生沟通的。

你会看到鲍恩先生在他的建议中没说增加主计员的工作量。他认为陈先生的工作负荷已到顶点了，不应该再让他做更多。这一点我或还有你都同意。

鲍恩一直对张承平[1]管理工厂和修理厂的能力很满意，也觉得他诚实。鲍恩觉得如果让他服从于某人的领导，无论是中国人还是外国人，将会引起大问题。因为他将会辞职，而那些在他手下协调工作的高级技工将有可能闹事。因为日本人拿走了或销毁了图纸，我们不得不经常依靠这些人对仪器设备的工作经验。如果没有他们，我们就真的无从下手了。（说到这儿，我想也许纽约办公室有一份这些仪器设备的图纸，包括电路、机器、水管、蒸汽管道和下水道？如果有的话，请把复印件寄到北平）

也许我们应该等到新的发电厂设备到了以后再聘用帕克先生建议的工程师，与此同时细心维护我们现有的设备。今天早上和鲍恩的交谈中，我向他指出因为工厂的花销占总预算的 40%，我们必须用最好的管理者。他重复了 Archie 有丰富的经验。

我准备周日开完会再写几句，然后让朱先生带回天津，请 12 日坐 B&S 船走的人带到韩国寄出，你就可以在走之前接到信了。我 6 号发出的电报中提到 B&S 船照常开到天津，我们已经通知他们你可以再入境，你可以把这些考虑在计划之中。我们会高兴地获知你从美国返回的确切日期的。

7 月 10 日，下午 2 点。

我们刚开完执行委员会会议，会议记录附上。一切都在其中，我无所附加。你会看到，鲍恩先生从月底他离开时开始退休。（他正努力在下周出发的船上找到一个位子，不然就要再等一个月）我庆幸董事们同意资金管理的办法只是暂时的。他们认为必须找到长期的解决办法。我明天电报通知你 Y.K. Feng 和 N.T. Chang 的旅行计划。我认为现在这样做是合理的。

李宗恩

[1] Archie Chang，协和医学院工程师（1930-1942，1947-）。

致施正信教授信[1]

August 2, 1949

Dear T.S.,

It is almost a month since I received your good letter of June 1st which came at a time when I was busily engaged in an interesting conference of a large group of natural scientists in Peiping. The gathering included many well-known educators as well as about 60% of the Academicians of the Academia Sonica. If you were here, you would have been glad to meet many old friends. It was only a preparatory conference; the actual congress of natural scientists will probably take place in the early part of next year and an attendance of about a thousand is expected.

It is practically certain that Peiping will be the future political capital as well as a national cultural center. Very soon the new National Political Council will be convened with a view towards the formation of a new coalition government sometime in October. It is, of course, impossible for one to keep out of all these activities. The greatest consideration continues to be the economic rehabilitation of the country which, I am afraid, will be a slow process.

Your analysis of the international situation was most interesting. I quite agree with you that we are going through a most critical stage in the evolution of human history. Your diagnosis of emotional immaturity and psychological imbalance is probably correct but, dear Doctor, what is your treatment? I refuse to agree that war can provide a solution. As far as China is concerned, whatever regime can improve the lot of 95% of the population must command support.

Your dissertation makes me feel that you may be interested in the enclosed summary of a series of discussions we have had during the past six months on the same subject among our faculty members. I would like to have your comments and criticism on our viewpoints. During the Science Conference mentioned above, we have had opportunities of getting fresh points of view from the Communist leaders who have been experimenting on methods of turning out large quantities of medical personnel to meet the immediate needs of the army and the rural population. Some of their experiments are interesting but not necessarily pedagogically sound. They appreciate nevertheless the importance of quality training and have a place in their scheme of things for institutions like the PUMC. We expect no interference in our educational program. Our difficulty lies rather in the acute shortage of qualified personnel to fill vacancies among our teaching staff.

I understand that you will be away for two years. I am looking forward to a visit from you on your return. By that time, we expect there will be new developments which will make it well worth your while to take a trip north.

With best of all wishes to you, Joan and your little girl,

Yours, C. U. Lee

[1] Letter Lee to T. S. Sze, August 2, 1949, PUMC Archive.

（译文）

亲爱的正信：

收到你6月1日的信快一个月了，那时我正在北平参加一个有意思的自然科学家会议。他们中有很多教育家及60%的中央研究院院士。如果你在这里，也一定会高兴看到这么多的老朋友的。这只是一个预备会议，正式的自然科学家会议大概会在明年初举行，估计会有上千人参与。

可以肯定，北平会是将来国家的政治和文化中心。新的政协会议即将举行，目标是在10月形成一个联合政府。置身于这些活动之外，几乎是不可能的。当务之急是国家经济的恢复，但这恐怕是一个缓慢的过程。

你对于国际局势的分析很有意思。我很同意你所说的，我们正处在人类进化史上最关键的时刻。你的所谓感情上的不成熟和心理上的不平衡的诊断也许是正确的，可是，我亲爱的医生，你的治疗方案呢？我绝不同意战争会提供答案。对于中国来说，不管谁当政，只要能改善95%的人口的生活的，就应该支持。

你的论文使我觉得你应该会对此信的附件感兴趣，这是过去6个月中我们的教职员对同一题目举行的一系列会议的总结。我很想听听你对我们的看法的意见。在上述的科学会议中，我们有机会从共产党领导人那里得知，他们正在寻找训练能够满足军队和农村所需要的大批医务人员的途径。他们有的方法有些意思，但不一定是系统的教学方法。不过，他们还是支持像协和这样一个高质量的学术机构的。我们的教学也不希望受到干扰。我们的困难是找不到合格教学人员来填补空缺。

我知道你要在国外两年时间。我很期待你回来能到此访问。那时，我们应该会有值得你北上的新的进展。

送上给琼和你的小女儿最好的祝愿，

你的，

李宗恩

致皮尔斯女士信[1]

1949 年 8 月 5 日

Miss A. M. Pearce
China Medical Board, Inc.
30 East 60th Street
New York 22, N.Y.
U. S. A.

Dear Miss Pearce:

This is my first letter to you since July 8th, there having been no opportunities to send any mail out during the interim. The last letter we have had from New York was dated June 3rd and received here on July 4th. We keep hoping that mail service may soon return to something like normal, but there are no early prospects for this that I can see. If the ships between Hongkong and Tientsin continue to run, as they have just begun to do, we will at least be able to watch our chances of sending letters to Hongkong by hand for forwarding to you. Unfortunately, there seems to be some block at the Hongkong end which prevents letters being similarly passed on to us here at the present time, but perhaps in due course this situation may improve. It is a great satisfaction anyway to have passengers able to come and go. Miss Wang Mei-ying left Hongkong at last on July 29th and should be here in a few days' time. Dr. Chiang and Miss Shen have announced their arrival in Hongkong and will be coming on as soon as they can get transportation.

With this improvement in the shipping situation we are hoping that it won't be long before we hear that Dr. Loucks is on his way back. With the interruptions in the mail services we will be eager for all the direct news which he will be bringing us.

The labor situation which caused us so many headaches during June and early July has come out of the acute stage, into a stage in which we will be concentrating on the task of educating the workers to apply their newly-found consciousness of the strength of united action to constructive ends. In terms of present-day techniques this means for us frequent and lengthy conferences and meetings, but if we can get the cooperation of our large group of employees in building up and strengthening the institution it will be worth it. The eleven men whose discharge at the end of May precipitated the difficulties have all been placed in other jobs in the institution, for which we had budget provision.

Ward K-II will be opened to receive patients on August 8th, half of the ward being for further beds for Obstetrics and Gynecology, and the other half for Pediatrics. The ward is so constructed that this division can be made satisfactorily as could not be done in most of our other wards. Dr. Chow Hua-K'and, Dr. Y. T. Tsur's son, is Assistant Professor of Pediatrics in charge of the Division.

The entrance examinations were held in Peiping the first week in July. Out of twenty-seven candidates for admission we accepted eighteen, fourteen of whom were

[1] Letter Lee to Pearce, August 5, 1949, RAC, CMB Inc, Box 48, Folder 335.

from Yenching, two from Peita, one from the Catholic University, and one from the University of Nanking. Of these seven are women. In addition, seven students have been taking examinations this week in Soochow and Nanking, of whom there will no doubt be at least one or two successful. Also there are two students from last year's first year class who will be repeating the year, so that our first year class will have not less than twenty in its enroment. Considering the unsettled conditions of the past year we are well pleased at this result.

One of the things we have to learn to get used to under the new regime is the number of meetings of all sorts which we are called upon to attend. The fact that this is the summer vacation has perhaps increased the number that have been scheduled, but there is no question that they have taken a great deal of time and sometimes physical endurance since the sessions are long. It is not uncommon for individual speeches to run for three or four hours! One extremely pleasant feature of these meetings has been the gathering together of many old friends and colleagues who have come from other parts of liberated China. There was for example such a large representation of physiologists at the meeting of scientific workers last month, that the Chinese Physiological Society was able to have a meeting and to plan to resume publication of their journal. Among these phosiologists was Dr. Feng Te-p'ei whom you will remember.

The economic situation has been greatly aggravated by the abnormally heavy rainfall of this summer which in many places has made flood, and which may have serious consequences to the autumn harvest. Prices have risen very rapidly during the past few weeks, commodity averages at the end of July being almost three times what they were at the beginning of the month. The bank of China continues to pursue a realistic policy on exchange, the rate on July 1st having been 1300, increased to 1500 on July 5th, 1600 on the 15th, 1800 on the 21st, 2000 on the 23rd, 2300 on the 28th, and 2700 on the August 1st. you will see, however, that this is not as fast an increase as the price increases I have quoted. We continue to be able to get coal in sufficient quantities so that we have no fear of not having enough to carry us through the winter. The price is not as low as we had expected but we hope to be able to keep within the budget for the year.

I am sending a copy of this letter to Dr. Loucks to await his arrival in Hongkong in case he has gotten away before it reaches New York.

With kindest regards and in the hope that you have had a good summer,

Sincerely yours,

C. U. Lee
Director

（译文）

亲爱的皮尔斯小姐：

自从 7 月 8 日的信后，还没有机会寄信的机会。我们从纽约收到的最后一封信的日期是 6 月 3 日写的，到这里已经 7 月 4 日了。我们一直希望邮路能够恢复正常，但希望总是落空。从香港到天津的船路刚刚恢复，如果不中断，我们至少能有机会把信带到香港，再转寄给你们。不幸的是，香港那边过来的信还不能过来，希望这一情况会很快改进。看到旅客可以自由进出，真让人高兴。Wang Mei-Ying 小姐 7 月 29 日从香港启程，这几天就会到这里了。蒋医生和沈女士也到了香港，应该不久就能找到旅行的办法。

船路一通，我们希望不久娄克斯医生就能回来了。邮路断了这么久，我们盼着听到他将带给我们最新的消息。

6 月和 7 月初的劳资纠纷使我们很头痛，我们不得不努力说服工人们把刚获得的那种集体的力量用在有益的地方。按现在的做法，这意味着多次长长的会议，但如果我们能够得到很多职工的合作，与学校协力，也许是值得的。这 11 个在 5 月底被解聘而造成问题的人，现在已经安置在学校其他部门工作了，我们也为此调整了预算。

K-II 病房将在 8 月 8 日开放，一半病床给妇产科，另一半给儿科。这个病房可以这样合理分割，但其他病房大多不行。周诒春的儿子周华康助理教授将负责这部分。

招生考试于 7 月的第一周在北平举行。27 个考生中录取了 18 人，14 人来自燕京、2 人来自北大、1 人来自天主教大学还有 1 人来自南京大学，其中有 7 个女生。此外，7 个学生在苏州和南京参加考试，肯定也会有 1-2 个被录取。加上 2 个留级学生，所有这一班新生至少会有 20 人。过去的一年时局混乱，我们对此很满意了。

在新政权下，我们不得不习惯被叫去开各种会议。会议可能因为暑假而增加，但这些会议占用了大量时间，而且这些冗长的会议也消耗体力。一个发言经常要讲 3-4 个小时！这些会议也有令人愉快之处，就是可以见到很多从解放区来的老朋友和同事。比如，上个月的科学工作者会议就有很多生理学家，中国生理学会召集了一个会议，计划恢复他们的出版物。这些人里有你认识的冯德培。

今年夏季很多地方降雨成灾，使经济形势恶化，很可能会影响秋季收成。最近几周物价上升很快，7 月底的物价几乎是月初的 3 倍。中国银行继续允许汇率随物价浮动，7 月 1 日汇率 1,300；5 日 1,500；15 日 1,600；21 日 1,800；23 日 2,000，28 日 2,300；8 月 1 日 2,700。不过你可以看出，汇率不如物价涨得快。我们继续为过冬储存足够的燃煤。虽然价格比期望的高，我们的今年的预算还可以勉强支持。

我把此信的复印件也寄到香港，如果娄克斯医生在纽约没有看到的话，一到香港就能看到了。

祝好，希望你夏季愉快！

你真诚的，

李宗恩
院长

致中华医学基金会主席帕克先生信[1]

1949 年 10 月 13 日

Mr. P.W. Parker
China Medical Boards, Inc.
30 East 60th Street
New York 22, N.Y.
U. S. A.

Dear Mr. Parker:

Your letter of June 14th was held up in the midsummer blockage of mails and reached me just as Dr. Loucks was due back, so I did not acknowledge it at once, thinking to wait for Dr. Loucks's later news before doing so, and then began the sessions of the Peoples' Consultative Council (PCC) to which I was a delegate, and again I have waited until in writing to you I could say something about these meetings and recent developments and their possible implications as far as the PUMC is concerned. Now I am taking advantage of Miss Ferguson's departure to send you a word of greeting and of reassurance as to the present state of the College.

The first months after the liberation of Peking were a period of marking time for most of us. We waited for policies to be formed and announced so that we could frame our own plans in the light of such policies – but no announcements were forthcoming, and we often felt we were working in the dark. Then came the period of intensive preparation for the PCC, and one was conscious of the release of a tremendous amount of energy not only in strictly political circles but in all walks of life. This was the time when labor problems began to loom up, when our workers union was formed as one of the expressions of the new-found strength that lies in organized group action. The fact that to begin with the workers were more concerned with what they could get than with their particular contribution to the development of the institution was not surprising, but after some two months of strenuous efforts on the part of both sides to find a reasonable meeting ground there are signs of a dawning consciousness of the fact that each person in the PUMC has a responsibility toward the institution. The period of the PCC meeting was one of carefully fostered and mounting enthusiasm, rising to the climax of the great mass meeting on October 1st when the establishment of the popular Government of the Republic of China was celebrated.

Now we are again in a period similar to that immediately following the coming of the Liberation Army. The new ministries are yet to be formed, and their policies are yet to be formulated – so once more we are likely to have a time of waiting for developments. For the current program of the College and Hospital this means going along without interference on our normal course. The working out of plans for the future must necessarily be held in abeyance until we know the framework of educational and health policies within which we will have to operate. For example,

---

[1] Letter Lee to Parker, October 13, 1949, RAC, CMB Inc. records, Box 48, Folder 335。

we do not yet know whether a medical school like ours which is attached to no university is to come under the jurisdiction of the ministry of education or the ministry of health. We do have considerable evidence, however, that the contribution of the PUMC in concentrating on quality rather than quantity is recognized and appreciated, and it seems reasonable to assume that this special function of the College will be encouraged as one of the important elements in the extensive planning for medical education and health services for the whole people.

It is therefore a great satisfaction to have the statements in your letter about the attitude of the CMB toward the continuance of support to the PUMC and to have Dr. Loucks' first-hand reports of the interest of the CMB in seeing the College hold its ground, political changes notwithstanding.

Last weekend we had Homecoming Day, something which we started last year for our graduates, and there was a splendid turnout of doctors and nurses, a number of whom had come from Tientsin for the occasion. At a round-table conference with the group it was encouraging and stimulating to sense their keen interest in maintaining standards, along with which there was a new appreciation of the importance of spiritual values without which standards alone would fail to achieve the purposes of the founders. Taken as a whole they are a group to be proud of, professionally keen and up to date, ethically conscious of their responsibilities, and tremendously interested in their alma mater. They have begun the raising of a loan fund for undergraduates to supplement the only such fund we have that survived the vicissitudes of the war. Miss Ferguson is carrying with her a photograph taken on Homecoming Day which makes quite an impressive showing and may interest you.

I attended the meetings of the PCC as one of the medical representatives in a group elected last summer by the All-China Science Association which was meeting in Peking. At the time of my election I was not very happy about it because I have always stayed out of political activities and also I could foresee that it might take a lot of time away from my duties at the College. As it turned out the session did not last as long as had been anticipated and I was able to keep my hand on things at the College without much trouble. Aside from the first-hand view of these historic events which was extremely interesting, it proved an excellent opportunity for contacts with a large number of people from other parts of China, some of whom were old friends. I am glad to say that I am not a member of the continuing committee of the PCC and my unsought excursion into the political field is over, but I believe I am justified in saying that my participation in the PCC did not weaken the independent position of the College but rather strengthened it by reason of the opportunity I had to explain our purposes.

Miss Ferguson will be able to answer many of the questions about the College and the general situation which will be in your mind and which may not have been covered in letters home. Changes of great magnitude have taken place in the past year, but I sincerely believe that there is still an important place for the College in the field of medical education and service in China in terms of the high purposes of the founders.

With warm personal regards,

Sincerely yours,

C.U. Lee, Director

(译文)

亲爱的帕克先生:

你6月14日的来信积压在了夏天被阻断的一大批邮件里，直到娄克斯医生该回去前才收到，因此我收到后没有马上告知，认为娄克斯医生能给你更新的消息。紧接着，我作为代表参加了连续几个人民政治协商会议（PCC），就想等到了解这些会议的情况及最近形势的发展对协和的影响后再写信。现在正好福美龄女士就要回美，我就顺便送上问候，再汇报一下协和的近况。

北平解放后的几个月对我们来说只是等待。我们在等待政策的制定和公布，然后按照这些新政策来形成我们的计划——但一直没有等到任何消息，所以我们经常感到在黑暗中摸索。然后是紧张准备的政协会议，不只是政治圈子，每个人都感到一种巨大的能量释放。就在这时劳资纠纷发生，我们的工会是一个新成立的“联合起来力量大”的组织之一。一开始，工人们只关心自己能获取什么，而不是自己能为学校的发展作出什么，这也无可厚非。双方经过两个月的努力终于得到了合理的解决，最后有迹象显示，协和的每一个成员都明白了对学校负有责任。政协会议期间，热情逐渐高涨，到10月1日的万众集会庆祝中国人民政府成立时达到了高潮。

现在，我们似乎又回到了解放军进城后的那段时期。新部门还没有成立，他们的政策还没有制定——我们又会有一段等待的时期。对于学校和医院的工作来说，这意味着一切正常，没有干扰。对于未来的长远规划，我们只有在知道了教育和医疗政策之后，才能相应地加以制订。比如，我们不知道像我们这样一个不隶属于大学的独立医学院，归教育部管，还是归卫生部管。不过确有迹象表明，协和的高质量教育的贡献得到了认可和欣赏，所以有理由相信协和的特殊作用将成为为全民服务的医学教育和医疗服务的具体规划的一个重要部分。

所以，您在信中表达的中华医学基金会继续支持协和的态度，并让娄克斯医生亲自代表基金会帮助学校在政权更替时稳定学校，使我们极为欣慰。

上一周我们举行了返校节，这是我们去年开始为毕业生举办的活动，很多医生和护士都来了，不少特地从天津赶来。在一个圆桌会议上，我很欣慰地看到他们要求保持标准，强调精神价值的重要性，认为没有这一价值的标准将不能达到创始人的目标。总的来说，他们是值得骄傲的一群人，专业上与时俱进，道义上勇于担当，而且对母校极为关心。他们已经开始为在校生筹款，存入我们唯一的一笔战后留下来的为同一目的的款项里。福美龄小姐会将返校节的合影带给您，您会对这张难忘的照片感兴趣的。

我作为医学界代表参加了政协会议，我是在夏季于北京召开的全国自然科学工作者代表大会上被选上的。刚开始时，我对此并不乐意，因为我向来远离政治，而且我觉得这会占去我为学校工作的很多时间。后来发现会议不像我想象的那么长，我可以管理学校的事务，没有遇到太大的困难。除了见证这一重要的历史时刻之外，我还有机会与来自中国其他地方的人取得联系，其中不少是老朋友。我很高兴自己不是政协常务委员，我介入政界的经历到此为止。但我相信我参加政协会议没有让学校丧失独立性，而且给了我强调其独立性的机会。

福美龄小姐将直接回答您对学校和一般情况的问题，她还会告诉您一些信中没有提及，但您可能感兴趣的事情。去年发生了巨大的变化，但我真诚地相信协和医学院仍可遵循奠基人为中国的医学教育服务的宗旨，在中国的医学教育界享有重要的位置。

顺致亲切问候，

你真诚的，

李宗恩

院长

致中华医学基金会主席帕克先生信[1]

1950 年 4 月 6 日

Mr. P. W. Parker
China Medical Board, Inc.
30 East 60th Street
New York 22, N. Y.
U. S. A.

Dear Mr. Parker:

With reference to your letter to Dr. Loucks dated December 16, 1949, I wish to express my deep appreciation for the decision of the China Medical Board to assume, as from the fiscal year 1950-1951, administrative responsibility for the present foreign staff of the College in respect of their salaries and furlough expenses. I understand that these appropriations will be in addition to the $600,000 for the operating budget of the College and that the above decision is an emergency measure on a year to year basis without affecting the basic principle adopted by the Board in 1947 relating to the assumption of responsibility by the College Trustees for all phases of college operation. I note also that you suggest two methods to implement the decision. Each is acceptable; and I think it may be advisable not to make a hard and fast rule but to consider each individual case separately, due regard to be given to special circumstances and requirement.

I have delayed writing to you because I have wanted to wait for the general situation to clear itself. The recent changes in the country are both profound and impressive. Perhaps the most noteworthy achievement of the new government is in the restoration of land communication. All the railways have been restored and construction is proceeding at a phenomenal rate. Measures aimed at price control and stabilization have been successful to some extent, while administrative integrity is on a high level. Much emphasis is placed on the welfare of the people. In Peking itself the old sewage system, unrepaired for twenty years, is being overhauled and a city-wide medical program is underway. The new social outlook has caught the imagination of the youth and the great changes now taking place have their whole-hearted support. While the road from theory to practice, from principle to application is long and arduous, every effort is being made to build up a new society, a new attitude of mind.

The College is gradually adjusting itself to its new environment. While solutions to many of our problems involve protracted negotiations and meetings, we are carrying on with the minimum amount of interference from the authorities. Organized labor in the College has been granted a greater measure of social security and improvement in working hours and medical care. On the other hand, our workers have shown a greater sense of responsibility, which is reflected in a reduction of coal consumption this winter, elimination of waste and of irregularities.

---

[1] Letter Lee to Parker, April 6, 1950, RAC, CMB Inc, Box 48, Folder 336

We are in the midst of preparing our 1950-1951 budget. The coming year will add fourth year students to the group receiving instruction in the Medical College and brings the necessity for expanding both academic activities and hospital capacity. We are attempting to make provision for these needs accordingly.

Taxes are a heavy burden; but high taxation is one of the government measures aimed at balancing the budget and controlling inflation. Payment in taxes is probably more than offset by losses which would be incurred from unchecked inflation. Entry or reentry of foreign members of the staff is a thorny problem. Nationals of all countries with whom China has not established diplomatic relations are faced with this difficulty. It is hoped, however, that exceptions will be made for technical personnel.

In conclusion, I have pleasure in reporting that our graduates continue to be much in demand in all parts of the country on account of their professional competence.

With warm personal regards,

Yours sincerely,

(signed) C. U. Lee

（译文）

亲爱的帕克先生：

您 1949 年 12 月 16 日的信已收到，请允许我感谢中华医学基金会决定负担 1950-1951 年学校现任外国教员的工资及休假薪酬。我明白这些费用属于学校的正常运行费用 60 万美金之外的临时紧急花费，不影响按 1947 年基金会规定的由校董事会对学校承担的责任。

我没有马上给您回信，因为我想等情况明朗一些再写。最近这个国家的变化，即深刻又震撼。也许新政府取得的最大成绩是恢复陆路交通。铁路运输现已全部恢复，建设的速度也快得惊人。稳定物价也获得了一定成功，管理的诚信度高，对人民的福利也很重视。在北京，已失修 20 年的旧下水道正在大修，全市的医疗系统也正在建立。现在社会上的新气象令年轻人很兴奋，他们对这些变化真心地支持。虽然从理论到实践，从原则到实施是一个漫长而艰苦的过程，但是新社会正在努力建设中，这是一种新的态度。

学校正在适应新的环境。我们现在解决问题需要反复交涉和很多会议，政府并没有对我们的工作进行干预。学校劳工组织的工作对社会安全、劳动改善和医疗保障都有所促进。另外，我们的工人表现出很强的责任感，所以去冬的燃煤消耗下降，浪费和违章现象减少。

我们正在做 1950-1951 年的预算。下一学年医学院将会有 4 年级学生，使学校和医院的费用增加，我们将做相应的预算。

税赋是一个很大的负担，不过高税收是政府平衡收支和控制通货膨胀的一个办法。缴税的支出比通货膨胀的损失总要少些。

外国教职员出入境很棘手。凡是没有和中国建交的国家都有同样的问题。但愿技术人员会算做例外。

最后，我高兴地向您报告，我们的毕业生因为他们的出色的专业能力，在全国都很受欢迎。

顺致亲切问候，

你真诚的，

李宗恩

致福美龄女士信[1]

1950 年 7 月 4 日

Dear Mary:

Your cable on June 7 and your letter of June 9 certainly brought us bad news. Like you we had also expected that you would be back to the fold by the end of this month. It is a great disappointment to me personally that the arrangements for your return were made to no purpose. However, I'm an optimist and I don't believe that you and Betty will be permitted, as you say, to "fall by the wayside". I feel that in all probability the Board after hearing H. H. L's report on conditions here will reconsider its decision and permit your return. Sitting in my office on this beautiful Summer's day, I resolutely refuse to subscribe to the view that Peking is not a safe and desirable place for anyone to be in. But what worries one is the latest development in the international situation; and here of course infinitely greater issues are involved, and their possible consequences are infinitely more serious.

I greatly appreciate your motive in abiding by the decision of the Board which, I note, recognizes its obligation to you in respect of your salary. You have taken the right and only possible course in the circumstances. My advice is that you remain where you are waiting patiently and have no plans but just a resolve to return. Your resignation, of course, cannot be considered.

We are all very busy, but the work of the office proceeds smoothly. We are fortunate at this stage in securing the services of Mr. Sun Pang-tsao as Recorder, concurrently acting for you during your enforced absence. Another newcomer is Miss K. H. Ch'en through examination. She is a graduate of Yanching University and an efficient typist. P.K. Ch'en had unfortunately to be terminated three months ago because of lung trouble. He was given a full year's salary. Lao Tang has transferred from the storeroom and is now here a full-time messenger. Chang Chun is now Dean in succession to H. C. Chang.

My best greetings.

As ever,

(Signed) C. U.
C. U. Lee

Thanks for yours of June 22nd, which has just come. C. U.

（译文）

亲爱的玛丽：

你 6 月 7 日的电报和 6 月 9 日的来信确实送来了坏消息。和你一样，我们

[1] Letter Lee to Ferguson, July 4, 1950, RAC, CMB Inc, Box 57, Folder 400.

也在盼着你本月底回来工作。对我个人尤其失望，因为为你返回作出的所有安排都白费了。不过，我是一个乐观主义者，不相信你和海丝典将向你说的那样“倒在路边”了。我觉得基金会在听取了娄克斯关于协和的报告后，会改变决定，允许你回来。在这个美丽的夏天，我坐在办公室旦，拒绝同意北京不安全和不宜人居的观点。但是，最近的国际局势确实令人担心， 重大的问题当然有，它们的后果也极为严重。

我感谢你服从基金会的决定，也明白你对所拿的二资应尽的义务。你在目前的情况下做了你唯一能做的事。我劝你别做其他计划，在那儿耐心等待回来。你的辞呈是不会被接受的。

我们都非常繁忙，但一切工作都还顺利。我们非常幸运的得到孙邦藻[1]先生在你离职期间代理你的记录员工作。另一个新来的打字员是燕京大学毕业的陈小姐，陈 PK 不幸因为肺病离开了，我们付给他一年的薪金。从仓库调来的老唐现在是全职通信员。张鋆现在接替了张锡钧担任教务长职务。

致以我最诚意的问候，

宗恩

刚收到你 6 月 22 日的信，谢谢。宗恩

[1] 孙邦藻，1921 年格拉斯哥大学硕士，上海交通大学英文教授，1927- 1939 年 Assiatant Chief in the Revenue Guards Department of the Salt Administration, 1946-1950 年任工业部代理秘书长。1950-1951 年任协和医学院代理秘书长。

致周诒春博士信[1]

1950 年 7 月 31 日

Dr. Y. Y. Tsur
HONG KONG

Dear Dr. Tsur:

I send you herewith a copy of the minutes of an Executive Committee meeting of the Board of Trustees held in the College on the 20th inst. You will see from it that as in the past we have our problems and difficulties. Before the College could be registered, we must have a properly constituted Board of Trustees. Four of the trustees have resigned and of the remaining ten the following eight are accessible: Keats S. Chu, C. C. Ch'en, Chu Fu-t'ang, A. M. Dunlap, Li Ming, George Sellett, T. A. Sun and your good self. The Executive Committee plans now to have first, by circular letter, a Nominating Committee appointed to make recommendations and then at a meeting of the Board either here or in Shanghai to hold the election of trustees. You doubtless know that according to precedent, if under extraordinary circumstances no meeting of the Board could be held, membership of the Board of Trustees could hold over unchanged until it becomes possible to secure a quorum. Hence, although your term has expired, you are still one of our trustees. Your offer to resign has not been considered.

Also, registration with the Ministry of Education necessitates certain modifications in the By-laws of the Colleges. Knowing your great interest in educational matters, I enclose a copy of the provisional regulation governing institutions of higher education both government and private.

Peking is still quiet and peaceful and a desirable place to live in. Perhaps as a capital its administrative importance has been somewhat lessened because of the existing decentralized form of government. But its old lethargy has gone, and, I hope, for good. The city is a veritable beehive of activity, and work is the general watchword. Roads are being widened and repaired, lakes drained, parts of the wall torn down, and there are programs for public health and sanitation – all these things which were the concern of a few are now the concern or work of all. There is today a new spirit abroad in the nation, and every endeavor is being made for the welfare of the people; and in spite of mistakes, considerable progress has been made with the active participation of the people.

May is well and your newest grandson is flourishing. Tsung-tsin is now assistant professor at Tsinghua under Liang Sze-ch'eng.

My brother has given me news of you and your family and he says that you may be returning. If this is your intention, may I add my little voice to many others to urge you to come as soon as possible. I know that much that has happened here has your sympathetic understanding and support. You will enjoy living in retirement in Peking, and it will be possible for you to limit your interest and activities to the PUMC, which

[1] 协和医学院档案室，周诒春档案

now need your help and guidance more than ever before.

With kindest regards,

Yours sincerely

C. U. Lee

（译文）

亲爱的周博士：

我随信寄给您 20 号在学校召开的董事会执行委员会会议记录。从中您可以看到我们仍有问题和困难。在协和登记之前，我们必须组成一个合法的董事会。四位董事已经辞职，剩下 10 位可联系到的 8 位是：朱继圣、陈志潜、诸福棠、邓勒普、李铭、席礼德、孙锡三，还有您。执行委员会现在正计划先用通函组成一个提名委员会，推荐下一任董事的名单，在比地或上海即将举行的董事会会议上投票决定。根据过去的惯例，您肯定了解，如因特殊情况不能召开董事会议，董事任期一直到下一次有法定人数开会时为止。所以，尽管您的董事任期已到，您现在仍旧是我们的董事，您的辞职信还没有机会被考虑。

另外，在教育部登记，要求首先对协和的某些规定进行修改。因为您一向热心教育，随信附上对管理公立和私立高校的暂时规定。

北京依然是一个平静宜居的城市。也许，作为首都，政府有去中心化倾向，北京在管理方面受到的影响减少了。不过，过去的懒散不复存在，我希望能够永远这样。整个城市都在忙碌之中，工作是最经常听到的字眼。道路被拓宽、湖泊被抽干、部分城墙被拆除，还开展了很多公共卫生运动。这些过去只有少数人关心的事，现在人人关心。目前全国表现出一种新的精神，努力为大众服务的精神，尽管错误也有，人民的积极参与确实获得了相当的成就。

珊凤身体很好，你的最小的孙孙也很健康。宗津现在是清华大学的助理教授，在梁思成手下工作。

我弟弟告诉我了您和您家里的情况，他说您也许会回来。您要是真有这个计划，我愿意加入其他人，期盼您尽早回归。我知道，您对这里发生的很多事都会同情和理解并支持的。您将会喜欢在北京享受退休生活的，您也可以参加一些协和医学院的活动，学校现在比过去任何时候更需要您的帮助和指导。

致以最高的敬意，

您真诚的，

李宗恩

致娄克斯医生信[1]

1950 年 11 月 16 日

Dr. Harold H. Loucks
China Medical Board, Inc.
U.S.A.

Dear Harold:

Mr. Sun in his letter to Miss Pearce today has given the latest news. I have urged him to write without delay to give all the facts concerning the decision we have made to lend a part of the College hospital to the Weishengpu for its temporary use. Having reached agreement on general principles we are now meeting daily with the representatives of the Ministry to work out the details. I believe, and many of us here share this view, that much good may come of the arrangement. We shall be in daily contact for many months to come with the Weishengpu personnel, not to mention the patients (all higher-ranking officials) in our midst, and a better understanding of the work of the College is bound to result. One hopeful sign is the insistence of the Weishengpu representatives that there should be no impairment of our standard of teaching and service. However, I do not wish to be unduly optimistic; difficulties are bound to arise and, maybe, even frictions. While I realize that the College administration has the full confidence of the CMB, I request that you will assure Board members that the best interests of the College will always be protected.

I hope these letters will reach you before irresponsible reports and wild rumors get abroad. I can well imagine the papers in the States giving the news that PUMC has been commandeered by the Government. I know that if such groundless reports should appear, and I hope not yet, you would act with your usual vigor and effectiveness.

With my warmest regards,

Yours sincerely

C.U. Lee
Director

（译文）

亲爱的赫拉德：

孙先生在他今天给皮尔斯小姐的信中报告了最近发生的事情。我让他在第一时间写信告知我们把部分附属医院暂时借给卫生部使用的决定及所有相关情况。达成一般协议之后，现在我们每天与卫生部代表开会研究具体细节。我相信，同时也代表这里其他人的意见，这一安排也许有好结果。在今后几个月

[1] Letter Lee to Loucks, November 16, 1950, RAC, CMB Inc, Box 48, Folder 336.

里，我们将每日接触卫生部的人和病人（都是高级官员），他们会对学校的工作有亲身的体验。一个好的迹象是，卫生部的代表坚持我们的教学和医疗标准将不受影响。不过，我不能太乐观，困难一定会发生，甚至摩擦。虽然我知道中华医学基金会对学校的管理工作给予绝对的信任，我请求你向所有董事保证，我们将确保学校的最大利益。

我希望你在得到国外不负责任的报告和谣言之前收到这封信。我能想像美国报纸会说协和被政府强占了。希望还没有这种毫无根据的报告，一旦发生，我知道你会立即采取有效行动的。

顺致亲切的问候，

你真诚的，

李宗恩，院长

致娄克斯医生信[1]

1950 年 11 月 26 日

Peking, China

My Dear Harold:

With the approach of Christmas our thoughts turn naturally to our friends far and near, and I feel I must not allow this opportunity to slip without showing some indication to my friends that although they have been neglected, they are not forgotten. Never a good correspondent, I find now writing individual letters to friends not so much a burden as an impossibility, since my "laborious days" (if I may call them so) seem all incessant work and interruptions. May I, therefore, resort to this circular note to wish you and yours a very Happy Christmas. And may 1951 bring Peace on Earth and Goodwill among Men. These are worn-out phrases but their sentiments have a renewed urgency.

Yours sincerely,
(signed) C. U.

（译文）

我亲爱的赫拉德:

在圣诞即将到来之际，我们自然想念起所有各地的朋友。我感到一定不能失去这个机会，告诉我的朋友们，虽然他们很久没有我的消息，但我从没有忘记他们。最好的莫过于一封信。我的"工作日"（如果我可以这样说）充满了无穷无尽的工作和干扰，但我觉得给每个朋友写信并不是个负担。所以，我用这封信祝你圣诞快乐。愿 1951 年为人类带来和平与幸福。虽然这是一句老话，但现在的情况为其赋予了新的含意。

你真诚的，

宗恩

[1] Letter Lee to Loucks, November 28, 1950, RAC, CMB Inc, Box 48, Folder 336.

我和协和医学院[1]

1952 年 1 月 9 日

不可否认的，我的出身和过去所受的教育对于我的思想有着极大的影响。我的家庭是旧中国典型的"士大夫"家庭。所谓士大夫，它是和官僚地主一而二，二而一的。虽然我是这大家庭中的长子长孙，但在我出国之前，家庭对我所产生的影响远不及我在国外所受的教育的影响之大。十八岁时，我偶然地出了国。当时我并未想到我为何出洋。到了英国，因为官费是指定给学医的人，我就学了医。及至学了医也就安心读书，安心做事；等到后来想到该回家的时候已经近三十岁了。在这十二年中，尤其是在英国，我的思想就深深地被个人主义、改良主义所支配，所以我读了斯大林同志"与英国作家威尔斯的谈话"后所得的感触也最深。

回国后到了上海，我不愿依附家庭，希望脱离家庭而独立。北京的协和是当时全国设备最充实的一个医学校，我认为它适合我个人的志愿和兴趣，就在这个小天地内一过又是十几年。我在这里执行着教学和研究任务，享受着"学者"的美名，而优厚的待遇、舒适的生活又充分满足了我个人的要求。

一九三七年抗日战争爆发以后，我的美梦被扰乱了。那时日本人的凶残无理，打击了我的自尊心。又想到日本人来了以后，我的"事业"将无从开展，于是对个人的前途有了顾虑，遂另找出路，远走贵阳办学。

我所以这样做，完全是从个人利益出发的。当时我俨然以医学教育专家自居，在抗日战争时期只管办我的医学院，却不问为谁办学，也不问办学的经费是从那里来的。除了取得国民党反动政府的支持以外，美军剩余物资我要，美国煤油大王的钱我也不拒绝。于是学是办起来了，学校里也就跟着来了国民党的特务分子训导主任。我就抱着不与人争的妥协态度和他相处。自己明明知道他很多事做得不对，但也没有及早反对。因为这样做会影响我的所谓"事业"。到后来他扰乱了我的整个教学计划的时候，我才把他解聘了。但也因此替我找来了许多麻烦。虽然如此，我并未认识到国民党反动统治的本质，国民党送来

[1] 《人民日报》，1952 年 1 月 9 日。

了党证我并未拒绝，甚至把我留在重庆国民党中央训练团随同其他大学校长一同受训时，我也就糊里糊涂地参加了。

后来美国洛氏基金委员会聘我做协和医学校校长，我答应下来了。这更充分表现出我对于为谁服务的问题是没有考虑过的。我认为这样可以更进 一步地发展我的"事业"。

由于我长期在英国学习，欧美资产阶级教育对我的思想有很大的影响。我对于社会发展的看法同威尔斯一样，认为社会制度是可以由渐变的方式变更的；旧秩序本身在瓦解着，可不用革命的方法来把它推翻，也不必用暴力的革命来建立新的社会。这种改良主义的看法使我走入"教育救国"的歧途，我自以为我所办的教育对社会秩序的变革产生着一定的作用；我认为提高了自己学校的质量就可以影响中国新医学的发展。及至学习了斯大林"与英国作家威尔斯的谈话"后，我认清了改良主义的反动的实质，它是不可能实现的。

我是学医的，褊狭的客观主义使我认为治病是医生的首要任务，而忽略了产生疾病的社会原因。教学生的时候，只知道传授一些医学学理和技术知识，至于学生将来为谁服务那就不管了，至多只是抽象地谈到医生的任务是为人类解除痛苦。我的这种"超阶级"、"超政治"的态度也就影响了部分和我相处的人们。

我是站在第三者的地位来处理事务的，对一切总是保持着所谓"客观"的态度。因此，我只看到事物的表面的现象，而未能领会其本质。对革命形势我采取这种态度，对同学们的爱国运动也是这样。就像处理学校行政工作时也不例外，这种处理问题的方法是不对的，在我过去所办的所谓"事业"中曾发生了不少错误。例如，我硬搬了资本主义国家的一套医学教育制度来做为我国的医学教育制度的准绳。

由于我常常孤立地看问题，钻牛角尖的习惯也就难免了。我对医学教育的看法就是如此，充满了单纯技术观点，而把人民对医学教育的要求忽略了。解放后很久我还提出过医学教育的国际水平问题，继续维持着协和的纯技术观点，一直到我清楚地认识到纯技术观点对我个人对协和教师的思想改造成了最大的阻力的时候，我才体会到技术必需和政治结合的正确原则。

我以为我在自然科学的范畴内是一个机械唯物论者，实际上并未摆脱唯心主义的羁绊。我虽非宗教徒，但常常以"博爱"去劝勉人们，对"以德报怨"的说法我是点头赞许的。我认为斗争和革命不是解决问题的最理想的办法。我也是从一切人都是好人这个前提来看问题的。我常常谈到一个人多多少少总还有他的好处，我们应该隐恶扬善。这种认识问题的方法是唯心的，因为我没有追究一个人的阶级本质。

在这次京津高等学校教师的思想改造学习中，听了报告，读了文件，通过小组学习及个人体验，我对我过去那些陈腐的、错误的、甚至反动的思想有了初步的认识。但这只能算是认识错误和改正错误的开始，至于如何在实践中去建立正确的立场观点和方法，做到全心全意为人民服务，还有待于我的主观努力。我愿意在同志们的督促和帮助下彻底改造我的思想。

在我离开学校致力于所谓“个人事业”的时期，多半的时间是在协和。及至一九四七年协和复校，我又负责协和的行政工作，这样协和对我的影响是很大的，而我个人对协和的影响也不小。检讨起来，解放以后协和所以进步慢，我是应该负相当的责任的。

协和是在一九〇六年由几个英美教会团体创办的，一九一五年由美国洛氏基金委员会接办，其中除在太平洋战争爆发后停办了六年，洛氏基金委员会统治了这个学校整整三十年。洛氏基金委员会是一个世界性的文化侵略机构，除了苏联及新民主主义国家以外，世界上几乎没有一个角落没有它的侵略基地，洛克菲勒建立这笔基金的动机从他个人方面说至少有两个很明显的目的，一是名利兼收，既可得到“大慈善家”的名义，又可扩大他的倾销市场。一是可以用办“教育事业”“慈善事业”为名而逃避一笔很大的所得税。但是要输出这一笔相当大的免税而无直接利润的美金（估计两亿五千万美元）到国外去必须通过国务院，而被认为是符合于国务院的整个侵略计划的。这充分说明了协和是美国的侵略计划在远东的一个重要环节。还有一个重要的事实更可证明美国国务院的文化侵略政策和洛氏基金是密切结合着的。在过去洛氏基金曾设立了很多“奖学金”的名额，来诱骗某些国家的部分学生。一九四九年美国国务院就吸收了这个经验，大量地设立这种“奖学金”，其名额较洛氏基金多达三十二倍，洛氏基金就这样为美国国务院创设了一种文化侵略的办法。协和的过去正如邓家栋大夫所谈，一切是特殊化，也就是说协和的一切制度、教学方法、工作作风和生活方式都是从美国原封不动地搬来的。也正如周金黄大夫说的，协和的一切教学、研究、医疗作风无不以资产阶级的水平为准绳。这样就训练出来一批高度个人自由主义和亲美、崇美的医护人员。他们强调个人兴趣、盲目研究和自由营业。他们对于社会发展的规律，革命的进展不但无动于衷，反而认为是扰乱了社会的安宁。总而言之，美帝国主义在短短的三十年中，以二千三百万元的美金达到了它的文化侵略的目标，在医药卫生工作者中造成了一批所谓“民主自由”分子，让他们服服贴贴地为它服务，要不是在人民政府和共产党的正确领导和教育下，我们恐怕要永远跌在深渊里而不知自拔。

过去我是一个彻头彻尾的改良主义者，因此处理协和的一切行政事务也是从这一个观点出发的。解放以后我也察觉到协和有些制度是应当改变的，可是不敢也不肯放手去改。对于那些应该改变的制度，我顶多认为不合潮流，而未站在人民的立场（那时我根本还是站在反人民的立场）去批判和否定协和过去的一切。我只肯定了一个大前提，就是协和固然有缺点，但是也有优点。这正好暴露了我的保守的惧怕变革的思想，根本否定了思想改造是一种革命。因此至今协和仍保留着很多的旧制度和旧作风，例如一年一轮的教务长制度、各系各自为政的自由作风、对苏联的科学理论未予以应有的重视。

我过去把“超政治”、“超阶级”的看法也贯彻到行政工作中，希望协和的一切人也超政治超阶级。我以为应该竭力使教授们可以安心地在实验室中工作，学生们闭门读书，而不被政治所“扰乱”。我认为对于技术专家的科主任的意见是应该尊重的，一切科内事务以及进修生的安排都本着他们的意见进行，但是我把窦威廉之流的帝国主义分子也认为是“学者”“教授”，竟不分敌我地一律看待。这种单纯技术观点也是阻碍协和进步的主要因素。

在这次思想改造学习运动中，协和不可否认地是已经动起来了，每一个人对自己的思想和协和的过去已经有了初步的认识。但是对过去错误思想的进一步澄清，还有待于更大的努力。

用实际工作来庆祝宪法草案的公布[1]

1954 年 6 月 18 日

我们的宪法草案公布了，它是一个历史文件，是真正属于人民的宪法。这是我国自古理论没有过的大事情，是值得我们庆祝的一件大喜事。我想每一个祖国公民看到这个宪法草案都会感到兴奋。

站在一个医务工作者的立场上，我愿意说几句话。自从解放以来，在我们的国家里，卫生事业是有很大成就的。在旧社会的时候，每隔四、五年必然要大流行一次霍乱，今天在我们国家里已被消灭。过去各个大医院最多见到严重的伤寒病，现在已很少看到了。过去蔓延最广的天花，现在也基本被消灭。这说明了我国公共卫生事业发展的非常快，它的成就也是惊人的。只有人民的国家才能这样，资本主义国家是不会有这种事情的。这次宪法草案中更给我们医务工作者指出了明确的努力方向，我们的责任更重大了，工作范围也更广大了。改善劳动条件、疾病的预防与治疗，劳动者的修养等等都是和医务工作者的责任不可分的。当然，这也是与结合群众运动，发挥群众力量分不开的。我们的国家很大，人口也很多，但是医务干部很少，为了很好地发展我们的卫生保健事业，培养大量的、合格的、能够解决问题的医务干部是文教卫生工作中很重大的一个任务，也是我们应该努力完成的任务。

在旧社会里，我是一个不懂政治也不大过问政治的人，反动统治政府也不要我们这样的人过问政治，这次我有机会参加了全国政协委员会所领导的学习和讨论，我感到这是我生平最大的光荣，我深深认识到了一个公民的光荣权利。讨论的过程中，充分地发扬了民主的精神，例如我们提到了科学研究工作的问题，这次公布的宪法草案中第九十五条就明确地规定了国家对科学研究工作的保护和鼓励。这次公布了以后，还要展开全国的民主讨论，这种充分发扬民主的精神，正代表了我们宪法的本质，它是为广大人民的利益而服务的，是人民的宪法，这是和资本主义性质的宪法根本不相同的。

我们的宪法草案是以马列主义为基础，参考苏联和各人民民主国家的经

[1] 《健康报》1954 年 6 月 18 日。

验，结合我国的具体情况创造性地制定的。 它不但总结了过去革命斗争的经验和成果，同时也指出了向前发展的方向，这是一个社会主义类型的宪法草案。我衷心地拥护这个宪法草案，并坚决用我的实际工作来庆祝宪法草案的公布。

在中国人民政治协商会议第二届全国委员会第一次全体会议上的发言[1]

1954 年 12 月 25 日

各位委员：

我这次能出席中国人民政治协商会议第二次届全国委员会第一次全体会议，不但感觉到光荣，而且怀着一种极兴奋的心情，因为这五年来我看到祖国在毛主席和共产党的领导下国民经济的迅速恢复，抗美援朝的伟大胜利，社会主义经济建设的突飞猛进，我国国际地位的空前提高，在保卫亚洲和世界和平工作中做出了杰出的贡献，国内人民和各民族之间关系的团结，全国人民代表大会的召开，宪法的公布，这一切都使我深深感到无限的兴奋和骄傲。

这种心情同我在五年前代表科学团体出席中国人民政治协商会议第一届全体会议的时候有很大的不同，当时由于我长期受美帝国主义的影响，同党有着很大的距离，甚至于可以说有一定程度的敌视，因此对新中国的成立采取观望和怀疑的态度。经过五年来在党的关怀和不断教育下，我在思想认识上有了基本转变，使我从美帝国主义文化侵略影响下解放出来。现在回想过去，我清楚地看到自己却是美帝国主义文化侵略政策所培养出了的典型人物。过去的协和医院可以说是执行美帝国主义文化侵略政策的典型机构。美帝国主义就是这样处心积虑地培养我这样的一群人来散布崇美亲美的思想，已达其侵略的目的，所以我今天要就我对于帝国主义特别是美帝国主义文化侵略的认识过程谈一谈。

我很早就到英国去读书，长期接受资本主义的教育和熏陶。回国后，一九二三年我就钻进了美国垄断资本家煤油大王所创办的协和医院，在十余年的过程中，我就被培养成为一个亲美崇美、敌我不分、忘掉祖国、忠实为帝国主义文化侵略服务的代理人。因此一九四八年我就被选为协和医院的院长，负责筹划协和医院的复校工作。当时美帝国主义为便于实施其文化侵略的政策，设有

[1] 《人民日报》，1954 年 12 月 25 日

协和董事会，董事长就是鼎鼎大名的战犯胡适。但是美国垄断资本家们还不放心，又派了一些披着科学家外衣的美国文化特务如娄克斯之流来协和监督和实际执行其政策。由于当时人民解放战争已进入反攻时期，华北局势有突变的可能，美国帝国主义分子是看到了这一前途的，因此，美国国务院就决定即使华北局势有变化，美国文化特务和战犯胡适之流必须退出的时候，还希望能够继续保持协和这一文化侵略据点。作为其卷土重来的基地，至少也可以在新中国继续产生影响。在这恶毒的计划下，我便被认为是它执行器计划的一个比较合适的代理人。而我呢，也就按照其企图，忠实地为保持这基地而效劳。所以从北京解放一直到一九五一年初接管以前这一阶段中，我一方面坚持美国“标准”和“医学教育制度”，一方面对政府的一些措施采取应付、拖延、抗拒的态度。当朝鲜战争爆发，美帝国主义文化特务娄克斯之流撤退后，我还向协和美国董事会汇报协和情况，并一再表示努力维持这样据点，甚至在一九五零年秋，军委卫生部都为志愿军伤病员向协和商借病床时，我在思想上还很抗拒，唯恐摧毁美国的“标准”和“制度”，怕丧失这块阵地。在一九五一年政府接管后，协和同美国的关系虽然断绝了，但我在思想上还是反动的。处处还留恋着美国的“标准”和“制度”。

接管后，在党和上级的领导教育下，在群众的督促下，经过一系列的政治运动，特别在思想改造的运动中所揭露的美帝国主义文化侵略的具体事实，我受到了深刻的教育，更由于党对我的关怀和信任，让我在原岗位上继续工作学习，我得到了进一步改造的机会。我的头脑逐渐清醒过来，认识到实质上我是在帮助美帝国主义执行其侵略政策。我痛下决心，彻底清除我亲美崇美的反动思想，坚决同美帝国主义划清界限，永远站在人民方面，全心全意为人民卫生事业服务。

几年来，协和回到祖国的怀抱之后，在党和上级的领导下，进入了一个新的历史时期，走上了为人民服务、为社会主义建设服务的道路，教学医疗方面都在不断的发展和提高。在教学效果方面，我仅举一个例子来说明，我们有一位教授在旧协和二十年培养了十三个专业人才，而其中五人现在还在美国。现在他一年可以培养至少十个专业人才，真正为人民服务的人才。换句话说，他的教学效果已经提高了二十五倍以上。在医疗方面也有很快的发展，拿门诊工作来举例，三年来门诊已经由七个分科增加到二十二个分科，一九四九年门诊的人次数为六万八千五百八十四人次，一九五三年则为二十九万四千六百二十五人次，增加四倍多。这些具体的事实教育了我，使我感觉到唯有在党的领导下，同全国人民在一起，科学和教育事业才能有光辉的前途。当我深切地体会到这些，我痛恨自己的过去，更痛恨美帝国主义的侵略本质。

美帝国主义在大陆上被中国人民赶出去之后，它不甘心于它的失败，又侵占我们的台湾，出兵朝鲜威胁祖国的安全和世界和平，但它处处遭到失败，最近又同蒋贼订立侵略性条约，处心积虑与中国人民为敌，这一罪恶行动遭到全世界爱好和平的人民的谴责。从我自己来说，我要坚决地站稳人民的立场，尽我一切的力量做好本岗位工作，支援解放台湾的斗争。

最后，我还要对在台湾美蒋统治下的医务工作者们说一句话，从我的惨痛教训中，你们可以认清美帝国主义侵略的实质和蒋介石集团的卖国本质。你们应当拥护祖国，在祖国人民解放台湾的斗争中献出自己的一份力量。

更好地向科学进军[1]

1957 年 3 月 23 日

党和政府提出向科学进军的号召，对科学家及青年们是极大的鼓舞。我愿意从一个医务行政工作者的角度，来谈谈对医学界向科学进军中的几个问题的体会，请各位指正。

做好本岗位工作是向科学进军的首要条件

首先，我想谈一下科学是个集体的事业，在这个事业中个人与集体的关系。

当科学进军的号召提出以后，青年们踊跃的响应这一号召，科学界表现出蓬勃的气象，这是一个极为可喜的现象。但是由于他们对这一号召的认识上的限制，就产生了不同的看法，至少在有的青年医务工作者中，思想上引起了一些混乱。其中比较突出而带有原则性的问题，就是不安心于现在的工作岗位的现象。例如，有的青年医务工作者，往往不考虑工作需要，个人的条件，争先恐后的报考研究生，向副博士进军。医院中有部分医师，轻视医务工作，而热心于钻图书馆，跑实验室，而对病人的关心及服务态度就不如从前了，以致病人反映医师的态度较以往冷淡，病房的护士们向领导提意见，要求明确护理工作人员向科学进军的方向。化验室的技术员们亦要求提高文化，准备投考大学，认为这是向科学进军的途径。青年们的这种热情是很可贵的，我也认为各级领导也必须明确在不同岗位上的医务工作者向科学进军的方向。但是在这里我感觉到应当首先解决的是对"科学"这一概念的几点基本认识有澄清的必要，否则会影响当前的业务工作，也达不到向科学进军的要求。

我们必须认识到，现在的科学工作是一个集体的事业，必须是各种有关的工作人员密切配合才能使科学得到发展。譬如在具体的医疗工作中，医师、护士、药剂师、技术员、营养师、行政干部、政治工作人员及勤杂人员等地密切合作，是完成医疗任务地基本关键，病人地诊疗成绩，是他们集体劳动地结

---

[1] 《人民日报》，1957 年 3 月 23 日。

果。一位医学专家地研究成绩中，也必然包括他的青年助手们地勤劳果实。由此可见，必须要求从事医学科学的整体事业中的每一个工作岗位的人员，专家、医师、护士、技术人员、药剂人员、营养师、行政干部、政治工作人员、勤杂人员等，热爱他们的工作岗位，不断提高工作水平，才能使整个的医学水平逐步提高。如果忽视科学必须是个集体事业的这一基本原则，不安心目前的工作岗位，则不但阻碍了医学科学的进展，也会减弱自己在集体中所起的作用。

也就是因为科学是个集体的事业，个人工作的好坏也就必定会影响整个的科学成果。因此就必定会影响整个科学成果。因此就必须强调在科学工作中要充分发挥每个工作者的实事求是的科学精神。要求严肃的、老老实实的对待每一件工作；不苟且、不马虎、脚踏实地的完成自己工作岗位上的任务，这样才能谈得到向科学进军。例如我们在进行日本血吸虫病、虐疾等传染病等防治工作的时候，就必须从疫区中收集大批数字材料，进行分析综合，找到这些传染病发生发展的规律，制订合理防治措施假如在疫区登记这些原始材料的工作人员，对数字不严肃，随便填表，则把这些材料收集在一起，任何第一流的统计学家都无法推算出科学的结论。再如，科学家在进行实验的时候，如果他的助手，技术员们地工作不细致，不准确，则他也无法得到正确的实验结果。

因此对青年医务工作者来说，热情的、实事求是的作好本岗位的工作，不断求得工作上的改进，是科学进軍的首要条件。我認为在这一方面我們有責任来进一步研究，分析、以及用实际事例来向青年們說明这一問題的重要意义。

各部门、单位要灵活而密切的配合

其次，我想談一下在科学的这个集体事業中，各个科学部門單位之間的关系及领导的关系。科学單位之間的关系是一个横的联系，而领导与各單位之間的关系是一个縱的联系。

既然科学是个集体的事業，因此在科学进軍中，各个科学部門及單位就必須有协调的步伐，灵活而密切的配合，才能完成这一进軍的任务。不論是那一項科学研究工作，必須要有有关部門的协調合作才能很好地进行。例如我們要进行猩紅热的防治研究工作，不但医学研究机構要在細菌学、病理学、藥物学方面进行，也必須有临床学家从診断、治疗等方面来协助，更須要防治机構从流行病学等方面来配合，而在进行調查时，还須要有兒童保健机構、居民地段的衛生組織的密切合作。只有在各个單位的紧密配合下，才能摸淸猩紅热这一傳染病發生發展的規律，制訂出合理而可行的防治办法。如果在配合中，有的單位考虑到本身任务比較重，对其他机構提出来的任务不能积極的配合，这样就对整个医学科学队伍的进軍不能不有所影响。因此，我認为在我国現有的人力物力的条件下，唯有加强各科学机構間的协調分工合作，互通有無，才能充分發揮現有的力量，符合勤儉办科学的方針。为了更好的协調，就必須要有統一的領导，在統一的領导下，不但可以使各科学机構間的步調可以一致，而且还可以使科学家們的工作安排的更为妥善。現在在这問題上是有缺陷的。例如，有些專家，就从多方面接到要求他完成的任务。如有一些医学專家，要求他負責編写医学院的高級教材，要求他完成一定的医疗任务，也要求他負担某一方面的專題研究工作。我不是說不可以对他們提出这些要求，也不是說他們不願意完成这些任务。而問題在于布置这些任务的不同部門之間是不是經过共同的研究，統一的布置安排。我認为这种“上面千条綫、底下一根針”的做法，在某种情况下，就不能不損害这些專家有計划、有重点的安排他們自己的工作。这对医学科学的进軍不能不說是一种損失。因此，我深刻的体会到，党所提出的向科学进軍这一号召中，进軍的重要意义。进軍就意味着有組織地，有紀律地，在統一安排之下的集体行动，而不是單干。这一号召只有在社会主义的集体思想的指导下才能充分發揮它的力量。

長远利益和当前利益的关系最后，我还想提一下在医学科学进軍中所存在着的如何恰当的安排目前利益和長远利益的問題。譬如，群众目前只感觉到医疗迫切的需要，因此單純的医疗任务就占用了医务工作者的主要力量，而就不能不影响医学科学的研究工作，这是一个矛盾。又例如，各地迫切的需要医藥衛生人材，因此各个医学院校就不得不付出絕大部分的力量来培养医学生、进修生，这样就使得一些目前为数不多的高級医学專家們的研究工作难于很好的开展，这又是一个矛盾。医疗是为了滿足人民的要求，培养和提高新生力量也是我們所需：而从長远利益来講，科学研究二作也不容有所忽視。因此，如何恰当的来对待它們之間的矛盾是需要我們很好的来研究的。我認为只有在有計划的統一領导下，在分工合作的协調基础上，做好我們当前的工作，不断地提高医学科学水平，就是解决長远利益和目前利益的关系的基本条件。

至于如何在具体工作中来全面体現向科学进軍的精神， 还須要我們大家来努力。

我的检讨[1]

1957 年 8 月 13 日

（一） 我和农工民主党的关系：我和章伯钧的关系除了听大报告和在公开的场合下吃饭外，没有私人接触过。我感觉他“能说、能讲、很有气魄”，这就使我愿意接受他的领导，为他作了以下工作：1. 给农工民主党招兵买马，不只北京，在其他地方也为他们介绍医学界的朋友和学生，利用我的地位发展组织，在我加入农工民主党前曾和政委谈过，说他们（指农工民主党）是要擒贼先擒王。2. 我为李伯球在北京市医药卫生界点火：5 月 10 号李伯球在文化俱乐部召开的西医座谈会的准备会上说：“可以说在本单位不便谈的话，如党政不分，有职无权等。”所以在 5 月 15 日，我主持的西医座谈会上，我叫大家踊跃发言向党提意见，讲不利于党的言论。不满党的领导。特别是对军委的不满，把协和当作童养媳，说军委把协和拆了，因为我的地位和煽动性言论，在校内引起了思想混乱，我应负主要责任。由于协和在医药界的地位，章伯钧、李伯球对我抓的很紧，我入农工后二月就把我放到农工民主党中央执行局，并把我推荐为反对英法侵略埃及委员会的委员。在5月15 日西医座谈会休息的时候，章伯钧亲自告诉我把我推荐为科学规划委员会的委员，章伯钧在休息时亲自告诉我，他们想把我摆在中央执行局，把李克鸿放到农工市委。在协和召开农工民主党的会议上，李伯球、李健生都参加了，那时我不但没觉得他们是两面派，同时和他们气味相投。在我参加农工之前，李伯球说：你们都忙，组织生活不一定很死，不必一定要开会。说“你担个名义就行”并与我说，通过组织提意见更有力些，我都点头称许。李健生对我说，共产党所组织的学习干燥无味，我也气味相投。我一方面在帮助他们发展组织，另外在西医座谈会上点了火。

[1] 《健康报》，1957 年 8 月 13 日，第三版。

（二） 我的政治野心：农工民主党借我点火，我也想利用农工民主党，在医药卫生界发展自己的政治野心，扩大我的影响。在校内想联系一批教授搞个组织。过去我认为自己提意见不被重视，要通过组织使我的意见和主张扩大影响，说明与党分庭抗礼，但我的政治野心不限于校内，我想通过医学教育委员会实现我的主张，解放后在高教部的一次会上就提出过，今年二月政协会上我提出组织一个医学教育委员会，妄想实现资产阶级医学教育，篡夺党的领导权。

6 月中旬向协和党委提出"我对协和发展方向的看法"，提出协和要作为全国医学教育的核心，想通过农工民主党实现我的政治野心。

（三） 我的立场问题：我所犯的错误的一切根本，是个立场问题，现在我还是牢牢站在资产阶级的反党反人民的立场上，对自己过去的反人民罪行，没有痛恨。思想改造后，虽与美帝国主义割断关系，但是立场未变，以致又犯反党反人民的罪行，在人代会上张锡均教授曾揭发了我的过去。我从资产阶级立场出发，处处对党不满，对军委卫生部有对立情绪，对党交给的任务消极敷衍。去年有一次周总理问我，对协和交地方有什么意见？我说对军委的领导很留恋。是因为军委在物质方面很优越。

几天来，我很沉痛，我愿意接受这场惨痛的教训，向人民低头认罪，接受对我的处分。我检查最近一年来为什么反人民的立场有所发展？

第一. 我长期受资产阶级思想熏染，资产阶级思想在我是根深蒂固的，在旧社会长期处在统治阶级地位。

第二. 主观上从未认真学习，甚至八大文件，邓小平的修改党章报告都没学习过，更谈不到学习方针政策了。由于不好好学习，不但没改变立场，反人民的立场还有所发展。对个别党员虽在业务上接触多，但思想上没见面，与党员站在对立的立场，所以看党员不顺眼，埋怨党的领导，我与党的距离越来越大，因我不热爱人民事业对之愈益严重，成为人民的罪人，尤其在苏共 20 次代表大会后，匈牙利事件后，我觉得共产党没有新的发展，在社会主义国家也出现这样事，所以反人民的立场有所发展。如果没有这次反右派分子的斗争，我将不知到什么地步。

（8 月 6 日在中共中国协和医学院党委召开的座谈会上李宗恩交代的三个问题）

李宗恩日记[1]

（1958年2月1日至1962年2月28日）

1958年

二月一日　　晴　　六

上下午：阅读报纸及哲学。

二月二日　　　　日

上下午：阅读报纸及哲学。

二月三日　　　　一

上下午：阅读哲学。

二月四日　　　　二

上下午：阅读哲学。

二月五日　　　　三

上下午：阅读哲学。

晚：王主任来电话说明天下午二时在十楼223号课室开会约我出席。

今日叔昭[2]去医院取安眠药。

二月六日　　　　四

上午：哲学。

下午：在十楼223传达国务院处理右派原则。

---

[1] 李维华收藏。

[2] 编者注：叔昭即妻子何晋。

二月七日　　　　　　五

上午：哲学。

下午：文件学习。

晚：出席农工民主党在和平宾馆开会传达中央关于处理右派分子的决议。

二月八日　　　　　　六

上下午：哲学。

帮助叔昭统计粮公节约材料。

二月九日：　　　　　日

上午：休息。

下午：整理购粮证。

二月十日　　　　　　一

上午：农工党市委会来电话说王人旋主委要约谈，时间未定。

下午：三时在辛寺的农工党北京市委王人旋主委约谈，在全国民主党派人士中有 96 名“标兵”，经过详细讨论后作出决定，包括本人在内。

二月十一日　　风四至五级　　二

上午：阅读周总理发言。

下午：哲学。

二月十二日　　　　　三

上午：今日觉得不甚舒服，稍有头痛。

下午：休息。

二月十三日　　　　　四

上下午：学习哲学。

二月十四日　　　　　五

上下午：学习哲学。

晚同叔昭出外散步，到东四大同酒家宵夜。

二月十五日　　　　　六

上午：阅读学习，政治部来电今日下午四至六时核对材料。

下午；到新楼会议室核对检查材料。

晚：寿复量血压 180/100。

二月十六日　　　　　日

上下午：哲学。

二月十七日　　　　　一

上下午：哲学。

二月十八日　　　　　二（春节，编者注）

上午：阅读斯大林时代，鲁陶[1]来拜年。

下午：胡正详及胡真来访。

二月十九日　　　　　三

上午：帮助叔昭打扫烧饭，胡正详太太及孟继懋太太来访。

下午：陈 XX（人民出版社）来拜年。

二姊来晚餐。

二月廿日　　　　　四

上午：函复刘良湛。

下午：读斯大林时代。

---

[1] 编者注：何鲁陶，何晋的亲戚。

二月廿一日　　　　　五

上午：哲学。

下午：*Studies in a Dying Culture* (Caudwell)

二月廿二日　　　　　六

上午：11:30，高血压门诊复诊。

下午：同苏苏讲故事，叔昭出去采购，汪嫂同苏苏之间有矛盾，同时照顾小华和苏苏有困难。

二月廿三日　　　　　日

上下午：学习哲学，参读 Caudwell's "*Studies in a Dying Culture*" 贵医同学陈 X 献来访。人民出版社。

二月廿四日　　　　　一

上下午：读完唯物辩证法的基本规律。

晚：180/104。

二月廿五日　　　　　二

上午：到院做心电图，政治部通知明日下午三时在礼堂前厅开会。

下午；休息，牙痛甚剧。

二月廿六日　　　　　三

上午：学习哲学。

下午：礼堂张政委向右派分子作报告。

二月廿七日　　　　　四

上午：阅读。

下午：家属委员会在楼下开会，牙痛稍好。

二月廿八日　　　　　五

上午：协助清洁。

下午：理发。

三月一日　　　北风，甚冷　　六

上下午：帮助清洁，顺三来做一天清洁工作，做得很不彻底。

三月二日　　　　　　　　日

上下午：帮助清洁。

三月三日　　　　　　　　一

上下午：帮助清洁。

三月四日　　　　　　　　二

上午：寄函苏州胡同国际书店关于医中华医学会代订的《日本医学通报》（三月三日）。

下午：阅读《澳洲医学报》合订本，下午东塘子胡同来院作卫生检查。牙根疼仍未消除。

三月五日　　　　　　　　三

上午：农工民主党来通知今晚在和平宾馆开会。

下午：去口腔科看牙床脓疱，切除并打青霉素一针，

晚：出席农工民主党召开的整风运动会。

三月六日　　　　　　　　四

上午：《人民日报》登出撤销本人的科学规划委员会的兼职。

下午：阅读文件。

三月七日　　　　　　　　五

上午：帮助清洁。

下午：去牙科复诊，并照相，取药。政治部电话，李政委或陈子扬这几天都很忙不能约谈。

三月八日　　　　　　　六

上下午：阅读。

三月九日　　　　　　　日

上下午：协助清洁。

同叔昭到大同酒家小吃。

三月十日　　　　　　　一

上下午：阅读。

三月十一日　　　　　　二

上午：院送来海关通知书一件。

下午：到公安街邮局取由伦敦热带病学院赠给领带一条，收税 250%（共合 3.23），如用包裹寄可能便宜些。

三月十二日　　昨晚撤销暖气　三

上午：阴，微雨，五六级风。

下午：阅读。晚：购得皮尺一具。

三月十三日　　　　　　四

上下午：阅读。

三月十四日　　　　　　五

上午：读报。

下午：到农工民主党阅看大字报，函复 Sir James Kilpatrick。

三月十五日　　　　　　六

上午：阅报。

下午：函复 Mrs. C. Simpson。

三月十六日　　　　　日

上午：阅报。

下午：阅读。

三月十七日　　　　　一

上下午：阅读。

三月十八日　　　　　二

上下午：阅读。

三月十九日　　　　　三

上午：赴院看大字报。

下午：起稿个人改造计划。

三月廿日　　　　　四

上午：读报。

下午：写个人计划。

三月廿一日　　　　　五

上午：政委谈话，关于我的处理，降级、降薪。

下午：购邮票将 Mrs. C. Simpson's 回信发出。

三月廿二日　　　　　六

上午：听彭真市长报告，二点半到家。

下午：休息。晚：出席漫谈会。

三月廿三日　　　　　日

上午：看报。

下午：植树。

三月廿四日　　　　一

上午：高血压复诊，看大字报，开始服用利血平（低压 110）。

下午：学习，到农工民主党市委同薛敏同志谈话。

三月廿五日　　　　二

上午：阅报。

下午：写自我检查。

三月廿六日　　　　三

上午：看报，电话宣传科请给一份大字报资料。

下午：阅读文件。

三月廿七日　　　　四

上下午：阅读文件，自我检查。

三月廿八日　　　　五

上午：到院参观浪费展览会，到政治部取大字报汇编，到管理科了解退房事，称下星期三开会将决定告诉我，到办公室寻高奇科长不在，王主任病假。

下午：看大字报，电话拆走。

三月廿九日　　　　六

上午：阅读文件。

下午：阅读大字报汇报，接到农工党寄来的政协全国委员会整风报告会入场卷（III28），因寄至科学院收发室，今日下午蒋予图先生转来，此信是 27 日下午 2 时发出，下午 6 时到。

三月卅日　　　　日

上午：读报及大字报。

下午：同叔昭到天文馆，天象厅票已售完，莫斯科餐厅晚餐。

三月卅一日　　　　　　一

上午：本院传呼电话是复兴食堂，5 · 5728，电话农工民主党冯书耕同志请他已后将通知直接寄至家中并告以上传呼电话。

下午：学习文件。

四月一日　　　　　　二

上午：《中华医学内科杂志》。

下午：《文艺报》 B.P. 190/96

四月二日　　　　　　三

上午：到院办公室清理书籍文献。

下午：阅读文件。

四月三日　　　　　　四

上午：到院办公室清理书柜。

下午：《文艺报》周扬报告。

四月四日　　　　　　五

上午：到院整理办公室书籍文件。

下午：阅读大字报汇编及《跃进报》。

四月五日　　　　　　六

上午：到院将清理办公室存在的问题交王荣全先生书面材料。

下午：阅读历史唯物主义。

四月六日　　　　　　日

上下午：协助叔昭核对选民表。

四月七日　　　　　　一

上下午：阅读历史唯（物）主义。

四月八日　　　　　　　二

上下午：学习。

晚：农工民主党市委召集市成员会介绍天津交心先进经验，范权报告。

四月九日　　　　　　　三

上午：政协礼堂听关于工业化的报告。

下午：学习历史唯物主义。

晚：家属开普选报告会。

四月十日　　　　　　　四

上下午：学习红与专问题。

晚：礼堂开会张院长报告本年基层普选意义。

四月十一日　　　　　　五

上午：到院看寄生物学系大字报。

下午：搬动房间。

四月十二日　　　　　　六

上午：政协医药卫生组开会。

下午：访问周诒春老先生。

四月十三日　　　　　　日

上下午：休息。

四月十四日　　　　　　一

上午：高血压复诊，低压控制得很好。

下午：收拾客厅。

四月十五日　　　　　　二

上下午：阅读文件。

四月十六日　　　　　　三

上下午：阅读文件。

四月十七日　　　　　　四

上午：到办公室整理档卷。

下午：礼堂交心大会。

晚：选民小组会。

四月十八日　　　　　　五

上午：到办公室结束交代，看大字报。

下午：生理科陈XX来谈李铭新教授交心问题。

晚：农工民主党交心会。

四月十九日　　　　　　六

上下午：围剿麻雀。

四月廿日　　　　　　　日

上下午：围剿麻雀。

四月廿一日　　　　　　一

上午：围剿麻雀。

下午：写交心材料一小时半。

四月廿二日　　　　　　二

上下午：写交心材料。

四月廿三日　　　　　　三

上午：写交心材料。

下午：阅读南共纲领草案批判。

晚：农工民主党交心会，检查者：李克鸿、刘士豪、陈桂光。

四月廿四日　　　　　四

上午：拟交心提纲。

下午：礼堂张政委报告，大争大辨，大整大改。

晚：选民小组开会。

四月廿五日　　　　　五

上午：拟交心会提纲。

下午：阅读文件。

晚：农工民主党交心会。

四月廿六日　　　　　六

上午：阅读文件。

下午：小组讨论。

晚：同叔昭到市场晚餐。

四月廿七日　　　　　日

上午：收拾由院取回书籍及文件。

下午：到天象馆，会到前贵阳医学院毕业生刘世曾大夫。

四月廿八日　　　　　一

上午：考虑科学前进中存在的问题。

下午：大扫除，小组停止一次。

四月廿九日　　　　　二

上下午：礼堂前厅召开教授交心会。

晚：时事报告，报告人陈子杨。

四月卅日　　　　　三

上午：写交心材料。

下午：出席解剖科小组讨论。

晚：同叔昭出外散步。

五月一日　　　　　四

上午：填关于吴明权、俞敏良的调查表。

下午：同叔昭外出散步。

晚上看花。

五月二日　　　　　五

上午：写检查两条。

下午：同叔昭去理发，买纸及书。

五月三日　　　　　六

上午：到卫生部听报告（徐部长）。

下午：解剖组小组讨论。

五月四日　　　　　日

上午：理发，熄火准备修理炉子。

下午：监督修理炉子。

晚：偕叔昭看电影“伪金币”。

五月五日　　　　　一

上午：高血压门诊复诊。

出外午餐，修理炉灶。

下午：解剖科小组宣布各自先阅读大字报汇报，并提出问题。

五月六日　　　　　二

上午：写交心材料。

下午：阅读大字报汇编。

五月七日　　　　　　　三

上午：写交心材料。

下午：阅读大字报汇编。

晚：出席选民小组。

五月八日　　　　　　　四

上午：政协礼堂听报告——孟用潜（国际关系研究所所长），讲美国经济危机。

下午：解剖科，小组讨论。

五月九日　　　　　　　五

上午：阅读。

下午：小组学习，政委办公室介绍王斌同志了解刘施青历史并将他的来信取去。

晚：农工民主党例会未开。

五月十日　　　　　　　六

上午：阅报，有关南共修正主义。

下午：小组讨论：薛先生检查交心。

晚：至市场采购卷宗夹，尺寸不合。

五月十一日　　　　　　晴　　　日

上午：研究形态实验系讨论提纲。

下午：文化俱乐部农工党交心运动经验交流会。

五月十二日　　　　　　一

上午：阅读文件。

下午：解剖科小组学习。

晚：农工党组会，我自己交心。

五月十三日　　　　　二

上午：阅读内科的重要问题。

下午：实验形态学小组讨论。

坐久后有头晕症状。

五月十四日　　　　　三

上午：阅读苏联干部政策。

下午：政协交心材料分析批判经验交流。

晚：选民小组会。

五月十五日　　　　　四

上午：阅读苏联干部政策。

下午：解剖科小组讨论（何助理研究员检查）。

五月十六日　　　　　五

上午：阅读苏联干部政策。

下午：2-4 阅读南共纲领，4-6 批判现代修正主义。

五月十七日　　　　　六

上午：写小字报一张。

下午：实验形态系小组讨论。

五月十八日　　　　　日

上午：投票。觉得头痛回家休息。

下午：头痛好转，同叔昭出外散步，到国子监图书馆。

五月十九日　　　　　一

上午：阅报，关于南共修正主义，苏联医务干部政策。

下午：小组讨论：学科发展与国家任务有没有矛盾?

晚：农工党支部会议。

五月廿日　　　　　　二

上午：阅读。

下午：小组讨论 - 继续，协调合作。

晚：大华电影，后在德昌厚遇宗津。

五月廿一日　　　　　三

上午：阅读。

下午：小组讨论：谈协调合作。

五月廿二日　　　　　四

上午：阅读《批判南共现代修正主义》（《真理报》社论）。

下午：小组进行讨论，"协调合作问题"。

五月廿三日　　　　　五

上午：考虑干部培养中的问题。

下午：小组讨论 —— 干部培养。

五月廿四日　　　　　六

上午：阅报。

下午：小组讨论。

五月廿五日　　　　　日

上午：同叔昭及苏苏到中山公园游览，参观除四害参展会。

下午：同苏苏讲书。

五月廿六日　　　　　一

上午：高血压门诊复诊，利血平每日一粒 0.25。

下午：前期辩论，J223。

晚：农工党交心会，付 1958 年党费，1 至 6 月底。

五月廿七日　　　　　二

上午：阅报，中共工作报告。

下午：前期辩论。

向李克鸿借《政治经济学》。

五月廿八日　　　　　三

上午：阅报。

下午：前期辩论继续。

晚：继续。

熏鼠运动。

五月廿九日　　　　　四

上午：理发、阅读。

下午：礼堂全院大辩论。

五月卅日　　　　　五

上午：阅报、看大字报。

下午：阅读《政治经济学》，小组讨论（形态系）。

五月卅一日　　　　　六

上午：阅读第七册大字报汇编。

下午：张政委传达总路线精神。

六月一日　　　　　日

上午：阅读人大第二次会议工作报告。

下午：在形态系小组讨论。

晚：患牙痛。

六月二日　　　　　一

上午：阅读帝国主义讲座。

下午：广播八大录音，扩大器发生障碍停止。

三时到口腔科看牙。

晚：农工党周会。

六月三日　　　　　　二

上午：干部处李子和处长同我谈云南医学院教学事。有位徐同志约谈关于蔡谦材料。到牙科上药，约定本星期五上午去拔牙。

下午：美术学院礼堂徐部长报告关于医院改革及中医学习问题。

晚：形态系小组讨论徐部长报告，因牙痛未去。

六月四日　　　　　　三

上午：阅读《帝国主义的基本经济规律》。

下午：形态科小组讨论通过跃进决心书。

晚：文化俱乐部农工党市委召开梳辫子的经验交流。

六月五日　　　　　　四

上午：阅读报纸，打电话约李处长谈话，不在。

下午：形态科小组讨论。

六月六日　　　　　　五

上午：拔牙。

下午：休息。

六月七日　　　　　　六

上午：《帝国主义经济规律》。去政治部取下午天桥剧场入场票。去牙科约星期一上午去看。

下午：天桥剧场中国医学科学院跃进誓师大会。

六月八日　　　　　　日

上午：阅读《帝国主义经济规律》。

下午：帮助叔昭腾写大字报。

六月九日　　　　　　一

上午：牙科复诊，同李子和处长反映情况。

下午：形态系小组讨论。

晚：农工党组织生活。

六月十日　　　　　　二

上午：阅读《帝国主义经济规律》，重读细菌战黑皮书。

下午：前期礼堂开会，比干劲、比精神、比指标运动开始。继续讨论。

六月十一日　　　　　三

上午：广西老三工作的林场主任来访。

下午：形态系小组讨论献礼。

六月十二日　　　　　四

上午: 将 Roll's Razor 借给形态系技术员参考。

下午：政协礼堂，大跃进大会。

六月十三日　　　　　五

上午：阅读《资本主义经济规律》。

下午：口腔科做模型。小组讨论。

六月十四日　　　　　六

上午：阅报，关于现代修正主义的反动性质。

下午：阅读《政治经济学》。

六月十五日　　　　　日

上午：同叔昭去参观纪念塔。

下午：阅读《政治经济学》。

六月十六日　　一

上下午：阅读《政治经济学》。

晚：农工民主党小组会。

六月十七日　　二

上午：去牙科补牙，党委介绍张同亮同志来了解林敦英事。

下午：草拟梳辫子稿。有一位姜同志来了解刘承元问题。

六月十八日　　三

上午：阅报，草拟检查提纲。

下午：去红星看《在总路线的光辉照耀下》。

六月十九日　　四

上午：开始写检查。

下午：继续阅读材料。

晚：张作干来谈修改英文稿件，开始修改。

六月廿日　　五

上午：继续修改。

下午：同张作干研究英文稿件。

六月廿一日　　六

上午：去口腔科拔牙，回家休息。

下午：休息，伤口疼，不能进饮食。

六月廿二日　　日

上午：去口腔科冲洗，假牙比较服帖。

下午：同叔昭出去散步。

六月廿三日　　　　一

上午：8:30 到口腔科冲洗，伤口良好。

下午：写检讨。

六月廿四日　　　　二

上午：理发，写检讨。

下午：口腔补牙，写检讨。

晚：预定农工党小组会未开。

六月廿五日　　　　三

上午：写检查。

下午：写检查，并读华教授关于争取长寿文章。

（汪嫂回家）

六月廿六日　　　　四

上午：读报，有关南共修正主义。

下午：抄检讨副本。

六月廿七日　　　　五

上午：阅读知识分子改造问题。

下午：补牙，修脚，洗澡。

六月廿八日　　　　六

上午：去高血压门诊，发现已改日子，重约星期一下午 3:30。回家阅读知识分子改造文件。

下午：《政治经济学》。

六月廿九日　　　　日　　　晚间大雨

上午：《政治经济学》，出外散步。

下午：《政治经济学》。

六月卅日　　一

上午：《政治经济学》。

下午：《政治经济学》。3:30 高血压门诊复诊，每日继续服一片。

七月一日　　二

上午：《政治经济学》。

下午：《政治经济学》。5:00 口腔补牙。

七月二日　　三

上午：给干部处联系，李处长开会不在。

下午：政治经济学学习。

七月三日　　四

上下午：修改张作干送来组织化学英文稿。

张先生准备本星期六飞基辅。

七月四日　　五

上午：口腔科修义齿，又去看黄宛大夫检查身体。

下午：华教授内科讲义。

根据黄宛教授意见利血平开始每日两片。

七月五日　　六

上午：到实验形态系拿院刊，购书。

下午：阅读中医理论。

晚：同叔昭到北海散步。

七月六日　　日

上午：随叔昭及苏苏到中山公园参观红专展览会。

下午：大雨，在家修改《实验形态系摘要》。

七月七日　　　　　　一

上午：口腔科修理义齿，除星期五上午，每日上午都可复查。去张鋆教授交英文摘要。

下午：上煤球一千斤（11.50）。

阅读中医概论。

农工党的小组会又改在星期一晚举行，但我未接着电话通知（本院守卫室忘却转告）未出席。

七月八日　　　　　　二

上午：电话刘国声同志得知农工党组会已于昨晚开过，刘士豪因调至北京医院已不参加矽肺研究。阅读《政治经济学》。

下午：去五楼访视李克鸿，回家碰见刘瑞华来宅闲谈。

七月九日　　　　　　三

上午：修改《实验形态学论文摘要》，叔昭去科学院取薪，图章存叔昭处。

下午：同卫生科取得联系，明早 8:30 去做 P.S.P. task，读华教授讲义。

七月十日　　　　　　四

上午：到卫生科做 P.S.P. task 及 N.P.N.

下午：读华教授讲义。

晚：张鋆教授来谈关于英文文摘。

七月十一日　　阴雨　　五

上下午：阅读华教授讲义，苏苏发烧（感冒）。

七月十二日　　　　　六

上下午：阅读华教授讲义。

七月十三日　　　　　日

上下午：阵雨，

晚：农工党小组长刘国声来宅并同至李克鸿室访问。

七月十四日　　　　　一

上下午：阅读文件（农工发下文件）。

七月十五日　　　　　二

上午：到政委办公室同兰同志谈施正信将来京，如他要拜访我，我应取什么态度，请党委指示。

购业务书籍，同黄宛大夫联系，关于身体检查结果。

下午：考虑个人红专计划。

晚：李漪来访叔昭。

七月十六日　　　　　三

上下午：草拟红专计划。

晚：同苏苏到市场散步，购买稿纸。

七月十七日　　　　　四

上午：写红专规划初稿。

下午：阅读文件，毛主席《两类不同性质的矛盾》。

七月十八日　　　　　五

上下午：阅读人民内部矛盾。

七月十九日　　晴，热　六

上下午：人民内部矛盾。

晚：同叔昭去国货公司购物并去访施正信（和平宾馆）。

七月廿日　　　　　日

上午：今早非常炎热，在家阅读业务书籍《日本医学通报》。

下午：阅读时事。

晚：王竹勤同志来访并去慰问李克鸿。

七月廿一日　　　　一

上午：时事阅读，同李处长联系不在。

下午：社会主义课程阅读。

晚：农工党组会。

七月廿二日　　　　二

上午：同李处长联系说去天津，约明天同兰助理员联系。理发。

下午：礼堂听报告，齐部长助理传达现场会议精神，破迷信，反保守在消灭血吸虫病的战线上所起的作用。

七月廿三日　　阴雨　　三

上午：电话党委办公室兰助理员关于今后工作安排问题，兰说李处长到阜成门外有事回来再同他谈。

阅读帝国主义殖民主义制度。

下午：阅读《前进报》，学习材料。

七月廿四日　　　　四

上下午：业务学习。

七月廿五日　　　　五

上午：到政委办公室取天桥剧场入场卷（总路线）。

下午：到新华书店购书。

晚：打滴滴涕。

七月廿六日　　　　　六

上午：阅读报纸。

下午：政协听报告，中东问题。

七月廿七日　　　　　日

上午：阅读报纸。施正信来访。

下午：政协报告，反殖民主义，反修正主义。

七月廿八日　　　　　一

上午：社会主义思想教育问题解答。

下午：高血压门诊，血压仍高。

七月廿九日　　　　　二

上午：社会主义思想问题解答，关于右派，关于资产阶级思想。

下午：继续。

七月卅日　　　　　三

上午：社会主义教育思想学习。

下午：继续。

七月卅一日　　　　　四

上午：去干部处访李处长不在，将信面交。

下午：学习国家资本主义。

晚：同苏苏去中山公园散步。

八月一日　　　五

上午：阅读报纸，孟继懋太太来访，修脚。

下午：休息，咳嗽。

晚：人民剧场——林海雪原（现代化京戏）。

八月二日　　雨　　六

上午：同李子和处长谈话，决定去昆明。

下午：阅读南共修正主义。

八月三日　　雨　　日

上午：休息。

八月四日　　一

上午：9-1:30 政协礼堂听艾思奇报告——专政与民主。

下午：阅读。

八月五日　　二

上午：到航空公司，前门车站。

下午：到前门车站行李代运处，崇外大街托运处。

晚：到文化宫散步，同叔昭及苏苏。

八月六日　　三

上午：去口腔科拔牙。

下午：休息。

八月七日　　四

上午：写信给昆明省委宣传部。

下午：阅读。

晚：农工小组会。

八月八日　　五

上午：访干部处李处长，收到行政介绍信。

下午：同叔昭去银行出售银器。

八月九日　　　六

上午：收拾东西，叔昭走访宗津，去托运公司。

下午：出售银器。

八月十日　　　日

上午：去琉璃厂，接洽出售字画。

下午：收拾楼上及楼下东西。

八月十一日　　　　一

上午：同苏苏到市场买物。

下午：琉璃厂人来看字画。

宗津来宅谈天。

八月十二日　　　　二

上午：修血压表。

下午：修理皮包。

八月十三日　　　　三

上午：收拾书籍及鞋子。

下午：取钢笔、血压表，及到人民市场；血压表臼八面槽医药公司实验工厂修理，19日可取。张有光来谈字画。

八月十四日　　　　四

上下午：收拾照片，学习。

八月十五日　　　　五

上午：学习。

下午：到人民市场接洽字画。

八月十六日　　　　六

上午：购绳子，收拾行李。

下午：收拾行李。

八月十七日　　　　日

上午：清理字画。

下午：同苏苏到吉祥看戏，王竹琴先生来访，张有光（荣宝斋）来谈字画出售事。

八月十八日　　　　一

上下午：收拾瓷器及字画。

八月十九日　　　　二

上午：到人民市场接洽字画，出售字画。取血压表。

下午：人民市场工艺品商店人来看字画。腾写检讨。

八月廿日　　　　三

上午：收拾画箱；腾写改造规划。鲁陶来。

下午：同叔昭到琉璃厂，荣宝斋。

八月廿一日　　　　四

上午：收拾文件。

下午：收拾文件，同叔昭去看《两姊妹》，宽银幕，大同晚餐。左臂首缓痛。

八月廿二日　　　　五

上午：理发。

下午：收拾文件。

八月廿三日　　　　　六

上午：收拾书籍及文件。

下午：收拾书籍。

八月廿四日　　　　　日

上午：收拾书籍。

下午：去崇文门外。

八月廿五日　　　　　一

上午：包装书籍。

下午：五弟妹[1]来访，心肾科复诊。

八月廿六日　　　　　二

上下午：到朝阳门外废品收购站。到管理科订票，收拾书籍（包装）。

八月廿七日　　　　　三

上午：到中国银行换去港币十元，每元 9021。

下午：荣宝斋张有光来取字画、砚、墨等。

晚：南河沿文化俱乐部晚会。

八月廿八日　　　　　四

上午：到电话李处长不在，政委亦不在。

下午：收拾书桌。

八月廿九日　　　　　五

上午：去中国银行换美元票（￥14.40）。

下午：去政协秘书处；晚张有平来访。

---

[1] 编者注：即李宗津的妻子，周珊凤。

八月卅日　　　　　　　六

上午：到民航公司及中国银行。

下午：同叔昭到故宫。

八月卅一日　　　　　　日

上午：廊坊二条 10 号荣宝斋珠宝门市部 3,2620. 刘。

下午：到孝顺胡同木器修理部。

九月一日　　　　　　　一

上午：中国银行金垣同志来谈保险费。

下午：收拾行李。

九月二日　　　雨　　　二

上午：去政协礼堂，到彼后因天雨去十三陵参观延期。

下午：收拾行李。

九月三日　　　晴　　　三

上午：第一批书籍寄出，中国银行金垣同志来访，收拾行李。

下午：电话政委约时会谈，王人旋主委有会约明日下午三时后，管理科通知飞机定于十五日。

九月四日　　　　　　　四

上午：寄书，看牙，政委办公室同蓝同志谈保险单事。

下午：到辛寺胡同访王人旋谈话。

九月五日　　　　　　　五

上下午：收拾行李，帮助寿复搬家，看牙。

晚：到孙邦藻家未遇。

九月六日　　　　　　六

上午：收拾行李，到中国银行谈保险问题。

下午：收拾行李。

九月七日　　　　　　日

上午：寿复搬家。

下午：同苏苏上街看游行，到百货公司运货。

九月八日　　　　　　一

上午：收拾行李。

下午：口腔科。

九月九日　　　　　　二

上午：陈子杨科长来谈。

下午：到寿复新宅。

九月十日　　　　　　三

上午：去托运公司，阅读北京市农工党代表大会工作报告。

九月十一日　　　　　四

搬运行李。

九月十二日　　　　　五

搬运行李。

九月十三日　　　　　六

政委约谈话。

九月十四日　　　　　日

晚在和平餐厅聚餐。

九月十五日　　　　一

乘飞机来昆明，住昆明旅馆。

九月十六日　　　　二

休息。

九月十七日　　　　三

上午：到省委报到并见到颜院长。

下午：医学院派车接到附属医院后指定医学院教职员宿舍住宿，但在附属医院食堂用膳。

九月十八日　　　　四

上午：拜访杜院长并同禤秘书接洽。

下午：到市内购置物件。

九月十九日　　　　五

上午：细雨路甚泥泞。

下午：休息。

九月廿日　　　　六

上午：休息，至医院寄信并遇见秦作梁先生。

下午：到南屏街理发并购买日常用品。

九月廿一日　　　　晴　　日

上午：清洁卫生工作。

下午：走访秦作梁先生及其爱人并同至圆通公园晚餐。返寓已七点半钟矣。

约今早去探望王党委书记。

九月廿二日　　　　　　晴　　　一

上午：阅读人民公社材料。

下午：秦作梁教授来谈，党委书记开会忙改日再约。寄北京王人旋主委信。

晚：到大街上买水果。

九月廿三日　　　　　　二

上午：到医院见陈科长并请代做一大便凳。在医院挂号并请秦医生开安眠药处方。

下午：学习人民公社文件。去访曹科长未遇。

九月廿四日　　　　　　三

上午：阅报，学习人民公社文件 。

下午： 到大观街购物及水果。

九月廿五日　　　　　　四

上午：阅报，23 日《人民日报》。

下午：学习陆定一《关于教育必须与生产劳动相结合》。

九月廿六日　　　　　　五

上午：学习，阅读《人民日报》（廿四日，廿五日）。

下午：学习。

晚：秦教授来告知图书馆人员均忙于积肥，图书馆仅于 12-2 时开馆两小时。

九月廿七日　　　雨（中秋节）　六

上午：阅读。

下午：同叔昭到医院寄信购饭票。

九月廿八日　　阴雨　　　　日

上午：休息。

下午：阅读阿英小说《闲谈》。

九月廿九日　　阴　　　　一

上午：阅读。

下午：清洁卫生。

九月卅日　　上午阴，下午晴　　　　二

上午：清洁卫生。

下午：到大观街买物。

十月一日　　阴雨　　　　三

上下午：阅报。

十月二日　　阴　　　　四

上午：阅报，业务学习，见童主任，去医院见到张师傅。

下午：去医院门诊部内科取安眠药。

十月三日　　晴　　　　五

上午：见王党委书记。

下午：业务学习。

十月四日　　晴　　　　六

上午：见梁院长，嘱明日开始在内科门诊工作，每日暂工作六小时，姚主任各方面介绍情况。

下午：至市内购物，听诊器等。

十月五日　　雨　　　　日

上下午：门诊应诊。

十月六日　　　雨，下午阴　　一

上下午：门诊应诊。

十月七日　　　　　　　　二

上下午：门诊应诊。

晚：门诊。

十月八日　　　　　　　　三

上下午：门诊，叔昭至文教部。

晚：文教部长来信及书包裹一个。

十月九日　　　　　　　　四

上下午：门诊，

晚：门诊，叔昭至巡津街邮局取书，共 22 包（连昨晚一包），并至南站及西站货运处，大概在南站。

十月十日至十月十七日

在这一期间天天在门诊工作有时晚间亦值班。

无特殊情况可记录。

十月十八日到廿二日

十月十九日星期日到南站取回行李。

1959 年

自 1959 一月二十八 至三月十六日（共四十八天）

右派分子集中学习总结检查。

十月十八日　　星期日

集体参加秋收工作。七时在门诊部集中，天阴下小雨，排队后步行至大观楼官渡。因走不快只能徐步跟在队后。过河因人多船小约半小时方渡。过河又经过一小村落方到达稻田，道路泥泞颇滑，时刻有摔跤之虞。

工作分工是将田里的稻束整理，倒下的树立起来。原则是稻束须排列整齐，束与束之间要有一定的距离，四周要腾出一公尺的边以便积肥。实际收割工作已完，我们的工作本来是将田里的稻束运经打谷场，但因天雨稻穗尚未晒干，只好做些整理工作。

还有一小学的捡粮队在田里捡拾落下的粳粒，使粳粒还家，节约粮食。

从工作的量，实在谈不上劳动，但从工作的性质来说，它的教育意义很大。当我在作这工作的时候，我浮浅的体会到，我为人人，人人为我的精神。这一工作不是为了哪一个人的吃饭问题，而是大家的福利事业，社会主义建设事业。儿童都组织起来，从小就参加增产节约的运动。它的教育意义又是何等重大。

这都是新社会的新事物，新风气，新精神，新道德。

1959 年暑假自九月二十四日至十月七日，十月十八日参加秋收，十一月二十七日星期五集中学习，1960 元月七日交总结——共 42 天。

1960 年

四月二十六日

调图书馆工作，每月初作书面汇报。

十月一日、二 日：学习，李富春的《高举总路线的红旗继续前进》，《人民日报》（八月十七日），及李维汉的《学习毛主席著作，逐步改进世界观》，《人民日报》（九月二十六日）。

十二月十三日：读《各国共产党和工人党代表会议声明》（《云南日报》60.12.7）抄录第五节：共产党和工人阶级的历史任务。（略）

十二月十四日：《会议声明》，《告世界人民书》。（略）

十二月十六日：《云南日报》

《红旗》社论《反帝国主义的伟大号召》（12/13）

《人民日报》社论《胜利的旗帜，团结的旗帜》（12/8）

《建立反对帝国主义侵略和战争的统一战线，防止世界战争，争取持久和平》（12/13）

《健康报》转载苏联《真理报》《关于各国共产党和工人党代表会议声明的社论》（12/10）

寿白：广西，平果县中共县委会工交部基建委员会

抄录鲁宾斯坦著《为美帝国主义服务的资产阶级科学和技术》丁夫译，生活·读书·新知三联出版社，1957 年北京

第十二章：为帝国主义服务的资产阶级医学

1961 年

2 月 28 日，读《拉丁美洲通讯集》第一集，世界知识出版社，1960 北京，介绍古巴革命后的新气象。

3 月 12 日：《云南日报》：《点面结合的工作方法》。

《红旗》1961 年 5 号 社论《在学术研究中坚持百花齐放百家争鸣的方针》

通过这一学习使我对于垄断资本的认识提高了一步。我已往的各种极端错误的看法和想法得到解决。例如，我曾认为科学总是知识的积累，知识总是真理或真理的一部分，与社会制度没有关系。我还认为一个科学工作者有他的"独立性"，与政治的关系不大。鲁宾斯坦通过大量事实的揭露把问题的本质介绍得很清楚，而有些现象我自己亦往往碰到或看到，但因为自己的反动立场以致自己曾一度做了垄断资本和殖民主义者的工具和帮凶。在这一点上我感谢党的教育，我的结论是：（1）虽然科学和技术本身是没有阶级性的，但社会制度决定着他的作用、发展方向和速度；（2）资本主义的总危机包括科学和艺术的没落，垄断资本的统治渗透到社会生活的一切领域中，使资本主义的总崩溃不可避免地到来。

近来图书馆工作比较忙，晚上总觉得有些疲乏，因而未曾抓紧自学时间。但为了进一步弄清楚垄断资本的本质，特别它对科学和技术的影响，还是阅读了一些有关这方面的资料。

5 月 8 日致农工民主党信：

农工民主党组织部：

我调来图书馆已一年了，服务一直在期刊组。年初以来，因人事调动，本来三个人的工作现在由我一人负责。

在党的领导下和同事们的帮助能够按期完成任务。以往每周参加园地劳动，身体有了锻炼。最近因关节常⽿隐痛，组织又让我做些室内清洁卫生工作，给我时间练太极拳，很有帮助。

在政治学习方面，除经常参加馆内布置的集体学习，利用业余时间参阅些有关帝国主义的侵略本质和它的经济基础、殖民政策及几方面的资料；对垄断资本的认识有所提高。最近对垄断资本统治下的科学发展方向的被歪曲和技术进步的被阻碍结合自己的思想写了一个小结汇报给组织。一个月前组织让我参加医学院教职员的神仙会学习，我有决心做好我的工作，加紧自己的改造来报答党对我的关怀，耐心的教育和各方面的照顾。

兹随函汇上人民币￥17.28 作为我的 1961 全年党费，请查收是可。61.5.8

对于改造：一方面有迫切愿望能够早日揭掉帽子回到人民的队伍里来：（1）年龄不让我一拖再拖，（2）改善处境，（3）改善家庭关系。另一方面：自己亦承认改造成绩不大，对自己要求不够迫切

寿白来函（61-5-21）自南宁

复信稿：

在检查方面肝细胞组织虽无特殊变化，但发现有血铁沉着，是与一般人不同的，对于身体有何妨碍尚不明确，胆囊造影都不显影说明肝的功能不够好。所幸者肝电波检查未发现肿大，因此证明不是合并性肝炎。

作了详细的检查很全面很好。我们的红血球血红蛋白在新陈代谢的过程中，分解为铁蛋白和胆红素，血铁沉着如不过多，一般来说并不是不正常的现

象。人体内胆铁经常以蛋白的形式或多或少地在肝脾及骨髓内存在着。既然肝细胞组织无变化，这一现象对于你的意义不大。你的黄疸是因为肝排泄不含铁的胆红素机能较一般人迟缓，或者说肝排泄胆红素的阈界较正常为高，以致正常应由肝排泄的胆红素留滞于血液内，引起黄疸。这类黄疸的临床表现为慢性波动性轻度黄疸、常因疲劳或偶发感染而加深，对于它的病因目前还没有一致的意见，但根据医学方面的实际经验，它的预后是好的，就是说它对于患者的一般健康与寿命无影响。文献中有此病状的患者活到七八十岁的高龄是常见的。我所知道就是这些。我希望你无论如何不要把轻度黄疸当作一个包袱，而影响你的工作。

至于割除扁桃腺的问题我的一般性意见是：对抵抗感染扁桃腺在正常情况下起着警卫作用，因此，除非它本身因反复感染而失去作用，没有割除的必要。这不过是原则，具体情况，具体分析。你的扁桃腺应不应去掉最好由专业医生做出决定；不好自作主张。

个人 61-62 学期的学习和工作计划：

在理论学习方面：根据政治经济学讲授提纲学习资本主义部分的基本经济规律，为提高政治思想水平并为将来学习打下基础。参加政治学习讨论会及民主党派的神仙会认真学习。

在业务方面：经常参加本院星期三的学术活动，特别注意有关内科方面的课题，了解各科的科研动向以便推荐有关最新资料。经常主动地帮助青年教师及同学查找资料及推荐各种索引文摘。

认真学习，做好工作，争取早日摘掉帽子，回到人民的队伍里来。

61:10.15

十月十七日：宣布朱、朱、缪摘去帽子

十一月十五日 七位同学摘去帽子

（第二稿）上月中旬，当朱锡侯、朱启照、缪安成三位先生被宣布揭去右派分子帽子，回到人民内部的时候，我很感震动，并在思想上出现一些不正确的看法。首先，我以为我之不能归队，原因恐是我以为我的罪名比较严重，影响比较大，危害性又深远。这一思想当然是不正确的，因为我只认识到问题不在于罪名的轻重，而在对于它的认识。

我对朱锡侯、缪安成两位先生的归队没有意见，但朱启照先生亦能在此次摘去帽子有些不解。我以为我的改造并不比他差，甚至比他强。这一思想当然更成问题。实际上对他的改造情况我却知道的很少，所见到的不过是些表面现象，怎能据此下结论，这种结论就是对党不信任。

另一个思想是如果需要我像朱锡侯先生那样写数十万言的书面检查才能揭帽子的话，我的希望就很少了。说来很惭愧。虽然小的时候我亦曾在私塾中读过些四书五经之类的古书，后因在国外年久对祖国的语言只有阅读的能力，以之表达思想或感情总觉吃力得很。以往写文章书信总有人代笔。最近精力较差，白天工作一天，晚上脑筋不听指挥，往往极容易写的字都想不起来了。

我想我的问题主要在于（1）虽然我在以往的检查中我已揭露过我的反党反社会主义的全部事实，但对于它的思想和阶级根源分析得不够，因而在认识方面不够深刻；（2）虽然我表面上听党的话但主动向党靠拢还是不够。

回忆我犯的反党反社会主义的罪行就是抗拒党的领导，走资本主义的道路，企图在医学教育方面建立我的独立王国。我的这种极端反动立场是与我的封建家庭出身（分）不开的，从小时候起就习惯于呼奴喝婢，游手好闲。整个青年时期又生活在英国资本主义社会环境，沾染了不少资产阶级绅士的气味和习惯，在表面上很有礼貌，不与人争、内心里总自以为高人一等，习惯于骑在别人头上，人生的最终目的就是个人能过着优越的和悠闲的生活。回国后拼命地向上爬，追求名位而更主要的是发号施令的权力。解放后不接受党的长期的和耐心的教育，执迷不悟，总以为在医学教育领域内我有一套，党离不开我。我所犯的罪行就是反抗党的领导，伸手向党要人事权和财政权。

自被划为右派之后又未能正确地对待周围群众对自己的严肃态度，感到精神上的压力很大；这种压力本身应促进自己的改造，相反在自己思想上产生一种自卑感，并使自己越来越孤立，对群众越来越疏远，经常生活在自我的小圈子里。三年来主动地向党靠拢不够积极，书面汇报既有困难口头汇报又不够主动，因循等待。总以为只要好好做好党委给自己安排的工作，遵守劳动纪律，不再犯错误就够了。

回忆 1957 当右派向党进攻的时候自己是如何狂妄和骄傲自满。现在体会到那时的骄傲和现在的自卑是同一思想根源，不外乎是处处从个人观点出发。今后只有少考虑个人的问题，而多关心国际国内的形势，时时刻刻把个人利益同集体利益结合起来看问题。

三年来党的教育和个人的感受亦能体会到我的那一套医学教育不但是少慢差费的资本主义的道路，完全脱离祖国的实际情（况）和需要并且最终是为帝国主义文化侵略服务的。今后这方面要在党的领导下，根据党的方针政策，批判地估计欧美科学发展的倾向和医学教育方面的经验。

12 月 8 日：胡科长来要对贵阳医学院学生朱庚尧的材料：朱庚尧大概是从河北医学院转学到贵阳医学院的，1944 或 1945 毕业。他是国民党员，但何时何地入党不清楚，可能是去贵阳前就入了国民党的。毕业后他怎样进入卫生署公卫讲习班不得而知。该班负责人是朱章赓，现在日内瓦世界卫生组织当雇员。当时教务主任贾魁（现在北京中华医学会中文编辑）对他的了解可能比我多些。骆瑞庭，不认识。

12 月 10 日，阅读《政治经济学》。

1962 年

1 月 31 日：近一个月来总觉容易疲乏，有时早晨头昏、头痛，多活动后气促，两腿稍肿。

2 月 16 日：自二月一日开始休息，至二月十六日复查。血压稍降（舒张压 120，降至 100），小便++蛋白，少许红血球及颗粒管型，周以信又建议两星期全休或必要时住院治疗，拟休息至 2 月底（12 天）

洋地黄——有两种

（1） 紫花洋地黄（Digitalis Purpura L, 中国产）

a. 洋地黄毒苷（吸收慢）

Digitoxin 1.0 mg 饱和剂量

（狄吉妥辛）0.05-0.10 mg 维持剂量

b. Gitoxin – 吉妥辛

（2）毛花洋地黄（Digitalis 中欧产）

a. Digixin 毛花洋地黄苷（狄乔克辛）

3.0 mg 饱和量 0.25 维持量

b. Lanatoside C （毛花洋地黄苷 C）

（静脉注射）

毒毛旋花子素（或苷）（吸收最快）静脉用

Strophanthus Kombe

Ouabain (哇巴因)与上相同

2 月 23 日，复查：情况同前。

2 月 27 日，踝部仍有些浮肿。

2 月 28 日，致农工民主党信：

北京后门，方砖寺，辛寺 0014 号，中国农工民主党中央委员会组织部：

我在昆明医学院图书馆服务已将两年，主要在中西期刊组工作；同时结合医学院教学和科研需要收集些医学文献资料。

最近身体较前衰弱，血压高，疲乏，有时腿肿，上了几岁年纪，血管有些硬化，影响心脏和肾脏功能。组织上给我很多照顾，春节前后让我休息了一个月；生活方面亦很关怀。我是非常感激和感动的。昆明今年冬季较往年寒冷，并下过雪，对我是一种考验。现已春回大地，觉得舒服多了。再有一两个星期总可以恢复工作了。

兹寄上最近的思想总结一份，请查收，并 1962 全年党费￥17.28.

1961 年第八期前进及 1962 第一期学习资料均陆续收到，以后如寄昆明六合村昆明医学院图书馆李宗恩收更为直接也。

同日：

致林宗扬信：

Dear C.E:

It will not be long before I pass out into the limbo. I am still labeled a rightest but when I see the country is making big stride forward and a radiant era ahead. I go in peace + comfort much

My wife will live long after me. I am asking you, C.H. Hu 胡正详 and P.C. Seng 孙邦藻 (home always Johnson) to be her adviser when she applies to any of you for advice. I am sure you will give her your wise counsel.

I also wish to thank you for the 1962 New Year greeting which you so thoughtfully sent me.

Adieu, my friend,

Yours always,

C.U. Lee

(译文)

亲爱的宗扬：

要不了多少时间，我就会去灵魂安息之所了。虽然我还带着右派的帽子，但我看见国家正在大踏步地向前，一个光明的时代就在眼前。我将安然而平静地离去。

我走后，我的妻子仍要活下去。我请求你，胡正详和孙邦藻（他总在家）在她需要的时候给她做个顾问。我相信你一定会给她明智的建议的。

我也想感谢你费心寄来的 1962 年新年祝福。

再见了，我的朋友。

永远是你的，

李宗恩

致孙邦藻信：

My Dear Johnson:

I fully expect to see you in person before very long but that is not to be. By the time this reaches you I shall be in the land of limbo. I shall for my lad on for there are things I do not understand but I do admit that there is a lot to be said for the new regime and I have no complaints.

Jean, my wife, will live long after me. I am asking you, C.H. Hu + C. E. Lin to be her advisers. If any time she has occasion consul to you I am sure will give her your wise counsel.

Adieu, my friend,

Yours always,

（译文）

亲爱的邦藻：

亲爱的邦藻：

本以为不久就会跟你见面，但现在已经不可能了。当你看到这封信的时候，我应该到了灵魂安息之所。应该说，有些事我并想不通，不过我确实承认新政府做了不少有善可陈的事情。我无所抱怨。

我走后，我的妻子，Jean，还要活下去。我请求你，胡正详，和林宗扬给她当当顾问。如果什么时候她咨询你们的意见，我相信你们一定会给她明智的建议的。

再见了，我的朋友。

永远是你的，

致胡正详信：

Dear C.H.

I am leaving this litter not for you in case I will not be seeing you again, for I feel tired and my time is approaching. Hardened arteries are troubling me again + my heart is weakening. However, I go in peace and contentment with no complaints.

My wife will live long after me. I am asking you, P.C. Seng (孙邦藻) and C.E. Lim to be her advisers. I am sure any of you will give her the wise guidance she may need at times.

Adieu, my friend,

Yours always,

（译文）

亲爱的正详：

我留下这封信，是怕没有机会再见到你了，我觉得累了，知道自己的大限已到。硬化的动脉又在给我找麻烦，再加心脏越来越虚弱。不过，我将平静而知足地离去，无怨无悔。

我的妻子在我走后还要活下去。我请你，孙邦藻和林宗扬给她当当顾问。如果她有需要，我相信你们任何一位都会给她明智的建议。

再见了，我的朋友。

永远是你的，

2 月 28 日

去北京等地航程

北京，星期 1、4、5、6

南宁 2、5

编后记

在协和医学院的百年历史中，有过三次关闭，三次复校。第一次关闭发生在太平洋战争爆发后的1942年1月，协和医学院被日军占领，变成其医学研究机构和伤兵医院。抗战胜利后，协和医学院于1947年秋季复校。第二次关闭发生在1953年初，协和医学院奉命停止招生，向干部进修学院过渡，为中国人民解放军培养高级师资和提高医务干部水平。在协和教授们的再三强烈要求下，协和医学院又于1959年恢复八年制医本科教育。第三次关闭发生在文革之初的1966年，动乱结束后于1979年复校。比较协和医学院的三次复校，要数第一次最艰难，也最关键。难就难在人去楼空，而且时局混乱、内战一触即发、恶性通货膨胀。在此承前启后的关键时刻，李宗恩在短短的三年中不但完成了首次协和复校，而且为协和医学院以后的两次复校和至今领先中国医学教育的地位奠定了坚实的基础。但是，在协和医学院迄今为止的14位校长中，李宗恩是唯一鲜为人知的一位。可幸的是，本书搜集的这些带有时代痕迹的文字尚存，而且随着时间的逝去越发厚重，无声地传递着历史深处的信息。

这些原始档案的获取，要感谢格拉斯哥大学医学院 Emma Wong 女士、伦敦热带病学院 Claire Frankland 女士、协和医学院档案室张霞女士、协和医学院图书馆王宗欣老师、贵阳医学院李晓芬女士、贵州省档案馆何君明女士及韩雯处长、中研院近代史所及洛氏基金会档案馆 Tom Rosenbaum 先生、清华大学校史馆副馆长金富军博士等的大力协助。

今年是李宗恩医生诞辰 125 年，本文集是李宗恩纪念系列丛书之一。让我们通过李宗恩留下的这些珍贵的文字来了解这一位民国医学教育家，在中国近代最为跌宕起伏、风云变幻的年代中，为中国医学教育呕心沥血、艰苦卓绝的奋斗历程。

李维华

2019 年 6 月

封面设计： 李维华

封面素描： 李宗津

李宗恩医生文存

李宗恩 著　　李维华 编

《亚美导报》出版　Asian American Today, Inc
美国　印第安纳　印第安纳波利斯
Indianapolis, Indiana, United States of America
www.yamei-today.com
印刷：IngramSpark
经销：Amazon.com & aatodayin@gmail.com
印张 7 X 10 英寸　字数 133,519
2019 年 6 月第 1 版　2019 年 6 月第 1 次印刷
ISBN: 978-1-942038-04-7

定价：$20 (USA)

www.ingramcontent.com/pod-product-compliance
Lightning Source LLC
Chambersburg PA
CBHW082125180726
48291CB00010B/2748